# Readings in Modern Theology

# READINGS IN MODERN THEOLOGY

*Britain and America*

Edited by Robin Gill

ABINGDON PRESS
*Nashville*

Published in the United States of America 1995
Abingdon Press
201 Eighth Avenue South
Nashville TN 37203

First published in Great Britain 1995
SPCK, Holy Trinity Church
Marylebone Road
London NW1 4DU

Library of Congress Cataloging-in-Publication Data
Readings in Modern Theology : Britain and America / edited by Robin Gill
p.  cm.
Includes bibliographical references and index.
ISBN 0–687–01461–1 (alk. paper)
1. Theology—Great Britain. 2. Theology—United States.
I. Gill, Robin
BT30.G7R33 1995
230'.09'049—dc20                                     95-774 CIP

Printed in Great Britain

# CONTENTS

## Part Two: Christ and Plurality

## Part Three: Spirit and Community

G: THE CHRISTIAN LIFE

H: CHRISTIAN COMMUNITIES

# Acknowledgements

The editor would like to thank the following for permission to include copyright material:

**Modern Theology** for:
Frederick Sontag, 'The Defense of God' (July 1985, Vol. 1, No. 4, pp. 292–301).
Geoffrey Wainwright, review of Lindbeck's *The Nature of Doctrine* (January 1988, Vol. 4, No. 2, pp. 121–32).
Stanley Hauerwas, 'Some Theological Reflections on Gutierrez's Use of "Liberation" as a Theological Concept' (October 1986, Vol. 3, No. 1, pp. 67–76).

**Theology Today** for:
John Polkinghorne, 'Creation and the Structure of the Physical World' (1987, Vol. 44, pp. 53–68).
Kathryn Tanner, 'The Difference Theological Anthropology Makes' (January 1994, Vol. 50, No. 4, pp. 567–79).
Gordon Kaufman, 'Models of God: Is Metaphor Enough?' (April 1988, Vol. 45, No. 1).
David Tracy, 'Theology and the Many Faces of Postmodernity' (April 1994, Vol. 51, No. 1, pp. 104–14).
David Kelsey, 'Whatever Happened to the Doctrine of Sin?' (July 1993, Vol. 50, No. 2, pp. 169–78).

**Theology** for:
Janet Martin Soskice, 'Creation and Relation' (January 1991, Vol. XCIV, No. 575, pp. 31–9).
Rowan Williams, 'Resurrection and Peace' (November 1989, Vol. XCIII, No. 750, pp. 481–90).
Sarah Coakley, 'Creaturehood Before God: Male and Female' (September 1990, Vol. XCIII, No. 755, pp. 343–54).
Stephen Sykes, 'An Anglican Theology of Evangelism' (November 1991, Vol. XCIV, No. 762, pp. 405–14).

**Cross Currents** for the following articles from *Religion and Intellectual Life*:
Rosemary Radford Ruether, 'Models of God: Exploding the Foundations' (Spring 1988, Vol. V, No. 3, pp. 19–23).
David Tracy, 'Models of God: Three Observations' (Spring 1988, Vol. V, No. 3, pp. 24–8).
Sallie McFague, 'Response' (Spring 1988, Vol. V, No. 3, pp. 38–44).

*Acknowledgements*

Rosemary Radford Ruether, 'Renewal or New Creation' (Winter 1986, Vol. III, No. 2, pp. 7–20).

**Journal of Theological Studies** for:
Ruth Page, review of McFague's *Models of God* (1988, Vol. 39, pp. 647–9).
David Ford, review of Lindbeck's *The Nature of Doctrine* (1986, Vol. 37, pp. 277–82).

**Journal of Literature and Theology** for:
Ann Loades, review of McFague's *Models of God* (March 1990, Vol. 4, No. 1, pp. 141–2).

**Fortress Press**, Philadelphia for:
Extract from Robert Jenson, 'The Christian Doctrine of God', reprinted from Geoffrey Wainright, ed., *Keeping the Faith: Essays to Mark the Centenary of Lux Mundi* (pp. 38–53) copyright © 1988 Fortress Press. Used by permission of Augsburg Fortress.
Extract reprinted from Edward Farley, *The Fragility of Knowledge* (pp. 171–83, 190) copyright © 1988 Fortress Press. Used by permission of Augsburg Fortress.

**T & T Clark**, Edinburgh for:
Catherine Mowry LaCugna, extract from 'Reconceiving the Trinity as the Mystery of Salvation' in the *Scottish Journal of Theology* 1985 (Vol. 38, pp. 1–3, 14–22).
Don Cupitt, 'After Liberalism' in Daniel Hardy and Peter Sedgwick, eds., *The Weight of Glory* (1991), pp. 251–6.

**Cambridge University Press** for:
Colin Gunton, 'Universal and Particular in Atonement Theology' in *Religious Studies* 1992 (Vol. 28, pp. 453–66).
Keith Ward, 'Truth and the Diversity of Religions' in *Religious Studies* 1991 (Vol. 26, pp. 1–3, 12–18).

**Journal of Ecumenical Studies** for:
Gavin D'Costa, 'One Covenant or Many Covenants?' (Summer 1990, Vol. 27, No. 3, pp. 441–52).

**Westminster/John Knox Press**, Kentucky for:
Extract from George Lindbeck, *The Nature of Doctrine: Religion and Theology in a Postliberal Age* (pp. 116–28, 135–7) copyright © 1984 George A. Lindbeck. Used by permission of Westminster/John Knox Press.

**Union Seminary Quarterly Review** for:
David Burrell, review of Lindbeck's *The Nature of Doctrine* (1984, Vol. XXXIX, No. 4, pp. 322–4).

**Harvard Theological Review** for:

Elisabeth Schüssler Fiorenza, 'Commitment and Critical Inquiry' (January 1989, Vol. 82, No. 1, pp. 1–11). Copyright 1989 by the President and Fellows of Harvard College. Reprinted by permission.

**Harvard Divinity Bulletin** for:

Extract from Ronald F. Thiemann, 'Toward the Integrated Study of Religion: A Case for the University Divinity School' (1992, Vol. 21, No. 4, pp. 15, 18–19). (Ronald Thiemann is Dean and John Lord O'Brien Professor of Divinity at Harvard Divinity School.) Copyright 1992 by the President and Fellows of Harvard College. Reprinted by permission. All rights reserved.

**Theological Education** for:

Rebecca Chopp, 'Emerging Issues in Theological Education' (Spring 1990, pp. 107–17).

**Heythrop Journal** for:

Nicholas Lash, 'Easter Meaning' (1984, Vol. XXV, pp. 7–18).

Ursula King, 'Women in Dialogue: A New Vision of Ecumenism' (1985, Vol. XXVI, pp. 125–35, 141).

**Exeter University Press** for:

Extract from Robin Gill, *Moral Communities* (1992), pp. 63–80.

**Darton, Longman and Todd** for:

Extract from Daniel Hardy and David Ford, *Jubilate: Theology in Praise* (1984), pp. 145 152.

# Introduction

This Reader attempts to give a snapshot of some of the best modern theology to emerge from British and United States academies over the last decade. It was tempting to include European, South American, Asian and African theology as well, not to mention recent Jewish and Islamic theology. Yet in the end it was decided that this would make the Reader too diffuse and too disparate. By concentrating upon British and American theology within the Christian tradition, it is possible to detect certain themes which have been dominant over the last decade and to trace some of the key points of agreement and disagreement between scholars.

The Reader is divided into three parts – God and Creation, Christ and Plurality, and Spirit and Community – and each of these is divided into broad (and sometimes overlapping) sections. Scholars from America and Britain frequently interact and some (like Dan Hardy, Janet Martin Soskice, Geoffrey Wainwright and Sarah Coakley) change countries. So it is hardly surprising to find that they often have similar interests and presuppositions. Yet there are some differences of focus between them. For example, the debate about the public role of theology in the academy is more American and the debate about worship and theology more English. Feminism has challenged both cultures, yet the influence may still be stronger in America. Conversely the extraordinary authority of John Polkinghorne's work is felt more keenly in Britain.

There are also two other differences between American and British academic theology which have become clearer over the last decade. The first is very evident. A generation ago many American theologians looked to Europe for direction. Even towering and original theologians such as the two Niebuhr brothers drew much of their original inspiration from Europe, especially from Barth, Troeltsch and Weber. British scholarship, particularly biblical scholarship, was often regarded with some awe by Americans. The British, and Europeans generally, seldom returned the compliment. Indeed, contemporary English theologians such as Raven and Temple tended to patronize the Niebuhrs. Few British theologians at the time thought that they had much to learn from America.

Today, however, this situation is almost reversed. There is a new confidence and vigour to American theology, and British scholars fail to keep up with this at their peril. It is no longer even clear that young

1

American scholars feel less educated than those who study also in Britain or Europe. In contrast, many young British scholars now feel a need to spend some time in America. Amongst British biblical scholars today there is considerable discussion of American scholars such as Wayne Meeks, John Gager and Norman Gottwald. And amongst British Christian ethicists today the Niebuhrs, Paul Ramsey and now Stanley Hauerwas are essential reading. However, within modern theology it is difficult to see how the debate between David Tracy and George Lindbeck can be avoided – although I regret that in Britain it often is.

The other major difference is linked to this. American theology seems recently to have become more communal than British theology. Certain themes – particularly those associated with postmodernism – have evoked a considerable debate amongst American theologians. Not surprisingly, if Americans no longer look quite so often across to Europe, they have generated internal debates instead. For example, George Lindbeck's *The Nature of Doctrine* or Sallie McFague's *Models of God* have both provoked an enormous literature and debate which have only sometimes impinged upon British consciousness. And David Tracy's *The Analogical Imagination* has been far more influential and contentious in America than it has been in Britain. There is almost a Tracy school and a Lindbeck school in America, but little comparable in Britain. Chicago and Yale seem to be distinct from each other in a way that Oxford and Cambridge today are not. In contrast, British scholarship can sometimes appear more fragmented and individualistic. For instance, it would be quite difficult to find common themes between the five Cambridge theologians represented in this Reader – Cupitt, Ford, Lash, Polkinghorne and Soskice. Those of us who head theology or religious studies departments in Britain sometimes feel as if we are in the business of attempting to herd cats!

Of course these differences can be exaggerated and many points of contact can be detected within this Reader. Dan Hardy and David Ford have been important mediators between the two cultures and even the 'distinctively English' connection between worship and theology is well represented in America by the British scholar Geoffrey Wainwright. Feminist theology has proved particularly exportable and Ann Loades' *Feminist Theology – A Reader* has done much to facilitate this. Perhaps the present Reader can also help this process of mutual communication.

There are several ways of compiling a Reader. The most obvious is to invite contributions from eminent scholars. All too frequently this becomes an editor's nightmare. Orchestrating scholars is difficult enough, but coping with their uneven contributions is the more serious problem. In the end the student suffers from many eminent, but some unintelligible, essays.

Extracting passages from carefully chosen books is an obvious way to avoid this. Yet this can sometimes fragment arguments. Vital explanations and clues, present elsewhere in the original books, can be absent from extracts unless there is an extensive commentary. A third method is to select pieces which were intended at the outset to be self-contained – namely journal articles and reviews. Scholars spend a great deal of time and energy producing them and yet, despite often being excellent, their readership is usually small.

To give greater interaction this Reader does have a few extracts from books, but most of the contributions come from journals. They can, as a result, be read independently of the books themselves. To represent differences of viewpoint some book reviews have also been added. And, to keep the Reader fresh, everything included was first published by active academics between 1984 and 1994. Inevitably this excludes some scholars who have retired and others who were less productive in this period. There is also a younger generation of scholars who are beginning to publish but are not included in the Reader this time. Perhaps next time they will be. Selection is always problematic.

The opening section is on *God as Creator*. The first contribution is from the philosopher of religion Frederick Sontag, Professor of philosophy at Pomona College, Claremont, California. This striking article encourages theologians to the defence of God in the modern world. As can be seen in this and other sections, apologetics at present is an increasing theme within modern theology. If a generation ago theology seemed to be academically isolated, especially in the wake of frequent attacks from philosophy, today the situation seems remarkably different. Logical positivism, and with it the certainties of intellectual atheism, is no longer the dominant voice within philosophy. Indeed, a surprising number of academic philosophers today have theological interests.

There are also a number of scientists with theological interests, amongst whom the most celebrated perhaps is John Polkinghorne. President of Queens' College, Cambridge, a Gifford Lecturer and formerly Professor of mathematical physics at Cambridge, he has unusual stature as both a theologian and as a scientist. In the second contribution he reflects his characteristic belief that we live in one world which can be described variously by theologians as well as by scientists. He believes that the very intelligibility of the world is important for apologetics.

Two younger theologians conclude this section. Kathryn Tanner, Associate Professor of religious studies at Yale University, argues that a distinctively theological anthropology – proclaiming the objective value of God's creatures – does make a difference to how we perceive and treat the world. Janet Martin Soskice, Lecturer in theology at Cambridge University, looks at the implications of the theological notion of creation for human relationships. Again the apologetic tendencies of both of these contributions are clear.

The second section, *God as Mother*, is unified around responses to Sallie McFague's book *Models of God* (1987) in which she defended at length the models of 'mother, lover and friend' for God. She is Professor of theology at Vanderbilt Divinity School and now one of the leading Christian feminists. It is clear from their responses that her colleagues do indeed find this a stimulating book. Contributions 5 to 8 were all published together in the journal *Religion and Intellectual Life* soon after the book's publication. Gordon Kaufman, Professor of theology at Harvard Divinity School, and Rosemary Radford Ruether, Professor of theology at the Garrett-Evangelical Theological Seminary, offer criticisms from radically different perspectives. The first has come to be suspicious of using personalist language about God at all, and the second is suspicious of McFague's reformist Christian feminism. They represent two important poles in the debate about God-language. David Tracy, Professor of Catholic studies at Chicago University, is more eirenic. His well known position on theological language – emphasizing the analogical and often elusive nature of this language – is much closer to that of McFague herself.

To conclude this section two short reviews of *Models of God* have also been included. Ruth Page, Senior Lecturer in systematic theology at Edinburgh University, and Ann Loades, Reader in theology at Durham University, offer contrasting feminist criticisms.

The third section illustrates some of the current, lively debate about models of the Trinity. Of course this debate often involves extended discussions of historical theology. Since this is a Reader in Modern Theology these discussions are only represented here in outline. The focus is intentionally upon the viability of Trinitarian models today. The most traditional approach is the first, by the Lutheran Robert Jenson, Professor of religion at St Olaf College, Northfield, Minnesota. The introduction to the article, written for a collection to mark the centenary of *Lux Mundi* from which this extract is taken, states his position as follows:

> It is the conviction of this essay that bewilderment about God, whether in the church or the polity, is not accidental to our civilization in this time. Rather, the ideologies that constitute late Western modernity are necessary and sufficient contexts of God's obfuscation. God suffers three disabilities in our age. In order of the following discussions: God is *useless* in the context of a community that interprets itself and its world

mechanically; God is *offensive* in the context of our pragmatism of historical liberation; and God is *particular* in the context of universal acquaintance. If mechanism, liberalism and universalism make God's problem in our time, then God's problem is the European-American Enlightenment.

The two extracts that follow show contrasting Catholic positions in the modern Trinitarian debate. Catherine Mowry LaCugna is Professor at The University of Notre Dame, Indiana. The article from which her extract was taken and her subsequent book *God for Us: The Trinity and Christian Life* have caused considerable interest. In the original article she defends Karl Rahner's axiom at length that 'the economic Trinity is the immanent Trinity and *vice versa*'. She stresses the importance of relating models of the Trinity to salvation history.

The task of James Mackey, Thomas Chalmers Professor of theology at the University of Edinburgh, is more polemical. He takes to task some of the recent social models of the Trinity. Adding to the position which he argued at length in *The Christian Experience of God as Trinity*, he maintains that such models tend to be highly speculative, unbiblical and dangerously linked to power. The hint about power at the end of this article links interestingly to his latest book, *Power and Christian Ethics* (in which he distinguishes between a Christ-like power as moral authority and power simply as coercion).

The next section is on the enormous theme of *Christ and Other Faiths*. Clearly this theme could have swamped the rest of the book. Instead four articles have been selected with distinctive viewpoints. A universalist and highly ecumenical vision is offered by Ursula King, Professor of theology and religious studies at Bristol University. She is well known for her interest in spirituality, especially in the work of Teilhard de Chardin, and for her expert knowledge of Indian religious thought. Writing here as a feminist and as a Catholic, she argues that feminist theology is capable of uniting women across different traditions and faiths. In contrast, Colin Gunton, Professor of systematic theology at King's College, London University, is more concerned to stress the particularity and distinctiveness of the Christian doctrine of atonement. Although Christianity shares with other faiths a sense of the need for redemption, it alone offers a dynamic of history that can effect this.

Keith Ward, then also a Professor at King's College London, but now Regius Professor of Divinity at Oxford University, offers a contrasting position. Whilst being unconvinced by John Hick's radically pluralist position, nevertheless, his own final position is clearly not as particularist

5

as that of his former colleague Colin Gunton. Gavin D'Costa, Lecturer in theology and religious studies at Bristol University, is fast becoming a leading expert on inter-religious relations. His work stresses both the plurality of religious traditions and their distinctiveness. In the contribution here his focus is specifically upon Christian–Jewish relations. In contrast to 'dual covenant' theories, he argues instead that there is just one normative covenant, because there is just one God, yet there can still be many further legitimate covenants.

The largest section in the Reader is that on *Christ and Postmodernism*. All of the theologians in this section seem to agree that we live in a post-modern or postliberal age. They assume that the secularist assumptions that once predominated in the intellectual world – based upon rationalist individualism and positivism – are now under attack. For George Lindbeck, Professor of theology at Yale University, there is a radical cultural-linguistic phenomenon which implies that there is no longer any common rational discourse, there are only specific communities which share languages and assumptions. A Lutheran, he argues that the Christian community is based upon, and fashioned by, Scripture. In that sense it is quite distinct from other communities and, as society at large becomes less Christian or, at least, less fashioned by Scripture, so Christians will become increasingly distinctive and distanced from the word. David Ford, Regius Professor of Divinity at Cambridge University, and David Burrell, Professor of theology at Notre Dame University, Indiana, offer thoughtful Anglican and Catholic summaries and appreciations of Lindbeck's seminal book *The Nature of Doctrine*.

Geoffrey Wainwright's analysis of this book is rather different. A celebrated liturgist, he is Professor of systematic theology at Duke University, North Carolina. Lindbeck himself had been highly involved in ecumenical relations for more than two decades before he wrote *The Nature of Doctrine* (he was a Protestant observer at Vatican II). So Wainwright's ecumenical perspective is very apt. However he is not finally convinced by Lindbeck's stress upon culture at the expense of propositions and experience in faith traditions. A more complex view of faith traditions, even in a postmodernist age is also offered by David Tracy. As might be expected from his analogical perspective, he is unconvinced by some of the most radical postmodernist perspectives (Lindbeck's will not have been too far from his thought). For Tracy, both modernist and postmodernist elements are inescapably part of our inheritance, and theology responds in many different and complex ways to them.

The complex ways that modernism and postmodernism affect theology are also evident in the contribution of David Kelsey, Professor of theology and colleague of Lindbeck at Yale. He argues that the doctrine of sin has not vanished in the modern world, but rather it has 'migrated'. He seeks to trace the differing ways in which this has happened. Finally, Don Cupitt, Fellow and former Dean of Emmanuel College, Cambridge University, offers a far more radical understanding of how postliberalism affects theology. For him it involves a process of radical deconstruction in which 'realist' views collapse. He concludes that any notion of objectivity – in the physical world, in metaphysics, or in morality – should now be abandoned. We can only 'gaze steadfastly into the Void'.

The next section, *Christ and the Academy*, draws back slightly from this vertigo, although the overall theme of plurality continues. It considers instead the current American debate about the role of theology in the academy. In some ways the position of theology (as distinct from religious studies) is more precarious in American than it is in British universities. The corresponding status of certain prestigious seminaries is conversely higher in America than in Britain. Allies to the general intellectual confusion and malaise expressed in various forms of postmodernism, a number of theologians in America have joined the debate about the public role of theology. Four have been chosen here, although several others could also have been chosen (for example, David Kelsey has been a major contributor in this area too).

The first contribution in this section is an extract from *The Fragility of Knowledge: Theological Education in the Church and the University* by Edward Farley, Professor of theology at Vanderbilt University. He argues that the aim of theological study is properly (even in a supposedly secular setting) concerned with a rigorous approach to the situation of faith, with what he terms 'the reflective life of the believer'. He does believe that the study of faith is a legitimate subject for the university, especially if the latter is critical of the presumptions derived from the Enlightenment tradition of value-neutrality or 'nonjudgmental neutrality' and is once more concerned about matters of 'truth'.

Two feminist contributions take Farley's argument further. The distinguished New Testament scholar, Elisabeth Schüssler Fiorenza, Professor of theology at Harvard, is also well known for her contributions to modern feminist theology. Her contribution here was first given as a Harvard Divinity School Convocation address. She has clearly been influenced by Farley's critique of much post-Enlightenment education. The institutions of so-called 'pure reason' often hide their own complicity in power relations. However both she and Rebecca Chopp, Associate Professor of theology at Emory University, wish theologians to hear the voice of the disadvantaged, whether women or minority groups. For both women it is important to hear the perspectives of liberation and feminist theologies. Chopp's analysis (extracted here from a longer article) of the present dilemma in Western education is particularly sharp. Knowledge seems to be becoming increasingly pluralistic and fragmented and yet most of us still cling to patriarchal forms of rationality to resolve this. Instead, she believes that theology ought to be showing the rest of the academic world new forms of communal flourishing. As theologians we ought to be challenging, rather than adopting, individualistic patriarchy.

Finally in this section the Dean of Harvard, Ronald Thiemann, reflects upon a more integrated model of theological education. As a dean he is well aware, not just of confusion within the academy, but also of much anti-intellectualism present within churches. Academic theology is under pressure on both fronts. Yet he believes that theologians have a crucial critical role to play in an academic world which is increasingly aware of, but puzzled by, values in what were once regarded as value-neutral areas. Despite pressure from churches, he also argues that critical ecumenism is essential to modern theology.

In the following section, *The Christian Life*, both Nicholas Lash, Professor of theology at Cambridge University, and Rowan Williams, until recently Professor of theology at Oxford University but now Bishop of Monmouth, make links between Jesus' resurrection and the Christian life today. They have in common a distaste for purely empirical approaches to the resurrection, although Williams appears to be less sceptical of the empty tomb than Lash. At the time of writing their articles Lash's book on this theme – *Easter in Ordinary: Reflections on Human Experience and the Knowledge of God* – was still to be written, whilst Williams' book – *Resurrection: Interpreting the Easter Story* – was already published. For both theologians the resurrection is an essential part of the whole Jesus story. Lash is particularly critical of those theologians who wish to separate incarnation and resurrection. And both theologians seek to use images, albeit elusive images, to explore the implications of resurrection faith today. For Lash it signifies that 'the story of human history is ultimately to be told in terms, not of death, but of life, not of chaos but of God's unconquerably effective love'. For Williams it signifies deliverance from our fantasies of control and that 'for God, no defeat is final, and that is the ground for *our* trust that no defeat is final'.

Had this been a Reader in South American or Indian modern theology the theme of liberation would have been far more prominent. It is present explicitly or implicitly in the feminist contributions here, but it is hardly a dominant theme elsewhere. Despite the centrality of liberation to discussions in the World Council of Churches over the last two decades, it has not been a dominant theme in much British and American modern theology. The article by Stanley Hauerwas, Professor of Christian ethics at Duke University, indicates some of the factors behind this crucial difference. A celebrated controversialist, he perhaps more than anyone else has been responsible for regenerating a distinctively theological emphasis in Christian ethics. He remains suspicious of Christian ethicists adopting the themes and agendas of secular ethics – whether in terms of liberation or anything else.

In contrast, Sarah Coakley, formerly at Lancaster University and now Professor of theology at Harvard, has clearly been influenced by secular feminism. She uses a feminist perspective to examine images of female dependence in both Christian iconography and theology. She does finally believe that there is a proper and more equitable representation of both male and female dependence and creatureliness before God. Like Hauerwas her position in the end is explicitly theological. However, unlike Hauerwas, she takes seriously secular critiques before reaching this final position. By now it will come as no surprise to discover that Hauerwas studied under Lindbeck, whereas Coakley moves far more in the McFague/ Tracy tradition of modern theology.

The theme of the last section is *Christian Communities*. Here again there are a series of contrasts. Within British and American modern theology there is a renewed sense of the theological importance of community. Secular society within both countries is often viewed by modern theologians as disastrously individualistic and fragmented. The theme of postmodernism has recurred repeatedly in this Reader. In the 1960s the theme of secularization was a dominant motif. Today, however, with the demise of secular confidence apparent in many areas of the academic world, the theme seems to be a varied combination of fragmentation, eclecticism, pluralism, isolated individualism, as well as nostalgias for the past – which together might be depicted under the umbrella term of postmodernism. The new theological stress upon community is often seen as a response to this. Yet the communities envisaged by modern theologians vary considerably.

For Rosemary Radford Ruether feminism is generating new forms of community and belonging. Her critique of the traditional denominations within Christianity, which she regards as deeply oppressive, has been more forceful than the other feminist theologians represented here. For some years she has been a part of an experiment to create 'feminist liturgies and communities rising from women of Christian heritage'. However, unlike feminist neo-pagans she is not convinced that there is a form of religion from the past which is free from patriarchy.

The theme of worshipping communities connects the final three contributions – all written by Anglicans. In this respect the work of Stephen Sykes, formerly Regius Professor of Divinity at Cambridge University and now Bishop of Ely, has been crucial. His thesis both in *The Integrity of Anglicanism* and in *The Identity of Christianity* is that worship is essential to the formation and understanding of Christian theology. This has clearly influenced my own understanding of churches as moral communities, as well as *Jubilate*, written jointly by Daniel Hardy (formerly Van Mildert Professor of Divinity at Durham University and now Director of the Center of Theological Inquiry, Princeton) and David Ford, from which the final contribution is extracted. Worshipping communities have implications for Christian ethics (my point), for evangelism (Sykes' point) and for hope and eschatology (Hardy and Ford's point).

Of course the intention of any Reader is to inspire others to dig more deeply into the literature and to read some of the many books referred to here only in passing. I hope that this snapshot inspires you to do just that.

# PART ONE

# God and Creation

# A: God as Creator

1 FREDERICK SONTAG's 'The Defense of God' was published in *Modern Theology* in July 1985 (Vol. 1, No. 4, pp. 291–301). Amongst his books are *A Kierkegaard Handbook* (Atlanta: John Knox Press, 1979) and *The Return of the Gods* (New York: P. Lang, 1989). He also edited with John K. Roth *The Defense of God* (New York: Paragon House, 1985).

2 JOHN POLKINGHORNE's 'Creation and the Structure of the Physical World' was published in *Theology Today* in 1987 (Vol. 44, pp. 53–68). Amongst his books are *The Way the World Is* (London: Triangle, 1983, and Grand Rapids, Michigan: Eerdmans, 1984); *One World: The Interaction of Science and Theology* (London: SPCK, and Princeton University Press, 1986); *Science and Creation: The Search for Understanding* (London: SPCK, 1988); *Science and Providence: God's Interaction with the World* (Boston: Shambala Publications, 1989); *Reason and Reality: The Relationship Between Science and Theology* (London: SPCK, and Philadelphia: Trinity Press, 1991); and *Science and Christian Belief: Reflections of a Bottom-up Thinker* (Gifford Lectures, London: SPCK, 1994: American title *The Faith of a Physicist*, Princeton University Press, 1994).

3 KATHRYN TANNER's 'The Difference Theological Anthropology Makes' was published in *Theology Today* in January 1994 (Vol. 50, No. 4, pp. 567–79). Her books are *God and Creation* (Oxford and New York: Blackwell, 1988) and *The Politics of God: Christian Theologies and Social Justice* (Minneapolis: Fortress Press, 1992).

4 JANET MARTIN SOSKICE's 'Creation and Relation' was published in *Theology* in January 1991 (Vol. XCIV, No. 757, pp. 31–9). Her book is *Metaphor and Religious Language* (Oxford: Oxford University Press, 1985) and she has edited *After Eve* (London: Marshall Pickering, 1990).

# 1

# THE DEFENSE OF GOD
## *Frederick Sontag*

### *The indecisive situation*

In modern times theologians have differed as to whether or not God is all-powerful (omnipotent). Still, few have ever doubted that, if a Divinity can be said to exist, it is at very least the most powerful being in the universe. To be responsible for the creation of galaxies and planets such as we inhabit, let alone to control every human activity, requires immense power. Moreover, most people think that God, or the supreme Divinity, works to achieve good in the world. Destructive forces are all around us. But even if they are not now under direct divine care, we picture God as possessing the power and the ability to control them where and when he chooses.

All this involves the age-old problem of theodicy. If God is that Being than which nothing more powerful can be conceived (to paraphrase Anselm), given his good intentions for his creatures, why does he not intervene to protect them and promote their good against every threat? That is an important question, and the answer we give hinges both on our notion of God's intentions and on his use of power. However, although it has not often been mentioned, what I want to stress is that God's failure to defend himself against attack is even more puzzling. Countless theodicies have been written to explain why God seldom protects helpless human beings from catastrophe, but little has been done to explore the divine reason for God's failure to provide for his own defense against the attacks upon him.

If the actions of human beings often offend him or thwart his plans, the standard response has been to say that God prizes human freedom and will not interfere with it, even though the price for such abstinence is high. However, this explanation is full of difficulties, at least two of which are: (1) the meaning of freedom, which is seldom agreed upon; and (2) the question of whether sufficient human freedom might be allowed and yet we could still exercise our volition with considerably less destructive effect. However, again I want to suggest that God's failure to speak out in his own defense is even more difficult to explain. In dealing with this, Judaism has its own special problem centering on Israel's covenanted relationship to

God, but let us use Christianity, with which I am more familiar, as an example.

Of course, God appears very little in the New Testament, except in the voice heard with the dove's descent at the time of Jesus' baptism. Also, one might argue, God was evident in his action to raise Jesus from the dead. And the Holy Spirit did descend upon the early disciples with the result of reshaping their dispirited zeal into an expanding Church. A voice to Peter did command him to eat 'unclean' food, and this released Christianity to become an international religion no longer confined within the Mosaic law. Even so, neither God's voice nor his actions are seen or heard in the New Testament in his own defense. Why? If Christians believe that Jesus came among us as God's incarnated presence, we might expect to find God's self-defense prominent at least in that life. But a reading of the Gospels leaves almost the opposite impression. Jesus seems defenseless and even unwilling to protect his divine mission from attack. He evidences no concern to defend himself.

Why should this be so? If God decided to enter the world to accomplish his will among us as Christians assert, why did he not do so with a show of force appropriate to the immensity, if not the omnipotence, of his power? Of course, we can read the temptation stories which concern the testing of Jesus' intentions as he begins his ministry. The moral we can draw from these stories is that Jesus feels impelled to take a harder path than the easy way he was tempted to use. He rules out as too simple unleashing a display of divine power to overwhelm the opposition. But why not use every weapon you possess to promote a divine plan? If our motives and intentions are good, why should we use anything less than the full power at our command? It seems foolish to lose a battle if you actually possess the power you need to ensure victory.

Even if Jesus had backed his divine cause with the power needed to secure its success, this need not have abrogated all human freedom as some suppose. God need not force compliance by the use of physical violence, but why does he not at least speak out more plainly in his own defense when the cause is threatened? Jesus came to teach us, and God never once raised a hand in his defense. Strange behavior for a powerful being to send a frail human into a nearly disastrous situation with no security guards or greater powers to back him up. True, Jesus performed miracles, and this is commonly taken as a sign of his access to divine powers. But when the time came for Jesus to rise to his own defense, why was he so silent, and why were his miracles so little in evidence when he needed them most? Such non-defensive posture persists right down to the last words of Jesus from the cross, which betray a sense of divine abandonment. To explain God's desertion, theories of the need for an atonement for human sin are invoked. On other occasions God's power to raise Jesus from the dead is pointed to.

Yet mystery still surrounds God's behavior, because God himself never explains these lapses of power and the failure to provide for his defense. This is left to human beings (theologians) to present theories after-the-fact to account for such strange divine behavior. God did not make his purposes clear, neither in these crucial instances nor in the records left behind. The whole divine salvific plan would be much more convincing if God defended himself and if he offered an explicit account of why he tolerated the abuse of Jesus, for instance. And why is this tactic of silence in the face of the need for a defense and then a later mysterious exercise of power in resurrecting the dead, a preferable divine strategy? Certainly Jesus' return was not totally convincing to all. Millions today and in every day have been unable to see God's resurrection of Jesus as a totally convincing display of divine power. Surely God could have been more explicit, and less mysterious, had he wanted to.

Like the argument designed to protect human free will, theoreticians have given God's apology for him by saying that a non-coercive display leaves room for 'faith.' Too much direct action on God's part, plus a power display and a dramatic self-defense, might overpower limited human beings and compel belief. That may be true, but even the desire to leave room for human assent (or for denial) does not fully explain God's silence. Moreover, in our world we have not been presented with one divine drama authoritatively translated which we are then free to accept or reject. We have been given at least half a dozen major dramas. Each has been interpreted as a divine disclosure and literally thousands of interpretations are still extant. Such confusion and multiplicity does not protect the human right to free assent. Rather, it often confuses and overpowers us and drives millions into silence.

Of course, we can and do provide solutions for these dilemmas regarding Divinity that last for a time. Those who satisfactorily explain God's lack of defensive behavior, or who accept the explanations which others offer, become believers in one of the world's theologically based religions. However, the problems involved with belief of this kind are two: (1) The religions of the world remain plural, which leads to 'the grass is greener on the other side of the street' tendency. That is, after a time we become unsure and think that believing another religious explanation is preferable. And, (2) Since convictions once reached can change, this leads to the famous love-hate relationship that exists between the once enthusiastic and the disappointed lovers and ex-lovers of a particular religion. Problem (1) promotes the vicious infighting that often exists between religious groups. We damn all others and assert the supremacy of the one we prefer. Conflict of this kind is the major disgrace in religious history. Problem (2) should convince us that no belief can ever be guaranteed against retraction.

God has not offered us simple alternatives. Rather, the complexity implicit in his action staggers the imagination. We admire clear lines of authority and an exact delineation of the limits of power in our human fathers. Why has God placed us in this less than optimum situation? The human will could decide and pledge itself so much more decisively, if only God moved less ambiguously and took action to defend the position he wants us to adopt. Those who believe one religion with conviction, and perhaps with great joy, can only do so if they simplify and overlook a great deal of detail and incredible variety. But for every person who can do this many find themselves confused by a God who cannot lay out a clear defense.

So his people wander.

## The human responsibility

God has set us in the midst of a religious drama full of alternatives and fascinating puzzles. But we could play his game with greater gusto if so many were not overwhelmed and even lost amid the complexity. So much destruction and venom is spread by religious zealots who try to be absolute in the face of our God-given uncertainties. All religions, every religion, must be pronounced 'a mixed bag', although each may at times rise to great heights and rescue countless individuals in the process. Each spreads good works at one moment, only to reverse all this by callous or destructive action in the next. Even the most religiously sensitive individual must wonder if God would be better off not to have used organized religion as his intermediary and dealt directly with human beings in one clear, consistent, open manner.

Nevertheless, both the religious practice and the theology of each religion offer an explanation for this through prescribed ritual action, recorded word, and divine symbol. All this is a vast and fascinating enterprise, sometimes magnificent, sometimes absurd. The Enlightenment proposal to create a rational religion does not seem to have counted on God's devious ways or his lack of directness, all of which thwarts clear, final, and single explanation. So the religious story continues, leaving millions to ignore it and millions to explore it. But my particular concern is to see if we can read some message from God's failure to provide for his own definitive defense. Since men and women act and speak to defend themselves every day, and some do so quite effectively, God must be able to defend himself if he should so choose. What can this decision not to provide for his own defense mean?

One clear divine message in all this is that, if there is to be a defense of God, we humans must provide it. Odd that what is divine evidently depends for its protection on what is merely human. This situation is a reversal of what many who come to a religion think is true. Most of us explore a religion seeking for a defense against our enemies, both internal and external. The great offer of most widespread religions has always been to grant consolation and solace and assurance. Those who seek out a religion often do so because they feel oppressed by a burden which needs to be lifted or by a mystery which needs to be explained. We come seeking God to defend us only in the end to find that the nearer we draw to Divinity, or the more we explore any religion, the more we find it is we who must offer a defense for God, if he is to have one. If God at all times spoke out with one clear voice, this semi-tragic situation could be avoided, that is, so many seeking from religion what is not finally available there. But God has not done this, and the multiplicity of voices raised in his name only underscores his silent inaction.

If we realize all this it may clarify our understanding of our religious life in one respect. *To seek God, to be a follower, means to be ready to defend God at any time and place* where *Divinity comes under attack*. But how can we recognize those special places and times when our defense is called for? And most important, how can we know exactly what action we should take for God's defense in a tense situation? The answers we give depend on our view of God and Divinity's demands. Since our visions of God vary, the actions we feel prescribed to carry out will vary too. If the uncertainties in the human situation were not as I have described them, a plan of action to defend God could be outlined more definitively. As it is, God seems to have left it to each of us, or at least to those who will take up the battle and are not preoccupied with other things, to outline his defense. We must each decide where God is under attack in our day and determine our own defense strategy on his behalf.

Nikos Kazantzakis has written about *The Saviors of God*.[1] He portrays God as badly in need of our assistance. Figuratively speaking, God bleeds and we must rush to his assistance in his struggle or all may be lost. This is a challenging view and very modern in its description of God's dramatic need for human help. However, this is not the picture I wish to draw for you, since I believe Kazantzakis is wrong in attributing failure to God. As he emerges in the issue I have raised over his lack of self-defense, God is a Divinity who retains full power to accomplish any task, although the time

17

of its use can be postponed. Nevertheless, in the world's history to date he has not put an overpowering defense into play against those who attack him, his causes, or his people. God needs our assistance, then, not because he is weak or subject to failure, but because he has refused to lift an arm in his own defense.

The test of our fidelity is that it is left to us to do what God will not do. This is what 'faith' or 'faithful action' really involves. We need not argue over the meaning of the Trinity, although we do need to decide what the nature of Divinity is like. What we must do is to act or to speak out when God's defense is lacking and needed. Our religious fervor has somehow been turned in the wrong direction throughout much of religious history. We spend energy on arguments over the sacraments, or vestments, or ecclesiastical authority, or buildings, or even over the interpretation of various sacred scriptures and crucial texts. All these issues must be dealt with, of course, particularly if they are critical to our understanding of what God demands of us. But it is a gross misplacement of religious direction if we misunderstand our situation over against God. The chief religious question is: Where are God or his people under attack, and what defense can we offer? What should be our primary concern in any religious life. It is a travesty of God's intent if, instead, we destroy other human beings in our own rush to achieve security.

God might have provided for his own defense in a painless and non-destructive way. Since he does not choose to do so, to put down or to harm anyone else in the name of God is to do what even God does not do for his own protection. Religiously, to harm another is always wrong. To say this does not solve the question of whether violence or force can ever be justified in the name of religion, but it does limit the question severely if we see that even God does not use direct force in his own defense. Certainly this means that any action we engage in the name of religion, whether peaceful or otherwise, must be done on our own responsibility and as a result of our decision. In no way can any action we take be argued as directly authorized by God, since he has provided no defense of his own. The actions we perform in the name of religion would be better if each act were argued on the basis of individual responsibility and decision and not as if it were God's own choice. It is true that Divinity's defenselessness means that we are left to act in his name, but we must be careful to say that it is *our* decision to act in this manner to defend God and never his direct command.

All this does argue for a certain gentleness and non-coercive quality in the divine nature, I think. No matter how destructive the consequences, a tyrannical God would surely not hesitate to use force whenever necessary.

The phrase we use against opinionated individuals when we say that they 'play God' is a misunderstanding. As it all turns out, it is actually the reverse. He fails to provide for his own defense and leaves that task to individual or group discernment. All this indicates that God is one who never issues direct orders to human beings, although perhaps he does to the stars and planets. Yet as our own non-violence and non-assertive qualities sometimes permit injustice to be done and destruction to take over because we are too reticent or too permissive, and so the gentle and non-directive quality we discern in the Divine has its disastrous side effects too when men run amuck and are not restrained.

Of course, the great issue and mystery in all this is: Has and will this non-defensive posture on God's part continue to be his silent form of behavior? Or, might he reverse himself at some future time and bring his defensive powers into play? The answer each of us gives will depend on his or her view of God and the religious story each listens to. Some theologies picture God as incapable of such a reversal or such an expenditure of power. But the mystery involved in the defense of God, which I have been talking about, stems from the conviction that he does have the power to enforce his will and yet allows himself to remain indefinitely defenseless. ('How long oh Lord, how long.') Of course nothing in our present experience, or at the least very little numerically considered, gives us a basis to predict that God will act differently than he does at present. However, much of our religious conviction rests on an assurance that he will do after all, on 'one fine day'.

## The future of God

If we believe that God will reverse his self-restraint some day and bring his power into play to achieve his goals, we must use the future as a key to interpret both past and present. We cannot use the past for a touchstone, as those engrossed in the historical quest would have us do, or the present as would the empirically minded advocate. But how is it possible to do that, that is, to use a not-yet-here future as a basis for expecting God to act differently than he now does? The future is not present to point to, as an empiricist might wish it were, nor can we compile exact evidence of its direction as historians would have us do. Yet when we consider it, much religion (particularly Christianity) is based more on an expectation about the future than on a certainty in the past or present. If so, this is one reason 'the historical quest' in religion has been so little able to succeed. It begins on a basis different from that projected by the religious message itself. Occasionally we have some present evidence, e.g. a miracle, a passage of

Scripture, or a conversion experience. But these infrequent events are not enough to out-balance the bulk of our present experience in which the majority of humanity remains in bondage and is subject to destruction.

God's 'eye is on the sparrow', a popular song tells us. But any God who would leave himself presently defenseless must have his eye on the future more than on the present or the past. His memory may be long and his perception omniscient, but the divine nature must be dominated by the future mode. That is, God depends more on what he will and can do than on what he has done or presently sees. The tale of creation may begin the biblical documents, but to use Genesis as a foundation to interpret God is to miss the major point.

## The freedom of God

If the defense of God I suggest is so important, why haven't philosophers and theologians urged it on us before this? The answer, of course, is that most views of God did not require it. Plato's God is persuasive against chaos but is not involved in deflecting the world from its present course. If you like the present action of God and think it adequate, there is no need for a divine defense. Aristotle's unmoved mover has a key position in the universe, but he does not concern himself with human affairs or with our anguish. Augustine and Thomas Aquinas, Luther and Calvin, each have changeless Gods who have directed the world's final outcome from eternity. But 'freedom' is the major social problem today, whether for men or for Gods. Human volition makes the future less predictable than the social sciences hoped for at their inception, but our human freedom is such that the future can never be determined by the past. In the modern world, it is Hegel who gave us the notion that reality could only be understood as 'process', but he is also first among those who thought the end could be discerned by charting a dialectic moving out of the past.

Instead, the past seems to roll on and to crush human religious hopes. Of course, this does not always happen but all too often it does. Our world does not demonstrate that it will achieve any purpose, at any rate certainly not a religious one, given its present course. Therefore, as disillusionment has set in over the Enlightenment hope to build its own new world, our ability to rely on God's future action has become crucial. Since history does not reveal the divine intent, we are thrown forward to the future. Along with this comes the realization of God's lack of defense. The modern world perfected the physical sciences. At the same time our insecurity in the world has increased rather than been eliminated, which is not what the social sciences hoped would happen. We are less secure and more alone now, psychiatrists tell us, than at any time in human history. Some want God to provide their lost security, but they do not realize that God himself has chosen not to live in that way. As our defenses have broken down and neither psychiatry nor the new social sciences have been able to provide our desired security, the defense of God appears necessary in ways it never did before.

If we must change our vision of God away from what it has been, can we ever say that any action we engage in is 'the will of God'? We can, but we must be careful to qualify our meaning, as those who destroy others in the name of God seldom do. No specific action can as such be called 'God's will'. All that God has willed, and all that we can claim by way of support for any action, is that we act in his defense. How we act, what we do, and the way we decide to carry out actions – all this is of our choosing not God's. So it is we who must bear the responsibility and we will all be evaluated on the basis of our choices. These decisions are our share of the responsibility as we work to establish new order, and God has given that project to us. It is God's to demand defense; it is ours to choose a specific course of action and accept responsibility for doing so. God will accept responsibility for having urged us to act in defense of his causes, but not for the specific means and the particular actions we propose on his behalf.

If so, can we ever claim that God speaks to us directly? Many individuals assert that God has done so as a way to explain their behavior. People often claim to act on specific instructions from God. Although it is not characteristic of Jesus, the biblical record abounds in stories of those instructed in specifics by God. I believe God may very well speak directly, but the interpretation of what we hear, how we translate God's heard word into action and even our claim to have heard him: for all that we must bear responsibility. This is particularly true due to the many conflicting reports we have about what God's direct instructions are. We know human beings can be deluded. Our decision that one putatively divine set of instructions is authentic and another false, this is up to us entirely. God's instructions appear in many places and on many lips, but none bears an official seal of guaranteed source. From out of the conflicting voices that come to us, it is our responsibility to say: This is from God; this is not. He has not yet broken his silence to confirm who has heard him correctly and who has grossly misinterpreted him. Such disclosure is for a future drama, and it should be an interesting scene when it is played out with God in the lead role.

21

## *Is it possible to achieve unity in defense of God?*

When we speak about 'the defense of God,' can those among us who follow non-theistic religions make any sense of all this? To support any religious way is to protect and uphold some values, goals, and forms of life which are not highly prized in the everyday world. Were this not so, did not some of us persevere along uncommon paths, religion would be unnecessary in society or in the lives of human beings. All religions, whether theistic or non-theistic, are called to a divine defense. That means: to protect, to uphold, and to follow pathways which might otherwise be trampled under foot or forgotten by the multitude. To return to theistic language for a moment, how odd of God not to establish clearly for us what is divinely valued so that secular society could recognize these as obvious values too.

No religion has a 100 per cent following among the peoples of the world. Thus, we face the need for internal campaigns to restore purity among the faithful, and we also hear about the need to drive out the infidels. Ironically, religious wars and intolerance and persecution come from the same source that drives us to the defense of God. Any religious goal is fragile, and we realize how easily its aims can be perverted. We ought to defend our particular religious goal with all our energy. But in our attempt to do this, too often we go astray and turn instead to destroy or to decry all who do not share our particular goal. Rage fails to distinguish between those who are antithetical to all religion and those who simply hold differently formed religious aims. All those who are religiously oriented (which is not everyone) should unite, theist and non-theist alike, in a non-tyrannical defense of those values the natural world is not attuned to. In these various plans to defend the sacred, we should pledge not to destroy or to denounce those whose religious visions differ from ours.

Quite obviously, if any program could count on receiving a majority support, it would need no special defense. However, we know religion will always be the concern of a minority. True, in certain societies and at certain times one religious form or another often ascends to a majority position. Then, carried away by victory, it may assume that the religious forces in the world should dominate in the secular domain. However, the history of religions shows us that triumphant and dominant religions tend to spoil and corrupt. When ecclesiastics control power, they become prey to power seekers just as kings do. When this happens, the religious consciousness of mankind, which is connected to a thirst for purity, rebels and strives to construct new religious forms. Then we launch an age of new religious movements just as we have recently. But this continual tendency to heresy, that is, to depart from the reigning orthodoxies, is never welcomed by the religious establishment. Too much is at stake, including the carefully cultivated religious security of dominant groups, for them to react calmly to the threat posed by new groups who form and drain away adherents.

Not every new religious movement is true and pure and good. Nor can any group or leader be all good, I believe, whether religious or political. But religious groups spring up in response to needs not being met by the already established religions. Of course, movements may be born partly out of the sense that, although religious celebrations are carried on, God has been left defenseless once again. The majority in any society hear other voices besides angels calling them, but the religiously sensitive should awaken whenever what they perceive to be God's goals are neglected. They should respond by issuing a call to his defense. All of us can answer to this alarm to salvage religious aims and goals from threatened prostitution, no matter what their religious orientation may be, theist or non-theist. To attempt to reconcile all theologies and their differences is another matter. Intellectual differences are important but are still a secondary concern. The practical issue is that we must not allow genuine religious life, no matter what its form, to be stamped out or lost by the lure of the secular world.

## The religious manifesto

In the late nineteenth century, Karl Marx and Frederick Engels issued a call to the workers of the world to unite. In rebelling, you have nothing to lose but your chains, Marx told them.[2] He thought that all workers would arise and form a worldwide community that bridged nationality and race. In this way they could free themselves from provincial concerns and lead a worldwide revolution to the benefit of all humanity. This call has had worldwide repercussions, some liberating, some destructive. Nevertheless, the vision Marx and Engels held out, that is to form a classless society based on a growing international community of workers, has not materialized. Realizing that corrupting forces and vested power structures would oppose this projected internationalism, Marx-Engels argued for the necessity to use violence as the only remedy strong enough to overcome existing barriers to human unity. Violence can tear down existing structures, it is true, but today we have come to think that it may also defeat the rise of the just society it seeks. In any case, I believe violence of any sort is unacceptable in defense of religious goals. Since the goals of religious life are so fragile that violence is sure to destroy the aim, we should pledge an abstinence from all wars.

Religious life needs to be defended from attack from those within as well as from those without, as Kierkegaard noted. Unfortunately, too much energy is expended within religious groups opposing those with whom they disagree religiously. Thus, those who rally to our call to defend both God and the goals of religion from secular attack know that they face opposition from friends as well as from enemies. But can we agree that religious ways are plural, that adherence to doctrine is not our main goal, but that the preservation of religious ways of life against their extinction is? If so, we can respond to a call for the defense of God on a worldwide scale. In doing so we know that we rise above race and class and nature, just as Marx projected for his society. If we take the pledge to abstain from violence, however, we also know we will never revolutionize the world's political and economic structures. Marx is right that such institutions both use and breed violence. Only a God whose whole being moves toward the future can achieve social change that is final and definite. Still, God needs our defense in our present hour against all attacks on that expected future which is yet to come.

All over the world religious life exists under the threat of destruction. God has taken a vow of silence. He has no voice or arms to defend himself but ours. Religious workers of the world, cease your age-old rivalries and internal strife. Unite, arise. Defend the Divine traditions in every land.

NOTES
1. Trans. Kimon Friar, New York: Simon and Schuster, 1969.
2. *Manifesto of the Communist Party*, English edn, 1888.

# CREATION AND THE STRUCTURE OF THE PHYSICAL WORLD
## John Polkinghorne

Our modern understanding of the structure of the physical world originates in the scientific revolution of the seventeenth century. It has been argued persuasively by Michael Foster[1] and others that it was the Christian doctrine of creation which enabled this step to be taken in Western Europe, a step which had not proved possible in the equally technically advanced setting of, say, Chinese culture. To the Christian, God is reasonable and so the works of the Creator are intelligible and open to rational inspection. Yet, because God is free, there is a contingency in creation which means that its order cannot be determined by a priori thought but must be discerned through experimental observation. Torrance puts this very well when he says: 'The intelligibility of the universe provides science with its confidence, but the contingency of the universe provides science with its challenge.'[2] The separation which Christian theology maintains between Creator and creation desacralizes the world and so makes its contingency open to empirical inquiry, free from the danger of impiety. Because the universe is God's creation, it is a fit subject for study. Thus it was that in the seventeenth century Christian theology provided the ideological setting in which science could embark on its task of investigating the pattern and structure of the physical world.

I

Ironically, the fledgling of the seventeenth century threatened to become a cuckoo in the nest as it grew up. The advance of physical understanding looked like demoting God to a detached deistic role. After the worlds had been set aspinning, Newton's laws took over and were perfectly competent to deal with the subsequent evolution of the universe. Sir Isaac had thought that divine intervention, angelically applied, might be necessary from time to time to preserve the integrity of the solar system and prevent its wobbling apart. His great successor, the Marquis de Laplace, showed that there was an inherent stability in gravitational interactions which enabled him to dispense with that divine hypothesis. Eventually, even the notion of the Divine Mechanic, the contriver of clever devices, proved unnecessary. Darwin pulled the rug from beneath the feet of Paley and his fellow apologists by showing how natural selection of random variations could provide the appearance of design without need for the intervention of a Designer. Science had come of age and seemed ready to disown its parent, Christianity.

To a very large extent, the problem had arisen from defective theological thinking. God had come to be regarded as a cause among causes, an agent at work alongside other agencies in the world. The sovereign Creator had become no more than an ingenious demiurge, restraining the teetering planets and assembling complicated creatures. The divine role was to explain the currently inexplicable, a time-dependent assignment, subject to decay with the advance of knowledge. There are always puzzling areas in our understanding of the world, but there is no reason to suppose that there are scientific no-go areas. Questions which are scientifically posable seem likely to prove to be scientifically answerable, however difficult it may prove at times to find what the actual answers are. The undeniable limitations of science arise from its self-imposed boundaries, its restriction to certain types of inquiry, that is, to issues of an impersonal and testable character. Within its own domain, it does not call for theological augmentation.

The God that Laplace and Darwin did not need to invoke was that straw deity, the God of the Gaps. The devout Methodist and distinguished theoretical chemist, Charles Coulson, who invented that phrase, once said briskly about murky areas in contemporary science: 'When we come to the scientifically unknown, our correct policy is not to rejoice because we have found God; it is to become better scientists.'[3]

God's activity in creation is not to be located with intervention in the world, either with or against the grain of physical law. Rather, it is to be found in those laws themselves, of which God is the guarantor. God is not a cause among causes but the sustainer and orderer of the world. Its regularities, discerned by science, are the pale reflections of God's faithfulness. To say that is not to assume a detached deistic role, so that once God had lit the blue touch paper of the big bang, the universe was left to get on with its own development. Such an understanding would attribute a false autonomy to nature and its laws. Those laws, and the universe that embodies them, are held in being solely by the *Logos*, the Word and Reason of God, eternally uttered.

But is all that just a flourish of theological rhetoric? After all, we can hardly put it to the test, as if we could withdraw the divine presence and see if the world collapses. All theological assertions partake of the nature of faith and so share in the risks inherent in such commitment. That does not mean, however, that the insights of faith are not rationally motivated. We do not shut our eyes and believe what we will. There is no unique way of proceeding from inspection of the physical world to the construction of a metaphysical scheme, such as the doctrine of creation, but, equally, it is not possible rationally to erect an arbitrary metaphysical edifice upon a given physical foundation. Questions of congruity constrain us. Our scientific and theological insights have to fit together. As a minister and a physicist, I am aware of that need for a consonant relationship between our understandings of the physical universe and of our encounter with God.

As far as the doctrine of creation is concerned, the proper place to look for such congruence is in the pattern and structure of the physical world, the nexus of law and circumstance which forms the *data*, the given, which science assumes in its theory of the world. Every intellectual endeavor must have its irreducible starting point, the unexplained in terms of which its explanations are to be framed. If the role of the Creator is that of the universal sustainer and orderer of the world, rather than that of an ingenious intervener in its processes, then it is to these foundational acts of scientific faith that we should look for consonance with our belief in God. The endeavor to do so declines to dispute with physics on its own territory (as the old style God of the Gaps tried to do), but it seeks instead to incorporate that territory in a wider realm of metaphysical coherence.

Such a quest seems to me to be obligatory, in one form or another, for all who wish to attain a unified understanding of the world in which we live. Quite frankly, science by itself is not enough. It leaves too many questions unanswered. But, you may say, are we not in danger of an intellectual infinite regression if we demand an explanation of everything, a regression which is only avoided by the trick of inventing an inexplicable God to put a stopper to it? After all, we have to start somewhere, and are not the laws of fundamental physics and the brute fact of the world's existence as good an irreducible basis as that provided by belief in a Creator? Certainly they seem to be better known and more widely agreed to than God is. I would reply that our intellectual restlessness can only find quiet where it also finds satisfaction. It is a remarkable fact that there has been a growing feeling among physicists that science, by the very character of its discoveries, raises questions which transcend its own power to answer. To their surprise, physicists feel an urge to concern themselves with metaphysical issues. In the homely language we scientists employ, there is a widespread feeling among us that there is more to the world than meets the scientific eye.

A number of books have been written recently putting forth this point of view. Perhaps such a book is most striking when it comes from the pen of someone who in other writings has shown considerable lack of sympathy with conventional religious thought. Such a one is Paul Davies. He recently went so far as to write: 'It may seem bizarre, but in my opinion science offers a surer path to God than religion.'[4] His book, *God and the New Physics*, is an account of those aspects of the structure of the physical world that lead him to this conclusion. The argument is innocent of any understanding of theology as an intellectual discipline, and it is indeed bizarre in its lack of balance. Davies, by declining to take account of the considerable body of claims to religious experience and insight, resembles nothing so much as a cosmologist who is only prepared to acknowledge what he can see through a telescope and who refuses the additional information about the nature of the universe offered to him by radio- and X-ray-astronomy. Nevertheless, within its self-limited terms of reference, the book is an interesting phenomenon.

## II

The feeling that there is more to the world than meets the eye finds its scientific motivation at two different levels. The first is that fundamental intelligibility of the physical universe which makes science possible. The fact that we can understand the world is so familiar that most of the time we take it for granted. Nevertheless, it seems to me that it is a highly significant fact about the way things are. What is perhaps more to the point, it also seemed so to Einstein. He once remarked that the only incomprehensible thing about the universe is that it is comprehensible.

At the articulate level of thought, it is mathematics that provides the perfect language with which to describe the pattern and structure of the physical world, the key to unlock its mysteries. Time and again, successful theories in fundamental physics have proved to be characterized by that unmistakable quality of economy and elegance which the mathematicians rightly call beauty. So frequently has this proved to be the case that a theoretical physicist, offered a putative theory which is clumsy or contrived in its mathematical character, will instinctively feel that it cannot be right. This power of mathematics to mirror physical reality has survived crises so grave that they might have seemed to threaten the subversion of science's rationality. The dilemma of the early years of this century that faced physicists when they realized that light behaved sometimes as a wave and sometimes as if composed of particles is a case in point. One might have thought that this was a clash of contrarities which would have defied rational synthesis. However, Dirac worked the necessary dialectical trick by his invention of the formalism of quantum field theory.

Human reason has always proved equal to the tasks set it by the phenomena of physics. It could so easily have been otherwise. Suppose we had access only to the geometrical rationality of the circle and that the analytic rationality of the calculus and the inverse square law was closed to us. Then our gropings after the structure of the solar system would have been condemned to an endless proliferation of epicycle upon epicycle (whether in the spirit of Ptolemy or in the spirit of Copernicus) with the pattern of Newton's great theory forever hidden from us. But it has not proved so. There is a remarkable congruence between the experienced rationality of our minds and the perceived rationality of the world around us. Dirac expressed his faith in this congruity when he wrote:

> It is more important to have beauty in one's equations than to have them fit experiment . . . because the discrepancy may be due to minor features which are not properly taken into account and which will get cleared up with further developments in the theory. . . . It seems that if one is working from the point of view of getting beauty in one's equations, and if one has a really sound instinct, one is on a sure line of success.[5]

In this passage, he draws our attention to a second aspect of the way in which human reason is so successful in exploring the physical world. The reference to 'a really sound instinct' – something which Dirac himself possessed in abundance – reminds us of that tacit side to scientific activity which Polanyi emphasized in his account of the scientific method.[6] The choice of questions to ask, the interpretation of experimental results, the elimination of spurious 'background' effects, the judgment when a discrepancy is serious or venial, all these call for the exercise of skills which are not exhaustively specifiable but which are essential for the scientific enterprise. I would wish to add to that list the skillful exercise of induction, for I do not think that mere falsifiability gives an account of scientific method which is adequate to actual scientific experience, whose fundamental character is that of discovery. The great success of science in settling questions to universal satisfaction (Is matter composed of atoms? Are atoms composed of electrons and nuclei? Are nuclei composed of protons and neutrons? Are protons and neutrons composed of quarks and gluons?), this success indicates that our tacit powers of judgment are as adequate for the successful discernment of the pattern and structure of the physical world as are our explicit mathematical abilities.

Some may feel that I am in danger of being carried away in scientifically triumphalist euphoria. Well, in my professional lifetime as a physicist, I lived through the advance in our understanding of the structure of matter which took us from protons and neutrons to quarks and gluons. It was a heady experience. And that experience was made possible by the marvelous intelligibility of the world, its transparency to human reason.

Is that just our luck or has it a deeper significance about the way things are? Let me return to Einstein. He once said:

> In every true searcher of nature there is a kind of religious reverence; for he finds it impossible to imagine that he is the first to have thought out the exceedingly delicate threads that connect his perceptions. The aspect of knowledge which has not yet been laid bare gives the investigator a feeling akin to that of a child who seeks to grasp the masterly way in which elders manipulate things.[7]

Although not a conventionally religious man, Einstein often spoke of God, whom he referred to in comradely terms as 'the Old One'.

If the congruence between the experienced rationality of our minds and the perceived rationality of the world is to find a deeper explanation, it must lie in some rational basis which is common to both. An elegant and persuasive understanding would be provided by recognizing the undergirding reason of the Creator, who is the ground of all that is. To refuse to take that step would be to leave oneself with an unresolved coincidence, an action that is contrary to all the instincts of the scientist. If the search for rational understanding is so successful in our exploration of the physical world, must it not also be pursued beyond that world of science into realms of wider metaphysical coherence? I am greatly in sympathy with the Bishop of Birmingham when he writes:

> Here I must declare myself and say that I believe very strongly in the Principle of Sufficient Explanation. . . . It seems to me extraordinary that many who spend their lives exercising their minds on human problems or on the investigation of the natural world . . . should state categorically that the mind has no right to ask 'Why' questions about the universe in which we live. To me, this is a dogma every bit as objectionable as religious dogma appears to rationalists.[8]

The great expositor of such a point of view has been the Jesuit philosopher, Bernard Lonergan. His whole metaphysics is built upon the analysis of, the centrality of, and ultimately the apotheosis of understanding. He does not hesitate to declare that 'since we define being by its relation to intelligence, necessarily our ultimate is not being but intelligence.'[9] That sounds like the creed of a professor! It often seems that for

Lonergan God is the Great Explanation, so that he proclaims that 'God is the unrestricted act of understanding, the eternal rapture glimpsed in every Archimedean cry of Eureka.'[10] Certainly, it is part of the attractiveness and coherence of theism that it offers insight into the rationality of the world, as well as into such features, indispensable to a whole view of reality, as the existence of beauty and of the moral order.

III

The second level of thought which motivates our feeling that there is more to the world than meets the scientific eye pertains to the character of the laws and circumstance revealed to rational inquiry. We have become aware in recent years of what appears to be a very delicate balance necessary in the *data* of our world if it is to be capable, in the course of its unfolding process, of evolving such interesting systems as you and me. In other words, if we played at God and wrote down a prescription for a universe – dictated its fundamental physical laws, prescribed the values of the physical constants which control the balance between the different forces described by those laws, specified the initial conditions from which the world derived its particular character – then, unless we had been meticulously careful in the mutual adjustment of the *data* of that prescription, our world would be one in which nothing interesting would happen. That is to say, it would not through its evolution prove capable of producing systems of the complexity which seems necessary if conscious beings are to appear upon its scene. Random twiddling of the 'knobs of the universe' will get you nowhere as a Creator. Fine tuning is necessary if humans are to come into being. This insight is sometimes called the anthropic principle.

Let me give some examples of the considerations which lead to this conclusion. In the very early stages of its existence, the whole universe was hot enough to be a gigantic arena for nuclear reactions. However, quite quickly – after about three minutes, in fact – the expansion of the universe had so cooled it down that nuclear reactions ceased, only to start up again much later in the interiors of stars, formed by local condensation. Thus, those hectic first three minutes[11] fixed the gross nuclear structure of the universe as we still find it today: three-quarter hydrogen and one-quarter helium. The precise proportion of these two elements depends upon the mutual relationship of the fundamental forces of physics, in particular the balance between the weak nuclear force, which causes some nuclei to disintegrate, and the other forces. Had this balance been only a little different from its actual value, then we should not be here, for either the world would be all helium and no hydrogen or there would be no supernova explosions in stars. Either would have disastrous consequences for the possibility of the existence of life. In the first case, if there were no hydrogen, there would be no water, and we cannot imagine life evolving without that vital substance. On the other hand, if supernovae did not explode, then the heavier elements, such as carbon and iron, which are also essential for life and which are only made by localized nuclear processes in the interiors of stars, would have remained locked up forever in dying stellar cores and so would have been unavailable for incorporation into living systems. We are all made of the ashes of dead stars. Thus, without that particular balance between strong and weak nuclear forces that we actually observe, we should not be here today.

A second example relates to the circumstance of the world, namely that it is very big. Our sun is just an ordinary star among the hundred thousand million stars of our galaxy, which itself is nothing to speak about among the thousand million galaxies of the observable universe. We sometimes feel daunted at the thought of such immensity. We should not. If the world were not about that big, we should not be here to be dismayed by it. A smaller universe would have run its course before we had time to appear upon its scene. It takes about eighteen thousand million years to make us the way we are.

A third example may relate either to the character of universal law or to particular circumstance, according to how things work out. The phenomenon to which it draws attention is the incredibly delicate balance between two competing effects in the early universe. One is the force of expansion, present in the singular explosion of the big bang, driving matter apart. The other is the force of gravity, pulling matter together. At a very early epoch (the Planck time), these two competing effects, expansion and contraction, were so closely balanced that they differed from each other by just one part in $10^{60}$. The numerate will marvel at such accuracy. For our innumerate friends, let us translate that into pictorial terms. If I took a target an inch wide and placed it on the other side of the observable universe, eighteen thousand million light years away, and took aim and hit the target, then I would have achieved an accuracy for one in $10^{60}$. Remarkable! But once again, if there were not this delicate balance between expansive effects and contractive effects, then we would not be here to be astonished at it. In a universe in which expansion predominated even a little bit more, matter would fly apart too quickly for it to be able to condense into stars and galaxies. In so dilute a world, nothing interesting would happen. On the other hand, if the forces of contraction predominated even a little bit more, then the universe would have collapsed in on itself again before there had been time for anything interesting to happen. Therefore, if you are going to play at Creator and set up a universe, make sure that you get the balance between expansion and contraction right if you want your world to have a fruitful history.

It is possible that this balance can be achieved, not by having to put it into the specification of initial circumstance but by a suitable choice of the universe's basic physical laws. An ingenious young American, Alan Guth, has suggested that there might have been what he calls 'an inflationary scenario' for the universe.[12] This is a process rather like the 'boiling' of space, in which a very rapid expansion of the world takes place. If that is correct, it would not only explain the delicate balance between expansion and contraction but also other puzzling properties of the universe, such as its high degree of isotropy. (It looks the same in all directions.) Guth's suggestion is highly speculative, and it would be wise to bear in mind the warning about cosmologists uttered by the great Russian theoretical physicist, Lev Landau, that they are 'often in error but never in doubt'. However, even if Guth is right, his inflationary scenario depends for its possibility on the form and balance of the basic laws of physics, so once again one would have to be careful in framing one's prescription for the world.

As with the intelligibility of the world, so with the anthropic principle: is it just our luck or has it a deeper significance about the way things are? Scientists have certainly felt uneasy about the question and have sought to carry its discussion further. Various lines of attack have been pursued.

One suggests that if we understood things properly, we should find that there is only one rationally coherent theory of the physical world that is actually possible, completely specified in all its characteristics. In other words, the cosmic 'knobs' cannot be twiddled after all. Relativistic quantum theory is very subtle and perhaps what seem like arbitrary quantities – the balance of strong and weak nuclear forces, for instance – may have to be exactly as they are if the theory is really to be totally consistent. Such a suggestion, if it were successful, would simply reduce our second consideration (the laws and circumstance of the world) to the first (the rationality of the world). The claim being made goes far beyond our present knowledge, and it also seems to me to be intrinsically improbable. Quantum electrodynamics, which describes the interaction of electrons and photons, is a beautiful and highly successful physical theory. I cannot see any rational impossibility in a world made up solely of electrons and photons, though we should not be part of it to enjoy its intellectual coherence.

A second suggestion is that perhaps there is a portfolio of different universes, each with a different setting of the cosmic 'knobs.' Then, if there were enough of them, it would scarcely be surprising if by chance in one of them the tuning were fine enough for us to appear on its scene. Of course, that is the one in which we live because we could not turn up anywhere else. This ample proposition is sometimes alleged to be supported by the notion of an oscillating universe, endlessly collapsing into a sort of cosmic melting pot and re-emerging thence, it is suggested, with its parameters changed by a mysterious process beyond the present power of science to investigate. Thus, a temporal succession of possible worlds would be generated. Alternatively, the highly contentious 'many worlds' interpretation of quantum mechanics is invoked.[13] This proposes that at every act of quantum measurement, the world divides into a series of 'parallel' universes, in each of which one of the possible results of the measurement actually occurs. However, that bizarre theory in no way suggests changes in cosmic parameters. The fact is that none of these ideas about multiple worlds is part of physics; they have no motivation at all in terms of our understanding of the pattern and structure of the physical world that we actually experience. In the strictest sense of the word they are metaphysical speculation.

The same can be said for the even cloudier proposition of the strong anthropic principle, which declares that in some unexplained way the emergence of human beings as observers forces the parameters of the world to assume values that permit that emergence. Here we would, with a vengeance, be hoisting ourselves by our own bootstraps.

There is nothing wrong with metaphysical speculation, but it should be recognized as such and not tricked out as pseudo-science. It seems to me that a metaphysical idea of much more economy and elegance is that there is just one world, which is the way it is, in its order and delicate balance, because it is the creation of a Creator who wills it to be capable of fruitful evolution.

## IV

The intelligibility and tightly-knit structure of the world provide the basis of a revived natural theology.[14] The feeling that there is more to the world than meets the scientific eye encourages the thought of an Intelligence behind its processes. It is the scientists themselves who have seen things that way while their theological colleagues have remained surprisingly unconcerned. The theologians are mostly either ignorant of what modern science has to say, or are so confident in revelation that they feel no need of ancillary help from general reason, or – mindful of the fate of Paley and the authors of the Bridgewater treatises – they are excessively wary of the whole enterprise of natural theology.

Such wariness fails to recognize that a revived natural theology is also a revised natural theology. It differs from its predecessors in two respects. Firstly, it is more modest in its claims. It presents itself, not as a demonstrative discipline, but as an insightful inquiry into the nature of the world. It does not assert that God's existence can be proved, but it seeks to persuade us that God provides that sufficient reason which can make satisfying sense of the remarkable world revealed to our investigations. It is in this search for an understanding of the world through and through, to its very fundamentals, that we discover the meaning of Augustine's claim that we must believe in order that we may understand.

Secondly, a revised natural theology looks for the source of its insight, not to particulars – the emergence of life, the structure of the eye, even the complexity of the human brain – but to the root structure of the physical world, the *data* of scientific inquiry. Its concern, therefore, is with laws and not with occurrences. Its God is not a God of the Gaps, competing with science as the explanation of events and continually being jostled off the stage of the world by the advance of knowledge. Rather, God is the Sustainer of the World, whose faithful will for material creation is expressed in those patterns of regularity which are the given of scientific inquiry. God is found, not in the gaps of knowledge, but in the fact of knowledge. William Temple once said that the fact of knowledge is more important than all known facts.

My case for a revived and revised natural theology rests ultimately on the order of the world. It would not be candid of me if I did not acknowledge the existence of three threats to that picture of wonderful order that I have presented. The first might seem to be posed by quantum theory, for it has dissolved the clear and determinate world of everyday into a cloudy, fitful world at its constituent roots.[15] For a subatomic particle, such as an electron, if I know where it is I do not know what it is doing, and if I know what it is doing, I do not know where it is. That is Heisenberg's uncertainty principle in a nutshell. Can the appeal to order survive such strange elusiveness in nature? Quantum theory deals in probabilities rather than certainties. At the level of elementary particles, it seems that God does indeed play at dice. In general, no cause is to be assigned to individual quantum mechanical events; their regularities are purely statistical.

There is a peculiar insubstantiality in the world. We may think that Dr Johnson had a point, in his bluff way, when he kicked the stone and asserted that he refuted Bishop Berkeley thus. However, that solid-seeming stone is mostly empty space and what is not is a weaving of wave mechanical patterns. Even logic is subject to modification in the quantum world. You tell me that Bill is at home and that he is either drunk or sober. Neatly employing the distributive law of classical logic, I conclude that I will either find Bill at home drunk or I will find him at home sober. Who could doubt so transparent a conclusion? Yet a similar argument applied to electrons would, in fact, be fallacious and von Neumann and Birkoff had to invent a special quantum logic to apply to their behavior.

I could go on telling weird travellers' tales of those who voyage in the quantum world. Its elusive and counter-intuitive character has seemed to some more suggestive of the dancing, dissolving thought of the religions of the Far East[16] than the sternly realist tone of the religions of the Near East. I do not agree. However idiosyncratic elementary particles may prove to be in their behavior, they have their own essential reality, even if it differs from the naive objectivity of everyday experience.

I reject the positivist views of people like Niels Bohr who treated quantum theory as just a highly successful manner of speaking about the behavior of laboratory apparatus. Such a view is an inadequate account of scientific experience. When physicists at CERN got very excited in 1983 because they considered that they had discovered the heavy W and Z particles predicted by elementary particle theory, they were not just rejoicing at an ingenious account of the behavior of an elaborate and expensive array of electronic detectors. They believed – and rightly in my opinion – that they had added to our knowledge of what *is*. If I am to defend this realist position about quantum entities, I think that ultimately I have to do so by asserting that it is our ability to understand them that assures us of their reality. In the unpicturable quantum world, we have to rely on intelligibility as the criterion of reality. That gives physics something in common with Western theology as the latter pursues its quest for insight into the nature of the Unpicturable, transcendent as well as immanent in the rational ordering of the process of the world.

A more serious threat might be thought to be posed by the realization that that evolving process of the world depends for its fruitfulness upon a delicate interplay between chance and necessity.[17] Chance – the random congregation of atoms or the mutation of a gene – is the source of novelty. Without its operation, nothing new would happen. But without the presence of a lawfully regular environment to preserve and select these fortuitous variations, all would vanish again like smoke in the wind. The role of chance has been held by some to preclude the possibility of meaning in the workings of the world. Its end point is not foreseeable from its beginning. Jacques Monod expressed this with Gallic intensity when he wrote: 'Pure chance, absolutely free but blind, is at the very root of the stupendous edifice of evolution.'[18] For Monod the universe is a tale told by an idiot.

Monod reaches this conclusion by his concentration on the chance half of the partnership. Let us consider for a moment the sphere of lawful necessity. The aspects of the behavior of atoms, relevant to the coming-into-being of life and its subsequent elaboration, are adequately accounted for by the laws of electromagnetism (which is the controlling force of interaction in this regime) and the laws of quantum theory (which is the appropriate form of dynamics describing the effects of that force).

When I first read of the speculations of biochemists like Monod about the origin of replicating molecules and life, I was bowled over by the thought of the astonishing fruitfulness of these simple laws – the thought that such equations could eventually lead to you and me. It spoke to me of a deep-seated potentiality present in the structure of the world, an insight of design which gripped my imagination. I am not a natural Teilhardian, but, for once, I could follow de Chardin in apostrophizing matter: 'You I acclaim as inexhaustible potentiality for existence and transformation.'[19]

The role of chance is to explore and realize that potentiality present in the pattern and structure of the physical world. To be sure, the final details of the end are not prescribed in the beginning. No doubt there are accidental features in humankind, such as the precise number of toes. But we have no reason to suppose that it is an accident that the raw material of matter is capable of evolving, in one form or another, into conscious beings, transcending their origin and capable of communion with their Creator.

I would argue that the balance between chance and necessity that we observe in the workings of the world is consonant with that balance between the gift of freedom and the reliability of purpose which should characterize Love's act of creation. I have written elsewhere:

> Theology has always been in danger of a double bind in relation to physical causation. A tightly deterministic universe, evolving along predetermined lines, seems to leave little room for freedom and responsibility. It is congenial only to deistic indifference or the iron grip of Calvinistic predestination. On the other hand, too loose a structure dissolves significance. Meaning can drown in the rising waters of chaos. A world capable of sustaining freedom and order requires an equilibrium between these rigidifying and dissolving tendencies.[20]

Chance signifies the vulnerability accepted by the Creator in making room for creation; necessity reflects the divine steadfastness in relation to it. No scientific umpire can adjudicate between Monod and my own view in our different judgments of the world. We agree on the physical circumstances (though he understood them much better than I do) but find conflicting significance in them. Both natural theology and natural atheism partake of the nature of faith and find their motivations from wider realms of understanding than the strictly scientific.

## V

The most severe threat to claimed significance is posed by the third matter which we must consider, namely the ultimate futility of the physical universe. We do not know for sure the future fate of the world. It depends on the precise nature of the near balance between expansion and contraction in the cosmic process. If the forces of expansion prove just to be the victors, then the matter of the world will continue to fly apart for ever. Within galaxies, however, it will contract under gravity to form gigantic black holes which, after almost inconceivable lengths of time, will decay by Hawking radiation. If, as some modern speculative theories in elementary particle physics suppose, the proton is an unstable particle with a lifetime in excess of $10^{31}$ years, then the nuclear pattern of the world will already have disintegrated long before this happens. By one route or another, according to this scenario, the universe will decay.

No less dismal is the prospect if the forces of contraction gain a marginal victory. Then the expansion that we presently observe will eventually be halted and reversed. The universe which began in the fiery explosion of the big bang will collapse in upon itself again to terminate in the fiery implosion of the big crunch.

Neither scenario that I have sketched seems encouraging to those who look for an ultimate purpose fulfilled within the history of the physical universe. Macquarrie was sufficiently dismayed by such a prospect to write: 'Let me say frankly, however, that if it were shown that the universe is indeed headed for an all-enveloping death, then this might seem to constitute a state of affairs so negative that it might be held to falsify Christian faith and abolish Christian hope.'[21]

Such a reaction strikes me as extreme. After all, Christian faith and hope have never been centered on utopian expectations for this present world. We cannot suppose that Macquarrie has never heard of the resurrection from the dead and the life of the world to come. Modern science simply makes plain with deadly earnestness the fact that if in this life only we have hope, the prospect is pretty bleak, not just for us individually but also for the whole of the physical universe. If there is a purpose at work in the world, it can only find its lasting fulfillment in a destiny beyond what we now experience. Such a destiny is unimaginable, but I do not think that it is an incoherent possibility. We know that what counts is pattern – not the particular realization of that pattern but the pattern itself. Our material bodies change their physical constituents every few years. It is the information content of their organization that is preserved as the expression of our personal continuity. It does not seem in the least irrational to suppose that the pattern might be reconstituted in a new environment of God's choosing. For us, that would be the resurrection of the body. For the universe, it might be what Paul was groping after in those mysterious words in Romans when he spoke of the creation 'subjected to futility' but also 'subjected in hope' that it might 'be set free from its bondage to decay and obtain the glorious liberty of the children of God' (Rom. 8. 20–21). I think the empty tomb might have something to say to us here if we would be willing to listen to its story, submitting ourselves to its insight rather than subjecting it to our prejudgment.

But if it's all going to be changed, why bother with the whole unsatisfactory process up to now? If fulfillment is in the new creation, what is the purpose of the old creation? Is not Macquarrie right after all to suggest that the decay of this present world is so negative a fate that it puts in question the hope of better things beyond it? The answer must lie in the preparatory processes of a God who chooses to work by unfolding development rather than by instantaneous decree. There is work for theologians to do in digesting these matters. I do not think the task is without clue or promise. Most of us Christians are content to face the prospect of the discarding and decay of our bodies without feeling that that denies the hope of a destiny beyond death. If that is true for us cosmic atoms, might it not be true for the cosmic whole?

It is time to face the question of what sort of God it is who is made known to us in the particularity of creation. Certainly this is not a God in a hurry. When one thinks of those eighteen thousand million years which elapsed from the big bang until conscious beings appeared, one can see that God is patient, content to achieve purposes through the slow unfolding of process. In that realization lies the small contribution that natural theology can make to that most agonizing of theological questions, the problem of the apparently wasteful suffering of the world.

The intelligible regularity of the universe reflects the rational reliability of its Creator. Its delicately balanced structure, intricately knit, evinces the subtlety of God's purpose to be achieved through the evolution of the world. The freedom which Love gives to its creation means that the potentiality with which the universe has been endowed is to be explored by the precarious interaction of chance and necessity and realized, not by the pronouncement of magical fiat, but by evolving development. If God's faithfulness implies that creation is orderly rather than fitfully manip- ulated; if the divine wisdom implies that creative purpose will be achieved by the anthropic potentiality inherent in the carefully adjusted balance of the universe; if love implies the acceptance of vulnerability by endowing the world with an independence which will find its way of development through the shuffling operations of chance rather than by rigid divine control; if all these things are true, then the world that such a God creates will have to look very much like the one in which we live, not only in its beautiful structure but also in its evolutionary blind alleys and genetic malfunctions.

We all tend to think that it would have been easy to have made things very differently, to have 'twiddled the knobs' of the universe so as to have preserved the good and eliminated the bad. The anthropic principle gives pause to such facile speculation. I am not quite daring to say with Leibnitz that this is the best of all possible worlds, but the idea is not as manifestly foolish as one might at first sight have supposed, if the world is to be one of lawful process.

## VI

What are the implications for theology generally of what we have been considering? I think they are considerable and need a sustained dialogue between scientists and theologians for their evaluation and digestion. If we believe in the unity of knowledge and experience, then advances in understanding in one realm of knowledge modify the tone and limit the range of acceptable insight in all others. There is an inescapable interaction between science and theology, as the whole of intellectual history from Copernicus through Darwin to the present day makes abundantly clear. That history is by no means one of continual warfare. Einstein once said that religion without science is blind and science without religion is lame. The two disciplines need each other.

Natural theology is alive and well and being practiced by scientists, however much it may be neglected or despised by theologians. It is important to recognize that there are reasons for believing in God which lie wholly outside our psyches. Such a realization would release contemporary theology from an undue dependence on existential analysis – a concern which, however necessary as part of a balanced exploration of experience is, in isolation, always liable to threaten to reduce theology to anthropo- logy. Natural theology also poses questions about the nature of God which general theological thought needs to take into account. For example,

Bartholomew, in his important discussion of the role of randomness in the processes of the world, calls for 'a doctrine of providence which, while allowing that God is ultimately responsible for everything that happens, does not require ultimate involvement in all things.'[22] In other words, God willed a world in which chance has a role to play, thereby both being responsible for the consequences accruing and also accepting limitation of God's power to control.

Natural theology is valuable, but it can only take us so far. People like Paul Davies, while they claim that physics provides a road to God, usually go on to say that they detect no sign of the personal God of Jews and Christians. The most they can assent to is the Divine Mathematician or the Grand Intelligence. We need hardly be surprised. Limited investigation yields limited insight. If one wishes to encounter the God and Father of Our Lord Jesus Christ, then one must be willing to take the risk of leaving the clear, beautiful, lunar landscape of science for the untidy, perplexing world of personal encounter. But to pursue that matter belongs to a different discourse.

NOTES

1. M. B. Foster, *Mind* XLIII (1934), p. 446; R. Hooykaas, *Religion and the Rise of Modern Science*, Scottish Academic Press, 1972.
2. T. F. Torrance, *Divine and Contingent Order*, Oxford: Oxford University Press, 1981, p. 58.
3. C. A. Coulson, *Science and Religion. A Changing Relationship*, Cambridge: Cambridge University Press, 1955, p. 2.
4. P. Davies, *God and the New Physics*, London: Dent, 1983, p. ix.
5. P. A. M. Dirac, *Scientific American*, May 1963.
6. M. Polanyi, *Personal Knowledge*, London: Routledge and Kegan Paul, 1958.
7. A. Einstein quoted in A. Moszokowski, *Conversations with Einstein*, Horizon, 1970.
8. H. Montefiore, *The Probability of God*, London: SCM Press, 1985, p. 8.
9. B. Lonergan, *Insight*, London: Longman, 1957, p. 677.
10. ibid., p. 684.
11. S. Weinberg, *The First Three Minutes*, London: André Deutsch, 1977.
12. A. H. Guth and P. J. Steinhardt, *Scientific American*, May 1984.
13. J. C. Polkinghorne, *The Quantum World*, London: Longman, 1984, chap. 6.
14. For a fuller discussion, see J. C. Polkinghorne, *One World – The Interaction of Science and Theology*, London: SPCK, 1986.
15. See Polkinghorne, *Quantum World*.
16. F. Capra, *The Tao of Physics*, Wildwood House, 1975 and G. Zukav, *The Dancing Wu Li Masters*, Rider/Hutchinson, 1979.
17. D. J. Bartholomew, *God of Chance*, London: SCM Press, 1984.
18. J. Monod, *Chance and Necessity*, ET, London: Collins, 1972, p. 110.

19. T. de Chardin, *Hymn to the Universe*, ET, London: Fontana, 1970, p. 64.
20. Polkinghorne, *One World*.
21. J. Macquarrie, *Principles of Christian Theology*, London: SCM Press, 1977, p. 256.
22. Bartholomew, op. cit., chap. 4.

# 3

## THE DIFFERENCE THEOLOGICAL ANTHROPOLOGY MAKES
## Kathryn Tanner

A theologian discusses human beings in relation to God. Discussion of this relation to God is the theologian's contribution to the understanding of human life, his or her pride and joy. But such a focus for discussing human life also marks the theologian's humility, signaling the limits of the theological enterprise and the dependence of the theologian upon other forms of inquiry and other contexts of investigation. I hope to offer here an account of humanity in relation to God that highlights the distinctive contribution of theological anthropology. First, however, I want to clarify, more generally, how the contribution of theology to the understanding of human life is both exalted and, at the same time, lowly.

I

Theology intends to be comprehensive. No element or aspect of the universe is really independent of a relation to God, since God is the Lord of all creation: 'The earth is the Lord's and all that is in it, the world, and those who live in it' (Ps. 24).[1] Thus, the theologian wishing to do justice to this relevance of God to the whole should exempt no element or aspect of the universe from theological comment. Within the purview of the eye trained on God come the stars in the sky, the trees and the oceans, wild beasts, creeping things of the earth, and certainly human beings, with whom God covenants, human beings with whom God chooses to be intimate in Jesus Christ. Because God's reach is universal, discussion about God is relevant, moreover, to more than the religious aspects of human life. God is a matter for concern not just in times of private prayer or within the walls of church, not just in ritual contexts when calling upon and praising God or bringing the bread and wine to one's lips, but in every affair of human life, no matter how mundane and trivial or seemingly profane, in one's workplace, on the street, in the home.

Theology does not try to insure this comprehensiveness by generating out of its own resources all there is to say on these matters.[2] A theological

43

discourse designed to cover the whole world is not entirely self-generated. It does not come forth from the theologian's mind in the way the world in itself comes to be from God's Word out of nothing. The theologian, as a theologian, is not an expert on plant growth, ocean tides, the molecular structure of biological compounds, human physiology and psychology, or group dynamics. Such topics, though included within the theologian's purview, are beyond theology's specific competence. The theologian does not have the resources – say, in biblical texts or church teachings – to render adequately informed judgments concerning them. The theologian depends upon other habits of inquiry and upon other disciplines for knowledge concerning such matters.

The theologian's specific concern is not so much to determine *what* is related to God – the height of the skies, the extent of the universe, the make-up of its inhabitants, their essential natures, accidental features or functionings – but *how* all things are related to God, a relation the theologian feels competent to discuss in light of the biblical witness, doctrinal pronouncements, church teachings, and the religious practices of Christians. Of course, if theology hopes to be comprehensive, the theologian's concern is not limited to this question of how God is related, bare and unadorned. Theologians make discussion of this question relevant to the whole world by taking up the best thought about the cosmos and its inhabitants and subjecting it to their particular angle of vision, by investigating how all this appears when one understands the world in its relation to the God of all.

The theologian who produces a comprehensive commentary is, there-fore, not like a self-determined creator of cultural artifacts – say, a writer of a novel or a composer of a symphony. He or she is, instead, is like an active reader or an orchestra conductor metaphorizing the artistic creation of others, diverting it from its intended course, transposing it into a new register or key. When producing a comprehensive commentary, the theologian does not provide his or her own place of habitation. The theologian engaged in such an enterprise is, instead, a perpetual renter, making do, making use of, working over the property of other disciplines, in the service of theology's own interests and purposes. The theologian producing a comprehensive commentary is, poor and incapacitated, a poacher or a parasite. Like those birds that lay their eggs only in other birds' nests, theologians bring their hope for a comprehensive commentary to fruition only by interjecting their own distinctive viewpoint within the spaces of other disciplines.[3]

Ironically, this lowly dependence on forms of knowledge not its own allows theology to intimate the way in which God's own Word is a word not simply for one time and one place, but for all. Theology has no special stake in any particular account of the natural world or of the human beings in it.[4] Theology does not become irrelevant, therefore, when its accounts of such things become obsolete. Claims made about the natural world and its inhabitants may come and go, influencing the theologian's commentary on them in this or that way. Unlike God's Word, every theological commentary on the world is transitory and fleeting; it shows its humanity by perishing, replaced by other human words for another time and place. Yet in and through this changing variety of theological production, there may continue to appear a distinctive theological *modus operandi*, particular patterns of poaching or styles of deflective transposition.

I intend to uncover a few of these patterns or styles of use in theological discussions of humanity.[5] I do not provide a full-fledged theological commentary on human life, informed as it would need to be by the best natural and physical science, sociology, and psychology of the day. Restrictions of space alone prohibit the attempt. Indeed, I try to minimize the degree of this dependence on other disciplines and sources of knowledge, focusing instead on the relation to God that is the basis for the distinctiveness of a theological viewpoint, merely indicating those places where the conclusions of other forms of knowledge might make an appropriate entrance. Even so, the account I offer is clearly influenced by a contemporary outlook on humanity – in its respect for human powers of self-determination, for example, and its sense of human life as inextricably embedded in wider worldly spheres, both ecological and socio-political. Moreover, the very stress in this account on the relation of human beings to God reflects a contemporary interest. This stress is the result of my judgment that, in an age of highly refined and well-respected sciences, theological anthropology needs to show not so much that it approves of their conclusions but that it has something of its own to say.

## II

At the most fundamental level, the human being is one creature among others. The relation that human beings enjoy with God, therefore, is one they share with all God's creatures. God's creatures are related to God as the recipients of God's good gifts or blessings. 'The Lord is good to all, and his compassion is over all that he has made' (Ps. 145.9). God holds creatures up in the palm of God's hand, bestowing upon them their existence in space and time, their living vitality and productive powers, their growth, increase, and capacities for communal fellowship in harmony with one another.[6] God acts bountifully in wonderful works; God expresses God's power in gifts of abundance:

> You visit the earth and water it, you greatly enrich it; the river of God is full of water; you provide the people with grain. . . . You water its furrows abundantly, settling its ridges, softening it with showers and blessing its growth. You crown the year with your bounty; your wagon tracks overflow with richness. The pastures of the wilderness overflow, . . . the meadows clothe themselves with flocks, the valleys deck themselves with grain, they shout and sing together for joy (Ps. 65.9–13).

God's solicitude and care extend to all God's creatures; God intends their well-being by seeing to their needs and satisfying their hungers. 'O Lord, how manifold are your works! In wisdom you have made them all; the earth is full of your creatures. . . . These all look to you, to give them their food in due season; when you give to them, they gather it up; when you open your hand, they are filled with good things' (Ps. 104.24–8). 'Satisfying the desire of every living thing' (Ps. 145.16), 'you save humans and animals alike, O Lord' (Ps. 36.6).

Faithful to this intention to bring about the creature's good, God works to uphold 'all who are falling' (Ps. 145.14), healing the sick, bringing captives out from their bondage, protecting the weak, easing the plight of the poor and the downtrodden.[7] God's blessings continue even under the disrupted conditions of sin:

> There is the beauty and utility of the natural creation, which the divine generosity has bestowed on man, for him to behold and to take into use, even though mankind has been condemned and cast out from paradise into the hardships and miseries of this life. How could any description do justice to all these blessings? . . . Think . . . of the abundant supply of food everywhere to satisfy our hunger, the variety of flavours to suit our pampered taste, lavishly distributed by the riches of nature, not produced by the skill and labour of cooks! Think, too, of all the resources for the preservation of health, or for its restoration, the welcome alternation of day and night, the soothing coolness of the breezes.[8]

Moreover, God's blessings to sinful humanity are not limited to those of the natural world: God sends God's own Word among us, to be born, to suffer, and to die for our sakes.[9] And more, Christ's coming is a prelude to even greater gifts of the kingdom: 'He who did not withhold his own Son, but gave him up for all of us, will he not with him also give us everything else?'

(Rom. 8.32). 'What blessings are we to receive in that Kingdom, seeing that in Christ's death for us we have already received such a pledge!' 'What blessings in that life of happiness will [God] provide for those for whom in this life of wretchedness he willed that his only-begotten Son should endure such suffering, even unto death?'[10] In some future time, Christ's compassion for the suffering, Christ's miraculous healings, Christ's feeding of the multitudes, will be brought to fulfillment in the well-being of a universal community in which the world and all its inhabitants will be reconciled for their harmony, peace, and security.[11] Enjoying in coming ages 'the immeasurable riches of [God's] grace in kindness towards us in Christ Jesus' (Eph. 2.7), we humans, along with the rest of God's creatures, will suffer no wants, becoming peaceful and harmonious with one another at a table set in glorious abundance by God.[12]

Human beings should rejoice in these gifts of God, given for themselves and for others, and esteem their goodness. Whatever a good God brings forth must be good in its own being. 'God saw everything that he had made, and indeed, it was very good' (Gen. 1.31). This gift-giving, value-producing, creative working of God cannot be limited, moreover, to some places or some times. 'My Father is still working, and I also am working' (John 5.17). 'God works ceaselessly in the creatures he has made. . . . This work is that by which he holds all things and by which his Wisdom "reaches from end to end mightily and governs all graciously." It is by this divine governance that "we live and move and have our being in him".'[13] Nothing of the creature's good is therefore exempt from the obligation to praise God for gifts bestowed. Everything that creatures have for the good, every precondition and means to their well-being, is to be attributed to God's giving: 'You are my Lord; I have no good apart from you' (Ps. 16.2).

This relationship between creatures and a gift giving God suggests a first, rather complex formality or pattern in theology's use of the sciences. The sciences may tell us about the creatures the earth contains, about their number and differences, about their natures, powers, and interrelations, about their inclinations, tendencies, and desires, and the manner in which they may or may not be satisfied in the present course of the world's compass. The theologian tells us, on the one hand, that those creatures are to be esteemed and their well-being valued. Creatures may be praised and respected without offense to God's glory, since this world and its inhabitants are the beauty with which God's glory clothes itself.[14] Praise for creatures does not detract from praise for the Creator, since all that is to be valued in the one is the gift of the other.[15] On the other hand, the theologian admonishes us that value is not to be ascribed to creatures apart from the continuous working of God in and for them. Esteem for the

47

creature apart from the God who makes it is idolatrous, a vain and empty esteem, since the good that is the creature's own remains dependent on God's giving. Dependent indeed, since, without God, the goods of created beings – their existence, nature, powers, perfections – cease to be.[16] Should God withhold God's gifts and 'take back his spirit to himself and gather to himself his breath, all flesh would perish together and all mortals would return to dust' (Job 34.14–15).

According to this first, complex formality, human beings must, therefore, be humble before God, even and especially for that of which they are most proud. Human achievements, for instance, come to pass only when God hears the plea that 'the favor of the Lord our God be upon us, and prosper for us the work of our hands' (Ps. 90.17). 'Unless the Lord builds the house, those who build it labor in vain' (Ps. 127.1). In adversity and opposition, it is not one's own arm alone, but one's own arm backed by the Lord's gracious giving that gives one the victory:[17] I worked harder than any of them – though it was not I [who achieved the success], but the grace of God that is with me' (1 Cor. 15.10). Joy in one's accomplishments is appropriate, then, only to the extent one continually boasts in the Lord's gracious help. 'Neither the one who plants nor the one who waters is anything, but only God who gives the growth. . . . For we are God's fellow workers . . . God's field' (1 Cor. 3.7,9).[18]

## III

Even though the human being is one creature among others, human beings are not merely one aspect of the created world; their relationship with God is not just that of any other creature. They have some special standing as the focus of God's concern. God may covenant with all the earth and its inhabitants (Gen. 9.10–17),[19] but God makes a special covenant with a particular people and, despite their continual failings, remains faithful to them with a steadfast love. God's Word may come into the world in order to bring about the eventual consummation of all things in a loving and just community, every one with every other and with God. God's Word nevertheless takes up humanity by becoming incarnate in Jesus Christ. Jesus Christ suffers and dies, first of all, for human sin and, by his death and resurrection, exalts human beings, first of all, to a new life in God in and through the Holy Spirit.

The creation of human beings in God's image (Gen. 1.26) may sum up this distinction. The biblical narrative remains silent, however, about any qualities of human nature that might account for their special standing. Creation in God's image is not a way of saying something about human beings as such; it is a way of pointing out a special relation between them and God. Human beings gain their unique dignity not by virtue of anything they possess in and of themselves but by being God's image – by reflecting, corresponding to, following obediently after, making an appropriate response to, the God who has created them for such a relationship.[20]

To be created in the image of God means, in other words, to have a particular vocation, one of fellowship and communion with God in which one uses all one's powers to glorify God and carry out God's purposes. Human beings may be alone among God's creatures in rendering conscious praise in word and deed for God's blessings in their own lives and throughout creation.[21] Unlike other inhabitants of the earth who are merely charged with furthering their own fecundity and prosperity,[22] human beings reflect God by adopting God's own project of universal well-being. Like the shepherd kings of antiquity, they mediate God's blessings, as best they are able, to both their own kind and the rest of creation[23] – for example, replenishing the earth and helping it to body forth bountifully,[24] furthering the prospects for human community by protecting and caring for the weak, the infirm, and the oppressed.[25]

As a second formality or pattern of use, then, the theologian takes up all that the sciences teach about human qualities and capacities in order to consider the manner and extent to which they may hinder or help human beings to fulfill their vocation of community and fellowship in relation to God. Thus, certain prerequisites might exist for that fulfillment: human beings might need to possess intelligence and will, powers of judgment and inner determination. They might require both spiritual and bodily aspects, self-consciousness and capacities for communication. Influenced by their varying cultural milieus, theologians over the centuries have offered these and any number of other characterizations of what makes human beings the image of God.[26] Indeed, they have often simply identified one or another such characterization with that image. The biblical text, however, simply talks of human beings without any distinction of aspects;[27] God creates in God's image the whole of the human in its entirety,[28] and the special relations that hold between God and human beings bear not on some aspect of humanity but on human beings as such, in and through all that they are.

## IV

This second formality specific to human life, which I have developed with reference to the creation of human beings in God's image, does not take away, however, from the first formality that concerned creatures as such.

This second formality presupposes the first: creation in God's image is just a further explication of what being created means for human beings.[29]

Bringing that first formality back into the discussion now produces a third formality: the distinction of being human, its special value and goodness, can be affirmed appropriately only against the backdrop of human unworthiness for it. Say what one will in praise of human beings – their special place in creation, their marvelous and unique qualities and capacities, the glorious nature of their partnership with God in the covenant and of their fellowship with God in Jesus Christ – none of it is appropriate apart from the affirmation of God's utter graciousness as the provider of such gifts. The general fact that the creature is not to be esteemed apart from a reference to God returns here in a new, more specific register.

First of all, the sheer extent of God's wondrous working, the universal scope of God's concern as the Creator of all, puts human distinction in perspective. God's hand is behind the course of the sun, moon, and stars, behind the grass that grows on the hills and the majestic rains that nourish them, behind the wild and fierce beasts of the seas, forests, and sky.[30] 'Although heaven and the heaven of heavens belong to the Lord your God, the earth with all that is in it, yet [something wonderfully strange!] the Lord set his heart in love on your ancestors alone and chose you, their descendants after them, out of all the peoples' (Deut. 10.14–15). Considered within the context of creation as a whole, the exaltation of the human in general is an unexpected grace: 'When I look at your heavens, the work of your fingers, the moon and the stars that you have established; what are human beings that you are mindful of them, mortals that you care for them?' (Ps. 8.3–4). Far from a matter of confident presumption, any special standing of humanity in relation to God requires the universal solicitude of God for its reassurance: 'Are not five sparrows sold for two pennies? Yet not one of them is forgotten in God's sight. . . . Do not be afraid; you are of more value than many sparrows' (Luke. 12.6–7).

The favors God bestows on human beings appear undeserved, in the second place, when considered in light of God's majesty. Who are human beings to be exalted by God, when, before God, 'even the nations are like a drop from a bucket,' 'inhabitants [of the earth] are like grasshoppers' (Isa. 40.15, 22), 'the whole world before you is like a speck that tips the scales, and like a drop of morning dew that falls upon the ground' (Wisd. 11.22)? 'Who can search out [God's] mighty deeds? Who can measure his majestic power? . . . When human beings have finished, they are just beginning, and when they stop, they are still perplexed. What are human beings, and of what use are they?' (Eccles. 18.4–8). The fleeting insignificance of humanity compared with God's eternity and everlasting might is the backdrop against which God's elevation of humanity is to be measured: 'O Lord, what are human beings that you regard them, or mortals that you think of them? They are like a breath; their days are like a passing shadow' (Ps. 144.3–4).

God's special gifts to human beings are discussed in biblical imagery of condescension.[31] Insofar as they are mere creatures of this world, human beings clearly have no capacity to storm heaven with a demand for God's favor. In bestowing blessings on human beings, 'the Lord our God, who is seated on high, . . . looks far down on the heavens and the earth' (Ps. 113.5–6). God reaches down from the heights to care for us in the depths.[32]

Although all human beings are lowly in this way before God in the heights, it is especially for the 'lowly' among human beings, those human beings with no status in the eyes of the world, that God comes down. The very ones with no claim to favor in human estimation – the sick, the despised, and the weak – receive God's special blessings. 'I am poor and needy, but the Lord takes thought for me' (Ps. 40.17). The Lord who is seated on high looks down upon the earth specifically to raise the poor from the dust, the sick from death, and the needy from the ash heap (Ps. 113.5–9). Those who boast before God of their health, prosperity, might, or social standing, considering all these the secure possessions of their own hands, fail to find such favor. God scatters them and exalts, instead, those of low degree with no illusions about the ultimate source of their favor in God's gracious giving.[33] 'Heaven is my throne and the earth is my footstool. . . . All these things my hand has made, and so all these things are mine, says the Lord. But this is the one to whom I will look, to the humble and contrite in spirit' (Isa. 66.1–2).

The special favors human beings get from God, moreover, can never be counted on as theirs by rights. God will remain faithful to God's loving intentions for us, but the gifts God bestows out of love remain just that – gifts. God is, therefore, never required to bless those that God does bless. God has, in fact, done otherwise on occasion, bringing affliction instead of blessings even to those people with whom God covenants.[34] God could yet do otherwise, tearing down in an instant the goods enjoyed by those who fail to see God as their refuge and source of strength.[35] 'So if you think you are standing,' Paul counsels, 'watch out that you do not fall' (1 Cor. 10.12) and lose God's benefits.

Finally, the special favors granted to human beings by God are undeserved in a more strictly juridical sense: they have not been earned. No one can stand before the God who made him or her and claim to be blameless, spotless and pure (Job 4.17). But much more than this, human beings have proven their unworthiness of special favor by piling up their sins. No one, therefore, has a valid claim on God's partnership and fellowship. Human beings cannot be said to deserve the love and concern displayed by God in becoming incarnate and living among us or the intimacy with God achieved through the workings of the Holy Spirit. God's special favors to human beings are, instead, the result of God's mercy and continued faithfulness to a partnership broken by its human participants. 'Since all have sinned and fall short of the glory of God, they are now justified by his grace as a gift' (Rom. 3.23–4). In acts of generous, unmerited invitation, God spreads out God's hands all the day to a rebellious people (Isa. 65.2). God 'does not deal with us according to our sins, nor repay us according to our iniquities' (Ps. 103.10); though our misdeeds multiply, God still considers our distress, hears our cries (Ps. 106), and returns good for evil. Dead through our trespasses, we are nevertheless made alive with Christ and exalted through him to sit with God in the heavenly places, only because of God's rich mercy and great love for us (Eph. 2.4–6).

Our infirmity and sin prove the graciousness of God's benefits to remedy our plight. We are all like Jonah in the belly of the whale – enjoying a deliverance from God that desperate straits make an unexpected and unhoped for surprise. We should therefore 'repeat that word which was uttered . . . by Jonah: "I cried by reason of my affliction to the Lord my God and He heard me out of the belly of hell" (Jonah. 2.2); . . . [so] that he [and we also] might always continue glorifying God, and giving thanks without ceasing for that salvation which he has derived from Him, "that no flesh should glory in the Lord's presence" (1 Cor. 1.29).'[36]

## V

I hope what I have said sufficiently demonstrates that a theological perspective on humanity exists that is not reducible to the conclusions of other habits of inquiry. There is something to a theological account of humanity even apart from its fleshing out by way of other modes of investigation. This kind of independence of other disciplines takes the shape of formalities or patterns for their use, and, therefore, it does not imply that a theological commentary on human life proceeds in isolation from other forms of inquiry. Theology has something of its own to say, which it does not need to prove by a procedure of that sort. A theological perspective on humanity has its distinctiveness, but it is not one that must be bought at the price of vain attempts at self-sufficient insularity. The other disciplines that discuss human beings are not foreign to a theological commentary on human life, since that commentary does not proceed independently of them. But neither does a theological commentary simply conform to those disciplines, since it does not receive its identify as a theological commentary from them.[37]

What may not yet be clear is the manner in which conclusions of other disciplines are altered when brought within a theological purview. Are they, for example, altered at all? Perhaps a theological formality merely leaves the conclusions of other disciplines alone, assimilating them as if within its own perspective. In that case, theological anthropology would assure its distinctiveness by leaving most of the field of inquiry about human life to entirely secular disciplines. Other disciplines would not encroach on theology's territory, but neither would theology encroach on theirs. Theology could provide a comprehensive commentary on human life, but people with no prior theological interest in life would have no reason to listen to it. They might know something more should they view what they know under a theological formality – something about God and the nature of our relations with God. In that sense, theological anthropology might make a difference to their understanding of human life, but a theological formality could neither challenge nor correct what they thought they knew before. Theological anthropology in this respect would make very little difference indeed.

The impropriety of such conclusions is hard to show on the basis of what I have provided here – a bare bones sketch of a few theological formalities themselves. The difference theology makes to the conclusions of disciplines it incorporates would certainly be easier to see if I had incorporated many such conclusions myself in order to produce a more fully-fledged theological commentary on human life. A few rejoinders are, nevertheless, possible on the grounds of the theological formalities I have discussed.

At a minimum, one can say that the relation between theology's contribution to an understanding of human life and that of other disciplines is more than merely additive. When incorporated in a theological commentary, the conclusions of other disciplines at least undergo transposition into a religious key. We know we are not alone in the universe as self-sufficient masters of ourselves. All that we are for the good is a gracious gift, for which we should render praise and thanks to God. Such a change in register marks more than simply a change in the way one maintains or holds the conclusions of other disciplines, that is, more than a change in one's subjective disposition or attitude with respect to what one knows on other grounds to be true of human beings. Thus, the first formality of creaturehood suggests human beings are properly understood only within the widest possible purview of the universe as a whole. Isolated investigation of the human makes little sense if human beings are part of a universal society of creatures held together by God's loving intentions. The second formality of human distinction implies, moreover, that human beings are made for a destiny of which the human and natural sciences may know nothing. The clearer that destiny in relation to God, the more theological anthropology will have to say of itself about human prerequisites for it. And the closer human beings are to fulfilling such a destiny, the more the qualities human beings display may require a reference to God in order to make sense.[38] Finally, the third formality of human unworthiness for God's favors saves scientific investigation of the human from self-interested conclusions. A theological anthropology that knows that human beings owe such favors to God's grace contests any effort by the human or natural sciences to glorify humanity by exaggerating our differences from, and superiority to, other beings within the world.[39]

The implications of theological anthropology for secular ethics are certainly material and more than merely formal. Insofar as it follows the three formalities discussed above, theological anthropology lodges an attack on both over- and under-valuations of human life, fostering instead a humble but healthy self-respect. Human life is genuinely valuable but not absolutely or unquestionably so in a way that would make all other beings of the universe mere means to human well-being. A theological contribution like this to ethics cannot be restricted, furthermore, to a counsel about proper individual attitudes, a restriction that would leave conclusions about politics and society to secular spheres. Theology, on the basis of its understanding of God, proclaims the objective value of God's creatures, a value that must, therefore, be respected in the relations human beings establish with one another and with other kinds of beings in the world. A whole socio-political and ecological ethics can be developed from this starting point, one that might differ substantially from any offered by non-theological disciplines.[40] At its most general, such an ethic would maintain that, since all human beings have been created in the image of God, the propriety of human behaviors is to be assessed within the widest possible frame of a universal human society. It would maintain, moreover, that, since the special standing of human beings is a mere modification of what it means to be a creature of God, the good of humanity cannot be furthered without attention to the good of all God's creatures – the whole world and all its inhabitants. In this way, the theological formalities I have discussed erase customary boundaries of moral concern. Even without contributing new ethical recommendations, theology, at a minimum, extends the application of those recommendations that exist so as to fall into conflict with every provincial and parochial ethic: 'Sparrows and sheep and lilies belong within the network of moral relations. . . . The line cannot even be drawn at the boundaries of life; the culture of the earth as a garden of the Lord and reverence for the stars as creatures of his intelligence belong to the demands of [God's] universal will.'[41]

NOTES

1. Translations of the Bible in this chapter follow the New Revised Standard Version.

2. See Clodovis Boff, *Theology and Praxis* (Maryknoll, NY: Orbis, 1987) on the dangers of what he terms 'theologism' (pp. 26–7, 36, 52, 107, 223, and elsewhere) and on his appeal to Thomas Aquinas' idea of theology's formal object (pp. 67, 75, 88–9). What makes a discussion theological is not its subject matter – theology can talk about any and everything – but its manner of treatment, its reference of all things to God. This is the sense in which I use the term formally. See also William Christian, *Doctrines of Religious Communities* (New Haven: Yale University Press, 1987) and his discussion of the way religious discourse can be occasion comprehensive without being topic comprehensive (pp. 186–92, 225–7). I am suggesting that theological discourse can also be topic comprehensive in a way William Christian does not envision. Theology can make a necessary place for what Christian would call 'secular claims' (p. 73).

3. See Michel de Certeau, *The Practice of Everyday Life* (Berkeley: University of California Press, 1984, pp. xxi–xxii, 29–42) on the creativity of 'consumers'. For further discussion of an appropriation of this for theological purposes, see Kathryn Tanner, *Theology and the Study of Culture* (Minneapolis: Fortress Press, forthcoming).

4. This is true even if some of these accounts are incompatible with a theological formality – something I am not ruling out.

5. I make no exhaustive or exclusive claims for these. There are others and the ones I develop, primarily on biblical grounds, are certainly contestable.

6. See Claus Westermann, *Blessing* (Philadelphia: Fortress Press, 1978) and Edward Schillebeeckx, *Christ: The Experience of Jesus as Lord* (New York: Seabury Press, 1980, pp. 515–30) for an interpretation of what material like this implies for the relation between God's action in creation and covenant.

7. See, for example, Psalm 146.

8. Augustine, *City of God*, New York: Penguin, 1972, 12.24.

9. ibid., 7.31 and 22.24.

10. ibid., 22.24.

11. See Ephesians 1.10 and Colossians 1.15–20; also Isaiah 11, 32, 35, 41, 60, 65; Jeremiah 31; and Micah 4.3–4.

12. See Irenaeus, *Against Heresies*, 4.32–7.

13. Augustine, *The Literal Meaning of Genesis*, New York: Newman Press, 1982, 4.12.23. The biblical quotations are Wisdom 8.1 and Acts 17.28. I am indebted to Kathryn Greene-McCreight for calling my attention to this passage of Augustine.

14. Psalm 104.
15. *'Quo major est creatura, eo amplius eget Deo.'* (Francis of Osuna, quoted by Henri Bremond, *A Literary History of Religious Thought in France*, vol. 1, *Devout Humanism*, New York: Macmillan, 1928, p. 11.) As Bremond remarks, this was a favourite quotation of St Teresa. *'Detrahere pefectioni creaturarum est detrahere perfectioni divinae virtutatis.'* (Thomas Aquinas, *Summa Contra Gentiles*, III, 69.15.)
16. See *City of God*, 12.26.
17. Psalm 44.4–8.
18. I follow the Revised Standard Version for verse 9.
19. The Noachic covenant. See Bernhard Anderson, 'Creation and Ecology', in Anderson, ed., *Creation in the Old Testament*, Philadelphia: Fortress Press, 1984, pp. 166–9.
20. For this account of creation in God's image, see Claus Westermann, *Creation*, London: SPCK, 1971, pp. 49–60, especially p. 56; Claude Stewart, *Nature and Grace*, Macon, Georgia: Mercer University Press, 1983, pp. 11–13; Vladimir Lossky, *The Mystical Theology of the Eastern Church*, Cambridge: James Clarke and Co., 1957, pp. 114–34; Jügen Moltmann, *God in Creation*, San Francisco: Harper Collins, 1991, pp. 215–33; Gordon Kaufman, *Systematic Theology*, New York: Charles Scribner's Sons, 1978, pp. 329–64.
21. See Moltmann, *God in Creation*, pp. 70–1.
22. See Genesis 1.22.
23. See Westermann, *Creation*, pp. 52–3.
24. See Genesis 1.28 and James Barr, 'Man and Nature: The Ecological Controversy and the Old Testament' in David and Eileen Spring, eds., *Ecology and Religion in History* (New York: Harper Torchbooks, 1974, pp. 61–75) for the meaning of 'dominion' and 'subdue' in this biblical passage.
25. This injunction runs throughout the prophetic books (e.g., Isaiah 1.16–17; Amos 5). In the New Testament, see, for example, Matt. 25.34–45. See also Westermann, *Blessing*, pp. 94–5, on the imitation of Christ's healing and helping as part of the commission to the apostles in Matthew 10 (Luke 10).
26. See, for example, the enormous variety of characterization even when discussion is limited to the early Eastern theologians. See Lossky, *Mystical Theology*, pp. 114–34. See also Westermann, *Creation*, pp. 56–8.
27. Lossky, *Mystical Theology*, p. 120; Moltmann, *God in Creation*, p. 221; Westermann, *Creation*, pp. 57, 59.
28. This can be affirmed despite the fact that a second creation story in Genesis (Gen. 2—3) permits some ambiguity.
29. See Westermann, *Creation*, p. 60.
30. See Job 34—40.
31. See Claus Westermann, *The Praise of God in the Psalms*, Richmond: John Knox, 1961, pp. 14, 117–22.
32. See, for example, Psalm 18.16.
33. See Luke 1.51–2.
34. See, for example, Psalm 66.
35. See Psalm 52.5–7.
36. Irenaeus, *Against Heresies*, edited by A. Roberts and J. Donaldson, vol. 1, *Ante-Nicene Fathers*, Edinburgh: T & T Clark, 1989, III.20.1.

37. An application to theology of de Certeau's account of the way 'the long poem of walking manipulates spatial organizations'. *Practice of Everyday Life*, p. 101.

38. That is, such qualities may have to be considered gifts of grace in a narrow sense according to which grace is distinct from nature. In the broad sense of God's giving developed in this essay all is grace, everything the creature displays for the good is grace. But in a narrower sense of God's grace, some gifts of God – for example, communion with God through the Holy Spirit – are not natural endowments and cannot be anticipated by reasoning from such endowments.

39. See H. Richard Niebuhr, *The Meaning of Revelation*, New York: Macmillan, 1960, pp. 126–8.

40. For a start at such a socio-political and ecological ethics and a discussion of its differences from some forms of non-theological ethics see Kathryn Tanner, *The Politics of God*, Minneapolis: Fortress Press, 1992, chapters 4—7; also my 'Creation, Environmental Destruction and Ecological Justice' in Rebecca Chopp and Mark Kline Taylor, eds., *Reconstructing Theology*, Minneapolis: Fortress, forthcoming.

41. Niebuhr, *Meaning of Revelation*, p. 122. See also the still helpful essay by Robert King, 'The "Ecological Motif" in the Theology of H. Richard Niebuhr', *JAAR*, 42/2, June 1974, pp. 339–43.

# 4

# CREATION AND RELATION
## Janet Martin Soskice

This article has three concerns: the relation of scientific insights to Christian belief and practice, the relationship of human beings to God, and finally our relationship, as human beings, to the rest of the created order. I will be defending anthropocentrism and attacking 'the Environment'.

One obvious place to begin to seek a theology of creation is the book of Genesis. Its very title means 'origins', but origins of what? Recent works on creation and theology have dealt extensively, sometimes almost exclusively, with questions about the origins of the physical universe and its life forms. The scientists deferred to have been astrophysicists, and the covers of the books bear pictures of swirling galaxies. For a whole generation of doctrinal theologians and philosophers of religion (my generation) this is what theology of creation meant – talk of big bangs and 'fine tuning' of the physical variables which make life possible. Certainly Genesis is concerned with the creation of the physical order but it is also concerned with the creation of the people, Israel. It is concerned, too, with order and right relation. In its first chapters we are given a schematic outline of the relation of the human being to God, the relation of man to woman, of human beings to plants and animals and to each other. Throughout Christian history these chapters of Genesis have been plundered to provide pictures of the ideal humanity, the ideal marriage, even the ideal State. The concerns of Genesis are then both wider and narrower, different from, those of the modern physical and biological scientist.

One common feature of this ancient religious text and modern science, however, is a concern with ultimate origins. Some of the earliest examples of biblical commentary we have are the Hexaemera, so called because they gave an account of the first six days of Creation. One of their objects was to insist that all that is was created freely by God. In posing their challenges to pagan creation narratives they sought to do so in ways compatible with the received scientific knowledge of their own day, a feature of the Hexaemera which impressed the nineteenth-century philosopher of science, Pierre Duhem. We can imagine that St Augustine, too, would have approved, for he thought that Christians made themselves ridiculous when they talked 'utter nonsense' about scientific matters while claiming to speak in accordance with Scripture. This makes Christian writers into laughing-stocks, he said, and does great harm, for when non-Christians hear a Christian making bizarre claims about the physical world and justifying them by appeal to Scripture, 'how are they to believe the same writings on the resurrection of the dead and the hope of eternal life and the kingdom of heaven?' According to Augustine, in a text much admired and appealed to by Galileo, 'whatever the [scientists] themselves can demonstrate by true proofs about the nature of things, we can show not to be contrary to our Scriptures'.[1]

This conciliatory attitude to natural science strikes us as modern on Augustine's part, for we have entered in recent decades another period of amiable relations between science and religion. In one way or another theology has come to terms with the challenges our great-grandparents faced in Darwinism – no longer do we find ourselves in the place of Ruskin whose faith wavered with each tap of the geologists' hammer. Indeed in recent decades some theologians have regarded science not as an enemy but as an ally and have called attention to strategies of scientific theory-construction and model-building in defence of their own strategies of theory-construction and model-building. As modern science has become more eloquent about its own limitations and the difficulty and tentative-ness of any truth-claims, theologians have been emboldened to make comparisons with their own tasks.[2] Advances in cosmology and evolution-ary biology have even encouraged the more reckless among the philo-sophers of religion in the ever-elusive hope that one day science will prove that God exists. A number of conferences have taken place on epistemo-logy, metaphysics, theology and astrophysics.

For those of us interested in science and religion this is all gratifying but also somewhat alarming. Why do our collections of essays always have that swirling galaxy on the cover, or a piece of electron-microscopal photogra-phy, and never a baby's foot, or a woman drawing water at a well, or – to use a biblical image of creation – a rainbow? As our essays on creation become ever more dense and theoretical there is a danger that they become ever more remote not only from what (if anything) the biblical books say about such things, but from what the Christian tradition ever wanted to say. Biblical scholars who somehow manage to 'gatecrash' science and religion symposia are often appalled at what passes for the Christian theology of creation. Is there not a danger that we are engaged in an elaborate parlour game which, however fascinating, is one which very few indeed will ever be able to play? Is this just a new scholasticism which, despite real merits, is as destined as its late-medieval predecessor for obsolescence?

As a contributor to some of these discussions I want to say, 'No'. These discussions are important in an overall Christian apologetic, and their obscurity to the non-professional is neither here nor there. (Few lay people understand modern astrophysics but they would understand well enough if someone claimed that modern astrophysics had decisively demonstrated that God could not exist.) But I wish to raise the spectre of the parlour game to highlight a kind of schizophrenia in the science and religion dialogue at present. For while doubt may be cast on the immediate impact of the lofty, metaphysical discussions currently taking place between scientists and theologians, there is no room to doubt the immediate impact science and scientific practice are having on all our everyday lives. One can scarcely even begin to list the areas of moral concern on which scientific theory and practice have some bearing: computer fraud, the disposal of industrial waste, *in vitro* fertilization, mad cow disease, the development and cost of armaments, the allocation of medical resources, the generation and limitation of world famine, AIDS, pollution, ante-natal diagnosis of genetic diseases. Wherever we turn we see possibilities, but also dangers. Even well-intentioned efforts may have unfortunate, even disastrous side effects. The hardy and disease-resistant crops that we hope will transform the lives of people in poor countries may need expensive fertilizers which only the rich can buy. Thus the introduction of the crops may serve to concentrate land and wealth in the hands of those already landed and wealthy, rather than aid the subsistence farmer who was originally supposed to benefit. These moral issues may not, as with positivist challenges of an earlier era, pose a threat to Christian belief *per se*, but they do represent a challenge to which Christianity, if it is to continue in its vision, must rise.

These issues are not issues for the Christians alone – they are all citizens' problems, and indeed all nations' problems, since many extend beyond the scope of a personal ethics. I may independently decide when pregnant not to take the alpha-feta protein tests which may indicate neurological disorders, but I cannot decide as an individual how to dispose of nuclear waste. However, even if these are not exclusively Christian problems, nonetheless may we not hope for some guidance from our religious beliefs as we move cautiously forward?

This is the point at which the schizophrenia in science and religion bites. After some time doing research in the philosophy of religion and philosophy of science I was a member of a working party in medical ethics. This group, composed in the main of medical doctors, philosophers and theologians, was discussing 'Quality of Life in Medical Decision-Making'. The contrast with my former involvement with science and religion was sharp. Whereas the science and religion debate at the 'swirling galaxies' level was fizzing with ideas and happy meetings of mind, one felt in the area of medical ethics that one was entering a conceptual wasteland, one where theological contribution was both peripheral and impoverished. Who was to blame? Not the scientists. They were coming simply with problems, one of the biggest of which was, 'On what basis do I make judgments about or between human lives?' One doctor said, 'I can't tell you exactly when a patient has died: I can tell you when her heart stops beating, or when she stops breathing independently, or when there's no pulse or no brain activity, but to say exactly when she has died – that's no longer a medical judgment.' The scientific contribution was, one could say, morally neutral. Blame, if there is blame, must be laid at the doors of the moral theologians (amongst whom for these purposes I place myself) for the signal failure to match with theologically compelling arguments the self-confident and increasingly aggressive views of moral atheism.

In such circumstances the cry goes up for the 'Christian opinion' – that is why theologians are asked on to medical ethics working parties in the first place. But 'Christian opinion' does not amount to theological argument; for example, a Roman Catholic theologian might be expected to express the 'opinion' that experimenting on embryos is wrong, but with no scope or opportunity to explain on what rational basis, in the light of their religious beliefs, Catholics might hold such a conviction. Rather this is seen as just one opinion thrown in by an interest group.

If the theologian should defend the opinion, she or he would be expected to do so on what was assumed to be the neutral ground of secular moral philosophy. From there these debates always proceed in a predictable way. The same questions perennially occur and perennially fail to be resolved: When does life begin? Is the embryo a 'person'? What weight should be given to potential?, etc., with scarcely a glance at what bearing Christian doctrine might have on such matters.

In such circumstances the theologian usually colludes in playing on ground which, far from being neutral, is home ground to secular moral philosophy and a wasteland for moral theology. No wonder, then, the impoverishment almost to the point of extinction of a distinctive theological voice. All the Christian can do in such circumstances is to offer their 'opinion' in a louder voice, but since there is no real conversation, no meeting of minds, the voice is unlikely to be heard.

Even in the Christian press today the discussion of controversial moral issues often takes the form of raised voices and embattled opinions, with little reference to the theological and biblical roots which gave rise to and make sense of these views. This shouting technique is unlikely to persuade non-Christians who do not share one's views, but even worse, it is increasingly unlikely to convince rank-and-file believers either, especially when the milieu in which they (for the most part) move is one increasingly alienated from Christian moral assumptions.

An example which to me demonstrates the gap opening up between Christian and agnostic moral assumptions comes from Peter Singer and Helga Kuhse's book, *Should the Baby Live?*, a book which deals with the problems of handicapped infants and the morality of infanticide. Singer and Kuhse go far beyond simply ignoring Christian views; they attack Christianity as the dominating and restrictive ideology which has, for so many centuries, curtailed human freedoms in the West. For more than 1500 years, they state, Christianity has dominated Western moral thought. Those who rejected it were persecuted. 'During this long era of totalitarian enforcement, Christian moral views gained an almost unshakeable grip on our moral thinking.'[3] We much detach ourselves from them if we are to address the moral issue of severely handicapped infants. In particular we must detach ourselves from the idea that human life has a special sanctity, a belief which may be defensible within certain religions but which cannot carry conviction in a pluralist state.

Let me remind you that Singer and Kuhse's argument is not directed towards abortion but infanticide – the killing of newborns who might otherwise live. If one includes in the definition of 'human' such indicators as self-awareness, self-control, sense of future and past, then Kuhse and Singer are content. But simply to be a member of the species *Homo sapiens* is not enough to make a being 'human' in the sense necessary for life to be preserved. Many disabled babies will never be 'human' in this more rigorous sense. Why, their argument continues, should being an *Homo sapiens* be so overridingly important? Is not this just species-ism, and much analogous to a racism wherein killing a black is less morally significant than killing a white? Species, like race and sex, Singer and Kuhse argue, is a morally irrelevant distinction.

They blame Christianity for the dominance in our culture of this morally irrelevant distinction, and in particular the doctrine that man (*sic*) is made in the image of God, licensed to kill other creatures but not his or her own kind. But according to Singer and Kuhse, 'an inquiring sceptic would wonder why an anencephalic infant (one born with little or no brain) more closely resembles God than, say, a pig.' Their conclusion is that 'to allow infanticide before the onset of self-awareness . . . cannot threaten anyone who is in a position to worry about it.'[4]

One should not dismiss their argument summarily. Singer's earlier book, *Animal Liberation*, was a considerable success amongst anti-species-ists, some of whom – one imagines – had little idea that advancing the cause of animals could have such radical implications for the claims of disabled human babies. But what is most interesting is that Singer and Kuhse place the essence of the debate in theology. While Christian ethics has been at pains to play on the grounds of secular philosophy, here we find two secular writers throwing the ball firmly into the theological court.

I would like now to sketch the beginning of a response to the accusation that 'the traditional principle of the sanctity of human life is the outcome of some seventeen centuries of Christian domination of Western thought and cannot rationally be defended',[5] and this brings us back to the theology of creation, a topic to which those of us interested in the debate between science and religion must now look with some urgency.

The theologies of creation which can be traced in the Old and New Testaments are not primarily interested in cosmology, and throughout Christian history, although theologians have occasionally pondered such questions as whether the universe had a beginning in time or whether it did not, these were never the central theological questions. Thomas Aquinas could suppose either possibility to be compatible with the Christian doctrine that God is Creator, although he believed, as a matter of fact, that the universe did have a beginning.

The biblical discussions of creation seem concerned not so much with where the world came from as with *who* it came from, not so much with what kind of creation it was in the first place as with what kind of creation it was and is *now*.[6] Creation in the Old Testament is, above all, order and it comes from God, exclusively from God. God is sovereign in creation and does not tinker with pre-existing matter like some demiurge. In Genesis God creates the universe from nothing and effortlessly. God pushes back the waters and separates light from dark. Creation is the triumph of order over chaos, and because creation is order it is law-abiding and, according to the Genesis story, it is initially both peaceable and just.

Later theologies posited that God, as creator of all that is, is both mysteriously Other (for God is not a creature) and also totally intimate to everything. God as both Otherness and Intimacy is, as Martin Buber insists, the 'You that in accordance with its nature cannot become an it'.[7] God, too, is mystery – the mystery by which we humans and all the rest of the created order are held in being. Christians believe that in Jesus of Nazareth the Word became flesh but not, as Karl Barth ceaselessly pointed out, that the God who is mystery becomes unmysterious in Jesus Christ. If we don't see Jesus Christ as mystery we see not God incarnate but a great man.

Human beings have a privileged role to play in God's creative love because, according to this story, they are made in the image of God. This, of course, is anthropocentrism, but not necessarily in a hostile form. One can distinguish two versions of Christian anthropocentrism, both of which have had their advocates. In what we might call 'divine hamster cage' anthropocentrism, God is the hamster owner and we are the hamsters. God creates the world as a kind of vivarium for human beings. The rest of the created order is our lettuce leaves and clean sawdust, completely at our disposal – quite literally, the world is our 'environment'. (This by the way is a very good reason for never speaking about 'The Environment' and talking instead of 'Creation'.) In what we might call 'divine servant' or 'divine regent' anthropocentrism, on the other hand, human beings are integrally part of the whole of the created order but they have a privileged responsibility within it; rights are attended by responsibility. Women and men are made 'in the image of God' not to ravage God's creation but to attent to it, both by caring for it and by praising it.

Whatever else it may mean to say the human person is in the image of God, it must mean, as Eastern Orthodoxy has insisted, that the human person, like the Deity, is in some sense a mystery. It is this doctrine of 'the person in the image of God' which, for the Church Fathers, keeps the human being from 'being finally dissected by reason'.[8] When we meet another person, however poor, lowly, diseased or dumb, we stand before something which holds the divine – we stand before someone who is mystery and must be reverenced as such, someone who, like Buber's God, is a 'You that in accordance with its nature cannot become an it'. Of course we can, and do, treat other people like 'its', as mere objects, but always to the loss of our own humanity. We do this in pornography, in harmful experiments on unwitting human victims, in indiscriminate killing in war. Ironically we can treat our neighbours as so many 'its' precisely in our eagerness to understand how they work. We are often, as Andrew Louth has said, bewildered by mysteries that remain mysterious even when disclosed. But, he continues:

> . . . if in our encounter with others we come to control and dominate them, and are not content to allow them their freedom in which they ultimately escape our understanding and control, then we have ceased to treat them as persons. In dominating them we depersonalize them, and ourselves. As Simone Weil put it, might's 'power to transform a man into a thing is double and it cuts both ways; it petrifies differently but equally the souls of those who suffer it, and of those who wield it.'[9]

God is mystery, and woman and man in God's image are mystery. The death of God will not, as Nietzsche thought, result in the glorification of man, but rather will take from women and men any claim they may have to be reverenced as participating in the divine economy. Without God and without the sanctity of the person made in the image of God, women and men will become not gods but mere objects to manipulate in a world of manipulable objects; and thus Singer and Kuhse.

It is both salutary and confusing that the Genesis story should tell us that it is this same creature, made in the image of God, through whom sin and violence disrupt the created order. Adam and Eve disobey God, Cain slays Abel. In the story violence spreads from the human realm to that of the animals. In the garden the animals live peaceably with Adam and Eve and with each other. After the Flood, we are told, they dread them. The point of these stories is that sin keeps us not only from right relation to other people but from right relation to the whole created order. But the earth and all its life are not, after all, destroyed in the flood, for the God who creates is also the God who saves – a theme strong in both Testaments. The God who saves Noah and the animals can save his people Israel, and – so Christians assert – save humanity in Christ. A God who creates can save. 'Our help is in the name of the Lord', says the Psalmist, 'who made heaven and earth' (Ps. 124.8).

The prophet Isaiah prayed for a just king who, as God's regent over creation, would be a saviour to his people, who would bring order and banish chaos. This king would judge the poor with justice and strike down the ruthless; and then, when there was justice, there would be peace. Then, only then, says Isaiah, lapsing into visionary language, 'The wolf shall dwell with the lamb . . . and the calf and the lion and the fatling together, and a little child shall lead them' (Isa. 11.6–7). This is a vision of Paradise, the New Creation, the Kingdom of God. We should not let the visionary nature of Isaiah's language distract us from the reality of the call. Robert Murray puts it thus:

> The Bible teaches us that neither sin nor salvation are affairs merely between us humans and God; sin entails alienation from our nature which relates us to God's other creatures, while salvation entails our re-integration in a vaster order and harmony which embraces the whole cosmos.[10]

Reverence for and right relation with God entail reverence for and right relation with other people who are made in the image of God, and further they involve right relation with the rest of the created order. The ethical imperative in this vision for the personal extends into the social and finally into the natural and cosmological.

On such a broad canvas religious writers from the biblical times onwards have painted a picture of God's creative and redeeming love. We might, I

believe, in our discussions of the moral issues in science and religion, paint
on a similarly broad canvas at least part of the time. Whatever we come up
with must have regard, as St Augustine would have insisted, for the best
science and for what we know of ourselves as creatures – of our biology,
our psychology, our natural genesis. Yet we remain mysterious, for we
stand in an odd position – fragments of the universe which are conscious of
themselves as precisely that. The pop-singer, Joni Mitchell, put it this way
in a song written about twenty years ago:

> We are stardust. Million-year-old carbon.
>> We are golden. Caught in the devil's bargain
>> And we've got to get ourselves back to the garden.[11]

She is basically right. Science agrees with Scripture in this – we are dust,
million-year-old carbon. But we are dust that has come to know itself as
dust, to know that dust can do right and commit wrongs. We are dust that
sees the possibility, in God's grace, of glorifying God along with the rest of
the created order. Let us start from there.

NOTES
1. Augustine, *The Literal Meaning of Genesis*, trans. J. H. Taylor, New York: Newman
   Press, 1982, 1.19.39; 5.3.3.
2. See Soskice, *Metaphor and Religious Language*, Oxford: Oxford University Press,
   1985, for a more detailed account.
3. Helga Kuhse and Peter Singer, *Should the Baby Live?: The Problem of Handicapped
   Infants*, Oxford: Oxford University Press, 1985, p. 117.
4. ibid., p. 124, p. 138.
5. ibid., p. 125.
6. It would be misleading, of course, to say that the Old and/or New Testaments
   have one unified 'theology of creation'. The reader must forgive me if I speak
   rather loosely here. My remarks however are based on recent work on creation
   themes in the biblical literature as studied by Old Testament scholars. See
   Murray below and also the essays in Bernhard Anderson, ed., *Creation in the Old
   Testament*, London, 1984.
7. Cit. Nicholas Lash, *Easter in Ordinary: Reflections on Human Experience and the
   Knowledge of God*, London, 1988, p. 232.
8. Andrew Louth, 'The Mysterious Leap of Faith' in Tom Sutcliffe and Peter
   Moore, eds., *In Vitro Veritas: More Tracts for Our Times*, London, 1984, p. 89.
9. ibid., p. 91.
10. Robert Murray, 'The Bible on God's World and Our Place in It', *The Month*, Sept.
    1988, p. 799.
11. Joni Mitchell, 'Woodstock', 1969.

# B: GOD AS MOTHER

5   ROSEMARY RADFORD RUETHER's 'Models of God: Exploding the Foundations' was published in *Religion and Intellectual Life* in Spring 1988 (Vol. V, No. 3, pp. 19–23). Amongst her many books are *Faith and Fratricide: The Theological Roots of Anti-Semitism* (New York: Seabury Press, 1974); *New Woman, New Earth: Sexist Ideologies and Human Liberation* (New York: Seabury Press, 1975); *To Change the World: Christology and Cultural Criticism* (New York: Crossroad, 1981); *Disputed Questions: On Being a Christian* (Nashville: Abingdon, 1982); *Sexism and God-Talk: Toward a Feminist Theology* (Boston: Beacon Press, 1983); *Womanguides: Readings Toward a Feminist Theology* (Boston: Beacon Press, 1985); *Women-church: Theology and Practice of Feminist Liturgical Communities* (San Francisco: Harper and Row, 1985); *Contemporary Roman Catholicism: Crises and Challenges* (Kansas City: Sheed and Ward, 1987); *The Wrath of Jonah: The Crisis of Religious Nationalism in the Israeli-Palestinian Conflict* (with Herman J. Ruether, San Francisco: Harper and Row, 1989); and *Gaia and God: An Ecofeminist Theology of Earth Healing* (San Francisco: Harper, 1992).

6   GORDON KAUFMAN's 'Models of God: Is Metaphor Enough?' was published first in *Theology Today* in April 1988 (Vol. 45, No. 1) and again in *Religion and Intellectual Life* in Spring 1988 (Vol. V, No. 3, pp. 11–18). His other recent books are *Systematic Theology: A Historical Perspective* (New York: Scribner, 1978); *The Theological Imagination: Constructing the Concept of God* (Philadelphia: Westminster Press, 1981); *Theology for a Nuclear Age* (Philadelphia: Westminster Press, 1985); and *In Face of Mystery: A Constructive Theology* (Cambridge, Mass.: Harvard University Press, 1993).

7   DAVID TRACY's 'Models of God: Three Observations' was also published in *Religion and Intellectual Life* in Spring 1988 (Vol. V, No. 3, pp. 24–8). His main books are *The Analogical Imagination: Christian Theology and the Culture of Pluralism* (New York: Crossroad, 1981); *Talking About God: Doing Theology in the Context of Modern Pluralism* (with John B. Cobb Jr, New York:

Seabury Press, 1983); *Plurality and Ambiguity: Hermeneutics, Religion, Hope* (San Francisco: Harper and Row, 1987); and *Dialogue with the Other: The Inter-religious Dialogue* (Grand Rapids, Michigan: Eerdmans, 1991). He also edited with Hans Kung *Paradigm Change in Theology: a Symposium for the Future* (New York: Crossroad, 1989).

8   SALLIE McFAGUE's 'Response' was also published in *Religion and Intellectual Life* in Spring 1988 (Vol. V, No. 3, pp. 38–44). The book which is discussed here is her *Models of God: Theology for an Ecological, Nuclear Age* (Philadelphia: Fortress Press, and London: SCM Press, 1987). Her other main books are *Speaking in Parables: A Study of Metaphor and Theology* (Philadelphia: Fortress Press, 1985); *Metaphorical Theology: Models of God in Religious Language* (Philadelphia: Fortress Press, 1982); and *The Body of God: An Ecological Theology* (Minneapolis: Fortress Press, 1993).

9   RUTH PAGE's 'Models of God: a review' was published in *Journal of Theological Studies* in 1988 (Vol. 39, pp. 647–9). Her books are *Ambiguity and the Presence of God* (London: SCM Press, 1985) and *The Incarnation of Freedom and Love* (London: SCM Press, 1991).

10   ANN LOADES' 'Models of God: a review' was published in *Journal of Literature and Theology* in March 1990 (Vol. 4, No. 1, pp. 141–2). Her book is *Searching for Lost Coins: Explorations in Christianity and Feminism* (London: SPCK, 1987, and Allison Park, PA: Pickwick Publications, 1988). She has also edited *Feminist Theology: A Reader* (London: SPCK, and Louisville, Kentucky: Westminster/John Knox Press, 1990) and with Michael McLain *Hermeneutics, the Bible and Literary Criticism* (New York: St Martin's Press, 1992).

# 5

∽∽∽∽∽∽∽∽∽∽∽∽∽∽∽∽∽∽∽∽∽∽∽∽∽∽∽∽∽∽∽∽∽∽∽∽∽∽∽∽∽∽

# *Models of God*:
# EXPLODING THE FOUNDATIONS
# Rosemary Radford Ruether

## The new human situation

It is the basic thesis of Sallie McFague's new book, *Models of God*, that most of the God-language of traditional Christian theology has become outworn. It is inappropriate to the new human situation in which we find ourselves. This new human situation has several major aspects. First, it is a time when all the 'others' of Western Christian society are rising up, gaining their own voice, becoming self-defining subjects, no longer willing to be defined as 'others'.

This rise of the 'others' is expressed both in social movements of emancipation and also in its cultural articulation, of which theology is one particular expression. Among these new subjects of history and culture are women, perhaps the most perennial 'others' of androcentric society; also non-Europeans, Blacks, Asians, Indians, Arabs; also the poor, or at least persons identified with the poor, for to be really poor is by definition to lack access to the means of culture as well as of physical sustenance.

Finally, there is a new pluralism of religion; or, rather, the breakdown of that Christian confidence that its religion is the one privileged expression of true Divinity destined to replace all others. We are entering into a new cultural situation of many-sided pluralism; pluralisms of religion, of cultures, of ethnicity, of gender and sexual orientation, of socio-economic class; each a case where the former invisible and silenced ones demand to speak as peers of their former masters; where the normative status of the Christian, white ruling-class male has been dethroned.

The second characteristic of this new human situation is 'nuclear knowledge', a radical expression of the knowledge of good and evil, for it is the knowledge of our capacity to do the ultimate evil, which is to annihilate, not only present life, but the very capacity of the planet to be life-giving. For the first time in human history human power *vis à vis* the world around it has potentially outstripped the capacity of the healing powers of nature to repair the damage wrought by humans. Before this time we have assumed that we can throw our garbage endlessly into fields and streams, and 'Mother Nature' would purify the mess. We have assumed that we could make war on our neighbors, killing other humans, destroying their means of shelter and livelihood, and, in another generation or two, this damage would be replaced by new births, new buildings, fields restored to cultivation. Today we face the stark possibility that our waste and war can do irreversible damage, destroying not only present life, but the very capacity of humans and other living beings to reproduce life.

## A new sensibility

This contemplation of the enormity of our new destructive power, a contemplation that we avoid assiduously in order to continue to do 'business as usual', demands a radically new cultural sensibility. This new sensibility must be one of awareness of the interconnectedness of all beings, an interconnectedness that reaches across not only all human enmities of race, class, gender, and religion, but also across the divide between the human and the nonhuman communities of beings.

This new ecological sensibility of interdependence with all other living things makes us aware of what is already the case, but which we have acted out (and are acting out) in destructive and denying ways. This new ecological sensibility both acknowledges and seeks to make benevolent that reality of interdependence that we have sought to deny and negate through dualistic and hierarchical modes of thought. This new sensibility is, literally, a reversal of the modes of consciousness that have governed patriarchal culture within our historical memory. For, if there were nonpatriarchal churches before the rise of patriarchy, they have, by definition, been cut off from the historical memory of the patriarchal traditions.

This new sensibility forces all those who have claimed to be 'above', dominating over that which is seen as inferior, whether that be male over female, white over black, rich over poor, or human over nonhuman, to realize not only their interdependence with, but their exploitative, parasitic dependency upon, that which they imagined themselves to 'rule over'. The conversion of our minds to the earth starts with a repentant acknowledgement that pyramids are built, not by trickling down from the top, but by each smaller layer in the hierarchy standing on a larger base that supports and upholds it.

For McFague, another crucial aspect of the new sensibility is an awareness of language, both the partiality of the linguistic gesture and also the capacity of language to generate reality. Linguistic worlds remain tentative and experimental, not absolute and final. But, also, language does not so much mirror the reality around us as generate relationships to it. Yet McFague also rejects a radical deconstructionist view of language as a self-enclosed 'game' without referent to an outside reality. Language generates various relationships to reality. This means there is a reality to which we relate ourselves in various ways through linguistic symbol systems. McFague also seems to assume that there is some ontology of right relationships of beings to one another. Right relationships of mutuality, care, and justice generate peace, harmony, a prospering of life energies. Wrong relationships create violence, destruction, alienation, impoverishment of life energies. We seek language systems that put us in right relationship, rather than wrong relationship, to the interconnection of beings. This suggests that there is an ontological basis of ethics. Ethics are not just arbitrary human constructions. Within a certain range of variability, there remain intrinsic ontological patterns of what kinds of relationality make for life-giving and what kinds of relationality make for destructive results.

## New symbols of God

This brings us to the center of McFague's project, the creation of new symbols of God to express this new sensibility, a new sensibility required by the new situation. What is wrong with the old symbols of God as patriarchal Father, Monarch of the Universe? Clearly the problem with this traditional language is not simply that it is politically and culturally *passé*, for we could easily find its social equivalent today; God as Boss, as Supreme Leader, as head of Central Intelligence. These are not sacral words, but, if we spend enough centuries pretending they are names for God, they might become so.

The problem also is not simply that the present names for God are non-inclusive of the human variety of race and gender, for, presumably, we could image God as a black Boss, as well as a white Boss, a female Boss as well as a male Boss. No, the key to what is wrong with patriarchal, monarchical God-talk is that it generates wrong relationships among living beings: dominating, impoverishing, destructive relationships, not life-giving relationships. God-talk based on relationships of domination and servitude generates bad ethics. Today it threatens to destroy us all.

## Coming clean

It is at this point that one must ask liberal relativists to come clean. Is this dominating God-language simply outworn, a language that was once right, but is so no longer? Or, was it, in fact, always wrong? McFague, like most liberal relativists, seems to straddle the fence. One aspect of her critique suggests that patriarchal God-talk is one metaphor among others, fine for its time, but no longer appropriate. Another side of her critique constantly exposes the evil ethical consequences of a God-language of domination that generates relationships of violence, illusionary separation, and impoverishing servility. If this is what this language does now, didn't it always do it? Wasn't it always wrong? Hasn't patriarchal God-language always been a countersign to the Christian claim of redemptive community, a sanction of evil, not a critique and liberation from evil?

It is not that this language was once appropriate and has now become inappropriate. Rather, it is that it can no longer mask its true nature, both because the victims have found voice and will no longer tolerate it, and also because we can no longer afford its destructive consequences. The violence and waste it generates now threaten to undo the healing capacities of nature to repair the damage. It is not that this type of relationship did not always generate violence and waste, but rather that the quantitative escalation of this violence and waste has become qualitatively different, because it now threatens, not simply some life, but all life. If this is the case, and I believe it is, then the blasphemous and idolatrous character of patriarchal, monarchical God-language is much more scandalous than McFague tends to suggest. Or rather the new God-language she suggests stands in much more radical judgment upon the tradition of Christian theology than she admits.

This does not mean that the continuity between the biophilic intention of Christian faith and her new God-language of loving, life-giving mutuality needs to be denied. But rather, we need to stand more thunderstruck and terrified at two or more thousand years of a Scripture and theology that sought to express redemptive hopes in language drawn from relationships of domination, war, and reduction of others to servitude. I think we need to pause longer in the gap between the old and new languages to stand aghast at this contradiction.

The Goddess, or post-Christian spiritualities that have arisen, precisely in response to the new sensibility of the danger of ecological, nuclear holocaust, are clearer about the radical scandalousness of patriarchal God-language. Yet, their desire to retreat to the world of preconscious natural harmonies prevents them from having an adequate ethical language for the radical evilness of patriarchy to which they testify.

Christians, who have a language for radical evil and fallenness, by contrast, are unable to acknowledge adequately that this contradiction lies at the very heart of the symbols they have used to express hope for redemption from evil. Our images of ultimate good have, in fact, generated the very evils from which we longed to be delivered. This is the scandalous discontinuity with past tradition that biblical feminists must acknowledge, even as we seek to ground ourselves on a deeper continuity with that true source of life-giving relationships which always and still yet upholds us.

This suggests to me that metaphorical theory is indeed engaged in a radical project of generating a new primary religious culture. If the Bible and the classical theological traditions are 'sedimentations of interpreted experience' and these sedimentations have, so to speak, been built on false foundations, then we are indeed not just redesigning the decor or even reconstructing the arrangements of the rooms in the house, but exploding the foundations.

We are calling ourselves into a new primal encounter with the disclosure of Holy Being and seeking a new religious poetic that will set us in right relation, life-giving rather than death-prone relation, to the nexus of living things. We are constructing, not simply a new theology, but a new spirituality upon which a new theology can be built. Without some real taste and experience of that new spirituality, new metaphors can easily slip back into being just covers for the same old relationships of domination and deadness.

# 6

# Models of God:
# IS METAPHOR ENOUGH?
# Gordon D. Kaufman

## A new construction

Sallie McFague's new book, *Models of God*, points us in the direction in which new constructive work in theology must move in coming decades – namely, toward a much more ecologically sensitive kind of interest and emphasis and toward the employment of new images and models in our thinking about God. Her understanding of all theology as metaphorical through and through enables her to free herself (and us) from slavish bondage to the patriarchal and monarchical models of the past, bringing her into a position to systematically develop metaphors neglected or rejected by mainstream Western religious traditions – the notions of the world as *God's body*, and of God conceived as *mother*, *lover*, and *friend*. Through these moves she succeeds in providing a wholly new and thoroughly refreshing ecological theological vision. Though McFague modestly denies that she is doing systematic theology in any grand sense, in my view what she has in fact produced is a new systematic theology, indeed a new way of thinking about systematic theology (she calls it 'metaphorical theology') together with a radical reorientation of basic Christian themes based on her analysis of the new theological models that she proposes. Moreover, she has done this compactly and economically: it is an exciting and illuminating book.

When I first learned that McFague was proposing a conception of God based on metaphors of mother, lover, and friend, I was quite skeptical. It seemed to me that the use of such images must inevitably lead to serious sentimental excesses, and that it could not help us address the really 'hard' issues with which theologians today must come to terms. But I was completely wrong in these judgments. McFague's examination of these models shows that they bear within them the potential for reorienting our theological tradition from its fixation on personalistic individualism – in its conception both of God and of humans – to an understanding of human existence more grounded upon and interdependent with the physical and biological orders of nature, and to a conception of God as thoroughly involved with all natural processes. Her analysis shows that many of the difficulties that modern theology has faced are dependent not so much on the *personalistic* character of the root metaphors of the tradition, as I had been inclined to believe; they are, rather, largely a function of the *patriarchal* and *monarchical* character of those metaphors – that is, it is the vision of the human (and God) as essentially dominating *will*, the powerful individual *ego*, the great 'I AM', that is at the root of many of our theological problems.

Theologians have not been sufficiently aware how much their thinking has been governed by a vision of the human grounded in these unquestioned notions. McFague's method of metaphorical analysis enables her to show what a difference it makes for the understanding of the human and of God if we conceive of God as, for example, mother and lover rather than father and king; and we thus are enabled to see how much our thinking has been unconsciously in the grip of metaphors that (however significant and appropriate they may have been in the historical situations in which they arose and were effective) have now become not only misleading but dangerously destructive. Her work clears the ground for a thoroughgoing examination of the models that have shaped Western religious thinking and for deliberate and self-conscious moves toward new root metaphors that will enable the Western religious sensibility more effectively to address the deepest problems of our 'ecological, nuclear age', as she so aptly characterizes our time. I shall try to give some idea here of the way in which her approach opens up and illuminates our thinking both about traditional theological perspectives and also with respect to the newer vision that she is attempting to introduce to us.

## The model and the metaphors

The notion of the world as God's body is, of course, very ancient, and in modern times it has been appropriated particularly by Whiteheadian theologians. For the most part, heretofore, I have not found this language particularly persuasive or illuminating. It has always seemed to me to involve an exceedingly anthropomorphic way of conceiving both God and the world, an anthropomorphism, moreover, that built upon and thus accentuated the unfortunate ancient dualism between mind and body. When one tried to think out metaphysically what all this might mean, our already difficult theological problems in conceiving God, and God's relation to the world, seemed to me only worsened. McFague's approach, however, opens up the questions in a new way. By reminding us that all of our language about God is metaphorical, and thus both *does* and *does not* assert what it seems to assert, she effectively loosens the tight conceptual grip that our theological language usually has upon us. The question now becomes: do the new metaphors being proposed illuminate matters that the accepted metaphors of the tradition – such as father, king, or lord – left in the dark? To examine this kind of question properly we need to set the various metaphorical alternative available to us side by side and see what each enables us to do.

This is exactly what McFague does in her book. Much traditional thinking has been based on the metaphor of the world as God's kingdom; what are the strengths and weaknesses of that metaphor in comparison with the metaphor of the world as God's body? As she says:

> A metaphor or model is not a description. We are trying to think in an as-if fashion about the God-world relationship, because we have no other way of thinking about it. No metaphor fits in all ways, and some are more nonsense than sense. The king-realm kind of thinking about the God-world relationship sounds like sense because we are so used to it, but reflection shows that in our world it is nonsense. . . . The metaphor of the world as God's body has the opposite problem to the metaphor of the world as the king's realm: if the latter puts too great a distance between God and the world, the former verges on too great a proximity. Since both metaphors are inadequate, we have to ask which one is better in our time, and to qualify it with other metaphors and models. Is it better to accept an imaginative picture of God as the distant ruler controlling his realm through external and benevolent power or one of God so intimately related to the world that the world can be imagined as God's body? . . . Is it better in terms of our and the world's preservation and fulfillment? Is it better in terms of coherence, comprehensibility, and illumination? Is it better in terms of expressing the Christian understanding of the relationship between God and the world? All these criteria are relevant . . . (70).

McFague goes on to argue that the intimate relation of God and world that the body metaphor suggests is much more appropriate to our modern ecological understanding of the mutual interdependence of all things. It

> encourages holistic attitudes of responsibility for and care of the vulnerable and oppressed [in contrast with the monarchical model which] . . . encourages attitudes of militarism, dualism, and escapism [and] condones control through violence and oppression [as well as] . . . having nothing to say about the nonhuman world. . . . Both are

pictures: which distortion is more true to the world in which we live and to the good news of Christianity? (78)

McFague examines the charge of pantheism leveled against the body model; she discusses the way in which the problem of evil can be interpreted in relationship to this metaphor; she points out the way in which this metaphor encourages us to think of God's relation to the world as caring for it, and the implications this has for our relationship to the world; and so on.

McFague reminds us that the negative theology has always emphasized that we really are in deep ignorance about who or what God is and how God is related to the world (xii, 61, 97); all of our claims, thus, are in fact our own *fictions* (xi, 182) — 'fiction' is understood here, I take it, in the etymological sense as our own 'fashioning' or 'forming'. It is, therefore, incumbent upon us to select with care the metaphors that we use and to see that they perform as effectively as possible the functions we intend them to perform. This is just as true if we continue to work with the patriarchal and monarchical metaphors of the tradition — with their unfortunate implications for our exceedingly fragile modern world — as when we take up new metaphors and attempt to construct our conception of God in ways more fitted to addressing the actual problems which we today face. In this light, and remembering that the idea of the world as God's body is to be understood as a *metaphor* — that is, that it both *does* and *does not* assert what it seems to assert — there is much to be said for the way in which it can help us reorient our theological thinking.

The same is to be said for the metaphors of mother, lover, and friend. McFague suggests that our deepest and most powerful images are not in fact those based on social and political order (which have been formative for Western religious traditions) but instead those referring us to the basic conditions of life itself,

> the beginning and continuation of life, imagery of sex, breath, food, blood and water. . . . This language continues to be powerful because images arising from the most basic level of physical existence the level of our tenuous hold on existence and what is needed to keep it going — are images of life and death (80).

With these considerations in mind, McFague undertakes to show how metaphors like mother and lover point us toward the deepest resources of our being and our well-being, and thus can provide the basis for a meaningful and powerful theological picture. The principal danger of these images, one might expect, is their highly emotional suggestiveness of a personalized, individualistic relationship of the soul to God. But McFague does not allow them to be developed in that pietistic direction. She has already argued that the world should be understood as an organic whole, God's *body*. We humans are related to God, therefore, not one-to-one, as individual ego to individual ego, but as constituent parts belonging to this organic whole. 'The Gospel of John gives the clue: for God so loved the *world*. It is not individuals who are loved by God as mother, lover, and friend but the world' (86).

> If the lover is God and the beloved the world rather than individuals, then the individualistic, dualistic, and other-worldly aspects dissolve. For now God as lover is seen to love not spirits individually in a world apart from the one we know, but all creatures, body and spirit, here and now. And we in turn do not love God one by one in vertical relationships of beloved to lover, but as we love the world, God's body – as we find it attractive and precious, valuable for its own sake – we are in this loving of the world loving God. With our model of the world as God's body, we avoid the dualism, individualism, and other-worldliness of the tradition's use of the lover model (128–9).

## The methodological and the material question

There is much that could be said about the transformation of sensibility and consciousness implied in the way in which McFague explores and unpacks her several models, but I cannot go into these matters any further here. I must turn in conclusion to a few questions I would like to raise with respect to her very suggestive proposals. The first is both a methodological and a material question – or rather, it is a material issue that perhaps calls for further methodological reflection. Let us grant for the moment McFague's central contentions (a) that theology is (and always has been) an attempt to develop a picture of the world and the human on the basis of certain root metaphors or images that provide structured patterns in terms of which the whole of reality, and the human place within that whole, can be conceived; and (b) that we should now select the metaphors we will use for this purpose much more self-consciously and critically than was done in the past, with a view to the major problems human beings face in the modern world. Does our recognition that it is always metaphors we are working with, and that therefore we never possess proper descriptions or definitions with tight boundaries, mean that we are free to juxtapose just any metaphors we choose side by side with each other as we construct a picture of the whole? Are we free to introduce into our theological constructing virtually any metaphors we find useful, regardless of how they relate to or cohere with each other? It is clear that a metaphorical theology will be much less tightly bound by formal demands for logical coherence than a theology that takes itself to be dealing with carefully defined concepts, but what are the limits here?

I raise this issue not only because of its formal methodological importance, but also because it seems to me to point to a problem in the book before us. There is a profound tension between the metaphor that provides the fundamental pattern for the overall theological vision that McFague is setting out – the metaphor of the world as God's body – and the three metaphors (or 'names of God') in terms of which the concept of God itself is elaborated: mother, lover, friend. McFague herself is aware of this problem and attempts briefly to dissolve it (75f.); but I continue to be troubled by it. The models of mother, lover, and friend all gain their force and meaning through their depicting a situation in which two persons are envisioned as distinct from and over against each other, even though they stand in very significant positive relation to each other. Are we supposed to think of God, now, as the *mother* of her own body? What could that mean? And haven't we notably transformed the meanings of 'lover' and 'friend' when we think of God's love and friendship as directed essentially toward her own body rather than toward a genuine personal counterpart? I am in full sympathy with McFague's desire to tone down the tendencies of all these metaphors toward an individualistic pietism, but I wonder if the remedy she has proposed – based on the metaphor of the world as God's body – doesn't give rise to such tensions with the other three metaphors as to make her overall picture incoherent. It is only through a skillful juggling act that one can keep all four of these metaphorical balls in the air at once; it is not entirely clear to me that they hang together well enough to provide a coherent theological picture. But perhaps *that* kind of coherence is not required – or even appropriate – in a self-conscious metaphorical theology. Or is it? I'm just not sure; and I'm not quite sure either just how we should proceed to answer this question.

## Metaphor or concept?

My second question is related to the first. Are metaphors like mother, lover, and friend in fact complex enough to provide the principal basis for a contemporary conception of God? Certainly they have the strengths of great immediacy and evocative power, and this is indispensable if they are to be the defining constituents of the central focus for worship, faith, and love in our contemporary highly pluralistic world. I am doubtful, however, if metaphors or models based primarily on the human person are adequate any longer to serve as the principal foundation for our conception of God: for in our world personal being is understood to be not the source or ground of the highly complex evolutionary, historical, and social processes of which we are aware, but rather their *product*. We, therefore, no longer have a way of thinking of personal reality – more specifically, of *a person* – as grounding the whole of reality (as the traditional theistic world-picture suggests when it posits God as the Creator); on the contrary it is the complex whole of reality that grounds and has brought into being all persons, according to modern ways of thinking. Is the image of mother or lover, then – any more than the images of father or lord – of a sort that can provide an adequate basis for a contemporary understanding of God? Is any *image* sufficiently complex to perform this function? Or is it only when we move to the order of *concepts* that we are able to hold before the mind the sort of complexity with which we are here concerned? (If there is any doubt that matters of great complexity can be dealt with more adequately with concepts than with images, consider the fact that we have no difficulty whatsoever in *conceiving* very precisely the difference between a pile of sand consisting of two million grains and another of two million and one; but it is difficult indeed to see how the *image* of two million grains of sand differs a whit from the image of two million and one. Highly complex realities can be entertained conceptually but hardly imagistically, however indispensable our images may be in much of our thinking.) If we are to think of *God*, then – the Creator or ground of all other reality, or the all-inclusive organic whole within which all other reality emerges and is sustained – it may be that *concepts* like 'evolutionary process' or 'life' or 'creativity' or 'universe' must be given centrality instead of powerfully evocative personal images of the sort that Sallie McFague (along with our ancient traditions) has suggested. I do not wish to make a dogmatic claim here, but I have some serious doubts that we have any images complex enough to do the work required. If we are serious about developing an adequate conception of God for our time, we will need to draw our metaphors from the conceptual order as well as from the imagistic order of bodies, mothers, and lovers. How all of these quite different sorts of metaphors are to be brought into significant and meaningful relationship to each other in our theological reflection and construction remains a difficult unanswered question.

Finally, pushing one step further this line about the questionableness of using chiefly personal models to provide theological foundations, I want to observe that the metaphor of friend (with which McFague brings her discussion to a conclusion) seems to be to offer fewer new theological insights than the other models she explores. This metaphor – the most emphatically personalistic of all those examined, in that it is based on and refers to *freely chosen associations* and the bonds that grow out of these, rather than inescapable biological dependencies or necessities (159ff.) – has actually been rather prominent in some versions of traditional piety, particularly in christological uses (one thinks of such hymns as 'What a Friend We Have in Jesus'); but it adds little to the understanding of God, or our relationship with God, that cannot be developed in connection with the metaphors of mother and lover.

In my opinion, a conception of God adequate to the contemporary ecological, nuclear sensibility can be most adequately completed not with a highly personalistic image like friend, with all the anthropomorphizing tendencies that suggests, but rather with a *conceptual* metaphor that is capable of taking up into itself the great complexity of reality as we know it today – the intricacy of physical patterns of energies; ecological interdependencies and the evolutionary development of life; the self-reflexiveness and intentionality of human consciousness and creativity. An image like friend is simply not equal to this task. More promising, perhaps, would be the concept 'trinity', which McFague briefly touches upon at the end of her book. But that concept will have to be developed much more fully than she has done here, if we are to see whether it is really adequate to this purpose.

There are other questions of detail that I might pose about Sallie McFague's new book, but I will leave the matter here. *Models of God* is an important new work in theology: important for the sketch of a new way to do theology that it provides; important for the new material theology, appropriate to an ecological, nuclear age, which is developed on the basis of a number of models that have been neglected or rejected in mainstream Western religious traditions; important for the issues that it raises for the theological community to engage in coming years. We are all in Sallie McFague's debt for showing us a way to move forward in the task of constructing a theology appropriate to the problems of our time.

# 7

# Models of God:
## THREE OBSERVATIONS
## David Tracy

## Introduction

I so respect and find myself in such fundamental agreement with Professor Sallie McFague's theology that it is difficult to find much to criticize. But since a truly critical spirit includes not only disagreements but critical agreements, my task is easier. Hence, I shall use the brief time to attempt three tasks: first, a statement on my fundamental critical agreement with her constructive project; second, a question about her methodological comments on 'heuristics' as distinct from 'hermeneutics' and 'constructive'; third, a suggestion for some further development of her New Testament reflections.

## *Sallie McFague's* Models of God: *an interpretation*

Sallie McFague's analysis of our situation as marked by the related crises of ecology, nuclearism, and global injustice is one good persuasive (i.e. situational) reason for her new constructive theology. That same situational analysis also nicely correlates with her theological construal of the 'heart of the matter' for Christian self-understanding: namely, that the vision of God and humanity rendered should be *destabilizing*, *inclusive*, and *non-hierarchical*. These characteristics, moreover, free her for certain important strategic alliances: (1) the destabilizing characteristic frees her to employ her own important work on the 'is not' or 'shock' aspect of metaphor as well as relate to some aspects of deconstructionist thought; (2) the inclusive characteristic frees her for alliances with much liberation and political theology, with the crucial proviso that 'inclusivity' be taken more radically to include non-human life (thus challenging the anthropocentrism of those and other theologies) in a manner similar to the earlier challenges to political theology from such different theologians as James Gustafson, John Cobb, and Schubert Ogden; (3) the non-hierarchical characteristic frees her to ally herself with much feminist theology with its emphasis on radical non-dualism, relationality, and, therefore, non-hierarchies (nature-spirit; male-female; soul-body; God as monarch-world as realm of the monarch).

These alliances are in no way extrinsic to McFague's project but flow naturally from her own construal of the heart of the Christian message as destabilizing, inclusive, and non-hierarchical in a situation marked by massive human injustice and suffering, ecological crisis, and nuclear threat. This theological construal of both 'message' and 'situation', in turn, frees her for a remarkable constructive project. The first major moment of such construction is, in her hands, both familiar and unfamiliar. What is familiar about her construal of the world as God's body is the metaphysics of radical relationality and process it entails. That position – now usually understood as process theology – moreover, finds clear traditional and scriptural warrants in much of the ancient *Logos* tradition (or, more exactly, as she makes clear, the *Sophia-Logos* tradition), in the Gospel of John, in later Pauline materials, in the Wisdom tradition, and in some aspects of the covenantal-as-radically-relational traditions.

What is unfamiliar here is equally important to emphasize: McFague's careful attention to metaphor, image, and the imagination could free process thought from its over-concern with concepts without equal attention to the relationship of those concepts to their grounding images and metaphors. This, in turn, would require, as McFague implies but could render yet more explicit, attention to the often *redescriptive* character of all process concepts as related to their grounding images and metaphors rather than an assumption of this purely descriptive character. This insistence is, I believe, no minor one as it involves the question of the very nature of the most basic categories and concepts we employ in all theological metaphysics. I believe McFague's position does entail a redescriptive position. Still, I cannot be entirely sure this is the case since her own comments on method are, to me at least, not entirely clear. Hence, my questions on method.

## *Heuristics: creative, constructive, and responsive?*

Hence, I must request a clarification: I am not sure exactly what the nature of theology as 'heuristics' as distinct from but related to 'hermeneutics' or 'constructive' is. In one sense, the use of the term is clear and fruitful. For as McFague makes clear, to call theology 'heuristic' highlights its experimental character and thereby emphasizes the need for pragmatic criteria on the fruitfulness of various metaphors, images, and models for our situation. With this pragmatic consistence, I concur. The question recurs, however, whether pragmatic criteria, though necessary, are sufficient for the theological task.

Sometimes McFague seems to suggest that pragmatic criteria are sufficient, as in her frequent appeals to 'trying on' the new models to see their fruitfulness and her equally frequent appeals to 'as if' language. But this latter language does not fit easily with her other frequent language of 'as'. More exactly, it is one thing to construe the world 'as if' it were God's body and quite another to construe the world 'as' God's body. In the first case, all one really needs is a kind of neo-Kantian understanding of the imagination (like Vaihinger's 'philosophy of as-if') and purely pragmatic criteria. This 'as if' claim is, to speak metaphorically, a 'soft one' for which either neo-Kantianism or pragmatism will suffice. In the second case, however, something more is needed. For to construe the world *as* God's body is to make a far stronger claim. To be sure, as McFague makes clear, to say 'as' rather than simply 'is' is to acknowledge a comparative element in the construal. More exactly, as she also makes clear, it is to acknowledge the metaphorical (is and is *not*) character of the interpretation.

Nevertheless, to construe the world as God's body is to make a claim for which, as far as I can see, pragmatic criteria, although useful and even necessary, will not suffice. In sum, we need to know more on whether this construal is not purely creative, purely constructive, and, at the limit, purely projective, but also has a responsive character. In all our theological construals of God, are we not also (as McFague in her discussion of the three models insists) both constructing models and responding to that ultimate power, however construed, which we name God? Wittgensteinians tend to highlight this aspect by their analysis of 'as' statements as logically distinct from 'as if' statements. Hermeneutics tends to highlight this aspect by appeals to such language as 'event of manifestation' (Ricoeur) or 'event of disclosure-concealment' (Heidegger), in order to indicate the nature of the 'as' claim as a claim of both 'response' and 'construction'.

Granted McFague's reluctance to follow the deconstructionists' dissolution of the hermeneutical 'as' into endless metaphoricity, I think she should say more on how her use of 'as' is not equivalent (as I presume it is not) to her use of 'as if' language. Without that further clarification, I fear that other readers will be left puzzled, as I was, with questions about the exact nature of the claim for the new metaphors and models for God that McFague develops and, therefore, with questions about what kind of criteria (purely pragmatic? or pragmatic-hermeneutic?) are appropriate here. 'Heuristics' clarifies the pragmatic side, but I do not see yet, without further clarification, how pragmatic criteria alone warrant her ontological claims (however 'modest' they are with Wheelwright, and however 'redescriptive' rather than 'descriptive' their concepts of 'relationality' and 'process' may be). In sum, will heuristics alone suffice?

## A thought experiment: nature in the story of Jesus

My final comments take the form of a brief thought experiment. The problem is this: granted our need to understand the Christian story as destabilizing, inclusive, and non-hierarchical, it is puzzling not to have the basic elements chosen from the story of Jesus Christ at the beginning of McFague's work display a relationship to nature on other than ethical-philosophical, prophetic grounds. To be sure, this purely prophetic portrait of Jesus is amply compensated for later in the book when the relationships to earth, body, cosmos intrinsic to McFague's brilliant analysis of her models of *mother*, *lover*, and *friend* (especially the analyses of mother and lover) are developed. But why not have those elements of our intrinsic relationship to earth, body, cosmos present at the very beginning, lest they seem only later reflections from a later New Testament or contemporary situation?

My suggestion is that, thanks to work like that of Eliade and several feminist theologians, one can show the presence of those natural elements even in the characteristics of the story of Jesus chosen by McFague as her candidates for the 'Christian paradigm'. This is not the place to develop these suggestions at length, but let me close by mentioning some possibilities for further reflection in each of Sallie McFague's candidates for the Christian paradigm: (1) In the parables, the frequency of agricultural, even earthy, metaphors is surely suggestive – even for rethinking McFague's or Crossan's seeming insistence on simply opposing the genres parable and myth; (2) 'The table fellowship with outcasts' suggests not only a prophetic liberationist strand but also, by the very choice of eating and food, our intrinsic relationship to earth as well; (3) Even the cross can also be construed (not improperly, I believe) as the Christian prophetic rendering of the mythic 'cosmic tree' and, hence, could relate us directly to earth and cosmos; (4) The 'appearance narratives' of the resurrection intensify those relationships by their relationship to both resurrected 'body' and cosmic reality.

If these suggestions seem worth pursuing to Sallie McFague, then, I believe, her models of mother, lover, and friend could receive even more warrant from her own interpretation of the Christian paradigm of the story of Jesus. At the same time, such development might lead to a new Christian theological construal of the Goddess traditions that could free us – as in Rosemary Radford Ruether's language of God/dess – to see how that model or metaphor need not be understood as merely pre-Judaic or post-Christian. Is that task not also suggested by the breakthrough to God as mother, lover, and friend so well portrayed in the groundbreaking work of Sallie McFague?

# 8

~~~~~~~~~~~~~~~~~~~~~~~~~~~~~~~~~~~~~~~~~~~~~~~~~~~~~~~~~~~~~~~~~~~

# RESPONSE
# *Sallie McFague*

## Introduction

I am deeply grateful for the careful, thoughtful responses to my book: no author could ask for better treatment. They vary considerably, however, some raising more issues than others for me to respond to. Rosemary Radford Ruether gives a stirring analysis of the basic thesis of the book and raises the issue of why I do not apply my critique of traditional language historically. Gordon Kaufman's response poses the greatest number of questions, most of them focused on the nature of and interaction among my alternative models of God. Speaking to these concerns will be a major focus of my response. David Tracy raises the critical question of the status of models in heuristic theology; he asks, does this theology have a responsive as well as a constructive character?

## Patriarchal God-talk

First, a response to Ruether's question asking me to stop straddling the fence and admit that, if patriarchal God-talk is oppressive now, it has always been so. I suspect it has. But let me make a distinction and give a rationale for why I waffle a bit in the book. The distinction is between patriarchal, monarchical, triumphalist models of God, which I suspect have always been oppressive, and *some* other models, such as the christological one of the king become servant, which, while irrelevant if not oppressive to us, may actually have been liberating in another era as a destabilizing notion. But why do I straddle the fence on patriarchal language, even when I suspect it has always been oppressive? For one thing, I didn't want the historical issue to become a red herring, diverting attention from the main project of the book: to persuade people that we must give up such models now. The pain of conversion to a new sensibility can too easily be avoided by arguing over points of historical accuracy. Moreover, insistence that what we now know to be the case, when asserted as historial generalization, can appear ideological. I very much like and in fact quote in the book Ruether's remark on avoiding 'the tyranny of the absolutizing imagination', which supposes that revolutions, theological or any other kind, are for all time.[1] I think that applies to the past as well as to the future. Just as we have to ask whether the model of the world as God's body, for instance, will be appropriate five hundred years from now – and be willing to consider that it may not be – so, I think we must be careful when generalizing about earlier historical periods. Or, to put this point positively, the case, if made, must be made carefully and historically: it was not the goal of this book to make that case (in fact, it would have been a diversion) and, in any event, I am not the one to make it. Ruether *is* a historian and claims that the patriarchal language has always been oppressive. Since I see theology as a collegial affair, I welcome her confirmation of my suspicion. If theology is not simply the *magnum opus* of a single individual or merely the translation of the community's traditional doctrines – if it is neither individual system building nor celebration of the Church's past – then we might entertain the notion that it is a collective, multidimensional enterprise with many different kinds of reflection and praxis. Many different tasks need to be done by many people with different abilities and interests: my task in this book is to try to convert sensibilities from models harmful in our time to others that will be helpful. *That* task does not, I think, depend on the historical issue.

## Divine relationality

Let me turn now to a topic raised by Gordon Kaufman: tension between the model of the world as God's body and the models of God as mother, lover, and friend of the world. The central issue, if I understand him correctly, concerns how divine relationality is perceived in the overall picture of God as mother, lover, and friend of her body, the world, or universe. One's initial response to that picture may be that the identification of God and God's 'other', the universe, is too close, for the universe is, after all, God's body. But the tradition has always struggled with monistic, indeed, narcissistic tendencies when attempting to speak of divine relationality. Consider orthodox Trinitarianism: here God's 'other' is God's own self, for the relationality of God is seen in terms of the relationships among the persons of the immanent Trinity. This solipsistic view is epitomized in C. S. Lewis's statement that God is 'at home in the land of the Trinity', and, entirely self-sufficient and needing nothing, 'loves into existence totally superfluous creatures'.[2] In our model, God's 'other' is the universe, which, to be sure, comes from God, but is not identical with God. Is not this understanding of divine relationality less monistic and narcissistic than the traditional one?

Let us look at the issues of relationality Kaufman raises: God as the mother of her own body, or the question of the source of that body, and God as interacting with it as mother, lover, and friend.

To say that God is the mother of her own body is, first of all, to recall that this particular 'body' is nothing less than all that is – the universe or universes that cosmologists speak of. The body of God, then, is creation, understood as God's self-expression; it is formed in God's own reality, bodied forth in the eons of evolutionary time, and supplied with the means to nurture and sustain billions of different forms of life. And what could that body be except God's own creation? Could some other Creator have made it? If so, then *that* Creator would be God. *We* give life only to others of our own species, but God gives life to *all* that is, all species of life and all forms of matter. In a monotheistic, panentheistic theology, if one is to understand God in some sense as physical and not just spiritual, then the entire 'body' of the universe is 'in' God and is God's visible self-expression. This body, albeit a strange one if we take ours as the model, belongs to God. God is mother of all reality; God is the source of all that is. As Julian of Norwich writes of God as mother: 'We owe our being to him and this is the essence of motherhood'.[3] The seeming incoherence here, I think, comes from the fact that our bodies are given to us, as are all other aspects of our existence. But as the creator of all that is, God is necessarily the source, the mother, of her own body.

Kaufman's second issue is concerned with how God interacts with the world: how can God as mother, lover, and friend relate to a *body*? Do not these models indicate the necessity of a 'genuine personal counterpart', he asks? We need to recall again the nature of God's body: it is nothing less than all that exists, which includes creatures with various levels of spirit and mind. In the model of God relating to the universe as mother, lover, and friend, there would be 'genuine personal counterparts', though they need not all be human ones. The body that God relates to in this model includes various levels of responsiveness – as the process theologians have pointed out, and as a sacramental perspective does as well. We think of ourselves as the only ones in the world who can respond to the mother, lover, and friend of the world, but that is simply another witness to our anthropocentrism. Medieval Catholic analogical thought knew better: each being, in its particularity and difference from all others, gives the creator glory as it fulfills its own being. Such response need not be fully intentional or even minimally so for a relationship to exist. Consider, for instance, how we can give motherly nurture to our houseplants or join an organization called 'Friends of the Library'. To be sure, these relationships are extensions of parental care and friendship in relationship to other human beings, but they illustrate how a body such as the entire universe, with creatures like ourselves who are highly responsive as well as others of minimal response, could provide 'genuine personal counterparts' to God as mother, lover, and friend.

## Personal models

A few words now about personal vs. conceptual models. Kaufman believes personal models do not fit with the contemporary scientific view of the universe and, in addition, are inadequate to deal with its complexity. Arthur Peacocke, the British physicist and theologian, disagrees:

> Does not the continuity of the universe, with its gradual elaboration of its potentialities, from its dispersal c. ten thousand million years ago as an expanding mass of particles to the emergence of persons on the surface of the planet Earth (perhaps elsewhere as well) imply that any categories of 'explanation' and 'meaning' must at least *include* the personal?

He goes on to say that an affirmative answer implies that 'the source and meaning of all-that-is . . . is least misleadingly described in supra-personal terms'.[4] I agree, however, with Kaufman's insistence that conceptual metaphors are necessary. Experimenting with that kind of model, however, was not the task I set for myself. I would refer him to my response to Ruether's plea that I do historical work: I see theology as a collaborative effort and welcome his contribution working with conceptual models, such as 'evolutionary process', 'creativity', and so forth. I don't find my models contradict his; in fact, I suspect they are complementary, though functioning at a different level. What I do disagree with, however, is the substitution of conceptual metaphors for personal ones, thus eliminating the latter. In his most recent work, *Theology for a Nuclear Age*, Kaufman speaks of God as 'the unifying symbol of those powers and dimensions of the ecological and historical feedback network which create and sustain and work to further enhance life'.[5] I essentially agree with this statement, but it lacks the imaginative power of the monarchical model it is intended to unseat. As they say in the South, 'It won't preach'. What Kaufman's conceptual metaphor needs, I think, is to be complemented by a model such as God as mother of the universe, which, I believe, is fully compatible with it.

## *Shy ontological claims*

Let us turn finally to an important issue raised by David Tracy: whether theology as 'heuristics' is only an 'as-if' venture or whether it includes an 'as' also. Is it all construction or does it include response and discovery as well? To be direct: the answer is Yes, response and discovery are assumed in this perspective. My position is epitomized in the statement by Paul Ricoeur: 'It would seem that the enigma of metaphorical discourse is . . . what it creates, it discovers; and what it finds, it invents.' He goes on to say, 'In the metaphorical discourse of poetry, referential power is linked to the eclipse of ordinary reference; the creation of heuristic fiction is the road to redescription; and reality brought to language unites manifestation and creation.'[6] This is the 'as' part: the models of God as mother, lover, and friend are meant to make ontological claims, albeit shy ones; they are offered as redescriptions (in place of God as monarch and patriarch) of God's relationship to the world. Notice that this position assumes that there are no *descriptions*; hence, there is no way to prove one's ontological claim; nonetheless, on the basis of the initial 'wager' or belief – that God is on the side of life and its fulfillment – one asserts that the alternative models are truer to that wager and better for expressing it.

The 'as-if' aspect of the project pertains to the overall method of heuristic theology; that is, to its experimental, inventive character, playing with novel possibilities to see what potential they may have. It suggests, 'Let us think as if God is mother or lover and see what happens'. The invitation to the experiment is the 'as-if' aspect, while the assumption of at least the partial success of the models is the 'as' aspect. Had I experimented with the models and found them to be inappropriate and unhelpful for expressing God's transforming love in our time, I would have made no ontological claim for them.

## *Pragmatic criteria*

What this comes to, I believe, is the importance of pragmatic criteria as the basis for ontological claims. Pragmatic criteria are central to my position as they are to other forms of liberation theology. The criterion of praxis is closely related to the tradition of Aristotle, for whom truth meant constructing the good life for the polis. In our time this must include the good life for the cosmos, but in both cases the assumption is that human life is fundamentally practical and hence that true knowledge is not basically correspondence with 'reality-as-it-is'; rather, it is reflection of many sorts that will contribute to fulfillment of life in its many forms.

But how does one escape the Feuerbachian critique that language about God is *nothing but* human projection? There is, finally, no way to ensure that some, indeed many, will not interpret it that way. If, with the apophatic tradition, we admit that we do not *know* the inner being of divine reality, then the hints and clues we have of the way things are, whether we call them religious experiences, revelation, wagers, events of manifestation, or whatever, are too fragile and too little for heavy metaphysical claims. However, those who are willing to enter the arena of interpretation and fight for one rather than another way of construing the God–world relationship are motivated to do so, not out of a sense of mere play, but because they believe the interpretation to be better and hence truer than its alternatives. Thus, I would say, a 'true' model of God will be one that is a powerful, persuasive construal of God as being on the side of life and its fulfillment in our time. It will be one that is destabilizing, inclusive, and non-hierarchical. So James Hart is correct, I think, when he calls my project 'evangelogic': 'the best is the true', 'ultimate justification . . . lies in the belief in creaturehood's vocation to the best and in the divine pole as the surety of this belief.' What is able to bring about this 'best' state – the transformation of all existence in inclusive nonhierarchical fashion in which the last and the least are included – is what I would call 'true'. Models based on this vision and expressive of it are 'true' models of the God–world relationship.

There are many other matters to be considered, but time is running out. I am deeply grateful for the stimulating questions and probing critique that my respondents have offered. I am just as grateful for their positive contributions to the task of proposing alternative models of God. I have mentioned a couple of times that I believe theology to be a collaborative effort: they apparently do as well, for each of them has suggested ways to advance the project I have suggested. Hart has illuminated its intent by re-envisioning it phenomenologically; Ruether has provided the historical case for alternative models; Kaufman suggests conceptual models as (I hope) complements to my personal models; and Tracy adds the claim that our intrinsic relationship to the cosmos can be found in the beginning of the tradition, in the New Testament story of Jesus.

I thank each of them for the collaborative dialogue in which I certainly felt my voice was heard and I hope I heard each of theirs as well.

NOTES
1. 'Envisioning Our Hopes: Some Models of the Future', in Janet Kalven and Mary I. Buckley, eds., *Women's Spirit Bonding*, New York: Pilgrim Press, 1984, p. 335.
2. C. S. Lewis, *The Four Loves*, New York: Harcourt Brace and Co., 1960, p. 176.

3. Julian of Norwich, *Revelations of Divine Love*, ed. Clifton Wolters, Harmondsworth, Middlesex: Penguin, 1966, pp. 166–7.
4. Arthur Peacocke, *Creation and the World of Science*, Oxford: Oxford University Press, 1979, p. 75.
5. Gordon Kaufman, *Theology for a Nuclear Age*, Philadelphia: Westminster Press, 1985, p. 56.
6. Paul Ricoeur, *The Rule of Metaphor: Multi-disciplinary Studies of the Creation of Meaning in Language*, Toronto: University of Toronto Press, 1981, p. 239.

# 9

# *Models of God*: A REVIEW
# *Ruth Page*

Sallie McFague calls her book an 'experiment' in the elaboration of models of God for an age whose sensibility is informed by a view of reality which is holistic rather than 'hierarchical, dualistic, external, unchanging, atomistic, anthropocentric (or) deterministic' (p. 13), and which lives in the shadow of the nuclear threat so that it accepts responsibility and has to rethink power. She proposes a trinity of models. First, God as mother, whose *agape* is delight in the existence of the other, whose activity is giving birth to creation and whose ethic is justice for all her children without exception. Then there is God the lover, whose *eros* is towards the world as the valuable other, whose activity is salvation in the sense of union and whose ethic is the healing, uniting process. Thirdly, God as friend is an inclusive, adult relationship of *philia*, a God who sustains relationship and preserves balance in an ethic of companionship, all with all. McFague brings a wealth of allusion and significance to her descriptions.

Central to her rendering is the metaphor of the world as God's body, not one I warm to, and which she herself acknowledges is 'experimenting with a bit of nonsense to see if it can make a claim to truth' (p. 69). I do not find her case convincing and there are other ways of finding God present and involved in the world, but she rejects the notion of spirit. Nevertheless, the *use* she makes of the metaphor is fascinating. The world as God's body becomes the locus and mediator of all relationship between humans and God so that the *agape* of the mother and the (otherwise potentially claustrophobic) *eros* of the lover are not for individuals but for the *world* – in which humans, of course, are included, still special for being the *imago Dei*. Again the human relation is not with God neat, as it were, but with her/his body, mothering it, loving it (finding it valuable), and befriending it. This, clearly is holistic thinking directed against individualism, but in the end I found both God and myself as entities rather negated in the reiterated emphasis on the world. Surely God's love can be for both the individual and the world, or we might as well stop using personal metaphors. Similarly when she writes that sin is not against God but against the world I want to say it is against both. Forgiveness does not feature. Mothers, lovers, and friends may forgive, but how does God's body the world forgive? In general the world is so large and so multiple that it dilutes the force of the relationships McFague describes so well.

In that her models are imaginative modes of faith they are tested by living with them: but in that they represent theological proposals they are open to argument. I find myself in disagreement over her description of salvation as the reunification of the world, already in place in that the lover finds it all valuable, but achieved in fact not only by Jesus (the paradigmatic saviour) but by all who bring about union. This depends first on seeing the world as a unity ('body') which has been fragmented – curiously traditional for so modern a theologian, for in the history of evolution the world is not a unity. She is aware, however, that total, simultaneous reunification is not possible in the world's diversity and changefulness. Further, union without possessiveness (she rejects that element of Nygren's *eros*) is so rare and fleeting a human condition (and not even a possibility among non-human male animals) that one wonders who can be saved, since we are the current potential saviours. Salvation is not presented in doctrine as an ideal or a momentary achievement, but as a steady state *given* to us. In her schema salvation should be 'being valuable'. But it turns into ideal and achievement precisely because the world in its entirety plays the mediatorial role compelling a total activism. Behind all this lies her Trinitarian structuring which is too a priori and constricting of her models. Union, for instance, becomes salvific while friendship and the quest for ecological balance are not – unless the *opera ad extra* are still *indivisa*. But in that case incompatible models – union with the lover, alongsideness with the friend – cause confusion.

The feminism in this book is not strident. What is pronounced is the modernity and reinterpretation of doctrine. Her question is: 'What should we be doing for our time that would be comparable to what Paul and John did for theirs?' (p. 30). Her answers are always interesting, thought-provoking, and illuminating.

# 10

# *Models of God*: A REVIEW
# *Ann Loades*

Professor McFague has written a theological treatment of language about God which is in its way quintessentially North American. She signals this by her own analogy for theology, as a 'house' to live in for a while, windows partly open and door ajar, a prison if it does not allow us to come and go, add a room, take one away, or even move out and rebuild. And she is scrupulously careful to acknowledge her own standpoint as white and middle class, living in a social context from which a few control resources as fundamental as food for so many others. Being female by sex and feminist by perspective is relevant because it has provided her with sufficient disorientation from the dominant symbol system of Christianity, loaded as it is with the assumption that there is a 'personal' deity who transcends sex, but not gender. Theology for her is a human construct for which we must take responsibility. We must be acutely sensitive to the 'cracks' that lie between the *little* we know, learn to live with the *via negativa*, work in a sceptical and heuristic manner, and endure uncertainty, partiality and relativity. We need to resist closure, coherence, identity and totality in our theology, and the identification of divine reality with our constructions. Theology *for our time* will work with an inclusive, non-hierarchical vision, stressing relationship and interdependence, transformation and openness, care and creativity, alert to human responsibility for our double-holocaust world.

The crucial move she makes after an explanation of her own method is to explore the metaphor of the world as God's body, a body to which 'God is present as mother, lover, and friend of the last and least in all of creation' (p. 87). The very phrasing of this summary (which leads to the separate expositions, of each, and thence to human conduct) immediately suggests an area of tension, which she would claim that a metaphorical, but not a systematic theology can tolerate. Of the problems with these metaphors, one need only at this point say that they continue to 'privilege' the human notwithstanding our inescapable knowledge that the human arises from very complex physical and environmental processes, and is arguably inadequate to provide indications of that which grounds the whole, unless one either defends the divine-human idiosyncrasy of classical Christian theology, or extrapolates from the human some conceptual schema which would take us away from imaginative metaphor. There is, too, a problem with what seems to be an unduly restricted understanding of 'metaphor' in her work. She herself gives the game away when she couples metaphors and models. Dr Janet Martin Soskice has argued for metaphor not merely as *re*-description, but as 'naming for the first time' and making cognitive claims. Models work roughly on the 'A is a B' pattern. And metaphors as naming work by catching all sorts of strands of association in a text or cluster of texts – though catching associations is what Professor McFague does for herself in her inventive experiments. The object is to edge us away from the idolatry we deny but in fact engage in when we make certain metaphors exclusive and come to view them as descriptions. There is a deep divide here about what can and cannot be claimed in theological 'knowledge'.

In her explorations, it is worth paying attention to her association of 'mother' with the pursuit of order, justice, and creativity, and with the life-giving instincts of our species, of which our response to the starving is but one indicator. And the exploration of God as friend is a much-needed attempt to reinstate a relationship of central importance in our dealings with one another and our relationship with God.

The book is provocative and problematic as many refreshing books are, and is in welcome contrast to so much of what passes for theology.

# C: God as Trinity

11   ROBERT W. JENSON's 'The Doctrine of the Trinity' is part of his longer article 'The Christian Doctrine of God' in Geoffrey Wainwright, ed., *Keeping the Faith: Essays to Mark the Centenary of Lux Mundi* (Philadelphia: Fortress Press, and London: SPCK, 1988, pp. 38–53). Among his books are *The Knowledge of Things Hoped For: The Sense of Theological Discourse* (New York: OUP, 1969); *Visible Words: The Interpretation and Practice of Christian Sacraments* (Philadelphia: Fortress Press, 1978); *The Triune Identity: God According to the Gospel* (Philadelphia: Fortress Press, 1982); and *America's Theologian: A Recommendation of Jonathan Edwards* (New York: OUP, 1988).

12   CATHERINE MOWRY LaCUGNA's 'Re-conceiving the Trinity' is part of her longer article 'Re-conceiving the Trinity as the Mystery of Salvation' published in *Scottish Journal of Theology* in 1985 (Vol. 38, pp. 1–3 and 14–22). Her position is argued at greater length in her book *God For Us: The Trinity and Christian Life* (San Francisco: Harper, 1991).

13   JAMES MACKEY's 'Social Models of the Trinity' is part of his paper 'Image and Metaphor in the Christian Understanding of God as Trinity', which he first gave at a conference at Trinity College, Dublin, in 1992. Amongst his books are *Jesus the Man and the Myth* (New York: Paulist Press, and London: SCM Press, 1979); *The Christian Experience of God as Trinity* (London: SCM Press, 1983); *Modern Theology: A Sense of Direction* (Oxford and New York: Oxford University Press, 1987); with James D. G. Dunn, *New Testament Theology in Dialogue: Christology and Ministry* (London: SPCK, and Philadelphia: The Westminster Press, 1987); and *Power and Christian Ethics* (Cambridge and New York: Cambridge University Press, 1994). He has also edited *Religion and Imagination* (Edinburgh: Edinburgh University Press, 1986).

# 11

## The Doctrine of the Trinity
### Robert W. Jenson

### The Cappadocians and the Holy Trinity

We now find God useless. That is or can be progress, for in fact God is *salvifically* useless. God is no use to us, because we are much use to him. What role does God play in our lives? It is an inevitable but wrong question. We shall be freed from it only by captivation to the right question: What role do we play in God's life? In the history we live, that question cannot but raise another: How can we play *any* role in God's life?

To both questions, only the full and unabashed doctrine of Trinity, in its original Cappadocian radicality, can answer. Jonathan Edwards, writing in America in the closest correspondence with Britain, reinvented the Cappadocian wheel, with what was already a true 'second naiveté'. In piety toward our theology's once achieved and then forgotten overcoming of the Enlightenment, I will cite him: 'There was, [as] it were, an eternal society or family in the Godhead, in the Trinity of persons. It seems to be God's design to admit the church into the divine family as his Son's wife.'[1]

The thought of the Cappadocian fathers is ecumenically celebrated for making possible the victory of Nicene Trinitarianism. Just as ecumenically, it is forgotten what their intellectual achievement in fact was. From the gospel's first penetration of the Hellenistic religious world, it had been presumed that Greece's interpretation of eternity was unchallengeable. Deity, said late Mediterranean antiquity, is immunity to time; God is the Rock of Ages who ignores time's river and in whose cover we too may hide. The Cappadocians, by an almost unimaginable break with their world's self-evidencies, trusted in an opposite eternity, thereby first conceptualizing the specific Christian identification of God.[2]

God's being, said Gregory of Nyssa, is a 'life [that] has neither interior measure nor compass, for no temporal ruler can keep up with it'. Gregory invoked eternity not as the motionless center of revolving time but as a *movement* that infinitely outruns and *so* envelops laggard time, that is 'infinite over against the past and infinite over against the future'.[3] He was aware of the break; he mocked the Arians for attributing the perfection of timelessness to the Father, thereby making him 'inactive'.[4] If the old conception of eternity located God's transcendence of time in the insurpassability of his past, in his status as the 'Unoriginate', Gregory challenged the Arians to 'reverse their doctrine and see infinite futurity as the mark of deity. . . , finding their warrants in what is to come and is real in hope, rather than in what is past and old'.[5]

A first Being who is real by perfect stability, and who is stable by perfect self-possession, can only exclude or absorb other beings that are real by relatively stable self-possession. If God is eternal by immunity to time, by perfect exemplification of primary substantiality, and if we therefore exist by relative resistance to time, by imperfect exemplification of substantiality, only two conceptions of our relationship to God are possible. We can stand over against God as separate and finally competing agents or we can vanish into him. A personal life, on the contrary, can receive other lives without absorbing them; indeed, this possibility belongs to the very notion of personhood.

I have introduced the concept of personhood. Before we dare to speak of our lives as lived in God, we must ask *whose* liveliness it is that the Cappadocian idea of eternity fits, whose liveliness it is that outstrips time.

To that question, the Cappadocians did not answer as mitigated Western Trinitarianism would: eternity is the property of God *simpliciter* who then is also three persons.[6] They held back the word 'God' and answered directly: time-outstripping Liveliness is the property of Jesus Christ and of the One he called Father and of their Spirit among us. *Then* they said: and these three are one God because this predicate of infinite futurity belongs mutually to all three.

This last must provoke the question: Why in that case are there not three Gods? Since the predicate of deity belongs equally to three something-or-others? The Cappadocians' answer to this question established the original doctrine of Trinity, the specifically Christian interpretation of God.

The name 'God', as Gregory of Nyssa said most bluntly, does not attach to sheer deity at all; a plurality of instances of deity does not, therefore, make a plurality of gods. 'God' is a word for the joint *dynamism* of the Father, the Son and the Spirit. Jesus Christ and his Father and their Spirit, precisely *by* the narrative differences and interactions that the Gospels recount, bear on us together. They achieve always one joint deed, by their mutual roles. And the one action is the supreme reality rightly adored and named as the one God.[7] 'All action which comes upon the creature . . . begins from the Father and is present through the Son and is perfected in the Holy Spirit. Therefore the name of the action ("God") is not divided among the several actors.'[8] God, we may say, is what happens between

Jesus and the Transcendence he called Father, and their Power who inhabits our future. He is the infinite life within which all created events are embraced and whose story is told by the Trinitarian discourse about divine 'proceedings'.

This doctrine of Trinity is Christian history's principal victory to date, in its continuing task of identifying the gospel's God. It is this doctrine with which we must press on if we are to apprehend the true God's blessed uselessness. And it is this doctrine which the Western Church never quite grasped, thus setting itself up for the crisis of Enlightenment mechanism. The Latin-speaking Church's failure to grasp the heart of trinitarianism can be displayed on many technical points; one is appropriate to my need.[9]

The maxim that the 'externally directed works of the Trinity are indivisible' could rightly have meant that the Trinity's *opera ad extra* are insurpassably the mutual achievement of Father, Son and Spirit and that this lively mutuality is real in God himself. In Western theology, to the exact contrary, the slogan has meant that the *opera ad extra* are *indifferently* attributable to any of the Three or to the Trinity as such. Thus God is again reduced to stability, his triune life pulled back into the interior of a monadic deity from which it can mean little to our religious life – as St Augustine himself, after all twistings and turnings, admitted.[10]

The gospel's promise is not that we shall be worked on by a monadic God's agency until we achieve some satisfactory state but that we shall rule with and in him. We will overcome the churchly and civil uselessness of God only by claiming our use for him, in the unmitigated audacity of the promise. We will be, as the Eastern Church has always said 'deified'; we will be taken into the Life as participants, obeying and loving the Father with the Son in their Spirit. The Christian God, the triune God, has room in himself for us, in our full communal and individual personhood as the spouse of the Son, the respondents of the Logos. And when now the Word is spoken not only about us but to us, and when we are not merely addressed but commanded to answer, to say 'Our Father . . .', then the triune Conversation opens already to include us.

I had next almost written, 'To do what we can do we do not need God, but to do what only he can do – live – God uses us'. But it is already too late in my argument for the penultimate truth of the first clause. To do what we truly can do we need God. But we will find what we truly can do only when we confess God as he is: the Triune *in* whom we live and move and have our being. Then we will see through the world's false metaphors, to the real human community and the real universe, in which there is much to be done and none of it but with prayer and praise.

A polity is no machine, and in no interesting way does it resemble one. A polity is the forum in which a moral community of persons deliberates its good. That we seek the mandate of heaven when it is needed, and are provided with organs of civil theology and liturgy by which to hear and respond in prayer and praise, but accords with the reality and destiny of human community.

Nor is the cosmos a machine, nor does it in any interesting way resemble one. Newton himself suggested that space is God's sensorium; and relativity theory makes the suggestion plausible. Perhaps the truth is to be sought on lines suggested by Edwards: the material cosmos allows the intersubjectivity of the uncreated and created community of persons. It is the 'between' by which we may be there for one another without absorbing one another.[11] I must break with these speculations and move on.

## Luther and the liberating word

We now find God offensive. That is or can be progress, for only when our assertion of freedom founded in ourselves is mortally offended can cracks of real freedom open.

What is it not to be free? Common-sensically, I am unfree when I choose and am prevented from doing or receiving what I have chosen. If it is another's choice that prevents me, I experience not merely unfreedom but subservience. Thus in most, common-sensical, contexts, the extent of our freedom is an empirical problem. Sometimes we are free and sometimes not, and the occasions are sorted out only by experience. The religious context poses a more principled question: Can we *ever* be free if there is God?

We experience God as an offense to freedom when we experience him as 'another' in the sense of the previous paragraph, and then necessarily as an *all*-choosing other. We experience God as an offense to freedom when we take his creating will as an interposing will athwart our choices. Precisely this experience is what the Scriptures mean by 'sin'. Its circular tyranny can be described as follows. First, we freely choose to put God at a distance, in order, we think, to be free. But if there is in fact God, just by this choice we become unfree with him. Then, to be free, we must deny him. 'Did God say. . . ?'

Reflective clarifications can help only so much. Western scholasticism did what could be done, with beautiful precision. Precisely *because* we are no competition for God in the matter of choosing, the greatest scholastics argued, his choosings do not cross ours. What God chooses to happen, happens. And if he chooses some things to happen because of creatures' free choices, that is how they will happen.[12] But such distinctions could not by themselves rescue their devisers from falling back into unfreedom with God, so soon as they turned to actual religious life and its explication. What was and is needed is speech in the Church that actually liberates, that effectively offends our false freedom. The needed reflection is reflection that prepares such speech.

The choice that Christian thought must soon make clearly has been nowhere more drastically posed than by Martin Luther. Luther's theological impetus was, above all, a passion to plumb the ecumenical correlation of God and faith. Faith, he found, is the liberty to which God offends us.

Luther set out his program in the nineteenth and twentieth theses of the set prepared for the 1518 convention of Augustinians, at Heidelberg. The pair is built around a rather elegant chaismus on *intellegere* and *conspicere*; the published translations ignore this. Let me try my hand.

> The true theologian does not come to see the invisible things of God by reflecting on the creation. The true theologian reflects on the visible and hinder parts of God, having seen them in sufferings and the cross.[13]

The theology rejected by the first thesis is what Luther took to be usual in the West. Provoked by the unsatisfactory character of the merely 'visible' creation, the theologian is launched on a reflective quest for its invisible Ground and Perfection. Insofar as we succeed, we arrive at a place from which we can 'see' – the sense now is mystic – God as this Ground. To the exact contrary, 'true' theology *begins* with seeing God, in that God intrudes himself as one of our objects, as a 'visible' event in our world, summed up as 'the cross'. This event is anything but the Perfection we seek beyond – or behind or below or be-whatever – this world; it is 'sufferings' *in* our world. The experience of God is thus not the end of a reflective enterprise; it is the beginning of one. Nor does the theologian make any journey away from this vision; in it he or she has an eternity's food for reflection, on the mystery that God makes himself our object, and that in cross and sufferings.

The reversal is precise. As the dogma of Nicaea laid it down: the incarnation does not, like the cult figures of antiquity, satisfy our need for a path to God; it obviates it. God was never abstracted from our temporal reality; he is eternally and self-definingly the Father of one of us. The religious quest is empty because God was not missing. He is all too present, for what could God present in our world be but cross and sufferings?

Luther evoked the offense along two lines. First, the God known in the way of 'true' theology is impenetrably *hidden*. That God is hidden, all Christendom has known. The usual interpretation has regarded God's hiddenness as the shimmer introduced by great metaphysical distance.

Therefore God's hiddenness is thought to be amenable to degree; revelation is God's lessening of the distance, and religion is our reciprocal movement. In truth, however, what hides God is precisely the offense that and how he makes himself a worldly object. That God presents his *posteriora* to us is both the event of revelation and what hides him from us. Therefore we never get past God's visible and hinder reality; his hiddenness cannot be ameliorated. And since God not revealed is anyway hidden, hiddenness is coextensive with deity.[14]

Second, the God known in the way of true theology pre-empts and obviates the attribution of 'the free will' to creatures. Over against him, we are free because we are freed. For the true God is, *Luthero referente*, first of all the God of promises.

All theology has said that God makes promises, but usually this has been taken for a contingent fact about a God initially interpreted otherwise. For Luther, that God makes promises is the fundamental proposition.[15] God is by platitudinous and materially empty definition somehow 'absolute'; the question is how. With Luther, the starting point of all understanding is that God makes absolutely reliable promises.

The God who is a promiser, and whose promises are reliable, must be an utterly free will, who allows for no contingencies in his intention. 'If you doubt . . . that God foreknows and wills all things . . . immutably . . . how can you believe his promises?'[16] A promise liberates its hearer from what would otherwise be the conditions of the intended future: 'I will see to the financing.' To make a promise is to claim to be free to do this. To say there is a promise-making *God*, and that he is God by making promises, is to say there is a promise-maker whose freedom encompasses *all* contingencies. If any created contingency can intrude between God's knowledge and his will, if there is ever a 'Yes, but . . .' with which we must answer a promise of God, it is over with faith and faith's God.

This God is therefore a will who '*omnia in omnibus movet et agit*',[17] a Will in which the good and the bad, life and death, are equally if very differently swept forward, who 'kills and makes alive'.[18] A promiser drives to a future; a promiser who is God 'moves' and 'agitates' all things. The root metaphor of more normal religious identifications of God is of a Governor who holds back a creation that threatens to get out of hand; Luther thinks rather of an Agitator who impels a creation that threatens to sink back into quiescence.

We return to the theme of God's hiddenness by noting the anguished question these last paragraphs must provoke. If all things are impelled by the will of God, then, given what actually happens, it looks bad for God's character. The point was starkly clear to Luther: 'For God so governs this corporal world in external matters, that if you follow the judgment of human reason . . . , you must conclude that God is not or that he is malicious.'[19] And externalities are the least of it. In God's specific relation to personal creatures, the offense of his freedom is the offense of predestination: 'By his will he makes us . . . damnable' and then 'saves so few and damns so many . . .' that 'he seems to delight in torturing his wretched creatures.'[20]

The offenses of experienced history and predestination are inescapable if we suppose the Bible's God; what is helpful about Luther is that he eschews every attempt to avoid them. Only in the Kingdom will we see how God's majesty and love are one. Now we honor God by withdrawing from the religious attempt to get closer and mitigate his hiddenness, by leaving to him that 'hidden and fearsome will' of God's mere unresisted impetus.[21]

If this were the whole story, I would just have described Satan, not God. But we were brought to the interpretation of God as absolute freedom by consideration of his *promises*. To turn away from God as he appears at the end of the religious quest is to turn back to God as he has already addressed us and taken us into community with himself, antecedently to all these torments. To turn away from God's incalculable mere will is to hearken to God as he has defined his will by the gospel.[22]

The gospel, to be sure, does not mitigate God's hiddenness; it redoubles it. If God in the world is hidden in inexplicability, in Christ he is hidden in sufferings and cross. But this redoubled hiddenness is just so a *speaking* hiddenness. The redoubling *defines* the mystery, as the mystery of love. That finally is faith: that we trust the loving word that God speaks, as the very God whose wrath repels us.

Can we believe the word of love, the word of God's hiding for us in the cross? Can we accept this word, from the God of this world's terrors? It is anyway clear that about this God, the real God, there is nothing else to do but believe him.

Christendom must finally come clean. The God we proclaim is irremediably offensive to 'the free will' of human religiosity. The offense can be overcome as faith, as a clinging to things not seen, but there are no milder options. God has identified himself by the crucifixion of Jesus. We have been fecund of theories about why this horrific event was necessary in terms of our self-chosen historical agency. All such theory now exposes itself as mythic. As to God's general rule of history, Christendom's mighty effort of theodicy has played out its moves. There is nothing to be done about God's hiddenness. That is always true, but surely we of all generations, indeed 'after Auschwitz', have no more excuse not to face it. The only alternative to the abandonment of theodicy would be worship of a

God himself subject to contingency; such a God would be another God than the one praised and feared in Israel and the gospel.

Since we have nothing to lose but our faith, we can in fact believe. We are free to trust the real God, freed by his utter freedom and the offense it is to us. We are free to live in history just because we do not rule it – or rather, because we rule in God.

## Karl Barth and our role in Christ's history

And what, at last, is to be done about God's *particularity*? The Christian God has an identity, and his identity is established by a historical particular: our God is whoever raised Jesus from the dead. Just so, as Karl Barth should have taught us if none did before, this God is truly encompassing, the God of all his creation. To see this requires a metaphysical wrench, which Barth accomplished, thereby dividing the theology of this century from that of the nineteenth.

Friedrich Schleiermacher had few imitators, but he pioneered the general way in which the nineteenth century tried to overcome the mechanism and historical pragmatism of the normal Enlightenment.[23] Specifically religious consciousness, he taught, is our unity with the whole of reality; indeed, only in religious consciousness is reality a whole, since only in it are we one with the rest. Thus Schleiermacher identified an encompassing whole that transcends mechanism, and so located us within it that religion is secured in its worth and necessity, and a clash between God's freedom and ours is made inconceivable. It was an ingenious and profound move. Only one cavil presents itself, but some may think it sizeable: Schleiermacher's teaching makes matters worse for our present problem.

Wholeness is constituted, according to Schleiermacher, in 'religion' sheerly as such. The theological question then becomes: What is Christ's role in our religion? The nineteenth century had many and various answers; none proved satisfactory, running out at last to Ernst Troeltsch's proposal that Christ is the religious inspiration we Westerners happen to be stuck with. As has been lamentably customary since about 1800, the English-speaking church has anachronistically imported also this German counsel of despair, discovering in it nothing less than 'Copernican' new insight. It is the question itself that makes the mischief, and against it that Barth protested.

In a confluence of pastoral responsibility, biblical study, and political outrage, young Barth, a great hope of liberal Christianity, was theologically and politically radicalized. We need not trace the steps, only record the outcome: Barth found his way by turning liberalism inside out. The question according to Barth is not what role Christ plays in our religious life and the totality constituted in it but what role we and our religion play in the totality constituted as Christ's history.[24] This reversal is very like that made by original Trinitarianism; and one effect of Barth's work was to renew the doctrine of Trinity for our century.

The story is not our story with a role for Christ. The story is Christ's story with roles for us. To state the most audacious of Barth's propositions straightway: the God-man, Jesus Christ, as a historical event, is the ontological foundation in God of all reality other than God.[25]

Therewith Barth only said of Christ what all theology has said of 'the Logos'. His purpose in saying it, moreover, was the same purpose that made the traditional Logos doctrine so central for the authors of *Lux Mundi*: determination that the world and human history not be abandoned to secularity but be understood as moved and shaped by the same eternal Logos that is in Christ. But the circle of *Lux Mundi* also shared what must now be seen as classical theology's great capitulation: we have been intimidated by uncriticized metaphysical dogma into detaching 'the Word' from its original role as a title of the man Jesus Christ and into making the *Logos asarkos*, a *not* yet incarnate extra metaphysical entity, be the inner-triune Ground of creation. We have taken it to be obvious that a historical particular cannot be ontologically foundational. But this axiom seems obvious only so long as we remain bound to Mediterranean antiquity's primal dogma, that eternity is immunity to time. Barth's achievement was to break this bondage. There never, he says, is actually a *Logos asarkos*; what is eternally actual as the Ground of creation is Jesus the Christ.

I must barbarously summarize Barth's elegant teaching. In all eternity, God chose to be one with us in the existence of Jesus Christ. This act of choice made covenant with us; and since the existence of Christ and the reality of this covenant are the same thing, God's eternal act of choice and the existence of Jesus Christ are the same event.[26] Thus what happened in Palestine between Jesus and the one he called 'Father' *is* God's self-determination. And that is, with this God, to say it is God's life, his eternity.[27] With that, metaphysics is stood on its head. Even the creation must be understood as an act of God-determined-in-Christ. To recite the famous doctrine: the covenant, established in the fact of Christ's existence, is the inner possibility and reason of creation; the creation is the outer ground, the stage and supporting players, of the covenant.[28]

God in and of himself is thus a historical being; in all eternity there occurs in him a meeting and a decision, and indeed a meeting and a decision between the Father and one of us.[29] Barth recovers the ability to play the full Cappadocian dialectic. History, as Barth analyzes it, involves self-transcendence, confrontation, and the possession of time in which to accomplish both.[30] Of the triune God it is therefore far from true that he is immune to history; it must, rather, be said that only he is fully historical and that we become historical by participation in his life.[31]

The system by which Barth carried out his insight is full of difficulties, and English-speaking theology has been mostly content to lament them. In my judgment, the difficulties reduce to one – which is shared by his critics. Barth did not fully overcome definition of God's eternity by the past tense. It continued to be an automatic epexegesis: 'in eternity, before all time'. We may ask, Why not 'in eternity, after all time'? It is a common outcome of all the theological openings I have pursued in this essay that the triune God's eternity is to be found in his infinite futurity, in the reality of 'hope, rather than in what is past and old'. We have still to catch up with Gregory.

Our theological times demand revisionary metaphysics. In this perspective, the real God is not the securely persisting Beginning; he is the triumphing End. God is Spirit, and Spirit in the Scriptures is the power of the last future, the anticipatory presence of the coming Christ, the 'down payment' on the Kingdom. God – any God – somehow rhymes past and future to create our present; both religious evocations and metaphysical interpretations of God must do so from one or the other of the temporal poles. The one possibility presents no greater logical difficulty than does the other; we suppose that an eschatological understanding of God's eternity is exotic only because we *pre*suppose the protological interpretation, because our thinking is precritically shaped by the metaphysics of Olympian religion, because it is unconverted by that very different discourse about God which derives from Israel's exodus and Jesus' resurrection.

If we take the plunge with Barth, and in this last respect past Barth, we shall be able to honor both Christ's particularity and the truth of humanity's total religious history.[32] For we shall then understand that the truth of all religions is to be established in the particular reality of Jesus Christ. Because Christ's story is the encompassing story, all history and, at history's center, all religious history belong *inside* the story of Christ. And since the encompassing story is impelled and shaped by its End, it is to Christ that the religions are carried.

The point, therefore, is not that all or some religions are, as historical phenomena, right or not right. Comparative study of religions is informative in many connections but tells us nothing about their truth. The religions are variously and truly apprehensions of God as and only as currents in God's universal history, as God creates it to be finally appropriated by Christ. Religious proclamations and rites are not justified as ahistorical items; it is by a word's or an action's place in religious history, by its temporally unique response to previous words and rites and enabling of future speech and practice that it is opened to the coming of the Truth. It is the *outcome* of humanity's religious history that will justify that history, when all our struggles will present a manifold object for Christ to interpret in and by that final address of love which will summon his eternal community.

If we keep it firmly in mind that the Spirit is Christ's spirit, and is never without that identity, we can even say that all religions are evoked by the Spirit. For we may then risk the dangerous proposition that the reality of God's Spirit and the fact that we live in time, that my achieved self is always threatened by I know not what, are the same. Since religion is our creaturely attempt to deal with the future's onrush, to evoke the continuity of achieved selfhood with the uncontrollable future, all religion is response to the Spirit. Or, what is the same, all religion is eschatological vision.

Apart from the gospel, of course, the way we deal with the Spirit's futurity is by erecting barriers against him, by building barns and burying talents. We posit gods whose deity is precisely their timelessness, resistance to the future more reliable than any we can muster on our own; we posit gods to protect us from God the Spirit. But the barriers cannot hold. They crumble before the impact of the future, and precisely in crumbling fulfill their Spirit-given reality. 'Thou fool' is said to us all, by and against all our religions; and each time a barrier falls, there is a flash of the Spirit.

The religions' direction to Christ does not occur over our temporal heads. The gospel about Christ, in all its specificity, is now spoken in the world of the religions and is now a power at work historically, urging all religions to their destined outcome. Thus religious history is innerhistorically directed to its final End; its relation to its coming Christ is an internal relation.

Because the gospel is a missionary message, the Christian religion is essentially syncretistic. Each time the gospel crosses a new cultural or epochal boundary it of course finds the ground already religiously occupied. Each time the pattern is the same: the religion of a time or of a people is invaded by the gospel, and a Christianity is created that is neither identical with the antecedent missionary Christianity nor a mere baptizing of the invaded religion. Each such Christianity, as a historical emergent, is fragile, wracked by incomplete syntheses. Its theological life will be spent sorting these out.

We need not go far for an example. It is the specific Christianity bred by the gospel on the soil of Olympian and Socratic religion which sets all the problems with which this essay and its many predecessors have struggled. If we can break through to an eschatological interpretation of God's eternity, we shall understand that our syncretism and its problems are not merely inevitable but are christologically ordained, instances of the gospel's transforming impetus amid the religions. There is a nice irony in our situation: what binds us to a static and comparative understanding of the religions, within which they must appear either as 'really' all the same or as merely competitive, is just that historyless interpretation of God which is the chief unresolved item of our particular syncretic task.

If God has history and is Lord from the future, our appropriate policy to other religions can be very simple: we should assert Jesus' resurrection and trust the Spirit. Christianity will be a syncretistic phenomenon with or without our consent; we should relax with this, not because all religion is equally right but because Christ lives to triumph. We need not regret the meeting of Athens and Jerusalem, for all its pitfalls into which we have fallen and from which we struggle to extricate ourselves. And we cannot and do not need to predict what will now come of Western Christianity's new confrontation with the resurgent religions.

When we speak with other religions, we should ask: What difference do *you* think it would make if Jesus Christ, this particular human being, defined by his particular life and death, should in fact have risen? Should the discussion become religiously creative, we need not determine in advance that the result will be congenial to either partner. We will indeed seek converts, but to the mission of Jesus' resurrection.

NOTES

1. Jonathan Edwards, *Miscellanies* (MS. collection containing the drafts of Edwards's planned major work, at Beinecke Library, Yale University), p. 741.
2. Robert W. Jenson, *The Triune Identity: God According to the Gospel*, Philadelphia: Fortress Press, 1982, pp. 162–8.
3. Gregory of Nyssa, *Against Eunomius*, in his *Opera*, vols. 1—2, ed. W. Jaeger, Leiden: E. J. Brill, 1960, book 1.366.
4. ibid., 3/10.36.
5. ibid., 1.666–72.
6. To the following, Jenson, *Triune Identity*, pp. 111–14.
7. Gregory of Nyssa, *Against Eunomius*, 2.34; *To Ablabius: That There Are Not Three Gods*, in *Opera*, vol. 3/1, ed. F. Müller, Leiden: E. J. Brill, 1958, §124.
8. ibid., §125.
9. To the following, Jenson, *Triune Identity*, pp. 118–21, 125–30.
10. e.g., Augustine, *On the Trinity*, 6.12; 5.10; 7.7–11.

11. Jenson, *America's Theologian*, chap. 3.
12. Thomas Aquinas, *Summa Theologiae*, 1a, Q. 22. art. 4: 'The efficacy of divine providence is not merely that something shall *somehow* happen; but that it shall happen either contingently or necessarily. And so that happens infallibly and necessarily which divine providence ordains to happen infallibly and necessarily; and that happens contingently whose reason in divine providence is such that it must happen contingently.' For a very useful compressed presentation of Aquinas on the whole matter, see Harry J. McSorley, *Luther: Right or Wrong?*, New York: Paulist/Newman Press, 1969, pp. 138–62.
13. Martin Luther, *Disputatio Heidelbergae habita*, WA 1.361–2.
14. See the splendid article by Eberhard Jüngel, 'Quae supra nos nihil ad nos', *Evangelische Theologie*, 32.219–22. The one side of the matter is in the cited passage from the disputation; the other side is in *De servo arbitrio*, WA 18:685.
15. Luther, *De servo arbitrio*, 614–21.
16. ibid., 619.
17. ibid., 709.
18. ibid., 709–10, 585.
19. ibid., 784.
20. ibid., 633.
21. ibid., 684–5.
22. ibid., 685–6.
23. It is, of course, the great *Speeches* that had this force: *Über die Religion: Reden an die Gebildeten, unter ihren Verächter*, Berlin, 1799.
24. For the formal dogmatic presentation, see Karl Barth, *Kirchliche Dogmatik*, Zollikon: Evangelischer Verlag, 1932, III/2:64–82, 158–241.
25. ibid., II/2.86, 109–214; III/1.44–103; 258–377; IV/1:54.
26. ibid., II/2:109–18.
27. ibid., II/1.294–305.
28. ibid., III/1:103, 258.
29. ibid., II/2.192–202.
30. ibid., III/2:189.
31. E.g., ibid., II/2.201: the divine life 'is the principle and being of all events whatsoever'.
32. Instead of picking through Barth, see Robert W. Jenson, 'Religious Pluralism, Christology, and Barth', *dialog* 20:31–8.

# 12

# RE-CONCEIVING THE TRINITY AS THE MYSTERY OF SALVATION
## *Catherine Mowry LaCugna*

If we move beyond venerable liturgical or dogmatic formulations about the Trinity, it is not at all obvious what it means to speak of the threefoldness of God. Certainly, Trinitarian theology is not obviously relevant for the life of most believers in this century. But while a Trinitarian framework is necessary for Christian theology, repeating dogmatic formulae simply will not serve us well today. Christians today are inclined to ask what the doctrine means in one's life as a Christian, and how each central facet of faith applies to the sociopolitical sphere. If the doctrine of the Trinity is really the central mystery of the Christian faith, ought we not more readily be able to answer such a query? The polite neglect of the doctrine of the Trinity in most contemporary theological works signals that something is wrong – either with the concept and confession of the triune God, or with its desuetude. Before discarding the doctrine altogether, one would be obliged to provide some sort of theological or exegetical evidence for such a move – some have done this.[1] But the future of Christian theism would seem to depend on the restoration of the doctrine of the Trinity to life and theology.

Among the several possible ways of re-conceiving Trinitarian theology, one is to revise the classical 'models' or analogies of the immanent Trinity. Instead of working with the 'three persons, one nature' formula, theologians construct new models of Trinitarian relations: interpersonal (H. Mühlen); society of persons (J. Bracken); processive relations of divine becoming (L. Ford); temporal unsurpassibility (R. Jenson); semiotic relations (G. Tavard); eschatological consummation (J. Moltmann).[2] This approach has many merits for it helpfully recasts archaic terms (e.g. hypostasis, subsistent relation) along with their accompanying metaphysics. But at the same time, this approach disguises a more fundamental problem: how is the reformulated inner Trinitarian analogy related to the 'economic' Trinity, that is, to salvation history? How does the new analogy convey God as being God *for us*?

Without intending to detract from the positive gains of such efforts, we may raise in addition to this theological question, a preliminary methodological and hermeneutical one: what is the reality to which any theoretical model of God refers, and how may we link up our speculations about God's 'inner' life with the divine reality? What are the theological warrants for seeing a connection between what we say about God and who or what God *is*? What is the connection between our experience of God in Jesus through their Spirit, and God's transcendent reality? What does it mean to speak of God as being threefold internally and constitutively, that is, as eternally prior to the divine excursion into history and time?

In Karl Rahner's monograph on *The Trinity*[3] he proposes an axiom accepted (in principle if not always without qualification)[4] by most contemporary theologians: 'The "economic" Trinity is the "immanent" Trinity and *vice versa*' (p. 22). The axiom can serve as a rich starting point for our reflection on the questions we have identified. It provides a grammatical and theological parameter within which one may re-conceive the relationship between God and all that is other than God ('the world'). *Prima facie* the axiom seems to provide the theological and hermeneutical correspondences we are searching for. According to it, who and how God is in the economy of salvation *is* (the same as) who and how God is eternally and transcendentally, and what one says or experiences of God's economic-historical activity is true as well of God's 'inner' history or immanent life. The axiom entails several far-reaching consequences not only for the doctrine of God/Trinity, but also for Christology and ecclesiology. For these reasons, we shall argue that Rahner's *Grundaxiom* is the precondition for re-conceiving the Trinitarian doctrine *as* the mystery of salvation.

But what is the meaning of the 'is' in the axiom? What is the justification for it? What are the consequences of postulating it?

Evidently an adequate Trinitarian theology, Nicene, Cappadocian, or contemporary, will adhere to the equivalence indicated by the copula. One could easily make a twofold historical observation: first, that the two classic distortions of Christian teaching on God, Sabellian modalism and Arian subordinationism, resulted from not taking seriously enough the equivalence indicated by the 'is'. Second, contemporary theologies likewise commonly run aground in one or other of these same directions.[5] Rahner's axiom stands in contrast to much 'orthodox' Western Trinitarian theology from Augustine onwards, for the precise reason that analogies were developed for the 'immanent' Trinity while the 'economic' Trinity largely passed out of theological and religious consciousness. This has the consequence of depriving the Christian doctrine of God of its salvific focus. . . .

Rahner's theology of the Trinity provides us with a soteriological focus which will help to reinvigorate the venerable dogmatic and liturgical formulations as we revise them in new theological models and analogies. I turn now to some concrete theological and methodological ramifications which I see entailed by Rahner's axiom.

## Theological implications

*Recovering the tradition.* The doctrine of the Trinity pertains above all to the *mystery of salvation.* This emphasis might better be served by retrieving other options in the Trinitarian tradition, specifically, the Greek rather than the Latin approach, the economic rather than the immanent, the Cappadocian rather than the Augustinian, the emanationist rather than the rationalistic. A more soteriologically oriented contemporary reformulation can shed new light on the problem of God and God-language. To bring this about, Jesus Christ must be at the heart of our Trinitarian theology. While dialectical and evangelical theology would put it in terms of the mystery of the cross (Barth, Jüngel, Moltmann)[6] and Roman Catholic theology in terms of the mystery of incarnation (Rahner, von Balthasar), there is only one mystery: 'God was in Christ reconciling the world to himself.' Trinitarian speculation, when it loses sight of this center, becomes onesidedly 'immanent'. It becomes a speculation, a mirror image, but a distorted one; it reflects the remarkable ability of the human intellect to construct analogies and theories of God, but not necessarily with reference to God's saving reality.[7]

*Missions and processions.* Second, a severe disjunction between missions and processions no longer can be retained. It was Augustine's genius to employ Neoplatonic categories to construct a Christian Trinitarian theology. But the attendant doctrine of divine timelessness, which entailed the metaphysical and temporal disengagement of eternal processions *ad intra* ('begetting' and 'breathing') from temporal missions *ad extra* (incarnation, sending of the Spirit) is problematic for us. Even though for 1500 years the Augustinian approach did not cause for Christian theologians difficulties of the sort we have today, it does explain why someone like Schleiermacher thought that he could make better sense of Christianity by relegating the doctrine of the Trinity to an appendix.

According to Rahner's Trinitarian axiom, any discussion of the Son or Spirit must be conducted in the context of their salvific missions, since the missions in history are constitutive of their divine 'personhood' and *vice versa.* Likewise, reference to what 'God has accomplished in Christ in their Spirit' must not be conceived apart from the inner-Trinitarian reality of which it is expressive. A remark of Rahner's bears repeating here: Roman Catholic theology in general 'is convinced that the Spirit might well exist without the incarnation' (p. 85). In this same connection we would have grounds for reversing the traditional *aporia* concerning the different appropriation of the creative and salvific events to the divine persons.[8]

*Contemporary challenges to Christian theism.* Third, a Trinitarian theology which is focussed on the *mysterium salutis* might respond quite differently to the contemporary challenges to theism. Feminist and Latin American liberation theologies, linguistic theory, atheistic theology and new metaphysical systems, notably that of process theology, have each already questioned classical Christian theism on various counts. These include its patriarchalism and imperialism, its frequent appeal to special or exempt linguistic and logical canons, its self-restriction to a static metaphysics, and its inability to articulate a 'real' relationship between God and world. I am suggesting that a reconceived *Trinitarian* theology would challenge the generally unitarian or Christomonistic character of most Christian theology as well as provide a fresh approach for answering the critiques generated by these contemporary theological challenges. A Trinitarian theology would point up the inadequacy of a Christian theology which in the west, from the fifth century on, has concentrated on the 'immanent' Trinity and developed its doctrine in a non-soteriological, a-historical fashion. New efforts in the area of the doctrine of God will need to be rooted in the mystery and death of Jesus rather than abstractly theistic or metaphysical or linguistic.[9] The closeness of God will become more important than God's incomprehensibility, for the second of these too easily becomes a metaphysical rather than a religious affirmation.[10] Similarly, God will continue to be worshipped as mystery yet not as anonymity in the style of a former apophatic theology[11] because Christian theology will concern itself with identifying *which* God – the God of the outcast or the God of the élite, the God who led Israel out of bondage or the God of Freud's illusion – it professes to know and love.[12] In this respect, Trinitarian theology helps us articulate the *who* and *how*, rather than the *whether* of God.

*Theological language and spirituality.* Fourth, the emphasis on the history of salvation has implications for our view of theological language. Presently we are witnessing a quite widespread interest in narrative theology, imaginative theology, symbolic theology, metaphorical and parabolic theology,[13] all of which have acknowledged that theology can become vapid when it is developed apart from the variety and richness of religious imagery. Certainly no one has suggested that theological language and religious language amount to the same thing, nor even that theological precision and conceptual reification are undesirable. As long as a soteriological concern is at the center of our doctrine of God, we ought to use the images and words which a community has used to describe its experience of salvation. All this implies a new kind of Trinitarian theology, one that is not only more self-consciously soteriological but one that is comprised of the various images, symbols, metaphors, parabolic experiences and narrative truths which gave rise to the doctrine in the first place.

Fifth, with respect to spirituality, there is a burgeoning movement back towards the center point of the intersection between theology and spirituality. Regardless of the difficulty of defining the latter term, at least we can say that the increasing separation of theology from spirituality since the thirteenth century has made each to some degree arid. A contemporary Trinitarian reformulation, were it to be the fruit of a contemplative theology (and all great Trinitarian theologians have been contemplatives – Augustine, Gregory of Nyssa, Bonaventure, Aquinas, Richard of St Victor), just might give us the combination of religious imagery, theological creativity, and soteriological rootedness we are seeking. After all, Trinitarian theology should be the prime exemplar of the encounter between speculative and mystical theology.

## Methodological implications

*The place of the Trinity in a dogmatic scheme.* First, if the doctrine of the Trinity concerns above all the mystery of salvation, then we might ask about its place in a theological or dogmatic schema. Were we to survey the tradition on this point, we would find two major methodological decisions; in the first, 'the triune God' is treated as a separate theme (e.g. Aquinas); in the other, the theologian creates an infra- or super-structure of threefoldness (including perhaps a theo-logic such as Calvin's or Barth's, or a theo-dramatik such as von Balthasar's). One would expect advantages and disadvantages in either case, and there is no intrinsic reason to prefer one to the other. Each approach is suitable for explicating the basic model, God-in-relation. But let us take note of some of the pitfalls of each.

If we elect the first course, which makes sense for the practical reason of the 'division of theological labor', still the temptation will be to formulate a doctrine of God, not a doctrine of the triune God, that is, a doctrine which has no soteriological focus. The questions we often hear now, such as 'Can we believe in God after Auschwitz?', indicate the yearning we have for a God who will save us and for a theology which will carry the assurances of a God who actively, assiduously, is 'for us'. In terms of Christian theology we are, I think, frequently deceived into thinking that if we could only get our house in order on 'the one God' we might be able to rehabilitate our rather dysfunctional theism and put to rest the liberation-theological, linguistic-theological, atheistic-theological and metaphysical-theological critics. At that point, we need never get around to 'the triune God', who would once more have been shown to be superfluous. *But salvation history forbids such a foreclosure.* Christian theists have to face up to the fact: either the Christian doctrine of God is first and foremost a truth about salvation in Christ and is therefore Trinitarian, or it is only yet another metaphysical theory. Christian Trinitarian theology is in fact both.

The second methodological option – a structural Trinitarianism – has the advantage of an undergird: it provides continual support. But the disadvantage lies in the tempting fascination of the number 'three', so that one is always trying to find three characteristics, three effects, three features, forms, or types. Whatever the doctrine of the Trinity might have meant in the first place, it comes to mean more of a numerical or dialectical arrangement. In this connection Rahner's overall theology is to be admired, for while it exemplifies the kind of structural Trinitarianism we are referring to, it resists the magic of threefoldness; in fact, one is surprised to find in his explitic thematic treatment of the Trinity, *four* aspects of *two* self-communications. There is a lot to be said also for any approach which resists easy correlation of Father, Son and Spirit with creation, redemption, and reconciliation, since the biblical and patristic records on this score are mixed.[14]

*The Trinity in relation to other doctrines.* If missions and processions are theologically in 'permanent perichoresis', then, methodologically speaking, three conclusions follow. First, both Christology and pneumatology ought to be developed in a manner which makes explicit the connection between the salvific missions of Word and Spirit, and their origin in the eternal divine processions. This is in order to uphold the axiomatic unity of 'economic' and 'immanent' Trinities, of missions and processions. Second, since the two *ad intra* processions of Word and Spirit entail and imply each other, then doctrines concerning the two *ad extra* salvific missions ought to be developed in tandem with, not independently of, each other. This would mean a more pneumatological Christology, and a more incarnational pneumatology.[15] The two 'modalities' of God in Word and Spirit need not work at cross-purposes with each other at the level of doctrine. And third, Christology and ecclesiology/pneumatology ought to be considered as *portions* of the more comprehensive Christian theological task. We might say that Christology and ecclesiology are 'tracks' within the wider enterprise of theology as such, which seeks to articulate the experience of salvation in Trinitarian terms.

*The Trinity and apophasis.* Third, the experience of salvation always entails some recognition of one's inadequacy before God, and therefore one sees the appropriateness of silence before God's ever greater reality. And when one breaks the silence, one recognizes the haltingness of one's speech and the smallness of one's imagination. We are in that respect like Moses who protests to Yahweh, 'I am a slow speaker and not able to speak well' (Exod. 5.10b). Now it is perfectly clear that a theology that would speak univocally or literally about God's being would run contrary to the whole of the biblical and patristic view of God as well as violate the most basic precepts of all theology and mystical experience.[16] Is the alternative utter silence?

The apophatic tradition in theology (whether that of mystical or negative theology) has tried to embody this distinctive dimension of the experience of salvation. However, negative theology in the Greek patristic tradition was entangled with a doctrine of God's immutability, impass-ibility, and non-temporality.[17] Today we need a positive incorporation of the spirit of apophasis without, however, its tendency towards agnosticism and certain attendant metaphysical assertions (at least, they cannot be all that is 'said' about God).[18] We therefore need a theological doctrine of God which is able to conjoin the insight of negative theology (in Augustine's words, 'a thing is not ineffable which can be called ineffable' – *De Doct. Chr.* I.6) with the urge of the theological *ratio* and *explicatio* which feel licensed actively to think and speak of God, and which produce content-statements about God ('There is one God in three subsistent relations'). Both an agnostic theology and a one-dimensional theology are flatly impossible. Images remind us that our abstractions tend to collapse the distinction between God's reality and our thoughts and words about God, and concepts serve to re-attach our images to the referent, God-in-relation. Notice that the Trinitarian framework preserves God's hiddenness and inscrutability (which is associated with 'Father') and God's manifestedness and concreteness (associated with the Son). The methodological result, then, is this: a theology of God in its totality must be both silent and forthcoming, just as God is both silent and yet utters a word. It must balance the two sides of the experience of salvation, just as it must conform to the God who saves. Torrance suggests the need for *apophasis* grounded on the *homoousion*; 'we must learn what is proper to "read back" into the eternal Being of God and what is not proper'.[19]

*The Trinity and religious imagery.* Fourth, I suggested above that a Trinitarian theology which takes seriously Rahner's axiom will be shaped by the religious imagery and symbols of our experience. Liturgies and creeds are already Trinitarian and often narrative in part; speculative theology must claim them for its own. But systematic theologians often are chary of the 'merely' symbolic and revert to a view of metaphor as mere ornamentation, thereby implying that non-discursive terminology is less precise than the technical.[20] However, even a superficial survey of doctrinal definitions shows a church not afraid to use metaphors: the 'Father' 'begets' the 'Son',[21] or, in an even more inventive vein, the Eleventh Council of Toledo (675) declared that the Son proceeds *de utero patri* (from the womb of the Father). The point is that since God is not directly graspable by human intellection or exhaustible by human locution, imagistic and ostensive language in all its forms (analogy; symbol; metaphor; parable; narrative) will have as decisive a role to play in theological formulations as will concepts and univocations. Models insure that all kinds of language are given hearing. Thus while it is true that 'Trinity' is a narrative truth insofar as it is the story of Christian salvation, it also can be given conceptual precision and systematic elegance when elaborated as a speculative and comprehensive theological *model*. This is to say nothing more than that our understanding of the economic and immanent Trinities gains by being articulated in several different modes of discourse.

*The Trinity and contemplation.* A final methodological corollary has to do with what we described as a 'contemplative' style of theology. Ordinarily, contemplative theology has been associated with the mystical Greek and the medieval monastic traditions, in contrast with the Latin speculative and medieval scholastic traditions respectively. History shows that the monastic and scholastic in fact complemented each other as theological styles. Today we should not want to drive such a hard distinction between the monastic-contemplative and scholastic-speculative approaches, perhaps by caricaturing the former as biblical, subjective, personal, liturgical, imagistic, moralpsychological, synthetic, and the latter as philosophical, objective, universal, scholastic, conceptual, intellectual, analytic.[22] Instead, if theology is above all a disciplined and faithful search to understand the mystery of salvation, then a theological style is called for which incorporates both emphases. In the modern theological context we are not suggesting that theology once again be the province of monks, but that theology be regarded as a participatory rather than spectator activity. Therefore it will not imitate the modern *scientia* which equates 'objectivity' with personal distanciation, nor will it surrender its passion for rigorous logic and precision.[23] In a contemplative and speculative theology, the theologian will be engaged with God affectively as well as cognitively, imaginatively as well as discursively, silently as well as expressively, doxologically as well as academically.[24] The style can perhaps be illustrated by the difference in English between 'conceiving' (the divine) and 'conceptualizing' it.[25] If I am correct, the contemporary task is to re-conceive the doctrine of the Trinity as the mystery of salvation, and to do so in a way that is both contemplative and speculative.

NOTES

1. For example, M. Wiles, *Working Papers in Doctrine*, London, 1976, and *The Remaking of Christian Doctrine*, London, 1974; G. Lampe, *God as Spirit*, Oxford, 1977; C. Welch, in *In This Name: The Trinity in Contemporary Theology*, New York, 1953, continues the Schleiermacherian view that only the economic Trinity can be the subject of theology; see also C. Richardson, *The Doctrine of the Trinity*, New York, 1958

2. See H. Mühlen, *Der Heilige Geist als Person*, Münster, 1963, and *Una Mystica Persona*, Munich, 1964; also R. Sears, 'Trinitarian Love as Ground of the Church', *Theological Studies* 37, 1976, pp. 652–79; J. Bracken, 'The Holy Trinity as a Community of Divine Persons', *Heythrop Journal* 15, 1974, pp. 166–82, 257–70; L. Ford, 'Process Trinitarianism', *Journal of the American Academy of Religion*, 43, 1975, pp. 199–213; R. Jenson, *God After God*, Bobbs-Merrill, 1969, and *The Triune Identity*, Fortress Press, 1982; G. Tavard, *Vision of the Trinity*, Univ. Press of America, 1981; J. Moltmann, *The Crucified God*, New York, 1974, and *The Trinity and the Kingdom*, New York, 1981.

3. *The Trinity*, New York, 1970, is a translation by J. Donceel of 'Der dreifaltige Gott als transzendenter Urgrund der Heilsgeschichte', in *Mysterium Salutis: Grundriss Heilsgeschichtliche Dogmatik*, Bd. II, hrsg. von J. Feiner and M. Löhrer, Einsiedeln. 1967. Hereafter pagination is given in the text. See also Rahner, 'Remarks on the Dogmatic Treatise "De Trinitate" ', *Theological Investigations* vol. 4, pp. 77–102, and 'The Mystery of the Trinity', *Theological Investigations*, vol. 16, pp. 255–9.

4. See the reservations expressed by W. Hill in *The Three-Personed God*, Washington, DC: University Press of America, 1982; also T. F. Torrance, 'Toward an Ecumenical Consensus on the Trinity', *Theologische Zeitschrift*, 31/6, 1975, pp. 337–50.

5. In contrast with the 'Arian' type of theology referred to in note 1 above, a 'Sabellian' type of imbalance is exemplified in P. Schoonenberg's theology; for him, God is not eternally self-differentiated but God 'becomes' triune in the event of Jesus Christ. cf. 'Trinität – der vollendete Bund. Thesen zur Lehre vom dreipersönlichen Gott', *Orientierung* 37, 1973, pp. 115–17.

6. This explains why Moltmann and Jüngel see the cross as an event which takes place in God's own being, not just in the economy of salvation. cf. Moltmann, *The Crucified God*, chap. 6, and Jüngel, *God as the Mystery of the World*, Grand Rapids: Eerdmans, 1983.

7. Hegelianism exemplifies that a Trinitarian theory need not be attached to the threefold God. G. Lampe's work (*God as Spirit*, Oxford, 1977) is, interestingly enough, explicitly soteriological yet not Trinitarian; he considers 'Spirit' to refer not to God's essence but to God's activity; salvation and creation are conflated as

one divine activity 'toward us'. Lampe's theory shows the consequences of not observing both the 'is' and the 'vice versa' of the axiom.

8. cf. the challenge of M. Wiles on the traditional way of appropriating activity to the divine persons, in 'Some Reflections on the Origins of the Doctrine of the Trinity', *Journal of Theological Studies*, n.s., 8/1 (1957), pp. 92–106.

9. Two recent examples of a christological Trinitarianism would be E. Jüngel, op. cit., and W. Kasper, *Der Gott Jesu Christi*, Mainz, 1982.

10. These remarks should not be construed as being anti-metaphysical since any reformulation along the lines I am suggesting cannot but be metaphysical in its own way. At the same time, the early history of Trinitarian theology demonstrates that the shift to the Augustinian preference for beginning with the divine nature and unity makes it impossible to introduce God's relation to the world into God's own being. Thus Aquinas, *Summa Theologiae*, 1a, Q. 13, art. 7, has creatures in 'real' relation to God but not vice versa since this would entail a lack in God.

11. cf. J. McLelland, *God the Anonymous*, Patristic Monograph Series, No. 4, 1976.

12. cf. R. Jenson, *The Triune Identity*, p. 115.

13. See R. Funk, *Language, Hermeneutic and Word of God*, New York, 1966; S. McFague, *Metaphorical Theology*, Fortress Press, 1982; I. Barbour, *Myths, Models and Paradigms*, New York, 1974; M. Black, *Models and Metaphors*, Cornell University Press, 1962; I. Ramsey, *Religious Language*, London, 1967; F. Ferré, 'Mapping the Logic of Models in Science and Theology', in Dallas M. High, ed., *New Essays on Religious Language*, New York, 1969; R. Scharlemann, 'Theological Models and Their Construction', *Journal of Religion* (1973), pp. 65–82; D. Burrell, *Analogy and Philosophical Language*, Yale University Press, 1963; D. Tracy, *The Analogical Imagination*, New York: Crossroad, and London: SCM Press, 1981; W. Lynch, *Christ and Apollo*, Notre Dame Press, 1960; A. Wilder, *Early Christian Rhetoric: the Language of the Gospel*, rev. edn, Harvard University Press, 1971; J. Crossan, *In Parables: The Challenge of the Historical Jesus*, New York, 1973; N. Perrin, *Jesus and the Language of the Kingdom*, Fortress Press, 1976; L. Keck, *A Future for the Historical Jesus: The Place of Jesus in Preaching and Theology*, Fortress Press, 1981.

14. Again, cf. Wiles' essay, note 8, above.

15. cf. the works of H. Mühlen cited in note 2 above; also Kilian McDonnell, 'The Determinative Doctrine of the Holy Spirit', *Theology Today*, 1982, pp. 142–61.

16. R. Brunner notes that Scripture has no doctrine of God of humanity *in se* (*Gott-an sich, Menschen-an-sich*) but only of God as approaching us and of us as coming from God (*Gott-zum-Menschen-hin, Menschen-von-Gott-her*). In *Divine–Human Encounter*, London, 1944, pp. 46ff.

17. McLelland notes that we need to recover the intent of the Patristic doctrine of God: 'Immanence asserts God's trustworthiness, impassibility his moral transcendence, anonymity his eminence beyond our linguistic and conceptual categories' (op. cit., p. 160).

18. Certainly T. J. Altizer's theology is shoulders above the rest; cf. *The Self-Embodiment of God*, New York, 1977, and *Total Presence: The Language of Jesus and the Language of Today*, New York, 1980. See also L. Dewart, *The Future of Belief*, New York, 1966 and *The Foundations of Belief*, New York, 1969.

19. Torrance, op. cit., p. 341.

20. We must remember that all philosophical terms (accident, form, substance, *et al.*) are themselves metaphors. See Black, *Models and Metaphors*, pp. 40ff.
21. I. Ramsey suggests that Arius' inability to see the figurative-imaginative dimensions of the metaphor of begetting accounts for his rejection of it (*Religious Language*, pp. 158ff).
22. Derived from the discussion in J. Leclercq, *The Love of Learning and the Desire For God*, Fordham University Press, 1961, pp. 233ff.
23. In contemporary science 'objectivity' is often understood to be present in proportion to one's distancing from the 'object' being studied. But if in theology the 'object' (who is really also a 'subject') is God-in-relation, such distanciation would involve a logical contradiction. If God can be known only in-relation, one could not prescind from this relation without invalidating one's method.
24. J. Leclercq contrasts contemplative and speculative theologies in this way: 'Monastic theology is a theology of admiration and therefore greater than a theology of speculation. Admiration, speculation: both words describe the act of looking. But the gaze of admiration adds something to the gaze of speculation. It does not necessarily see any further, but the little it does perceive is enough to fill the whole world of the contemplative with joy and thanksgiving' (op. cit., p. 283).
25. There is support for this distinction in the study by J. Gibbons, 'Concept and Verbum: Reproductive Metaphors and the Inner Life in the Twelfth Century', Unpublished paper, presented to the 1983 Medieval Conference at Kalamazoo, Michigan. She contrasts the monastic-devotional and scholastic-technical approaches to God. In general, the monastic use of the conception metaphor refers to conception in the heart, which is maternal. The monastic attitude stresses the change in one's life brought about by conceiving God's word in the heart. The schools, on the other hand, saw conception as an intra-mental process, the mind being in this case the image of God.

# 13

∿∿∿∿∿∿∿∿∿∿∿∿∿∿∿∿∿∿∿∿∿∿∿∿∿∿∿∿∿∿

# SOCIAL MODELS OF THE TRINITY
## James Mackey

The most prominent feature of contemporary Trinitarian theology has been the re-emergence of so-called social models of the Trinity, due mainly to the work of Jürgen Moltmann. These have been subject to persistent suspicion, sometimes expressed quite mildly as the suspicion that they do not sufficiently protect the unity of the divine Being, sometimes as brashly and openly as in charges of tritheism. But they continue to recommend themselves, and to be defended, on the grounds of their alleged influence for creative improvement upon the structures of society in churches and states: they nourish more humane social relationships, it is said, than the more metaphysical doctrines of the Trinity in which, traditionally, the threeness was abstruse in formulation and, hence, quite submerged in more dominant impressions of a monotheistic, monarchical unity of the divine Being.

When I first read Moltmann's *The Trinity and the Kingdom of God* I was impressed by his critique of the abstruseness and consequent practical irrelevance of traditional Trinitarian theologies, and I felt that, in the absence of anything else, his social model might do some of the good he expected it to do. I have since become convinced that the introduction of the social model has resulted in a very great deal of damage indeed, done not only to Trinitarian theology, but to the whole task of seeking a relevant Christian theology; and that the Trinitarian theology of Augustine, for instance, did at least have the advantage of running out of meaning just at the point where we ought to be apophatic, that is to say, in attempting to describe the immanent structures of the divine Being. For it is not the need for a social model as such that does the damage – the relationships between God, Jesus and those who make up the body of the Church in the world provide a model as social as the most ardent socialist could desire; and the damage that is done is not exhaustively invoked by those who press the charge of tritheism – for, unless it happens to be false, as Christian monotheists think it is, there is probably nothing intrinsically unacceptable about belief in a happy, productive and harmonious Trinity of divine persons in the heavens. What is wrong, and can be very wrong in practical implications as well as in itself, is the projection of current ideas of human relationships into the divine Being, resulting in an 'immanent' Trinity which then, of course, becomes normative (and not merely inspiring) for the reconstruction of human relationships in civic and ecclesiastical societies. This process turns our present perception of 'good relationships' into absolutes, and that is not a good thing even for our present perception of the good 'Christian' relationships, that is, those we believe that Jesus as risen Lord still tries to foster in our midst, for of such processes ideologies are made.

But do the more recent Trinitarian theologians construct an immanent Trinity in addition to the Trinitarian structure of this divine 'economy'? Have they not rather moved beyond the addition of extra referents? Do they not all now accept with enthusiasm Rahner's axiom: 'the immanent Trinity *is* the economic Trinity, and the economic Trinity *is* the immanent Trinity'?[1] I can only say that they all leave me in considerable doubt about this, and some more than others. For Rahner, the economic, free self-communication of the divine reality to Jesus, and the 'immanent' self-communication of the divine reality, are still two things, even if the dual process is described as 'two things at once'.[2] In Kasper much the same impression is given of the procession of the Spirit. He explicitly evokes the 'transcendental-condition-of-the-possibility-of' clause, the very hallmark, whether in this or in comparable phrasing, of the Platonic dualism within which most Trinitarian theology still appears to be trapped. 'On the one hand, then', says Kasper, 'the immanent love of God reaches its goal in the Spirit. But at the same time . . . the love of God in the Spirit also moves beyond God himself,' and that constitutes the activity of God the Spirit in the world.[3] One begins to notice how often words like 'often', 'both', and 'too' occur even where Rahner's axiom rules.

Even Jüngel, who follows Moltmann in seeing the death of Jesus as the central 'economic' event in which the Trinity is revealed, cannot, for all his insistence in seeing only one event in God's 'coming to himself' and 'coming to us', avoid all impressions of duality. 'This death', he writes, 'is the seal of that event in which God comes both to God and to man.'[4] And what of Moltmann himself on this matter? His is the intriguing suggestion that 'the economic Trinity completes and perfects itself to immanent Trinity when the history and experience of salvation are completed and perfected.'[5] This, if he meant it fully, could give acceptable substance to one reading of Jüngel, to the effect that the events of the economy implement, effect, and finally confirm the relationality of the triune divine life; but, of course, in view of the empirical fact that we are still on the way to full stature of children of God, that God as Spirit has not yet brought everything 'in God' so that 'God is all in all', it follows that there is not just now available to us any 'immanent' Trinity on which we could model our changing relationships, in fact there will be no immanent ('remaining in') Trinity properly speaking until all has returned 'in' to God, and God also, after a real history, will finally be all 'in' all of a real body, that of Jesus, and that of his extended 'Body of Christ' in the world, and that of the extended body of those who make up the Body of Christ, the physical world. Meanwhile, the only Trinity that is, and so the only Trinity that can be known, is that of the dynamic (the economy) in which the God that Jesus prayed to as Father, came into Jesus ('I am in the Father, and the Father is in me'; 'God was in Christ reconciling the world to himself'), and is still active in the world as the risen Lord Jesus, the life-giving Spirit (as Paul calls him in 1 Cor. 15.45 – just the phrase used to describe the 'divinity' of the Holy Spirit in the Creed: the Lord and giver of life).

But is Moltmann happy to have his position described as such a move from a protological to an eschatological account of immanent Trinity? He must, of course, answer for himself. I can only say that when questioned on this point at the conference, he wished to make a distinction between doxological formulations and more general theological ones, and this leaves me with the impression that all of these contemporary theologians would have us operate with some presently available distinction between an immanent and an economic Trinity; and while we do so, the serious faults incurred by the new social models will continue to damage both our theology and our practical prospects. What are these faults?

First there has been a great deal of bowdlerizing of both scriptural and Patristic materials, neither of which can ever be made to yield three immanent divine persons in even the minimal sense required for a social model. It would take far too long to illustrate this in detail, but one example of a common mistreatment of Patristic material is worth giving. The social modelists appear to assume that if monarchy or undifferentiated monotheism predominates over a society of real persons in our imagery of the divine, imperial, if not indeed sexist types of authoritarianism, and consequent oppression of people, are bound to occur in human societies under such ideological influence. But this ignores both the more intelligent analyses of power (which can see it abused as much by majorities in a democracy, as the Irish should know, as by sovereign monarchies or oligarchies) and more seriously, the liberating effects of Christians simply opposing to the lordship of Caesar, the sovereign lordship of the servant Jesus (after all, Tertullian's much maligned 'monarchy' principle was exercized in his view through, and only through, the 'economy' of Jesus and the Spirit of Jesus).

Second, charges of tritheism are never quite dropped, nor would it appear, can they be. It does not really matter how improved are the ideas of personhood with which we feel we can now operate as compared to less wise predecessors, or how superior these are thought to be in their understanding of the essentially relational nature of the process of becoming and of being a person. The fact of the matter remains that persons on these newer models can still be counted, and when these models are applied to immanent divine persons, there will be three of them in a way so similar to the sense in which there are three (or more) of us, that no subsequent enthusiasm for the relational unity of the three and no amount of emphasis on the uniqueness of a process which secures simultaneously unity and distinction in the coming to be of persons in community, can ever suffice to obviate a charge of tritheism. That much at least the Fathers knew, and never forgot.

Additional moves made in recent Trinitarian theology to divert the charge of tritheism are really futile. For example, Colin Gunton seems to think he will avoid that charge if he rejects the idea that the three persons have three wills, and talks instead of such interanimation of Father, Son and Spirit, that what is done is done by all three.[6] In fact, as McDade unwittingly perhaps illustrates, such detailed stories are now being told about the interactive roles played by the Son and the Spirit in the immanent process of the former's 'generation' and the latter's 'spiration' (partly to reconcile East and West on the *'filioque'* problem), that social modelists could well find cover in quite generally conveyed impressions of three immanent agents up there, each with their own well differentiated jobs to do, albeit all converging on the process of inter-relational person-forming. Perhaps what is happening now is that the social modelists are simply expressing the closet tritheism of so much of our uncritical impressions of the Christian Trinity, due in turn to our forgetfulness of what Rowan Williams called the rigorous and austere logic of the classical Patristic writers. In any case, it borders on the amusing to find David Brown upbraiding Gunton for his harshness towards Augustine when Brown himself offers us the picture of three divine persons as three consciousnesses, each having such a unique and different 'personal history' that we can actually envisage the other two persons being 'in full charge, as it were, of the running of the universe' during the (brief?) period when the Son of God was dead.[7]

At this point, of course, the enterprise of seeking a 'Trinity as a community of persons in relation' as a clue to 'a proper non-hierarchical understanding of society and the Church and to our own and the divine relation to creation', has resulted in such unadulterated nonsense as to bring the whole of Christian theology into disrepute. On the one hand,

Moltmann can hardly be blamed for these excesses of the social model; on the other, once one leaves open a possible distinction between immanent and economic Trinity, and with that the possibility of applying the things said of Jesus in the Scriptures to a 'second referent', an eternal Son of God who was a fully constituted person, as we know persons to be constituted, 'before' Jesus was conceived, then, at what point can you call a halt to a process which clearly can arrive at the plain nonsense which Brown had at the very least the courage to publish?

But I should like in conclusion to return to the ideological dangers of this social model of the Trinity; for whereas the alleged tritheisms may result in the end in no more than a relatively harmless piece of nonsense which only those who are payed to do so may be expected to read, the projection on to an immanent divine society of structures of social relationships destined thereafter for re-entry into our human task of building a better world can carry by this very detour an absolute normativeness and a foreclosure on other options, which are the hallmarks of ideology everywhere. I am intrigued, and better informed, when one of my students uses Levinas's *Otherwise than Being or Beyond Essence* in order to arrive at a truer understanding of the mutual vulnerability involved in the very coming-to-be of persons-in-relation; I can anticipate being even better informed when the call of one member of the conference, Mary Condren, is answered, for a finer, psychoanalytic analysis of personhood; and I can simply discount the damage then done by trying to project these on to immanent divine persons; for I know that all these finer insights derived from watching real human persons. I will have all I need before that projection takes place, and I can use it in my own thinking about persons in relation. But when some concrete 'non-hierarchical understanding of society' is finally produced, and I remember Marx's statement that such religious visions are man's recognition of himself by a detour ('*die Anerkennung des Menschens auf einem Umweg*'), what will then protect me from the absolute claims which this vision will have picked up on its detour? Who will then allow me even a suspicion of its truth and finality, any more than the present hierarchs want to allow me?

Finally, then, if no substantial trace of an 'immanent' Trinity in any way distinct from an 'economic' Trinity is currently available to us, just what kind of Trinitarian theology can we now have? Of what referents can it now be composed?

The first referent is the God to whom Jesus prayed, calling him 'Father'; the second referent is Jesus of Nazareth, 'in' whom was this same God who was also in the world before Jesus, but who is now so much 'in' Jesus (and Jesus in God) as to enable us to say that in and through this human person of Jesus, God experiences a human destiny in the very process of shaping human destiny (saving, revealing);[8] the third referent – if it can really be called third, for at this point one realizes that arithmetic has nothing to do with the matter – is now the same Jesus-Immanuel, but now as risen Lord/ life-giving Spirit of his 'body' in this world: this Jesus who was also in the world before this body, as the God active in and through him, was in the world before him.

We could use the same term for all three referents. God is Spirit; the risen Jesus is life-giving Spirit; the Body of Christ is the life-giving Spirit still incarnate in the world, but now as community rather than individual, but still being brought by the indwelling Spirit, now in the 'character' of Jesus, to the fulness of grace and truth. Such use of terminology would give us a Spirit-Trinity, much as one finds in Paul if one reads, say, 1 Cor. 12— 15, paying particular attention to 12.4–6 (the parallelism), 12.12–13 where 'members' are made into one body by being, as natural bodies are, animated by one Spirit, which, or who is identified in 15.45 as the 'second Adam', the risen Lord, Jesus. The word 'person' is not really apt as a name for naming all three referents simultaneously, for answering the question: three what? We believe the Father of our Lord Jesus Christ is a divine person, and Jesus is certainly a human person, but it would stretch the word person beyond all recognizable content to go on to talk of three persons. As it always did, of course. Read Book 7 of Augustine's magisterial work on *The Trinity*, and watch the word person lose *all* that would enable it to describe a human person. So, in answer to the question: three what? First refuse the rule of arithmetic, for a triadic rather than a 'biadic' structure is suggested by the *history* of salvation, the economy itself in which God was before Jesus and Jesus before his 'body' in the world, rather than by any possible discovery of three divine persons in any way similar to a community of three (or more) human persons. Then, if absolutely necessary, take refuge in some such phrase as 'three modes of being' or 'modes of origin' (*tropoi hyparxeos*) of God, whose being is in becoming, and who becomes what God freely wills to be, the God who is all in all, in this very process known as the 'economy' (of salvation).

The term 'Spirit', of course, is not usually, and has not traditionally been used for all 'three', nor is there any reason why it should lay exclusive claim to that function, though it could well fulfil it. First, words such as 'Word' and the feminine 'Sophia' (Wisdom) are fully fledged alternatives, fully authorized in the common religious tradition of Jews and Greeks. It was, then, something of an accident of history that 'Word' was chosen as the cipher for the indwelling in Jesus by the first apologists, who recognized in it the obvious bridge-term for coming to grips with the dominant religious claims of the educated Graeco-Roman world. Second, since each 'mode of being' reveals the same divine being (here is the need for the *homoousios*) as each other 'mode', and yet is not altogether identical with any other mode, a variety of terms is indicated as an alternative to a repetition of one term – so 'word' and 'spirit'.[9]

In the Patristic era when Christian theologians borrowed all of the metaphysics for their Christologies, and ready-made 'binities' and 'trinities' from predominantly Platonic religious philosophers,[10] they naturally shared a dualist worldview, and the ideal/empirical divisions of that era, and were thus prone to duplicate referents in just those ways which give us immanent in addition to economic Trinities. The best theologians of East and West, however, managed to find formulae to defeat the Arians (who in respect of Platonic dualism, were as prone to immanent divine speculation as themselves), without incurring the charge of tritheism. They did this with great difficulty – for the schemata borrowed from Porphyry and company were never designed for use of a person like Jesus – and in the end their relational formulae for immanent 'threes' were so abstruse as to convey no conceivable information about the inner divine reality. So, if only by default, their successors were driven back to the story of Jesus and the history of his 'body' in the world, in order to find content for a divine revelation that would inspire and gradually improve; and Trinitarian doctrine was left to slumber, seldom disturbed, in theology's back bedroom. That was not all a bad thing, one now recognizes, especially when faced with modern efforts to renew the doctrine by trying to give it concrete relevance without exorcizing the old dualism of ideal and empirical, immanent and economic. There are good reasons, then, to prefer Augustine's austere grammar of orthodoxy, utterly uninformative as it turns out to be on God's inner being, to any of the social models more recently produced.

Unless, of course, Rahner's axiom is finally taken in its fully radical sense: in the sense that we have only our economic Trinity, in the midst of which we now are, or half are. Then we are left to glean our vision for a better communal future in our extended body, this physical universe, from the concrete lessons that Jesus taught in his ways of relating to others and to things, in all of his life, death, and destiny. And that in turn is available to us, of course, only in the ongoing history of those scattered communities of his followers (and even outside of their formal boundaries), some of the earliest shapes of which are chrystallized in the Scriptures.

Furthermore, since this 'body' is still being built up to the point of God being all in all, to the stature of a fully immanent Trinity of God, Jesus and human community; and since it is quite blatantly nowhere near that happy consummation as yet, there is plenty of room for us to heed the warning to us to pay more attention to *ta erkomena*, the things that are (yet) to come, as a result of Jesus' 'other paraclete' in the world; and there is no room at all for the crypto-ideologies that must always lurk in those social Trinities which have not quite abjured all knowledge of the inner being of God. Sustained fidelity to the rule of metaphor (the 'second' metaphor being: the followers of Jesus are the body of the divine Christ) must be one of the ways of achieving this happy result; though it is not, of course, the only way.

NOTES

1. K. Rahner, *The Trinity*, London: Burns and Oates, 1970, p. 22.
2. op. cit., p. 64.
3. W. Kasper, *The God of Jesus Christ*, London: SCM Press, 1984, p. 226.
4. E. Jüngel, *God as the Mystery of the World*, Edinburgh: T & T Clark, 1983, p. 383.
5. J. Moltmann, *The Trinity and the Kingdom of God*, London: SCM Press, 1981, p. 161.
6. C. Gunton, *The Promise of Trinitarian Theology*, Edinburgh: T. & T Clark, 1991.
7. David Brown, *The Divine Trinity*, London: Duckworth, 1985, p. 251. See his review of Gunton's book in *Theology* March/April 1992.
8. In short, God becomes human, incarnate; provided incarnation is not thought to refer merely to some moment of conception – becoming human takes a little longer than that – but refers to all of life and death and, if there is such, beyond death.
9. To avoid repeating myself I beg to draw attention to an extensive account of the manner in which such symbolic terms of their nature allow the expression of distinction-in-identity, in *The Christian Experience of God as Trinity*, London: SCM Press, 1983, pp. 68ff.
10. See John Dillon, 'Logos and Trinity: Patterns of Platonist Influence on Early Christianity', in G. Vesey, ed., *The Philosophy in Christianity*, Cambridge, CUP, 1989.

# PART TWO

# Christ and Plurality

# D: CHRIST AND OTHER FAITHS

14   URSULA KING's 'Women in Dialogue: A New Vision of Ecumenism' was published in *The Heythrop Journal* in 1985 (Vol. XXVI, pp. 125–35 and 141). Her main books are *Towards a New Mysticism: Teilhard de Chardin and Eastern Religions* (London: Collins, 1980); *The Spirit of One Earth: Reflections on Teilhard de Chardin and Global Spirituality* (New York: Paragon House, 1989) and *Women and Spirituality: Voices of Protest and Promise* (Basingstoke: Macmillan, 1989, and Philadelphia: Pennsylvania State University Press, 1993).

15   COLIN GUNTON's 'Universal and Particular in Atonement Theology' was published in *Religious Studies* in 1992 (Vol. 28, pp. 453–66). Among his books are *Becoming and Being: The Doctrine of God in Charles Hartshorne and Karl Barth* (Oxford and New York: Oxford University Press, 1978); *Enlightenment and Alienation: An Essay Towards a Trinitarian Theology* (Grand Rapids, Michigan: Eerdmans, 1985); *The Actuality of Atonement: A Study of Metaphor, Rationality and the Christian Tradition* (Grand Rapids, Michigan: Eerdmans, 1989); *The Promise of Trinitarian Theology* (Edinburgh: T & T Clark, 1991); *Christ and Creation* (Carlisle: Paternoster Press, and Grand Rapids, Michigan: Eerdmans, 1992); and *The One, the Three, and the Many: God, Creation, and the Culture of Modernity* (Cambridge and New York: Cambridge University Press, 1993).

16   KEITH WARD's 'Truth and the Diversity of Religions' was published in *Religious Studies* in 1990 (Vol. 26, pp. 1–3 and 12–18). Amongst his many books are *Ethics and Christianity* (London: Allen & Unwin, 1970); *The Development of Kant's View of Ethics* (Oxford: Blackwell, 1972); *The Concept of God* (Oxford: Blackwell, 1974); *The Divine Image: The Foundations of Christian Morality* (London: SPCK, 1976); *Rational Theology and the Creativity of God* (Oxford: Blackwell, 1982); *Images of Eternity* (London: Darton, Longman and Todd, 1987); and *A Vision to Pursue* (London: SCM Press, 1991).

17   GAVIN D'COSTA's 'One Covenant or Many Covenants? Toward a Theology of Christian–Jewish Relations' was published in *Journal of Ecumenical Studies* in Summer 1990 (Vol. 27, No. 3, pp. 441–52). His book is *Theology and Religious Pluralism: The Challenge of Other Religions* (Oxford and New York: Blackwell, 1986) and he has edited *Christian Uniqueness Reconsidered: The Myth of Pluralistic Theology of Religions* (Maryknoll, New York: Orbis, 1990).

# 14

# WOMEN IN DIALOGUE:
# A NEW VISION OF ECUMENISM
## *Ursula King*

Our age is an age of ecumenism. Numerous movements around the world are working for the closer coming together of people, whether in the religious or secular sphere. These attempts to bring about greater unification are in stark contrast to the equally growing particularistic and divisive tendencies we find everywhere around the globe. How can we achieve greater unity and universality and yet maintain our individual and collective particularities? This is a central question in ecumenism.

'Ecumenical' in general means worldwide, universal or catholic in the sense of inclusive and comprehensive. In a narrow, more specific sense ecumenism has been associated with the movement for unity in the Christian churches. On 21 November 1964, the Second Vatican Council promulgated the 'Decree on Ecumenism'. The Decree describes the ecumenical movement as 'those activities and enterprises which, according to various needs of the Church and opportune occasions, are started and organized for the fostering of unity among Christians'.[1] A similar definition is given in the *Oxford Dictionary of the Christian Church* which speaks of the ecumenical movement as 'The movement in the Church towards the recovery of the unity of all believers in Christ, transcending differences of creed, ritual and polity. The aspiration for unity can be traced from New Testament times and has found various expressions at different periods, but it has never been so potent as in the present century'.[2] This description raises the question of how far Christian origins, as recorded in the New Testament, implied already a situation of pluralism and diversity which subsequent interpreters misunderstood as a monolithic uniformity.

The word 'ecumenism' also refers beyond the movement for Christian unity to a wider, global ecumenism which relates to the coming together of people from different faiths in a new spirit of openness and trust. It thus points to the important role of interfaith dialogue within the religious life of the world today, not least the Christian churches who are closely involved in this wider ecumenism. Let us keep both the specifically inter-

135

Christian and the wider interfaith understanding of ecumenism in mind and reflect upon our cumulative ecumenical experiences in the Christian churches in general and in the Roman Catholic Church in particular.

Many see in the movements towards greater Christian and interfaith unity the Divine Spirit at work trying to heal our divisions by creating a new sense of coming together in community. From a situation of ignorance, exclusion and condemnation of each other we have come to one of mutual acceptance and cross-fertilization. This is only possible in a pluralistic situation where we recognize our differences yet seek a convergence of frontiers, a unity and universality beyond the particularities of our individual religious groups. To reach this insight requires a continuous process of growth, made possible through the practice of both intrareligious dialogue – dialogue among ourselves and within our particular religious group – and the practice of interreligious dialogue which crosses over and transcends the traditionally established boundaries of religious institutions.

Over recent years the vision of ecumenism has grown in clarity, strength and inspiration. It has reached ever wider circles of people; it is fed by the springs of faith and the deep desire to come together in what unites rather than what divides us – whether in action, thought, or worship. The ecumenical movement represents perhaps the liveliest and most dynamic outreach of institutionalized religion today. Ecumenical and interfaith dialogue provide much substance for contemporary theological thought; they are of vital importance for the future of religion. And yet one can ask whether this attractive vision of ecumenism does not remain too narrow, too organizationally rigid and exclusive, too little based on the grass roots experience of the trials of faith lived by ordinary women and men? To gain greater wholeness, to develop more inner strength and outer integration, it may help to pursue a somewhat different perspective and reflect on ecumenism from the vantage point of experiences which seem to have been overlooked or deliberately excluded, namely those of women.

It is certainly legitimate to say that the contemporary women's movement is also a global ecumenical movement which brings together women from all races, nations, and religions. This more recent movement has created an equally inspiring vision of quite a different world and quite a different Church. If we look at ecumenical and interfaith dialogue from the perspective of the lively dialogue among women today, what can we see and learn?

136

## *Where are the women in ecumenism?*

The question 'Where are the women?' has been asked many times before, but it is still the crucial question. On 12 January 1984, *The Times* showed a photo of the 'Historic meeting on church unity' at New Hall which brought together Roman Catholic bishops and leaders of the Anglican and Free Churches. As Janet Morley commented recently: 'The photo made one very striking visual point; for whatever problems the churches face on the way to unity, we seem effortlessly to have reached consensus on what "authority" looks like in the Church. Every single leader in the picture was white, middle-aged, and male.'[3]

Is this photo of the all-male ecumenical leaders in this country a symbolic expression of the powerful limitations of ecumenism in practice? How truly universal and inclusive can such an ecumenism be?

The question 'where are the women in ecumenism?' soon leads to the more basic question 'where are the women in the churches?' Many contemporary studies highlight the marginality and invisibility of women in our religious institutions and structures. There may be plenty of tea ladies and plenty of women saints and mystics – but there are few, if any, women in the visible positions of authority in the Church. Women always seem to take second place; they are kept in a state of subordination and dependence. Enforced by what has been called the Christian 'ideology of obedience' (Dorothee Soelle), women's role has always been defined by others, by men, not by women themselves. In the teaching and practice of the Church it has largely been restricted to the role of wife and mother, or to that of the dependent woman religious. When I was asked to speak about 'the *role* of women in ecumenical and interfaith dialogue', I accepted the subject but consciously rejected its formulation.

We are no longer at a stage where women's role can be defined in a situation of heteronomy, where women obediently accept what may or may not be granted to them. Women today experience themselves as fully autonomous, self-reflecting human beings who wish to define their contribution themselves, whether in ecumenical dialogue or elsewhere. This may be difficult to understand for people in a traditional position of authority with power entirely on the side of their sex, and dependence on the side of women. The idea of mutuality and partnership, whether at the personal level in family and marriage, in society at large or in the churches, is something quite new. We have yet to create a society in which women live on equal terms with men with regard to the distribution of power and responsibilities. Yet this ideal of a community of equality provides a powerful possibility to put into practice the Christian teaching on the community of the people of God.

The call to Christian discipleship is the same for women and men. Women, like men, are equally created in the image of God; they are called to the same freedom of the spirit and share the same sacraments of baptism and Eucharist as foundational experiences of the Christian life. From the times of Jesus women have come forward in great numbers to give their life to the way of Christ and to the diverse ministries of Christian service.

Much questioning occurs today as to what these Christian ministries are and how they can best be practised in our society. Contemporary society and consciousness are undergoing profound changes which also include a critical reflection on the meaning of sexual differentiation. Much of the traditional understanding of women's and men's roles, as culturally and religiously defined and limited, is now perturbingly called into question. This requires a new, more probing exploration of what it means to be human as women and men, to be embedded in and nourished by personal relationships, all of which require mutual ministry and service.

There are many reasons for the profound changes in our society. One important aspect is represented by the modern women's movement which has dramatically transformed the self-understanding of many women worldwide, including women in the Roman Catholic Church. This was perceptively documented by the global *Pro Mundi Vita* Report on 'The Situation of Women in the Catholic Church' produced in 1980.[4] From the perspective of contemporary women, many earlier ecumenical ventures can be found wanting, from the many activities of the World Council of Churches to the Vatican Council and the numerous ecumenical meetings since then. Women, if they have been there at all, have usually been at the margin, just as the few women observers at the Vatican Council were. On many occasions the officially recorded dialogue has been between the different representatives of the hierarchical and priestly structures of the churches who are exclusively male. But contrary to the official picture of ecumenism, women have been far more active in ecumenical meetings at parish and local level than what has been visible in public. The public lack of recognition of women's work and women's participation in the churches is truly scandalous.

For example, if one looks at the language of the Vatican 'Decree on Ecumenism', one cannot but be hurt as a woman, as one is by so many other official church pronouncements. The decree speaks only of the Church and 'her sons', but not of the daughters; it also refers exclusively to the 'separated brethen' but not to the separated sisters. Only ten years after the 'Decree on Ecumenism', Cardinal Heenan judged that the language of the decree 'may already appear cold and grudging'[5] because the ecumenical outlook had developed with such speed since the Council. He did not recognize that the consciousness of women had developed and changed equally speedily.

The 'Decree on Ecumenism' did not include women in its address. But that was in 1964. Somewhat more surprising is the fact that the recently published *World Christian Encyclopedia*,[6] a comprehensive and splendid reference work, is virtually silent about Christian women in the world. Is this due to the fact that all the detailed statistics about organized, empirically visible Christianity are collected by male church officials?

We learn from this first global investigation of Christianity that during the 1980s Christians of all kind numbered 1,432,686,500 people, representing 32.8 per cent of the global population. During the twentieth century Christianity has become present in every one of the 223 inhabited countries of the earth and 'the church is therefore now, for the first time in history, ecumenical in the literal meaning of the word: its boundaries are coextensive with the oikumene, the whole inhabited world'.[7] The surprising outcome of this world-statistical survey is the fact that although Christianity is divided into seven major blocs, if every separate Christian group is counted, world Christianity includes as many as 20,800 different denominations – a plurality which not even the investigators suspected. This information should make us aware of the need to take into account the extraordinary diversity and complexity within Christianity itself. There is not only the pluralism of religions in the world today but there exists an amazing pluralism within Christianity itself.

The *World Christian Encyclopedia* pays much attention to this diversity, especially in Asia, Africa, and Latin America, the churches of the Third World where the majority of Christians will soon live. Christians in the Encyclopedia are counted according to different races; they are distinguished into clergy and laity, adults and children, but not into women and men! One section gives some general description of 'women lay workers', 'women religious' and 'women ordained' but no detailed statistics. However, it contains the informative comment that there are 'over 200 organizations of major significance' in the world 'for women in the ordained ministry, diaconate or priesthood'.[8] It so happens that this is exactly the same number as that of significant ecumenical commissions and agencies.

The same invisibility of women is documented by this year's *Catholic Directory* in Britain. It lists the exact number of members of each male religious order and congregation whereas female orders and congregations are simply listed by name. This list is more than twice as long as that of the

139

men but numbers are not important. Statistics are given for the number of priests of each diocese, the number of male religious, of permanent deacons and candidates for the priesthood but the women religious of each diocese disappear as individuals behind their institutions which are simply listed as 'Convents of Religious Women'. And yet we know that there are about three times as many women religious as there are priests and men religious together in the Roman Catholic Church worldwide. We also know that a higher proportion of women than men are practising Christians.

These few examples, which could easily be multiplied, highlight the largely unacknowledged and little officially visible participation of women in the churches – their insignificance, not because of a lack of numbers or a lack of dedication, but because of a lack of authority and recognition which has been withheld from them by men.

The issue of women's full participation in all Christian activities and ministries, including the ordained priesthood, is of central importance in ecumenical dialogue. In some churches women already take a much larger share of activities and the ordination of women has been practised by some groups for considerable time now. It is perhaps true to say that the larger the churches are, the more conservative they tend to be. It comes as a shock to discover that the first woman minister was ordained by American Congregationalists as long ago as 1853! Forty years later, at the well-known World Parliament of Religions in 1893 which marks the first ecumenical gathering of world faiths, she was one of the very few women speakers who took up the cause of Christian women in her lecture on 'Women and the Pulpit'. To think that one hundred years later we are still struggling with the same issue!

No doubt many people, not least the members of the Movement for the Ordination of Women who worked so hard for years, were overjoyed by the majority vote of the General Synod in favour of the ordination of women. At the same time one cannot but be depressed by the great many complications and the years needed to have this decision implemented. Is this not over-cautious, half-hearted as well as demoralizing for women? Even more discouraging is the statement by one Roman Catholic bishop that the decision of the Church of England in favour of the ordination of women is an 'obstacle' to unity between the two churches.[9]

Why should the genuine vocations of women be considered as 'obstacles' in the life of the churches? If the ordination of women is seen as a controversial issue in ecumenical dialogue, it might be pointed out (if indeed it is necessary to point out) that this dialogue takes place only between men: for all intents and purposes, women are excluded. Are women merely pawns in the ecumenical negotiations for church reunion?

As if the unity of the churches and the understanding and practice of Christianity did not concern women as much as men. Where is the truly inclusive ecumenism here which concerns not only all churches but also both sexes?

Perhaps no man can share the feeling of hurt and humiliation, the sense of repudiation and refusal which women experience when they are excluded from full Christian responsibility and treated as if they were children, not adults. Is this Christian love, charity, and understanding? Can there be full Christian fellowship if one sex is dominant and the other dependent?

The situation in interreligious dialogue is not much more encouraging than the developments in Christian ecumenism. Women are very active in local interfaith meetings and do much to cross over traditional barriers. The British Council of Churches has set up a new 'Women in Interfaith Dialogue' group and the committee for interreligious dialogue created by the Roman Catholic hierarchy has some women members. But in my experience of dialogue in England and India women are never the official representatives or 'spokes-women' for dialogue because they are not the bearers of official religious authority and it is often, though not always, the authorities which take the initiative in dialogue. With the exception of a few women religious and women theologians the people who speak and write on ecumenical and interfaith dialogue are mostly male. The structures, authorities, and hierarchies in the world religions have been and are dominantly male, and this is precisely what women today are no longer willing to accept. This is why women have created their own dialogue, their own groups and, one might almost say, their own *oikumene*.

## Women's oikumene: *what is women's dialogue about?*

We hear a great deal about the Third World and its suffering, about the need for development, justice, and peace and for a more equitable distribution of the world's resources. Perhaps few are aware that there exists also a 'Fourth World' of deprivation, injustice, subordination, and suffering – and that is the world of women who experience themselves as the alienated 'other' in Church and society.[10]

In many parts of the world Christian reflection has created a vigorous liberation theology born out of the experience of the suffering and struggle of the poor and oppressed. Some consider liberation theology as a new point of ecumenical convergence for different traditions, experiences, and struggles. In trying to overcome their oppression, women have created another liberation movement. This is not only concerned with their own liberation but that of all people by affirming the full humanity of all women.[11] Christian women see this as a genuine possibility to express an authentic Christian universalism. It is significant that a recent theological consultation organized by women was entitled 'Called to Full Humanity: Women's Responsibilities as Members of the Church Today'.

The roots of the women's liberation movement go deep into history – a history of struggle for equality, justice, and human rights. In the nineteenth century the women's movement was closely interwoven with the fight to abolish slavery whilst the new feminism born in the sixties grew out of the campaign for equal rights and against racism. If we adopt an inclusive definition of feminism, then every person who recognizes the subordination of women and aims to overcome it, is a feminist, whether woman or man. Feminism is not a unitary, but diverse movement, not without its internal contradictions and tensions. Yet over the last twenty years women have spoken out with ever increasing strength and entered into a new dialogue. They have discovered themselves and each other; they have learnt to perceive and criticize the deep injustices done to them; they have also developed an amazing ability to envisage alternatives.

Through sharing their experiences women have discovered consciousness-raising as an adventure and systematic method. By working together in small, non-hierarchical groups women have deliberately fostered a change in awareness. This has sometimes led to a radical conversion experience of such intensity, that it can only be likened to the profound *metanoia* of a religious experience. It may be difficult for men – and some women – to realize what it means when women experience their own strength and power by learning to speak out, to name and define themselves and make independent decisions in a newly found freedom.

This ecstatic self-discovery has also led to a new celebration of community, of the bonding among women. Sisterhood, vividly described in poems, songs, and other artforms, is the term used to express the solidarity of all women – their relatedness in suffering, in giving birth and life, in nurturing and caring, in joy and ecstasy. Sisterhood is an experience and powerful symbol among women today against which many of the vague references to the general 'brotherhood of man' pale into insignificance. Sisterhood can of course be used in an exclusive all-female sense but it has the potential of widening out into larger circles of community. It implies the vision of a new, more equal and just community of partnership between women and men, a newly found wholeness. As Sheila Collins has written:

The wholeness that feminists are proposing is a wholeness based on a multidimensional vision of the world, rather than on the single vision which has dominated Western culture and most theological thought. Such a multidimensional vision means the ability to grasp complexity, to live with ambiguity, and to enjoy the great variety that exists in the world. Wholeness does not imply the eradication of differences . . . or . . . the fear of a monotonous unisexual creature. . . . On the contrary, wholeness of vision may lead to a multiplication of differences, as people are able to choose freely the person they want to be rather than following a pattern of one they are *expected* to be. Only through an affirmation and celebration of our differences can we come to an understanding of the ties that bind the total creation together.[12]

This is not only a vision of a 'New Woman – New Earth' (as Rosemary Ruether entitled her book) but for Christians it includes the vision of a 'new woman – new Church'.

Several feminist theologians have pointed to the elements of prophecy and revelation in modern feminism, to its implicit religious dimension. Anyone who has close contact with women's groups will recognize this. Here a spirit is alive which is vibrant, joyous, loving, caring, and compassionate; a warmth of human feeling, a sincerity of purpose and existential commitment, a sharpness of vision rarely found elsewhere. Sometimes I think this experience must be like the joy of the early Christians, their love and fellowship, their sense of belonging together and sharing all things.

These positive, life-enhancing and community-strengthening aspects of feminism are probably less well known than the negative aspects of feminist anger, protest and critique, much publicized by biased reporting in the media. Feminism challenges the structures of sexism, androcentrism and patriarchy embedded in our institutions, our language, our thought. Its critique addresses all religions as presently practised; it is a critique which also applies to ecumenical and interfaith dialogue.

Sexism has been defined as a way of ordering life by gender, as 'any kind of subordination or devaluing of a person or group solely on the ground of sex'. In Christian terms sexism can be understood as a collective form of sin, a social oppression which exists in society and church. It is the particular merit of the World Council of Churches to have called as early as 1974 a consultation of 170 women from different countries and churches, including the Roman Catholic Church, to discuss 'Sexism in the 1970s'.[13] Pauline Webb introduced that consultation by saying that sexism is not just a matter of acknowledging the physical difference between men and women but rather

> recognizing that alongside this difference there have been different histories, different expectations, a different sense of identity, and an association with the structures of power that have created a male-dominated order in almost all human society and certainly within the Church, making it impossible for the Church to foreshadow the truly human community. So it is for the sake of that community that we Christian women come now to examine the heresy of sexism and to explore ways of overcoming it that will liberate both men and women for a new partnership in the gospel.[14]

Androcentrism takes male examples and practices as the basic norm for everything human without taking into account the view of women. In order to be fully human we have to be truly inclusive and bring together the insights of both men and women. Many men do not realize that their understanding of humanity is one-sided because it is only male-defined. Feminists uncover this androcentric perspective in all areas of our culture. For Christian feminists it is particularly important to read the androcentric passages of the Bible in a new light, to examine the language of liturgy and prayer, and to uncover the androcentrism of many theological premises.

The strongest feminist critique is addressed to patriarchy, the exclusively male-dominated structures and powers which have shaped all aspects of society. A growing number of Christians is becoming aware of this critique which is also exposing the patriarchal assumptions of much Christian teaching and the sexist practices of church life, language, and organization. However, the greatest challenge of all posed by the dialogue of contemporary feminists is the question: Can religion, can theology and the churches still speak convincingly to women today? Can women still find the divine spirit in the churches as we know them? The history of the Church, from New Testament times onwards, seems to be shot through by a pattern of the promise and betrayal of women. In spite of their significant contribution to the life and mission of the early Church women were soon excluded from official positions. But the history of Christianity is rich with examples of powerful 'Women of the Spirit'[15] who exercised spiritual leadership through the authority of their own experiences in searching for and discovering God.

Many voices today speak of the divine concealment in our world, the loss of transcendence. For women this is often connected with a distorted, blemished image of God and with the restrictive practices of a powerful male church. It has been asked whether the churches are in fact destructive of religious experiences for women. In answer to this one can point to the spiritual quality of and the spiritual quest within the women's movement which has drawn many women out of the churches, but one can also point out that women's conversion experiences in the past have often been away from the conformity of established religious practices in search of new ways and alternative models. The medieval Beguines are a good example of this.

Today there exists a new spirituality in feminism which is rooted in women's own experience. Some even speak of a 'spiritual feminism'. It consists of a new relationship to body and nature and of a search for wholeness, integration and peace. This new feminist spirituality is mostly found outside or on the margin of official religious institutions. But it is important for Christian feminists too, as they experience how the existing church structures deny full equality and space to women and thereby restrict and dehumanize, not only women, but men too.

Many women ask themselves: can I remain at home in the traditional Church and still be a contemporary woman? The awakening to feminist consciousness has led Christian women to form subcommunities in their churches where they are in dialogue with other Christian women and with the Church if the Church will but hear them. This is an ecumenical dialogue across denominational boundaries. Best known are perhaps the women's groups which have worked in close conjunction with the World Council of Churches, but there are other examples. Latin American women founded a group of 'Women for Dialogue' (Mujeres para el Diálogo) in 1977 at Puebla with the explicit aim 'to get the voice of women heard within the Church'.[16] They work for the liberation of Latin American women and strive to develop a feminist theology within the Latin American context. Many different Christian feminist groups exist in England. To name but a few, there is 'Christian Women's Information and Resources' at Oxford; the 'Catholic Women's Network'; 'Women in Theology' as well as the 'Movement for the Ordination of Women', focused on a particular issue. There is also 'The Society for the Ministry of Women in the Church' founded as long ago as 1929 and, in the Catholic Church, St Joan's International Alliance which dates from the beginning of this century.

Women of today have developed a newly sharpened awareness which challenges the sexist and patriarchal assumptions of religious and social institutions and proclaims the vision of an alternative community and world. For Christians it is important that the feminist movement is not seen at the fringes of the Church but as the central embodiment of the vision and incarnation of the Church as the people of God. Feminists have discovered a new sense of divine immanence and transcendence closely related to the experience of the wholeness of body-spirit, of the closeness to nature to which we all belong and of the bonds of community. In seeking new paths of spirituality women are drawing on old and new sources commensurate to their own renewed experience of self, world, and Divine. In this sense the dialogue and *oikumene* of women bears the potential for transforming spiritual and theological thinking, including the thinking on ecumenism.

NOTES

1. See 'Decree on Ecumenism', §4 in W. M. Abbott, ed., *The Documents of Vatican II*, New York: Herder and Herder, and Association Press, 1966, p. 347.
2. F. L. Cross and E. A. Livingstone, eds., *The Oxford Dictionary of the Christian Church*, Oxford: Oxford University Press, second edn, 1978, p. 443.
3. J. Morley, 'Reflective Report', *The Community of Women and Men in the Church*, Report of BCC Working Group 1982–4, p. 3.
4. *Pro Mundi Vita Bulletin*, 'The Situation of Women in the Catholic Church: Developments since International Women's Year', No. 83, Brussels, October 1980.
5. See J. C. Heenan, *A Crown of Thorns. An Autobiography 1951–1963*, London, 1974, p. 322.
6. D. B. Barrett, ed., *World Christian Encyclopedia. A Comparative Survey of Churches and Religions in the Modern World* AD *1900–2000*, Oxford, 1982.
7. ibid., p. 3, column 2.
8. See ibid., p. 967, 'Women in the Ordained Ministry' and p. 848, 'Women, ordained'; p. 825, 'ecumenical commission'.
9. 'Women priests "obstacle" to unity', *The Times*, 17 November 1984, p. 36.
10. This theme has been movingly explored by the Indonesian woman theologian Marianne Katoppo. See her book *Compassionate and Free. An Asian Woman's Theology*, Geneva: World Council of Churches, 1979.
11. The insights of liberation theology and feminist theology are brought together in L. M. Russell, *Human Liberation in a Feminist Perspective – A Theology*, Philadelphia, 1974.
12. S. D. Collins, 'The Personal is Political' in C. Spretnak, ed., *The Politics of Women's Spirituality*, New York, 1982, pp. 362–7. The quotation is from p. 366.
13. *Sexism in the 1970s. Discrimination Against Women. A Report of a World Council of Churches Consulation, West Berlin 1974*, Geneva: World Council of Churches, 1975.
14. ibid., p. 10.
15. See R. Ruether and E. McLaughlin, eds., *Women of Spirit, Female Leadership in Jewish and Christian Traditions*, New York, 1979.
16. *Pro Mundi Vita Bulletin* (see note 4), p. 27.

# 15

~~~~~~~~~~~~~~~~~~~~~~~~~~~~~~~~~~~~~~~~~~~~~~~~~~~~~~~~~

# UNIVERSAL AND PARTICULAR IN ATONEMENT THEOLOGY
*Colin Gunton*

## What are we talking about?

The unique philosophical problems of Christianity derive from the fact that it is not a philosophy, but a gospel. That is to say, its teaching and institutions are distinctively what they are by virtue of their relation to particular divine acts rather than because they are primarily a general teaching or philosophy. Whatever general teaching there is is rooted in particularities. It is not, then, difficult to come to a provisional understanding of the reference of the 'particular' in the title. Christianity as a particular religion, distinct from other religions and philosophies, is a distinctive way of appropriating what is believed to be salvation, deriving from a centre in a specific pattern of divine action. That centre, to be sure, gives rise to a range of conceptions of salvation sharing a family resemblance, but is none the less common to all those that are recognizably within the Christian fold.

The particularity of the conception of salvation derives from the particularity of its saviour, for all Christian theologies of atonement are in some way necessarily linked to Jesus of Nazareth: usually to his death in the first instance, but by no means solely so. The first great systematic theology of salvation, that of Irenaeus, located the work of salvation in the whole of the history of the incarnate: birth, life, death, resurrection and ascension; while Origen, because of an emphasis on salvation as a teaching, is the father of those who in modern times have centred the matter on the life rather than the death. Despite all the variety and complexity, however, there is no doubt about what in general we mean when we simply refer to – as distinct from articulate systematically – the particularity at the heart of Christian atonement theology.

That historical particularity gives theology a number of gains and losses. Its gain is its concreteness and personal character. One is not saved first of all by learning a teaching or assimilating a philosophy, but by being brought into relation with a particular person as the route to or mediator of reconciliation with God. Particularity thus aids identification, specification and distinctiveness. Salvation is *identified* by reference to the person, Jesus of Nazareth, it is *specified* in terms of a number of images and concepts interpreted by reference to the life, death and resurrection of Jesus of Nazareth – satisfaction, justification, sacrifice and the rest – which in turn gain their *distinctive* meaning from the connection with him.

The losses involved in the christological particularity of Christian atonement theology also have to be made clear if we are to see what is at stake in the discussion. The first is a necessary limitation and hence apparent loss of universality. It appears that those prevented by time or space from entering into relation with the particular person Jesus are to that extent barred from salvation, so that in practice God appears to offer salvation only to a limited range of human beings. The second loss is one in principle, not just practice, for particularity appears to deprive of philosophical universality. This is particularly apparent in a milieu dominated by Platonism, but by no means only that. How can one hang one's hope of heaven, or whatever, on a mere historical contingency? A third loss, perhaps a combination of features of the first two, was faced by Paul. Linking salvation to that particular human being appears to deprive it of respectability in other respects than the philosophical, especially in view of the apparently unconvincing character[1] and less than respectable origin and end of the saviour. To the scandal of particularity is added that of what to some minds appears the disreputability or the nondescript character of the saviour.

There are a number of moves by which the philosophical drawbacks of particularity are countered or made a positive advantage in Christian theology. They all center in one way or other on that most universal of concepts, *God*. If the acts by which the particular Jesus-history is distinctively what it is are acts of God, then it is in some way or other made or shown to be universal by the one who is the author of all meaning and truth. But when we come to ask how that universality is made to be what it is, we reach the beginnings of a real complexity, for different ways of seeing the matter locate the universality in different places. More than that, they lead to different conceptions of that in which the universality consists. In the next section of the paper we shall explore some of the different types of universality.

## Types of universality

The chief move by which the drawbacks of particularity are overcome is by making the particular to be in some way universal. God is by definition universal, so that if the work of Jesus is understood to be in some direct way the work of God, it is rendered by that very connection also in some way universal. But what is the form of the moves in support of the claim that the particular is more than particular? Here we must be aware of the fact that conceptions of the putative universality of the atoning significance of Jesus theology are manifold and various. An attempted classification would go something as follows.

1. Universality by the overcoming of temporal and spatial limitation.

a. Universality can be achieved protologically, by an act or decision of God in the beginning, or in some way before time. According to this move, the historical atonement is the outworking of some kind of universal plan or decree. God's intent is some form of universal salvation, some way of bringing the whole world into fellowship with him. The particular history of Jesus then becomes the factual way in which the relationship is brought about. The advantages of this view are at least two. First, it obviates some of the cruder theories of atonement according to which it is seen as largely a repair job, cleaning up so to speak after the unfortunate incidence of sin. It thus roots historical particularities in the universal will of God for salvation. What is often called the Scotist form of Christology holds that the Son of God would have become incarnate whether or not there had been a fall. The fall then becomes a formal rather than the efficient cause of the historic atonement, the latter being supplied by the universal love of God for his creation. Second, in general the protologically weighed conception of universal salvation does leave room for human freedom. It says that God's will from the beginning is for the salvation of all, but, unless the doctrine is contaminated by determinist views of predestination, leaves a space for human freedom to be damned. On many conceptions of the matter, human agents may reject the willed salvation.

What this approach does not do without assistance from other considerations is to cater during their lives for those born before or outside the geographical influence of the saving history. One way of saving its universality here is to show or claim that although the universal will for salvation became uniquely particular in Jesus, it was anticipated elsewhere and at other times. Here, a great deal of difference is made by the teaching that the one who realized salvation in time is the incarnation of the eternal Son of God, the one through whom the world was made and is upheld. In this case, the historical particularity of Jesus is supported by a doctrine of his ontological continuity with the eternal Son of God – one, that is, who is eternal and omnipresent. This means that although the incarnate Word is historically particular, by virtue of other things we might say about him it can be claimed that his significance is temporally and spatially universal. This point will recur under other heads (see below).

b. Universality can be achieved 'performatively'. According to this approach, the historically particular life of Jesus takes on universal significance by virtue of certain universalizing features. Thus Anselm held that the satisfaction wrought by Christ was of such infinite weight that it served for those who lived before it or outside its spatial influence.[2] That is a characteristically Western approach, tending as it does to invest universality largely in the cross. But there are other ways of making a similar point. Thus it might be argued, after Pannenberg in recent times, but probably Paul originally, that the logic of resurrection is necessarily a universalizing one. The idea of resurrection belongs conceptually in a universal context, so that the resurrection of Jesus might be said to confer or indicate his universal significance, a significance relating him to all creation from its end, so to speak. Similarly, the Letter to the Hebrews bases Jesus' universal significance as God, on the one hand, in his eternal sonship, but his universality as man, on the other, both in the achievement of his life and death and in his ascended state, the ascension here referring to the transcending by divine gift at the end of his earthly ministry of the limitations of time and space.

c. Eschatologically. As the reference to Pannenberg suggested, there is also a third way of overcoming temporal and spatial limitation, and that is eschatologically. According to this view, which probably takes its beginnings from Origen, the final destiny of things is the *apocatastasis*, the redemption of all things in Christ. If all are ultimately to be saved, the view that only some participate in salvation in the present may still be troublesome, but is relieved from the apparent unfairness of making the discrimination absolute. In the end, all will be saved even though there are apparent injustices during this life.

It is probably true that all traditionally orthodox theologies of atonement draw on most if not all of the considerations outlined here. This is because there are two thrusts to the universalizing of the atonement: its basis in the eternal love of God and its outworking in a historical event features of which are held to transcend, by virtue of their universal significance, mere historical particularity.

2. Corresponding to and in places overlapping with the move to spatial and temporal universality are moves designed to overcome what might be called ontological limitation, the objection that salvation based on a particular era or person is not universal for it leaves some people or realities outside its range. The chief counter to the charge is a move which we have

already met in another context, by which the historical Jesus of Nazareth is identified with the eternal Word or Son of God through whom all things were made. In the words of the Fourth Gospel, the light which comes into the world at the incarnation is the light that enlightens everyone, of all times and places (John 1.9,14). Because Jesus of Nazareth is the incarnation of the creating and redeeming Word, it is part of the being of all things to be in some positive relation to him. There are, of course, problems with this view, because if it is taken to its extreme, the branch on which it sits is sawn through, for the historical Jesus becomes redundant. If all are automatically enlightened by the eternal Christ, the historical Jesus appears to have no function, and the gospel is reduced to a form of knowledge. (Thomas Erskine of Linlathen appears to have moved to a position rather like that under the impact of his views about universal salvation, and Origen was suspiciously near to it.) On such a view the doctrine of the atonement disappears, for the cross which is its center is replaced by an immanent or universal divine principle which makes it redundant. What is missing in such a reduction is a historically formed doctrine of sin: that atonement is necessary because the universal human relatedness to God through the eternal Christ is disrupted with consequences that can be dealt with only through a personal incarnation of the eternal Son. (That has been the theme of orthodox atonement theology at least since Athanasius.)

This brings us to an important reason for the particularity of the atonement, that its necessity – indeed, universality – is logically linked to historical contingencies, and not only the one that human sin is. Underlying that motive for holding to the importance of historical particularity is the broader teaching that the eternal purposes of God are worked out in time and history. According to it there is an *economy* of creation and salvation, not merely the instantiation in the universe of timeless Platonic principles. The world is teleologically ordered, that is, it is created by God for a purpose whose outworking requires time. It is for this reason that the relation between universal Christ and particular Jesus is not treatable simply christologically or trinitarianly, but requires support by other dogmatic theses. One of them is predestination or election. In its biblical form, linked with the historical Israel and visible Church, election has been a way of linking the eternal will of God with historical particularities and the movement of creation to its end. Thus the election of Israel, certainly in the more universalistic strands of Old Testament theology, is the way by which God wills to realize in time his purposes for all the earth.

In such a way, particular election serves universal divine purposes. It is one of the disasters of the Western theological tradition that that polarity

151

became lost, so that election served an opposite purpose, becoming in effect a denial of universality. According to the Augustinian view shared by Anselm, Aquinas and Calvin, there was introduced into atonement theology a strict limitation on the universality of the atonement, for it was taught that only a limited number were fore-ordained to be saved: in Anselm's view, sufficient to fill up the complement of heaven after the expulsion of the fallen angels.[3] (An interesting tangential point here is that, as Barth's theology shows, an inversion of this view leads to a similar loss of the polarity of particular and universal, and so to a virtual universalism. Barth's theology is an example of a universality based upon a particularity: the whole human race apparently hurried off to heaven by virtue of a pretemporal divine decision to elect all people in Christ. Because in eternity God elects his Son, and so in him the whole of humankind, it takes a special kind of determination to avoid ending up in heaven.)[4]

That point reminds us, however, that to overcome the typical problems of this dimension of the problem, we must separate conceptually the themes of atonement and election and locate them within their appropriate systematic and economic space. Atonement is, as an act of God, directed to the redemption and completion of the creation, universal in being concerned with the reconciliation of all things. Because, however, it is located in time and is historically particular, its universality is not that of a timeless principle, but of the historical event that decisively shapes a universality which works itself out in time. There is therefore in Christian theology no room for a Platonic or timeless principle of atonement because atonement is the way by which the order of time and space is restored and brought to perfection. According to this view, created reality is temporal, and therefore becomes itself only through process of time. Particularities are necessary parts of the process. Ontological universality will therefore be achieved only eschatologically, at the end. That is the heart of Christianity's particular concept of universality, and the reason why its operation appears to be unjust: to exclude certain people by virtue of their placing in time and space.

We return to that with which we began. The philosophical problems of Christian theology arise out of its particular character. It is not a philosophy or moral teaching, but a gospel, a faith bound up with particular divine acts, because it is by such that the temporal teleology of the creation is realized. The enquiry about the form of those acts has led to a further specification of the problem of particularity and universality. Because the world is temporal, takes place as process, the relation of particular and universal in atonement theology is bound up with the way in which we see the atonement as located in relation to temporal process: to creation, to the particularities of the human fall, to redemption and to the final perfection of things. The atonement is a particular event which is decisive for the outcome of things, for it concerns the decisive act of God in the midst of time to reorder the teleology of, to recreate, a world that through evil had become threatened with a loss of its teleology. It is there that talk of the universality of the atonement must be located.

In the above discussion, a wide range of considerations came into view. At the centre is the way in which a contingent historical figure may be supposed to be of universal significance. Other questions are bound up with it, but can only be mentioned here. Central among them are two. The first concerns the scope of redemption. In what sense is the atonement a matter of human moral (rather than cosmic) reconstitution, and therefore in that respect of less than universal import? That is to say, is its universality human or more than merely human? The second question concerns the matter of human freedom, and of whether and in what way a supposedly universal atonement might be conceived to override or establish human freedom. If the atonement necessarily avails for all, whether we wish it or not, are we free to be what we are? But if it does not avail for all, in what sense is God unjust to those who appear not to obtain its benefits? The questions, of course, are bound up with a larger number of other beliefs about the nature of God and of divine action in the world.

All of those questions are important ones. However, there is an air, if not of unreality, then of something unsatisfactory about the way in which such discussions are conducted. The reason is, I believe, that all of the questions and answers carry a fideistic air: the whole problematic arises from within Christian belief, and in terms of a too limited range of intellectual possibilities. They raise philosophical questions in a rather restricted sense, and appear to cut little ice in contexts outside the Christian theological circle. (Indeed, in parts of that circle, too, the terms of the questions would appear far too restricted.) I shall therefore now develop the matter of the particular and the universal, expanding the range of the discussion, by means of a currently fashionable dispute in philosophy, and return by that route to what I hope will be a broader consideration of the specifically Christian concern.

## Foundationalism and the doctrine of the atonement

The philosophical dispute to which I want to refer is that over foundationalism, by which I mean the doctrine that a discipline's claim for rationality and truth must be based on some generally accepted intellectual foundations. There have been since the Enlightenment two rival candidates for being the universal foundations for thought, the rational and the empirical: universal and certain structures of concepts or some indubitable data of sense experience. On the whole it may appear that Christian theology has much to gain from the recent assaults on foundationalism, because the form that foundationalism took in the Enlightenment was generally hostile to a faith that appeared not to conform to the Enlightenment's narrow conception of rationality and experience. Indeed, foundationalism has more generally come into question because neither of the favoured candidates has succeeded in delivering what it promised. There are no certain and indubitable sets of concepts, no certain and agreed reports of sense experience. The Enlightenment project has failed to produce the certainty it sought, and there are those who would suggest that there are therefore no universal bases for thought, so that anything goes. (That would appear to be the teaching of Feyerabend on scientific method.)[5]

The more rational responses to the failure of the project have taken the form of a quest for non-foundationalist rationalities. These responses take the form of arguing that the basis and criteria of rationality are intrinsic to the disciplines concerned, which should not have imposed upon them in a procrustean way the methodologies which are appropriate for other forms of intellectual life. In particular, it is widely recognized that the tendency to take the natural sciences as models for cognitive respectability and to dismiss as non-cognitive all enterprises which do not conform to their particular standards has led to reductionism and a constriction on free intellectual enquiry. In theology, two models for a non-foundationalist epistemology have been Barth and Wittgenstein, and their links are indicated by the fact that both tend to be labelled fideist by foundationalist opponents. In this light, the methodological aspects of Barth's attack on natural theology can be seen as an assault on foundationalism and a claim for theology's intellectual autonomy.

The appeal of anti-foundationalism to theologians groaning under the oppression of demands to justify their discipline before the bar of allegedly universally valid scientific method is immense. It liberates a celebration of the rights of particularity. It enables the theologian to say that theological method must be different from other methods because it shapes its approach from the distinctive content with which it has to do – just as, indeed, other disciplines shape their approach in the light of their distinctive content. Anti-foundationalism, that is to say, advocates the individual autonomy of intellectual disciplines, thus ironically deriving an Enlightenment value from an otherwise anti-Enlightenment claim. Theologically it also has much to be said for it. Foundationalism appears to derive from an excessive confidence in human intellectual powers, to be too titanic an enterprise. According a place to human fallibility and sin allows historical and cultural particularity to be friends rather than foes of an appropriate rationality. We can see only so far, and must limit ourselves to what we can handle rather than attempt to roam in realms of speculation from which little reliable knowledge is likely to be forthcoming. The appeal of such a doctrine in connection with as particular a doctrinal locus as the atonement is immense.

It must be realized, however, that the anti-foundationalist song is the voice of a siren. The allusion to fideism indicates the perennial weakness of non-foundationalist epistemologies. They can appear to be attempts to render their contents immune from outside criticism and so represent intellectual sectarianism. In other words, they can appear to evade the challenge of the universal, and to run the risk of the rank subjectivism and relativism into which their extreme representatives have fallen. Theologically speaking, they evade the intellectual challenge involved in the use of the word *God*. If part of the meaning of that word is to refer to the universal source of being, meaning and truth, then those who would use it must be prepared to take some account of intellectual enterprises which impinge upon theirs from 'outside'. Here two illustrations bring out something of the point. The first is that although Barth is by no means subject to a temptation to play down the universal implications of his use of the word *God*, he is most in danger of appearing to make unsupported assertions precisely where he evades the challenge of the links between theological and other epistemology.[6] The second is that a favorite move of postmodernists like Cupitt is to withdraw some of the universalistic implications of the concept of God. *God* loses its ontological universality and becomes a word to express particular and therefore possibly diverse modes of human experience of the world with no relations between them. That seems to me not a serious option, because it is an evasion of the question of truth.

The quest then is for non-foundationalist foundations: to find the moments of truth in both of the contentions, for something like what Putnam has called realism with a human face.[7] If that appears to be a characteristically English quest for a middle way, then so be it. But the underlying intellectual issue is too important to be construed merely in that way. What underlies the quest is not a belief in some middle way so much as a conviction that both foundationalist and anti-foundationalist share certain presuppositions that are false. On the one hand, it can be argued that the problem is not the quest for foundations, for some understanding of the unity of the world and of the thought with which we attempt to come to terms with it, so much as the form the quest has taken from the Presocratics and Plato to the present day. The quest may be for foundations, but it is a quest engaged in by fallible, finite and fallen human beings, and the quest has failed because this fact has been overlooked. On the other hand, the anti-foundationalist position, certainly in its extreme postmodern form, depends on the failure of the discovery of certainties, as if to say that a failure to find certainty of a particular kind is a failure to find anything at all. There is reason to hold, therefore, that there can be a fallibilist quest for foundations, whose success is consistent with the provisionality of its conclusions.

A discussion of the matter of the atonement in this context will prove illuminating both for the atonement and for the matter of foundationalism, for it will enable closer attention to be paid to the relation between the particular history and its relation to the truth of the universal human condition. I have suggested elsewhere that the Christian theology of the atonement draws upon at least three families of metaphors by means of which it gives rational account of its view of human life in relation to God.[8] It could further be argued that these three clusters of metaphors appear elsewhere than simply in Christian theology, and it is precisely there that we come upon elements of universality, because the Christian usages in some way or other share in a widespread human analysis that might almost be claimed to be transcendental. In this context, that is to say that they reflect a universal human orientation towards and habitation of reality.

Thus many religions and philosophies share a tendency to understand the moral life as a sharing in a cosmic battle between the forces of light and those of darkness. That is why, I believe, that although Tolkien's *Lord of the Rings* does not set out to teach a specifically Christian theology, there are underlying that modern myth many themes that appeal both to the Christian and to the human moral consciousness in general. The war of light against darkness is a theme of many religious traditions, including Jewish intertestamental literature and that attributed to Zoroaster. When the life of Christ is depicted in the gospels in terms of a battle with the demonic, and when other New Testament writings, particularly perhaps the Book of Revelation, see the cross and resurrection also as a divine battle against the forces of evil, they are drawing on a motif that is common to human beings of many religious traditions. Their particular theology draws on what I suspect are transcendental features of human being in the world.

So it is with the second set of metaphors, that to do with legality. The notion of the moral life as life in obedience to a legality that comes from beyond the individual agent is likewise deep-seated within the human mind. Indeed, it is one of the interesting features of the thought of Kant that his central concept of autonomy is in the first instance a legal concept, while his conceptual troubles in attempting to reconcile the demands of objective legality and subjective autonomy are well known. But it is not simply a case of seeing the moral through the focus of the legal. Behind many uses of the metaphor is a belief that at stake in the tragedies as well as the moral successes of human life is more than a matter of individual right and wrong but something to do with universal justice, with the justice of Zeus or the righteousness of God. In some way or other, there is a drive in the human mind to link the regularities and irregularities of human behaviour with the very fabric of the world. The notion that Jesus dies under the law incorporates within itself both of these general themes; that he dies a judicially imposed death, but one also mysteriously prescribed by the law of God.

The link between behaviour and transcendentality comes out more strongly still in the third great area of metaphor. The common human concern with dirt and pollution, spelt out in Mary Douglas' *Purity and Danger*,[9] may be argued to point to a universal human way of being in the world. In a broad conspectus of human culture there is a view that in some way or other associates moral evil with pollution, so that breaches of morality are more than breaches of the law or of ethics, but in some way or other disrupt the very relation between the agent and the universe. Classic is perhaps the treatment in the Oedipus cycle of the intrinsic relation between moral pollution and the fate of the whole communities unknowingly caught up in it. It may be that since the Enlightenment some of the rooting of these concerns in the structure of being has been lost, and with it a sense both of our common humanity and of the rootedness of our moral life in the cosmic context. But one has only to survey some of the vocabulary of environmentalism to note what it has in common with a long and venerable religious tradition, and rightly so, for the ecological question is essentially the same as that which is at the heart of many religious concepts of sacrifice.

Here I could cite Václav Havel's reflections on the need to live in harmony with nature and his scathing rejection of the Western ideology of consumption. He links the environmental pollution wrought by Communism with its more general moral crisis, but with that of the West also, which he chides for believing implicitly that the consumer society reflects the order of the universe:

> As a boy, I lived for some time in the country and I clearly remember an experience from those days. I used to walk to school . . . along a cart track through the fields and, on the way, see on the horizon a huge smoke-stack of some hurriedly built factory. . . . It spewed dense brown

smoke, and scattered it across the sky. Each time I saw it, I had an intense sense of something profoundly wrong, of humans soiling the heavens. . . . It seemed to me that, in it, humans are guilty of something, . . . arbitrarily disrupting the natural order of things, and that such things cannot go unpunished.

Interestingly, Havel compares his experience with that of the medieval peasant who would probably think it the work of the devil. 'Both the boy and the peasant are far more rooted in what some philosophers call "the natural world" '.[10] Thus, again, in seeing in the death of Christ a metaphorical sacrifice which freed from pollution, the New Testament writers were drawing on experiences deep in the human consciousness, arising as they do from the most fundamental – foundational – human realities, of being set in a universe with whose structures and destiny we are closely bound.

What we find in these brief analyses is not a number of identical and context-independent characterizations of the plight of fallen humanity, but interpretations of reality sharing family resemblances. What I want to suggest is that we have 'open transcendentals', analyses that suggest that there is a universal kind of human concern at work in widely different cultures. All these analyses are particular, for they belong in different historical, religious and cultural contexts. But because they share in a common concern to identify the human plight or need and to heal it, and because they do so in language that overlaps interestingly, they show that the particularities of Christian atonement theology do not operate in a fideist vacuum. Plato's concern with justice and Paul's with justification belong therefore in the same family, share in the same transcendental enquiry despite their marked differences of analysis and prescription. Discussions of redemption, *salus*, human wholeness, are of universal moment, because they arise from the structures of human being in the world, that is, from human and worldly transcendentality. What culture has not, even at its most optimistic, revealed a concern for human healing and a sense of the deep flaws in human nature and the world that require it? What culture has not conceived that in some way human misdeeds have upset something of the fabric of the universe, so that a Greek tragic view that the pollution incurred by an unavenged murder has led to plague is not so far from a modern view that the pollution of nature has led inexorably to the paying of a price?

In the context of what can be claimed to be universal features of the human condition (its concern for victory over evil, right living under the law and integrity of life in the world) Christian theologies of atonement appear as particular analyses of and prescription for these universal ills. They are a particularizing of a universal human concern, rooted, as I have suggested, in the structures of human and worldly transcendentality. Similar themes appear in it as in other philosophies and religions: universal justice, pollution and sacrifice, the war of good against evil, human moral lapse and restoration. But because the Christian particularizing is based upon the historical contingencies of Israel and Jesus, it takes a particular shape. It therefore has a distinctive analysis and prescription. It holds that the basis of the human placing in the world is not a matter of appearance and reality, or weakness of will, or chance, but a personal relation: a relation between a personal God and the creatures he has made in his image. Shared in most Christian views of the matter is a view that creation involves some kind of moral responsibility for the created order, that the rejection of the relation to God on which that moral responsibility is based has led to destructive consequences; and that the love of God is such that he has ordained means, at personal cost to himself, whereby that relationship may be restored.

The distinctive character of a Christian position can be seen if we glance at two analyses both of which claim in different ways to be articulations of the human condition aiming at a kind of transcendentality. The first is that of Anselm of Canterbury, who sets out to give proof of the rationality of the atonement by 'necessary reasons'. In speaking of the need for atonement, *remoto Christo* – Christ being set on one side – Anselm has two sets of intellectual opponents in view: the adherents of other religions than Christianity and Christians who deny the need for a rational account of salvation. In order to found his particular theology of the atonement, Anselm draws, as a recent discussion has convincingly shown, on what was the universal intellectual framework of his world, a theory of the order of the universe maintained in being by God and disrupted by human misdeeds.[11] (That, of course, is the only universal intellectual framework there can be, if foundationalism is wrong in seeking one that is universal independently of historical context.) In its light, satisfaction, which should be understood not as its rationalistic detractors have done, but as a wholly positive form of dynamic moral overcoming of evil by good, is shown to be a universal requirement. Having established this, Anselm then proceeds to show the intellectual and moral necessity of the particular satisfaction achieved by the God-man.

Anselm thus uses a universal analysis in support of a particular theology of the atonement, believed by faith. As is now generally recognized, there is in Anselm a holding in tension of faith seeking understanding and the support of Christian beliefs by 'necessary reasons'. By contrast, Kant, in his

*Religion within the Limits of Reason Alone* draws, as is increasingly being recognized, upon certain particular features of the Christian tradition, and especially aspects of the theology of the Reformation, in a general theory of human moral redemption. As Gordon Michalson has recently pointed out, the difficulties of Kant's philosophy in this work derive in part from the fact that he cannot accept the more general Enlightened view that it is ignorance, rather than a defect of the will, that is at the root of the human moral plight. This means that his account of radical evil draws upon themes coming to him from the Christian past rather than the Enlightenment return to a rational or Platonic analysis of the human condition. It also means that the tension in his thought derives in part from the attempted combination of an anti-Pelagian or Augustinian analysis with a Pelagianizing concept of redemption.[12]

Kant's account of radical evil is therefore a kind of Christian transcendental analysis of human fallenness, to which is added a generally rationalist account of redemption. Its failure as an account of salvation is that it achieves a diagnosis that represents the human condition as beyond self-salvation, and appends to it an account that, in general, appeals to innate human power for a solution. That is to say, it is an account factually dependent upon a particular historical analysis of the human condition which is then transmogrified by what looks like a category mistake into a philosophically universal account. It thus moves in the opposite direction to Anselm's account, and ends up in a failure to give a clear account of the relation between historical particularity, which for ideological reasons it has rejected, and universality.

Anselm and Kant thus present alternative approaches to the particularity and universality of the theology of the atonement. The latter attempts to *overcome* particularity by means of a rational and transcendental analysis, the former to *support* it by a trascendental analysis which reveals interesting common features with that of his modern successor. Thus a choice of ways of conceiving the relation between universality and particularity is presented to us. The implication is that the discussion of the problems outlined in the second section, those internal to Christian theology, need not result in fideism. The alternative to that is not to go the way of Kant and the Liberal Protestantism that has followed his lead in rationalizing away the particularities. Rather, there is need of a continuing dialogue between the particularities of Christian theology and the various questions about universal meaning which it raises and on which it impinges. (That would include, of course, the question of the relation between Christianity and the theologies of salvation of other religions and philosophies.) If foundationalism is wrong, there is no other way, for there are only particularities. The questions to be asked are then what forms of universal meaning arising from and are related to what forms of particularity, and in which way.

The distinctiveness of the Christian theology of the atonement, its particularity, derives from the distinctive way in which it construes the human condition and identifies its redemption: its unique combination of historical dynamic and moral realism. It shares with other faiths a sense of the need for redemption, but sees evil as deriving indeed from a flaw in the will, but one that cannot be understood merely immanently, only in relation to God. The reason is that human being is what it is in relation to God, the Creator and redeemer of all that is. When that relation is disrupted, so is the order of the universe, in such a way that only the Creator, present in person, can restore things to their true end. On any account, as I have already suggested, God, as the source of being, meaning and truth, is a crucial focus of universality. On this account, the universality is historically focused because only so can the dynamic of history, the nature of man and woman as created in the image of God, the radicality of evil and the redemption of the world be held together. That is Christianity's peculiar claim to truth: its way of seeing the human condition as fallen, but fallen from its true destiny which is restored in the one who went to the cross.

NOTES

1. For an example of how the life and teaching of Jesus as recorded in the gospels appear to a skeptical secular mind, see Richard Robinson, *An Atheist's Values*, Oxford: Oxford University Press, 1964.
2. Anselm of Canterbury, *Cur Deus Homo*, 2.16.
3. ibid., 1.16–18.
4. See Karl Barth, *Church Dogmatics*, translation edited by G. W. Bromily and T. F. Torrance, Vol. 2, Part 2, Edinburgh: T & T Clark, 1957, chapter 7, 'The Election of God'. It must be noted that the author does not accept that his position entails universalism, although many critics have argued that it does.
5. Paul Feyerabend, *Against Method. Outline of an Anarchistic Theory of Knowledge*, London: Verso, 1978, first edn, 1975.
6. See Colin Gunton, 'No Other Foundation. One Englishman's Reading of *Church Dogmatics*, Chapter 5', in Nigel Biggar, ed., *Reckoning with Barth. Essays in Commemoration of the Centenary of Karl Barth's Birth*, London: Mowbray, 1988, pp. 61–79.
7. Hilary Putnam, *Realism with a Human Face*, edited by James Conant, Cambridge, Mass., and London: Harvard University Press, 1990, esp. pp. 1–29.
8. Colin Gunton, *The Actuality of Atonement: A Study of Metaphor, Rationality and the Christian Tradition*, Edinburgh: T & T Clark, 1988.

9. Mary Douglas, *Purity and Danger. An Analysis of the Concepts of Pollution and Taboo*, London: Ark Books, 1984, first edn, 1966.
10. Václav Havel, *Open Letters. Selected Prose 1965–1990*, selected and edited by Paul Wilson, London: Faber and Faber, 1991, pp. 249f.
11. Helmut Steindl, *Genugtuung. Biblisches Versöhnungsdenken – eine Quelle für Anselms Satisfaktionstheorie?*, Freiburg: Universitätsverlag, 1989.
12. Gordon E. Michalson, Jr, *Fallen Freedom. Kant on Radical Evil and Moral Regeneration*, Cambridge: Cambridge University Press, 1990.

# 16

## TRUTH AND THE DIVERSITY OF RELIGIONS
### Keith Ward

I will be concerned with only one problem about truth which is raised by the diversity of religions which exist in the world. The problem is this: many religions claim to state truths about the nature of the universe and human destiny which are important or even necessary for human salvation and ultimate well-being. Many of these truths seem to be incompatible; yet there is no agreed method for deciding which are to be accepted; and equally intelligent, informed, virtuous and holy people belong to different faiths. It seems, therefore, that a believing member of any one tradition is compelled to regard all other traditions as holding false beliefs and therefore as not leading to salvation. Since each faith forms a minority of the world's population, all religious believers thus seem committed to saying that most intelligent, virtuous and spiritually devoted people cannot know the truth or attain salvation. This is a problem, because it is in tension with the belief, held by many traditions, that the supremely real being is concerned for the salvation of all rational creatures. How can this be so if, through no fault of their own, most creatures cannot come to know the truth and thereby attain salvation?

Among those who have seen this as a problem and have proposed a philosophical defence of one solution to it, John Hick must take a foremost place. His book, *An Interpretation of Religion* (London, 1989), is a statement of the position which has come to be known as religious pluralism. This major work, filled with illuminating discussions of the phenomena of religious belief and with fresh and lucid insights, is meant to be, not the end of the debate, but an opening up of discussion which might clarify the problem and its solutions further, and might establish a coherent framework for developing inter-faith dialogue and for a credible religious faith held in full awareness of and with full respect for the beliefs of others. My aim is to contribute to this discussion; and I shall do it by using the time-honored philosophical technique of niggling and irritating criticism of various theses Hick presents. My argument will be that Hick's position is philosophically unacceptable as it stands, though it would be unwise simply to reject it wholesale; and I hope that my attack, such as it is, will be taken as a tribute to the force of the issues Hick places before us.

The pluralistic hypothesis is that religions provide different valid but culturally conditioned responses to a transcendent reality, and offer ways of transcending self and achieving a limitlessly better state centered on that reality. Thus no one tradition possesses a set of absolute and exclusive truths, while all others are delusory and ineffective for salvation. All will, or at least can be, saved by adhering to their own traditions, which purvey differing, but authentic, responses to the ultimately real. All can know the truth and attain salvation in their own traditions; so believers no longer have to condemn all others as mistaken, and no longer have to wonder why their God leaves the majority of creatures in mortal error. Here is an elegant and morally attractive solution of the problem of error in religion; and it is one that has great appeal for those who are reluctant to say that they alone are right and everyone else is wrong.

Nevertheless the hypothesis is riddled with difficulties; and the most obvious one can be put very forthrightly. To believe a proposition is to think that it is true. To think that it is true is to affirm that reality is as it is described by that proposition. Insofar as our affirmations are fallible, it is always possible that reality is not as some proposition asserts it to be. Thus an affirmation by its nature excludes some possible state of affairs; namely, one which would render the proposition false. If an assertion excludes nothing, it affirms nothing. In that sense, all truth-claims are necessarily exclusive.

It immediately follows that, where any truth-claim is made, it is logically possible to make another truth-claim which the first claim excludes. It is logically impossible for all possible truth-claims to be compatible. So it is possible for religious traditions to contain incompatible truth-claims, claims which exclude one another. Since this is a matter of logical possibility, it is a necessary truth that not all possible religious traditions can be equally true, authentic or valid. One can easily construct traditions which are strictly incompatible and of them, at least, pluralism must be false. That is, they will not consist of equally valid concepts of ultimate reality. One does not even need to invent such traditions, since, for example, Satanism and Christianity are fundamentally opposed both morally and factually.

But if this version of pluralism, which we might call 'extreme pluralism', is incoherent, it might nevertheless be the case that many religious traditions, and maybe all the major ones that exist on our planet, do not contain mutually exclusive beliefs, but are equally valid paths of salvation and of authentic experience of the Real. This is 'hard pluralism'; and it is a contingent hypothesis; whether or not it is true will be a matter for careful investigation. But it certainly looks as though many claims exclude one another. The Buddhist assertion that there is no creator god excludes the Christian assertion that there is one all-perfect Creator. The Muslim assertion that Allah has no son excludes the Christian assertion that God has an only-begotten Son. What is the pluralist to do about these *prima facie* incompatible claims?

Hick's strategy is to retreat from discussing particular religious beliefs and to talk instead of 'religion'; to retreat from discussing specific truth-claims and to talk instead of 'religious traditions'. This may seem innocuous, but it can be, and turns out to be, very misleading. It is well known that definitions of religion are hard to find; and Hick proposes that we regard 'religion' as a family-resemblance concept, so that there is no essential core definition. Yet he is concerned with only one sort of religion or one feature of religious beliefs. He characterizes the central strand of religion with which he is chiefly concerned as 'awareness of and response to a reality that transcends ourselves and our world' (p. 3). Fairly rapidly, he nominalizes the verb 'transcends', and speaks of 'belief in the transcendent', saying that 'most forms of religion have affirmed a salvific reality that transcends human beings and the world' (p. 6). What he is doing is to pick out one class of religious beliefs, or one set of religious phenomena which can be defined in terms of belief in a transcendent salvific reality. There is nothing wrong with that; but it should be noted that it picks out one area of agreement in truth-claims by definition. Faiths which lack that central belief are not going to be counted; conversely, faiths which are counted are assured of a minimal degree of agreement to begin with. They will all agree on something, so they will not be incompatible in all respects. But, so far, this is not really pluralism (the acceptance of very different beliefs as equally valid); it is exclusivism at a relatively abstract and general level (those are excluded who do not believe in one transcendent salvific reality). It is also an acceptance of some truth-claim – the claim that there is such a reality which can bring creatures to a limitlessly good state – as 'absolute', or true for everyone, regardless of their point of view or cultural situation.

Hick argues at length in *An Interpretation of Religion*, that we cannot reasonably claim 'that our own form of religious experience . . . is veridical whilst the others are not' (p. 235). He allows that virtually every religious tradition has done so; but then proposes the following argument:

(1) By something akin to Swinburne's Principle of Credulity, *A* is justified in thinking that what seems to be the case probably is the case,

in the absence of strong countervailing reasons. So if *A* seems to apprehend God's presence, she is justified in thinking that God is in fact present, and therefore that God exists.

(2) By the principle of universalizability, however, *B* is similarly justified in believing that reality is non-dual, on the basis of her experiences of *samadi* or enlightenment.

(3) Since the fact that '*A* is me' is not a relevant reason for giving *A*'s views greater force than *B*'s, it seems that *A* and *B* are equally justified in believing contradictory things.

(4) Therefore it is implausible to believe that all religious experience is delusory except one's own.

(5) This suggests the Pluralistic Hypothesis, that different types of religious experience are veridical but partial responses to a reality which cannot be adequately described by any set of beliefs alone.

This argument is plainly invalid. The trouble lies with step (4). A sharp distinction is to be made between justification and truth. I can be justified in believing something false (e.g. that the earth is flat) due to imperfect knowledge. In complex situations, given rather different initial information, people may be justified in believing contradictory things. But contradictory beliefs cannot both be true; so all that follows is that at least one person is justified in believing something false. Hick has already argued that both atheists and theists can be rationally justified in adopting the views of the world they do adopt, given the ambiguous nature of that world. But it does not follow that each must accept the other's view as equally true. The very reverse is the case. If I am rationally justified in believing *X*; and you are rationally justified in believing not-*X*; then we are both justified in believing the other to be deluded, or in some other way mistaken.

Now something *does* follow from this about the character of such beliefs. I must admit other believers may have reasons which seem just as strong to them to accept their views as I have to accept mine. Therefore I cannot claim that they are obviously or detectably mistaken. And I cannot seriously claim that my view is obviously or clearly true. So I must admit the equal right of others to exist and hold the views they do. And I must admit the fallibility and theoretical uncertainty of my view. To accept this might in itself be a great advance in religion, but it does not constitute a reason for accepting hard pluralism. It could be a reason for denying any right to believe any view in this area. However, one can argue, as Hick does, that the matter is so important that I am justified in making some choice. It may even be that I *must* believe something in this area, though it is hard to say how detailed my beliefs must be. In fact Hick vacillates, sometimes saying that, because conflicting views have so little to choose between them, it is not important to hold such views, and one should concentrate simply on the practical matter of salvation. But at other times (e.g. as between realist and non-realist religious views) he says that it is important to choose a realist and cosmically optimistic view, because only that offers good news to all.

Whichever he says, it *is* reasonable to claim that our own experiences are veridical whilst all others are not. It is unreasonable to claim anything else. But the situation does not have to have this all-or-nothing character. Surely we do not wish to say that centuries of prayer, meditation, sanctity and devotion in other traditions are founded on illusion? Surely they must be putting people in touch with the real spiritual reality, whatever it is? Hick himself gives the answer: 'There seems to me to be no difficulty in principle in the thought that a person may be correctly experiencing some aspects of reality whilst falsely experiencing others' (p. 220). That is, there may well be something veridical in what great religious traditions experience; but also (very often) something false. He even tells us how to discriminate: we accept some belief as veridical 'because it evokes a confirming echo within our own experience' (p. 220). We reject others because they clash with our experience. There are many echoes of our experience in the religious experiences of others; and we may take these to be veridical. By parity of reasoning, we may think that our own tradition, even our own present experience within that tradition, is liable to contain many mistakes, though we will not know what they are. Humility is certainly in order; it does sound arrogant to say 'my religious experience is perfectly correct; all others are totally false'. But we can say: 'My religious experience is correct in important respects, though it may contain many errors. The experiences of others may contain many veridical elements; but there are important misinterpretations, too'. The veridical elements will be those which seem to echo my own, the errors those which clash with my own; nor will I be able to identify the errors in my own. I can be on the lookout for such errors, and look to other traditions to help me identify them. And I can look for elements other traditions have which may complement, rather than contradict, my own. Thus my beliefs are always revisable; and others may always be capable of disclosing new insights. Yet those beliefs which lie near the core of my belief-system must be given preference over competing beliefs.

Hick does precisely this, of course. He identifies many errors in the Christian tradition – belief in Hell and literal belief in incarnation are just two which he takes to be morally undesirable and rationally insupportable.

His core-beliefs are that one should turn from selfish egoism to attain a limitlessly good end-state by some sort of relation to a reality of supreme value; and he is only prepared to accept beliefs which are compatible with these. The suggestion is that any set of beliefs which result in such an end-state is likely to be true; others are not. The trouble is that this criterion is quite unusable, as Hick's discussion makes very clear. Some of the most obviously deluded, restrictive and exclusive belief-systems produce astonishing commitment, assurance, love and self-sacrifice. On the other hand, as Hick points out, the great scriptural traditions have histories replete with hatred, intolerance and violence; so that none of them emerges as much better than any others, in the long sad history of human fanaticism. It seems, then, that either the suggested criteria of adequacy do not enable us to choose between many different beliefs; or that they are in tension with the criterion of consistency with other well-established knowledge. Hick tends to dismiss metaphysical speculations, together with particular historical claims, as unsettlable and unnecessary to salvation. But of course his whole book is a metaphysical exploration of what can be intelligibly said about the object of religious faith; and the fact that his version of pluralistic religious realism is unsettlable and highly disputable does not stop him from asserting both its truth and its importance for a correct (non-exclusive) understanding of salvation.

This brings us to the question of whether unsettlable beliefs can be necessary for salvation. Hick finds this 'implausible' (p. 369); but it is rendered immediately more plausible by the consideration that the very concept of what salvation is involves beliefs which are theoretically unsettlable in practice. If one asks what is necessary for salvation, one might be asking whether any beliefs are requisite for the final attainment of wholly fulfilled human life. Atheists, of course, will deny that there is any such final attainment, or even any such possible notion as that of a wholly fulfilled life; 'do your own thing' might better be their motto. So the mere acceptance of the concept of a wholly fulfilled life presupposes the very contestable belief that there is a proper goal of human activity. If there is such a consciously attained goal, then one cannot achieve it without having the correct belief about what it is, and how one has come to achieve it. In this sense the possession of some particular beliefs is necessary to salvation. People without those beliefs will not attain salvation, for the simple reason that salvation consists in attaining a state which entails possessing such beliefs; i.e. it entails that one knows what salvation is and that one has attained it. At such a point, of course, one may suppose that religious disputes will finally be settled. As Hick says, 'To participate knowingly in fulfilment would confirm the reality of God beyond the possibility of rational doubt' (p. 179). In other words, at least some important metaphysical claims about the existence and nature of God are settlable by experience in principle.

But one might also ask whether any beliefs are requisite *now* if one is to have a reasonable hope of attaining salvation later, or if one is to be on the right path towards salvation. Different views exist on this question; but Hick seems to me correct in thinking that if there is a God of universal love, he will not make our loss of eternal life dependent merely upon making an honest mistake. So one might suppose that a positive response to whatever seems to be good and true, by a conscience as informed as one can reasonably expect, and a commitment to seek truth and realize goodness, is sufficient to dispose one rightly to salvation. Some beliefs are requisite; but they will depend on particular circumstances, since what one is justified in believing at one time may well be different from what one is justified in believing at another. Nevertheless, if one believes in such a God of love, one will also think that he will eventually bring rational creatures to know what he truly is, so that the search for truth will issue in a specific set of true beliefs sometime. Thus it is misleading, though in one sense true, to say that no metaphysical beliefs are essential to salvation. It may not be essential to your eventual salvation that you hold them now; but it is essential to your actual salvation that you come to hold them. Metaphysics, however difficult and disputable, is important to faith (I don't mean anything very grand by this; just beliefs about the nature of what is ultimately real).

In a recent paper, Hick refers to the 'novel', 'astonishing' and 'bizarre' doctrine that 'the salvific power of the dharma taught five hundred years earlier by the Buddha is a consequence of the death of Jesus'. But one need not deny that the dharma is an effective way of overcoming egoism and attaining inner peace and compassion, when one asserts that it does not bring one into a conscious loving relationship with a personal God. Nor is it bizarre to hold that one can be brought into such a relationship only by the saving activity of God uniting human nature to himself in the life and death of Jesus, and subsequently in those who come to accept Jesus as Lord and Saviour. It is not that Buddhists attain salvation by the Middle Way, though somehow the efficacy of this way depends on something that had not yet happened. Buddhists do not attain Christian salvation, since their Way does not lead to that personal relationship with God which is salvation. They attain a high degree of compassion and inner peace; and their unselfish devotion to the truth as they see it will surely fit them to receive salvation from a personal God when his saving activity becomes clear to them. There is a salutary reminder here that metaphysics is not what saves us; for Christians, the act of God, establishing creatures in knowledge and love of him, does that. But metaphysics is needed to set out the coherence of the concept of a God who can so act in a world like this.

It may help at this point if we distinguish what we may call soft pluralism from hard pluralism. Soft pluralism is the view that the Real can manifest in many traditions, and humans can respond to it appropriately in them. I think this view is defensible and important, and it is certainly different from the view, held by many, that there is only one God, who only reveals himself in one tradition and only saves those who belong to that tradition – the restrictive interpretation of the decree of the Council of Florence, 'Outside the Church there is no salvation'. It is coherent to hold that there is a God who is infinite and beyond human comprehension in his essential nature, who discloses something of that nature, as it stands in relation to us, in many religious traditions. It is coherent to hold that in many (though not all) religious traditions, believers aim to overcome selfish desire in relation to a supreme objective value which promises bliss, knowledge and freedom; and that this does constitute a positive and appropriate response to God, as disclosed to them. It is also coherent to hold that no tradition has the completeness of truth about God; that all contain many revisable and corrigible beliefs, and that we should look to other traditions to complement, correct or reshape our own. This is certainly part of Hick's thesis.

But another form of the thesis is also at work; a thesis both more intolerant of virtually all actual religious traditions and sliding at times into incoherence. The intolerance surfaces in many stringent remarks about the bizarre, primitive and astonishing beliefs held by orthodox believers. The incoherence appears in the claim of hard pluralism that all (or at least all 'great') traditions are equally valid paths to salvation and equally authentic modes of experience of a Real which is a completely unknowable postulate of the religious life. It is the stress on equal validity, equal authenticity and complete unknowability which is incoherent. These three claims constitute an inconsistent triad of propositions, since one cannot assert all of: (1) There is something wholly unknowable; (2) all experiences of it are equally authentic; and (3) all paths to fuller experience of it are equally valid. If (1) is true, (2) and (3) cannot be asserted. Not only is there no way of knowing if they are true; they cannot be true, if they entail (as they do) experiential knowledge of the wholly unknowable. If there are any criteria of authenticity at all, it must be possible to distinguish more and less authentic experiences. But this can only be done by means of some concept of the Real which can be described more or less adequately. Once one has such a concept, there may indeed be experiences which give equally authentic knowledge of it; but that can only be so if those experiences are complementary, not contradictory. That means (as is the case with the often quoted wave–particle duality of light) that competent observers must agree that both of two descriptions of an object can be true, in different conditions of observation. Unfortunately, most Buddhists will not agree that it is true that there is an omnipotent personal agent who brings about changes in history; and most Christians will not agree that the idea of God is an imaginative projection which needs to be overcome in the recognition of one non-dual reality. Hard pluralism is as strongly falsified as any contingent hypothesis is ever likely to be.

Yet it might be insisted that this situation must be changed. There is another version of pluralism, which might be termed 'revisionist pluralism', which asserts that all the scriptural traditions need to be radically revised, in consequence of the rise of the natural sciences, of biblical scholarship and of post-Enlightenment critical thinking in general. The idea of an infallible scriptural revelation will need to be discarded, and many particular beliefs revised in the light of new knowledge of the world and of human psychology. Now if this is done in all the great scriptural traditions, one will be much less clear about which beliefs are essential or even central to each tradition; and the revised beliefs may well turn out to be compatible with similarly revised beliefs in other traditions.

If a Buddhist is prepared to regard belief in re-incarnation as a myth, a Christian thinks of the incarnation as a mistaken fourth-century doctrine, and a Muslim agrees that the Koran is a fallible and morally imperfect document, they might well be able to agree much more than they used to. One can see the scriptural faiths, defined by their acceptance of infallible revelation (and even the Buddhist scriptures are regarded in that way by many orthodox believers), as belonging to past history just as surely as their tribal predecessors do. Religion can move to a more universal phase, in which insights are selected from many traditions, while most of their differences are relegated to the museum of dead beliefs. I suspect that Hick wishes to commend revisionist pluralism, too. There is much to be said for it; but it cannot be said that it sees all existing traditions as equally valid perceptions of truth. On the contrary, most existing traditions have to be radically purged of error, in the light of the more adequate views of a post-Critical age. It is ironic that this view, which sees the great traditions as 'earlier stages in an evolution of which it is the culmination' is precisely of the type which Hick earlier characterizes as unacceptably arrogant (p. 2). Revisionist pluralism makes it own absolute and exclusive claim – it is just true that there is one Reality of supreme value which will bring all

171

creatures to good; and anything which denies this or tries to restrict the ways in which this may happen is false.

Revisionist pluralism is incompatible with hard pluralism, since it denies that unrevised traditions are equally adequate forms of religious truth. It is compatible with soft pluralism, but not entailed by it, since it is possible that one existing tradition characterizes the Real most adequately; that is, that its central truth-claims are more adequately descriptive of the Real than competing alternatives. To the extent that the Real is a personal and active self-disclosing agent, one might think that an existing tradition which claims to have witnessed the self-disclosing acts of this agent is more likely to be adequate than the conclusions of a highly abstract and speculative philosophical hypothesis. But that is a question of the acceptability and coherence of particular conceptions of ultimate reality, which needs to be argued out in detail. One thing is certain, that revisionist pluralism is not in a position to assert moral superiority, greater tolerance or greater impartiality over any particular tradition as such, when traditions are taken as not excluding ultimate salvation for others; since the claims each must make for itself are logically on a par.

Religious believers do not have to suppose that the majority of the human race are excluded from salvation, as long as they have a view which allows for a development of knowledge after death. They are, however, committed to thinking that most people are mistaken in their beliefs about the ultimate nature of reality. That is, after all, not a very surprising thought, though it is a sad one. It should lead to a keen sense of one's own fallibility, a deeper appreciation of the attempts of others to understand human nature and destiny, and a firm stress on the primacy of moral and spiritual practice in religion. These are the leading themes of John Hick's recent work, which he formulates in the pluralist hypothesis. I have suggested that in at least one sense (soft pluralism) his case is persuasive. There are other senses however which, if I am right, are not sustainable. On this, at least, truth is exclusive, and one of us must be wrong.

# 17

# One Covenant or Many Covenants? Toward a Theology of Christian–Jewish Relations
## Gavin D'Costa

## Introduction

For many post-war theologians the events of the Holocaust have dictated the theological agenda. There are many areas of controversy in the Jewish–Christian debate, but for the purpose of this essay I wish to examine an emerging consensus among a group of theologians on a single issue.[1] The problem can be summarized as follows: for nearly 2,000 years, Christianity has defined itself as the fulfilment of Judaism. The 'new covenant' and 'new Israel' were formed in the person of Christ and the Church that he established. Israel's history reached its completion and fulfilment in these events. Judaism should have flowered into Christianity – but (and here there are variations) through ignorance or hard-heartedness the Jews rejected their true destiny. Hence, for most of Christian history Judaism has been seen as an anachronism. Some argue that this view heralded the theological extinction of Judaism and that the subsequent attempts at historically liquidating the Jews was an inevitable corollary.[2]

In response a number of Christian theologians have argued for what has been called by some the 'dual covenant' position. These theologians, with various nuances, have urged that Christians should view the Jewish and Christian traditions as two distinct yet complementary covenants. Jews, in remaining Jews rather than becoming Christians, are being faithful to their covenant with the same God who forged a further complementary covenant into which the gentiles were grafted. Neither negates the other; they are, rather, two distinct, complementary, and related ways to God. The fulfilment model should be abandoned as should mission toward the Jews. Both are anachronistic and theologically unjustified.[3] Some theologians further suggest that this particular case raises more widely applicable principles regarding the world religions. Colonialist imperialism bears analogy to the political and social anti-Judaism fostered by a fulfilment theology. Blindness to the revelatory events in the world religions bears analogy to the theological obliteration of post-New Testament Judaism.[4]

If the dual covenanters are correct, one must indeed review Christianity's attitude toward Judaism (and toward the world religions). The challenge is a bold one. I will examine just some of the arguments of some dual covenanters, acknowledge important differences among them, and, by means of a critique, tentatively suggest an alternative approach. This alternative is aptly reflected in the subtitle of this essay: '*Toward* a Theology of Christian–Jewish Relations'. It is an alternative requiring substantial amplification, and here I can only sketch the beginnings of such an approach. I should also state that my reflections come out of the Roman Catholic tradition.

## The arguments of the Dual-Covenant School

I shall outline what I take to be some important arguments put forward. Such a list is clearly not exhaustive, nor can it reflect the nuances of various stances.[5]

(1) A fulfilment theology has entailed the theological negation of Judaism and eventually (and possibly inevitably) the historical liquidation of Jewry. This thesis can be sub-divided into two aspects, theological and sociopolitical. They can be held together, although this is not always the case.

(a) The theological negation of Judaism entails the denial of God's covenant and, therefore, *fidelity* with and to God's people. This is un-Christian, as it contradicts the fidelity of God affirmed within Christianity.[6]

(b) The theological negation of Judaism is intrinsically related to the sociopolitical negation of the Jews. This is un-Christian, as it amounts to genocide![7]

(2) Jesus cannot be proclaimed as the Jewish 'Messiah' for a number of reasons. One is that he is not the Messiah because he has clearly not inaugurated the reign of God – as is expected of the Jewish Messiah. To quote Ruether: 'For Judaism, Jesus cannot have been the Messiah, because the times remain unredeemed and neither he nor anything that came from him has yet altered that fact. In short, Judaism, in rejecting Jesus' messianic status, is simply reaffirming the integrity of its own tradition about what the word *Messiah* means.'[8] Given this, Christians can dismantle the claim that has been primarily responsible for anti-Judaism: 'Jesus is *the* awaited Messiah.'

174

(3) An objection put to the dual covenanters may be framed as follows. If Judaism is an alternative and valid path to salvation, what of Christian claims regarding Jesus as the only way to salvation: 'I am the way, and the truth, and the life. No one comes to the Father except through me' (John 14.6 [*NRSV*]; see also John 3.18 and Acts 4.12)? Here again, there are a number of responses. One such is that the New Testament language above represents Christians' experience of their encounter with the Divine through Jesus. It should not be interpreted ontologically and metaphysically but seen as confessional language expressing the normative encounter with God *for Christians*, and not for Jews (or others).[9] This position emphasizes the importance of the *experience* of salvation, outlawing universalized claims based on particular experiences. Hence, Jesus' death and resurrection form the determinative *paradigm* for Christianity and not for other religions. Ruether claims: 'The cross and the Resurrection are a paradigm for Christians, not for "all who would be a part of Israel" or necessarily for "all men". That is to say, it is a paradigm for those for whom it has become a paradigm.'[10]

(4) The fourth argument concerning mission is related to earlier arguments. Again, there are important distinctions.

(a) Christians must abandon mission to the Jews, for the Jews are already in a covenant relationship with God. It is theologically self-contradictory to proselytize among God's chosen people.

(b) Some supplement 4a, arguing that Judaism's existence is required to maintain the true balance of the covenant tradition. Parkes, for instance, wrote of two distinctive covenantal traditions' being preserved by Judaism and Christianity respectively. If one is negated, the other loses its dialectical partner in an ongoing revelatory history. The Sinaitic covenant embodies community and complements Calvary, which emphasizes the individual.[11] Rylaarsdam argues for a similar tension with a different typology.[12]

(c) Some theologians further argue that Christian attitudes to Judaism should encourage a rethinking of Christianity's attitude to other religions. One such theologian is Gregory Baum. He analogically applies the lessons of Christian anti-Semitism to Christian mission in general so that the Christian 'message of hope does not imply that people are called to become Christians out of the great world religions. The Church's claim to be the unique source of saving truth is a judgment on the systems of the world, not on the great world religions.'[13] This is distinguished from those who argue that, while there is no legitimate place for mission to the Jews, mission is valid to the other world religions as they are not analogous to Judaism.[14]

These four areas raise serious questions about Christian identity and

Christianity's relationship to Judaism. These questions revolve around the themes of 'covenant' and 'fulfilment'.

## An examination of the arguments of the Dual-Covenant School

(1) With regard to the theological and sociopolitical negation of Judaism (1a), while it would be difficult to deny anti-Semitism in the Christian tradition, it would be problematic to show an *intrinsic* and necessary link between fulfilment theology and sociohistorical liquidation. My contention is *not* meant to deny that there is and should be justified Christian guilt about the Holocaust. Christian complicity and responsibility for anti-Judaism throughout history is undeniable. No theological or historical arguments can eradicate this fact. My point is to raise the question: Has Christianity the resources to make normative theological claims concerning its universalist nature? More importantly, can it make such claims while preserving the integrity and rights to exist of those from other religions – and especially Judaism?

One may tentatively point to a way of maintaining normative claims and at the same time preserving the integrity and rights of those from other religions. Among the documents of Vatican II is *Dignitatis humanae*, the 'Declaration on Religious Freedom' (1965). This document is important as it stands alongside *Ad gentes*, the 'Decree on Missionary Activity' (1965), which affirms the universal mission of the Church. Based on Christian revelation, the former document affirms 'that the human person has a right to religious freedom' so 'that all men are to be immune from coercion on the part of individuals or of social groups and of any human power, in such wise that in matters religious no one is to be forced to act in a manner contrary to his own beliefs.' It continues: 'The Synod further declares that the right to religious freedom has its foundation in the very dignity of the human person, as this dignity is known through the revealed Word of God and by reason itself' (para. 2).[15] From this it follows, and this is all important, that any form of mission that violates the rights of an individual or community (para. 4) to practice their own religion is against the teachings of the gospel. The document (too timidly) acknowledges that Christians throughout history have fallen short of this requirement (para. 12). Regarding Judaism these statements should be read in conjunction with those in *Nostra aetate*, the 'Declaration on the Relation of the Church to Non-Christian Religions' (1965), wherein there is a solemn condemnation based on 'the gospel's spiritual love' of 'the hatred, persecutions, and displays of anti-Semitism directed against the Jews at any time and from any source' (para. 4).[16] Although these are Roman Catholic documents, I believe that the argument put forward is in keeping with teachings based on the gospel and, therefore, relevant to the wider Christian community.

In light of these reflections I would suggest that Christianity has within its theological resources the ability to affirm the fundamental rights for the existence and practice of Judaism (or any other religion), while at the same time claiming a normative and universal status, including the claim that Christ is the fulfilment of all longings for God and is God's normative self-revelation. I will return to the nature of 'fulfilment' shortly. Here I want to suggest that the thesis that a fulfilment theology is *intrinsically* related to sociohistorical negation is problematic without detracting from Christian complicity and responsibility for the Holocaust.[17]

What of the related argument that a fulfilment theology negates the fidelity of God's covenant with the Jews and the Christian understanding of God requires and ensures such fidelity (that is, argument 1a)? First, it can be said that there is no ambiguity in mainstream Christianity about the valid covenant made with Israel. The inclusion of the 'Old' Testament (more properly, the Hebrew Bible) in the Christian Bible testifies to God's saving and revelatory covenant with the Jews. Second, *if* God develops and seals this covenant through Jesus, then it does not necessarily follow that those who remain Jews and who do not follow Jesus after this time have *actually rejected* the fulfilment of the covenant in Jesus and the Church. This second point can be posited on historical and theological grounds. To take a clear example, during Jesus' time and the subsequent few centuries there were many Jews who would never have heard of the sect of the Nazarenes or their preaching. It is absurd to say that their commitment to the old covenant *after* the time of Jesus was wanting or dishonest. They rightly believed that they were keeping faithful to a valid covenant relationship.

Employing a distinction between the *historical* and *existential* confrontation of the gospel, we can pursue the matter further. By historical, I mean the explicit social and historical encounter with the preaching of the gospel – which many have never experienced. This could be because a person has never been in contact with a Christian (the traditional undiscovered Amazonian tribesperson) or that Christians have obscured the gospel in their preaching through their words, thoughts, and deeds. By existential, I mean the *inner* and personal confrontation with the gospel that should accompany successful historical preaching but is not necessarily concomitant. It may be the case that the gospel is preached, but for many *legitimate* reasons the hearers of this proclamation are resistant to it. For example, the gospel proclamation may be historically associated for them with the

177

destruction and denigration of their own religion and heritage, or it may be associated with the political and economic domination of their kin. This whole area clearly involves a complex network of historical, social, and psychological issues. It also implies the possibility of rejecting Christianity in 'good faith', a matter to which I will return shortly. My point is that for a number of legitimate reasons it cannot always be assumed that when the gospel is preached the listener is truly and existentially confronted by the truth proclaimed in Christ.[18]

It is clear that there were and are many Jewish people who have never been historically or/and existentially confronted with the Christian gospel, and, in this context, the continuing legitimacy of God's faithful covenanting relationship with Judaism cannot be denied – especially within the fulfilment view. As to the Jewish faithfulness to this covenant, it is not appropriate for a non-Jew to pronounce on this matter.

Here I want to make an important qualification regarding the word 'fulfilment'. It has for too long been erroneously assumed that Christianity's 'fulfilment' of another religion is a *fait accompli*. Fulfilment is wrongly seen as a task completed rather than historically enacted and thus ongoing and dynamic. 'Fulfilment' rightly expresses two important aspects of Christianity's meeting with another religion. First, from their time of encounter, all that is worthwhile within another tradition is incorporated into Christianity, not necessarily on its own terms but within a christocentric Trinitarianism. This is precisely the way in which many of the early church Fathers incorporated the heritage of Greek philosophy, and it is the process so well documented by Cardinal Newman in *The Development of Christian Doctrine*. Quite simply, it is the process of indigenization.[19] Second, the fulfilment that takes place should primarily be focused on Christianity's own partial fulfilment, not on the denigration of another religion. In the process of indigenization, many aspects of Christianity's existing tradition and practice may come into question and be subject to penetrating cricism. With indigenization can come purification as well as universalization and growth, and only through this process does Christianity fulfil itself. Much more can be said on this issue, but it is important to correct the triumphalist sense of 'fulfilment' before proceeding to the second set of arguments.

(2) Some dual covenanters have argued that a rejection of Jesus as Messiah was perfectly legitimate on Jewish grounds because God's reign did not accompany Jesus and has not accompanied his followers; evil, suffering, and injustice still prevail.

There has been much recent research on Jewish messianic expectations. The fruits of that research indicate a single point of agreement – that there was no single agreed notion of the Messiah prevailing in Jesus' time.[20] Contrary to Ruether, there was no period of Judaism in which there was an 'integrity of its own tradition about what the word *Messiah*' meant – and, consequently, no easy dismissal of a possibly genuine messianic claim. After all it was the *Jewish* writers of the New Testament who first made this claim. Why, a priori, should their interpretation be rendered illegitimate as against other Jewish interpretations? My first point is to counter simplistic reductions of complex issues and allow for the possibility of authoritative inspiration in the interpretation of tradition.

However, one must admittedly acknowledge considerable scholarly disagreement over: (a) whether Jesus regarded himself as Messiah, (b) in what manner the New Testament writers viewed Jesus as Messiah, and (c) whether the answers to (a) and (b) result in a fulfilment theology. Interestingly, Mussner positively answers (a) and has a high regard for (b), while rejecting a fulfilment view![21] The issues are indeed complex, and here I wish only to point toward a path forward for future exploration.

I would follow Mussner in arguing that Jesus viewed himself as the promised Messiah, while being well aware of nationalist and political messianic expectations, the latter of which he had no wish fo fulfill. (See, for example, John 6.14–16; 18.36–8; Acts 1.8ff.; Pet. 2.13.[22]) Scholem is partly right in discerning an interiorization and individualization of the messianic idea in Christianity. However, through Jesus' social preaching and ministry he proclaimed the imminent reign of God (see, for example, Mark 1.15; 1.21–8; Luke 7.22), and, through his resurrection and the Pentecost event, Christians have properly come to view the beginnings of the eschatological reign, which is to be fulfilled and completed in the second coming. Where I agree with the dual covenanters (and perhaps this will justify my cursory treatment above) is that the reign of God is *not yet* complete. Jesus' messianic ministry has been inaugurated but is not yet fulfilled. Where I disagree is in regard to the significance of this recognition. I would like to propose the following:

First, one cannot simply say that Jesus was not the awaited Jewish Messiah if there is a possibility that Jesus understood himself thus, but, more importantly, his *Jewish* disciples used this term of him. Van Buren acknowledges a once legitimate messianic affirmation while the first followers of Jesus remained Jews. It is only when the Church became predominantly gentile that the Jewish character of the term was misused against the separated siblings.[23] However, it is difficult to imagine that this Jewish sect that preached the Messiah's arrival was not already thereby proclaiming a distinctive element, which caused many of them to be fervent missionaries among their own Jewish communities. Proclaiming the Messiah was part of a complex and multifaceted perception that in some way the longings of Israel had arrived.[24]

Second, while Christians have every right to argue that their particular interpretation of the Messiah is definitive regarding this common history, they must nevertheless acknowledge the plurality of beliefs and expectations held by Jews *in good faith* concerning the Messiah. Hence, a Jewish rejection of Christian claims may be made entirely in good faith and cannot be attributed to sinfulness or wilful error. However, in terms of demonstrating their interpretation, Christians can only point to the Church's messianic ministry and the awaited second coming. Upon this latter event Christians can only hope. There is *no* clearcut evidence. Regarding the Church's messianic ministry, it is often difficult to identify the reign of God through the Church's life! And, in light of Christian participation in the Holocaust, Christians require deep self-inspection and cleansing before they can have any confidence in pointing to the messianic ministry entrusted to the Church. Hence, it is difficult to maintain unambiguously that Jews, past or present, have rejected the Jewish Messiah.

Third, Christianity's messianic claim should be understood in a self-critical fashion. It is primarily a mirror for Christianity to reflect upon and purify itself so that it may truly take the messianic form and shape determined by its founder. Historically, the Church is guilty of constantly falling short of this goal. Rather than abandoning its messianic self-understanding, this very element may lead it out of its anti-Jewish history and into one of true service and solidarity with those who suffer, who are oppressed and downtrodden. Nevertheless, even such attenuated messianic claims leave us with the difficulty of the third set of arguments.

(3) The third argument suggested that biblical language concerning exclusive claims for Jesus be interpreted: (a) confessionally (as expressive injunctions) rather than ontologically, and (b) that the Christian paradigm is only determinative for Christians. (I have dealt with these issues elsewhere and will only briefly outline my counter-arguments here.[25]) First, it should be said that passages like John 14.6 and other seemingly 'exclusivist' texts can be read in a wider biblical context, so that on exegetical grounds a viable inclusivist interpretation is permissible.[26] One need not subvert the entire ontological import of what is admittedly confessional language. However, my main disagreement with this transposition of ontological language into expressivist language is the way in which 'experience' is exalted at the cost of the ontological implications of such experiences. If one experiences God's self-disclosure in Christ, then propositional statements generated from this encounter cannot be entirely

relativized. They are, of course, culture-bound and historically particular expressions, but when the 'object' of reference is God (analogically), these statements, if they are true, must be objectively true and not true just for the believer. Whether they are universally intelligible is another matter entirely. Through revelation the nature of God, humankind, and the world are disclosed, however dimly. Most theists, for instance, resist the suggestion that such disclosures are true only for them but not for others. Others may, for example, deny God's existence, but various explanations are given for this. It would not be usual practice for Christians or for any other religious persons simply to retract their ontological claims, because there may be other contrary or apparently contrary claims.

If we turn to Ruether's comment that the Christian paradigm is 'a paradigm for those for whom it has become a paradigm', we can see that on one level this is tautologous. Ruether is, of course, getting at the fact that only when one uses and accepts this paradigm can it be deemed authoritative. The point, however, is that an authoritative paradigm then affects the understanding and interpretation of other, often competing paradigms. Ruether's use of the word 'paradigm' is significant. When the Copernican paradigm battled with and eventually replaced the Ptolemaic paradigm in the history of science, it was because each paradigm made literal claims about a universal worldview! They could not mutually complement each other in any *ultimate* sense. Similarly, with religions that make cognitive claims about the nature of God, humankind, and the world. If the cross and resurrection truly disclose a triune God, then a person shaped by the Christian paradigm reads off all history from within this paradigm. Only if paradigms were radically incommensurable would Ruether's point carry weight, but then we would not be talking about any relationship – complementary or otherwise.[27]

To relate the discussion to my argument: I have acknowledged the legitimacy of viewing Judaism as a continuing covenant with *God*, but after the Christ event this relationship, as is all of history, is viewed from a Trinitarian perspective. The Christian Bible, in Lindbeck's terms, 'supplies the interpretative framework within which believers seek to live their lives and understand reality. . . . Traditional exegetical procedures . . . assume that Scripture creates its own domain of meaning and that the task of interpretation is to extend this over the whole of reality.'[28] Paradigms inevitably interpret other paradigms and reintegrate them within their own structure of meaning.

My agreement and disagreement with the dual covenanters can now be sharply focused. With them, I have no reservations in acknowledging God's activity throughout creation and history, especially focused in God's

181

covenant-relationship with God's people Israel. Where I part company with them is in my contention that Christianity can do nothing but view salvation history, wherever it occurs, as christological and Trinitarian in its orientation. Furthermore, a christocentric Trinitarianism is not a form of 'closed' revelation, so that the insights, riches, and criticisms from other religions will deepen, purify, and enrich the Christian understanding of God and may, of course, concomitantly involve judgment upon various aspects of Christian practice and theology. Hence, while contact with other paradigms (religions) will challenge and critically develop the articulation and understanding of the Christian paradigm; nevertheless, the Trinitarian and christocentric paradigmatic center will be criteriologically decisive for evaluating and incorporating other paradigms within Christianity's own self-understanding and understanding of the other. If one relinquishes the normative christological criterion for talk of God, one must adopt some other organizing criteria and thereby opt out of 'Christian discourse'. My own view does not deny the presence of other revelatory events but relates and evaluates them in terms of christological and Trinitarian criteria. Hence, it can properly be said that there is only *one* covenant within which there are *many* covenants.[29]

(4) Concerning the argument on mission, much of what I have to say here has been said above. Christians cannot abandon their call to *universal* evangelism on the grounds that they are negating the acknowledged fidelity of God's covenant relationship to the Jews (4a). (I have dealt with this in relation to 1a.) If Christians are to acknowledge elements of a valid covenant relationship within Judaism while remaining faithful to their commitment to Christ, it is clear that they must preserve, respect, and reintegrate much of their own Jewish theological roots in their encounter with Judaism. Hence, the polarities spoken of by Parkes and Rylaarsdam (4b) should be integrated *within the Christian paradigm itself* – as was argued earlier.

In regard to extending the no-missions principle (4c), I would suggest that Christianity's mission to Judaism bears qualified analogy to its relation to the other religions. The lessons from Christianity's anti-Jewish history should be a gruesome reminder of the imperialism latent within the fulfilment model. In this respect missionary activity must be challenged by and reminded of Christianity's past history. Hence, in a sense not intended by the dual covenanters, I would agree that Christianity's relation to Judaism should act as a catalyst in reorienting Christianity's attitude toward the world religions. However, Baum's argument that Christianity's critical 'judgment' refers only to the 'systems of the world' and not to other religions is theologically unbalanced and arbitrary. He fails to be radical enough! In a Barthian sense I would extend the arena of judgment to encompass the world religions as well as the systems of the world and, most importantly, also to Christianity itself. Baum's proposal neutralizes the crimes of Christian history at the cost of relativizing the claims that are part of that history.

If I have rejected the theological restraint on mission to the Jews proposed by dual covenanters, there is yet another major objection to mission that is independent of the fulfilment debate. Rabbi Abraham Heschel reminds us that history, and especially the history of the Holocaust, shapes Jewish perception of Christian mission: 'To the Jew such an attempt to "convert him" appears as an attack on the very existence of the Jews, a call to self-extinction.'[30] As long as such perceptions validly exist, it would be crass insensitivity to proselytize among the Jews. This is not a pragmatic restraint on mission but one founded on theological grounds. If mission violates the 'psychological freedom' of an individual and suggests 'external coercion', then theologically it is questionable and unjustified.[31] All Jews may not agree with Heschel, but, as long as there is even one voice of protest, Christians must seriously consider the appropriateness of mission to the Jews, in view of the Holocaust.

## Conclusion

In this essay I have only begun to develop an alternative approach to the dual-covenant schools. It is an approach that tries to take cognizance of the perplexing issues raised in Jewish-Christian encounter. I have tried to propose a revised version of the fulfilment model that steers clear of the sociopolitical imperialism so often related to this approach. I have also tried to indicate a path by which the legitimate covenant relationship with Judaism is affirmed – as well as the possible legitimate revelations within other religions. However, in contrast to the views examined, I have suggested that it is most theologically coherent to view the many possible covenants within a single revelatory history reaching its normative but proleptic fulfilment in Christ. Christians need not deny other covenants, but their evaluating criteria for discerning such events can only be christocentric, Trinitarian, and ecclesiocentric. Furthermore, in this process of evaluation, Christianity cannot simply claim to be the fulfilment of other religions but will itself be fulfilled through encounter, dialogue, and indigenization.

My closing suggestion is that there is only one normative covenant, within which there are many further legitimate covenants. This is because there is only one God who is self-disclosed in many ways, but for discerning these ways there is only one criterion available to Christians: a christocentric Trinitarianism.

NOTES

1. See John Pawlikowski, *What Are They Saying about Jewish–Christian Relations?*, New York: Paulist Press, 1980, for an overview of the many aspects of the debate.
2. See Rosemary Radford Ruether, *Faith and Fratricide: The Theological Roots of Anti-Semitism*, New York: Seabury Press, 1974, and also the resultant debate: Alan Davies, ed., *Anti-Semitism and the Foundations of Christianity*, New York: Paulist Press, 1979.
3. Some theologians who argue this are: Ruether, *Faith and Fratricide*; James Parkes, *The Theological Foundations of Judaism and Christianity*, London: Vallentine-Mitchell, 1960; J. Coert Rylaarsdam, 'Jewish–Christian Relationship: The Two Covenants and Dilemmas of Christology', in *Journal of Ecumenical Studies* 9, Spring, 1972, pp. 249–68.
4. See, e.g., Ruether, *Faith and Fratricide*, p. 256; Gregory Baum, 'Rethinking the Church's Mission after Auschwitz', in Eva Fleischner, ed., *Auschwitz: Beginning of a New Era? Reflections on the Holocaust*, New York: Ktav Publishing House, the Cathedral of St John the Divine, and the Anti-Defamation League of B'Nai B'rith, 1977, pp. 113–14.
5. I shall mention some theologians classified as 'single covenanters' in the notes, as their arguments sometimes overlap with those of dual covenanters.
6. See for instance, Franz Mussner, *Tractate on the Jews*, London: SPCK and Philadelphia: Fortress Press, 1984, pp. 16–36.
7. See for instance, Ruether, *Faith and Fratricide*, pp. 214–25.
8. ibid., p. 245; see also Monika Hellwig, 'Christian Theology and the Covenant of Israel', *Journal of Ecumenical Studies*, 7, Winter, 1970, p. 49.
9. See Hellwig, 'Christian Theology', p. 49.
10. Ruether, *Faith and Fratricide*, p. 250.
11. See Parkes, *Theological Foundations*, pp. 30ff.
12. See Rylaarsdam, 'Jewish–Christian Relationship'.
13. Baum, 'Rethinking', p. 124.
14. See Hans Küng, *The Church*, London: Search Press, 1981, pp. 132–50.
15. Walter M. Abbott, ed., *The Documents of Vatican II*, New York: Herder and Herder, and Association Press, 1966, pp. 678–9.
16. ibid., pp. 666–7. See also John Oesterreicher's commentary on this document, originally intended to address the Jews, in Herbert Vorgrimler, ed., *Commentary on the Documents of Vatican II*, Vol. 3, London: Burns & Oates; New York: Herder and Herder, 1969, pp. 1–136.
17. See Yosef Hayim Yerushalmi's critical response to Ruether in Fleischner, *Auschwitz*, pp. 97–107; and Alan Davies, 'On Religious Myths and Their Secular Translation: Some Historical Reflections', in Davies, *Anti-Semitism*, pp. 188–207.
18. See Yves Congar, *The Wide World My Parish*, London: Darton, Longman and Todd, 1961, pp. 121–7.
19. The wider historical dynamic and cross-fertilization resulting in such a process is

well illustrated in Arnulf Camps, *Partners in Dialogue: Christianity and Other World Religions*, Maryknoll, NY: Orbis, 1983; and Gavin D'Costa, *Theology and Religious Pluralism*, Oxford and New York: Basil Blackwell, 1986, ch. 5.

20. See especially Gershom Scholem, *The Messianic Idea in Judaism*, London: George Allen and Unwin, 1971.

21. See Mussner, *Tractate*.

22. See also Oscar Cullmann, *The Christology of the New Testament*, London: SCM Press, 1963, pp. 113–33; and especially C. F. D. Moule, *The Origins of Christology*, Cambridge: Cambridge University Press, 1977, pp. 31–5.

23. Paul van Buren, *A Christian Theology of the People Israel*, Part 2, New York: Seabury Press, 1983, pp. 276–7.

24. See Moule, *Origins*, ch. 5.

25. See Gavin D'Costa, *John Hick's Theology of Religions*, Lanham, London and New York: University Press of America, 1988, chs. 3—4; and *Theology and Religious Pluralism*, ch. 2.

26. See for instance, Kenneth Cracknell, *Towards a New Relationship*, London: Epworth, 1986, chs. 1—2.

27. See Gavin D'Costa, 'Elephants, Ropes, and a Christian Theology of Religions', *Theology* 88, July, 1985, pp. 259–68, for an example of the use and abuse of the notion of paradigm in an interreligious context.

28. George Lindbeck, *The Nature of Doctrine*, Philadelphia: Westminster Press, 1984, p. 117.

29. See my 'Christ, the Trinity, and Religious Plurality', in D'Costa, ed., *Christian Uniqueness Reconsidered: The Myth of a Pluralistic Theology of Religions*, Faith Meets Faith Series, Maryknoll, NY: Orbis, 1990, pp. 16–29.

30. Cited in António Barbosa Da Silva, *Is There a New Imbalance in the Jewish–Christian Relation?*, Uppsala: Teologiska institutionen, 1985, p. 113.

31. See *Dignitatis humanae*, para. 2.

# E: Christ and Post-Modernism

18  GEORGE A. LINDBECK's 'The Nature of Doctrine: Toward a Postliberal Theology' comes from his *The Nature of Doctrine: Religion and Theology in a Postliberal Age* (Philadelphia: Westminster Press, and London: SPCK, 1984, pp. 116–28; 135–7). His other book is *The Future of Roman Catholic Theology: Vatican II: Catalyst for Change* (Philadelphia: Fortress Press, 1970). He also features in Bruce D. Marshall, ed., *Theology and Dialogue: Essays in Conversation with George Lindbeck* (Ind.: University of Notre Dame Press, 1990).

19  DAVID F. FORD's '*The Nature of Doctrine*: a review' was published in *Journal of Theological Studies* in 1986 (Vol. 37, pp. 277–82). His books are *Barth and God's Story: Biblical Narrative and the Theological Method of Karl Barth in the 'Church Dogmatics'* (Frankfurt: Lang, 1981); with Daniel Hardy, *Jubilate: Theology in Praise* (London: Darton, Longman and Todd, 1984: American title *Praising and Knowing God*, Philadelphia: Westminster Press, 1985); and with Frances Young, *Meaning and Truth in 2 Corinthians* (Grand Rapids, Michigan: Eerdman's, 1989). He has also edited the two volume *The Modern Theologians: An Introduction to Christian Theology in the Twentieth Century* (Oxford and New York: Blackwell, 1989).

20  DAVID B. BURRELL's '*The Nature of Doctrine*: a review' was published in *Union Seminary Quarterly Review* in 1984 (Vol. XXXIX, No. 4, pp. 322–4). His books include *Aquinas: God and Action* (Ind.: University of Notre Dame Press, 1979) and *Freedom and Creation in Three Traditions* (Ind.: University of Notre Dame Press, 1993). He has also edited *God and Creation: An Ecumenical Symposium* (Ind.: University of Notre Dame Press, 1990).

21  GEOFFREY WAINWRIGHT's 'Ecumenical Dimensions of Lindbeck's *The Nature of Doctrine*' was published in *Modern Theology* in January 1988 (Vol. 4, No. 2, pp. 121–32). His books are *Eucharist and Eschatology* (London: Epworth Press, 1975);

*Doxology: The Praise of God in Worship, Doctrine and Life: A Systematic Theology* (Oxford and New York: Oxford University Press, 1980); and *The Ecumenical Movement: Crisis and Opportunity for the Church* (Grand Rapids, Michigan: Eerdmans, 1983). He has also edited *Keeping the Faith: Essays to Mark the Centenary of 'Lux Mundi'* (Philadelphia: Fortress Press, 1988) and with Max Thurian, *Baptism and Eucharist: Ecumenical Convergence in Celebration* (Geneva: WCC, and Grand Rapids, Michigan: Eerdmans, 1983).

22    DAVID TRACY's 'Theology and the Many Faces of Postmodernity' was published in *Theology Today* in April 1994 (Vol. 51, No. 1, pp. 104–14). For his books see entry (7).

23    DAVID H. KELSEY's 'Whatever Happened to the Doctrine of Sin?' was published in *Theology Today* in July 1993 (Vol. 50, No. 2, pp. 169–78). His books are *The Uses of Scripture in Recent Theology* (Philadelphia: Fortress Press, 1975); *To Understand God Truly: What's Theological About a Theological School?* (Louisville, Kentucky: Westminster/John Knox, 1992); and *Between Athens and Berlin: The Theological Education Debate* (Grand Rapids, Michigan: Eerdmans, 1993).

24    DON CUPITT's 'After Liberalism' was published in Daniel Hardy and Peter Sedgwick, eds., *The Weight of Glory: A Vision and Practice for Christian Faith: The Future of Liberal Theology* (Edinburgh: T & T Clark, 1991, pp. 251–6). Amongst his many books are *The Leap of Reason* (London: Sheldon Press, 1976); *The Debate About Christ* (London: SCM Press, 1979); *Jesus and the Gospel of God* (Guildford: Lutterworth Press, 1979); *The Nature of Man* (London: Sheldon Press, 1979); *Taking Leave of God* (London: SCM Press, and New York: Crossroad, 1980); *The World to Come* (London: SCM Press, 1982); *The Sea of Faith* (London: BBC, 1984); *Christ and the Hiddenness of God* (London: SCM Press, 1985); *Life Lines* (London: SCM Press, 1986); *The Long-Legged Fly: A Theology of Language and Desire* (London: SCM Press, 1987); *The New Christian Ethics* (London: SCM Press, 1988); *Creation Out of Nothing* (London: SCM Press, and Philadelphia: Trinity Press, 1990); and *After All: Religion Without Alienation* (London: SCM Press, 1994).

∽∽∽∽∽∽∽∽∽∽∽∽∽∽∽∽∽∽∽∽∽∽∽∽∽∽∽∽∽∽∽∽∽∽∽∽∽∽∽∽

# 18

# THE NATURE OF DOCTRINE: TOWARDS A POSTLIBERAL THEOLOGY
## George A. Lindbeck

The importance of texts and of intratextuality for theological faithfulness becomes clearer when we consider the unwritten religions of nonliterate societies. Evans-Pritchard[1] tells of a Nuer tribesman who excitedly reported to him that a woman in the village had given birth to twins, both dead, and that one was a hippopotamus and had been placed in a stream, and the other a bird and had been placed in a tree. There are in that society no canonical documents to consult in order to locate these puzzling events within the wider contexts that give them meaning. Is the equation of dead twins with birds and hippopotami central or peripheral to Nuer thought and life? Would the religion and culture be gravely disturbed if this equation were eliminated? Even the wisest of Evans-Pritchard's informants might not have understood these questions, and even if they did, they presumably would have had no idea of how to reach a consensus in answering them. In oral cultures there is no transpersonal authority to which the experts on tradition can refer their disputes. This helps explain why purely customary religions and cultures readily dissolve under the pressure of historical, social, and linguistic change, but it also suggests that canonical texts are a condition, not only for the survival of a religion but for the very possibility of normative theological description. In any case, whether or not this is universally true, the intrasemiotic character of descriptive theology is inseparable from intratextuality in the three Western monotheisms – Judaism, Christianity, and Islam. These are pre-eminently religions of the book.

We need now to speak in more detail of how to interpret a text in terms of its immanent meanings – that is, in terms of the meanings immanent in the religious language of whose use the text is a paradigmatic instance. On the informal level this is not a problem; it becomes so, as we shall see, only when theology becomes alienated from those ways of reading classics,[2] whether religious or nonreligious, which seem natural within a given culture or society. Masterpieces such as *Oedipus Rex* and *War and Peace*, for example, evoke their own domains of meaning. They do so by what they themselves say about the events and personages of which they tell. In order to understand them in their own terms, there is no need for extraneous references to, for example, Freud's theories or historical treatments of the Napoleonic wars. Further, such works shape the imagination and perceptions of the attentive reader so that he or she forever views the world to some extent through the lenses they supply. To describe the basic meaning of these books is an intratextual task, a matter of explicating their contents and the perspectives on extratextual reality that they generate.[3]

These same considerations apply even more forcefully to the pre-eminently authoritative texts that are the canonical writings of religious communities. For those who are steeped in them, no world is more real than the ones they create. A scriptural world is thus able to absorb the universe. It supplies the interpretive framework within which believers seek to live their lives and understand reality. This happens quite apart from formal theories. Augustine did not describe his work in the categories we are employing, but the whole of his theological production can be understood as a progressive, even if not always successful, struggle to insert everything from Platonism and the Pelagian problem to the fall of Rome into the world of the Bible. Aquinas tried to do something similar with Aristotelianism, and Schleiermacher with German romantic idealism. The way they described extrascriptural realities and experience, so it can be argued, was shaped by biblical categories much more than was warranted by their formal methodologies.

In the case of Aquinas especially, however, the shaping was in part methodologically legitimated. Traditional exegetical procedures (of which he gives one of the classic descriptions[4]) assume that Scripture creates its own domain of meaning and that the task of interpretation is to extend this over the whole of reality. The particular ways of doing this depend, to be sure, on the character of the religion and its texts. One set of interpretive techniques is appropriate when the Torah is the center of the Scripture, another when it is the story of Jesus, and still another when it is the Buddha's enlightenment and teachings. For the most part, we shall limit our observations on this point to the Christian case.

Here there was a special though not exclusive emphasis on typological or figural devices, first to unify the canon, and second to encompass the cosmos. Typology was used to incorporate the Hebrew Scriptures into a canon that focused on Christ, and then, by extension, to embrace extrabiblical reality. King David, for example, was in some respects a typological foreshadowing of Jesus, but he was also, in Carolingian times, a type for Charlemagne and, in Reformation days, as even Protestants said, for Charles V in his wars against the Turks. Thus an Old Testament type, filtered through the New Testament antitype, became a model for later kings and, in the case of Charlemagne, provided a documentable stimulus to the organization of the educational and parish systems that stand at the institutional origins of Western civilization. Unlike allegorizing, typological interpretation did not empty Old Testament or postbiblical personages and events of their own reality,[5] and therefore they constituted a powerful means for imaginatively incorporating all being into a Christ-centered world.

It is important to note the direction of interpretation. Typology does not make scriptural contents into metaphors for extrascriptural realities, but the other way around. It does not suggest, as is often said in our day, that believers find their stories in the Bible, but rather that they make the story of the Bible their story. The cross is not to be viewed as a figurative representation of suffering nor the messianic kingdom as a symbol for hope in the future; rather, suffering should be cruciform, and hopes for the future messianic. More generally stated, it is the religion instantiated in Scripture which defines being, truth, goodness, and beauty, and the nonscriptural exemplifications of these realities need to be transformed into figures (or types or antitypes) of the scriptural ones. Intratextual theology redescribes reality within the scriptural framework rather than translating Scripture into extrascriptural categories. It is the text, so to speak, which absorbs the world, rather than the world the text.

There is always the danger, however, that the extrabiblical materials inserted into the biblical universe will themselves become the basic framework of interpretation. This is what happened, so the Christian mainstream concluded, in the case of Gnosticism. Here Hellenism became the interpreter rather than the interpreted. The Jewish rabbi who is the crucified and resurrected Messiah of the New Testament accounts was transformed into a mythological figure illustrative of thoroughly nonscriptural meanings. Nor did the mainstream wholly escape the danger. It creedally insisted that the Jesus spoken of in Scripture is the Lord, but it often read Scripture in so Hellenistic a way that this Jesus came to resemble a semipagan demigod. The doctrinal consensus on the primacy of Scripture, on the canonical status of the Old as well as the New Testament, and on the full humanity of Christ was not by itself enough to maintain an integrally scriptural framework within which to interpret the classical heritage which the Church sought to Christianize. Better theological and exegetical procedures were needed.

Up through the Reformation, this need was in part filled through the typological methods we have already noted. As one moves in the West from Augustine, through Aquinas, to Luther and Calvin, there is an increasing resistance to indiscriminate allegorizing and an insistence on the primacy of a specifiable literal intratextual sense. Whatever the failures in actual execution, and they were many, the interpretive direction was from the Bible to the world rather than vice versa.

In the Reformers, it should be noted, the resistance to allegorizing and the greater emphasis on intratextuality (*scriptura sui ipsius interpres*) did not diminish but heightened the emphasis on proclamation, on the preached word. Scripture, one might say, was interpreted by its use,[6] by the *viva vox evangelii*. In the intratextual context, this emphasis on the living word involves applying the language, concepts, and categories of Scripture to contemporary realities, and is different in its intellectual, practical, and homiletical consequences from liberal attempts, of which Ebeling's is the most notable,[7] to understand the Reformation notion of the word of God in terms of an experiential 'word event'.

As the work of Hans Frei shows,[8] the situation has changed radically in recent centuries, and new difficulties have arisen. Typological interpretation collapsed under the combined onslaughts of rationalistic, pietistic, and historical-critical developments. Scripture ceased to function as the lens through which theologians viewed the world and instead became primarily an object of study whose religiously significant or literal meaning was located outside itself. The primarily literary approaches of the past with their affinities to informal ways of reading the classics in their own terms were replaced by fundamentalist, historical-critical, and expressivist preoccupations with facticity or experience. The intratextual meanings of Scripture continue informally to shape the imagination of the West (even atheistic Marxists think of history as the unfolding of a determinate pattern with an ultimately ineluctable outcome), but theologians do not make these meanings methodologically primary. Instead, if they are existentially inclined, they reinterpret the notion of providential guidance, for example, as a symbolic expression of confidence in the face of the vicissitudes of life; or, if they objectivize, they might, as did Teilhard de Chardin, interpret providence in terms of an optimistic version of evolutionary science. Whether it will be possible to regain a specifically biblical understanding of providence depends in part on the possibility of theologically reading Scripture once again in literary rather than nonliterary ways.

The depth of the present crisis is best seen when one considers that even those who doctrinally agree that the story of Jesus is the key to the understanding of reality are often in fundamental theological disagreement over what the story is really about, over its normative or literal sense.[9] Is the literal meaning of the story the history it is on some readings supposed to record, and if so, is this history that of the fundamentalist or of the historical critic? Or is the real meaning, the theologically important meaning, the way of being in the world which the story symbolizes, or the liberating actions and attitudes it expresses, or the ethical ideals it instantiates, or the metaphysical truths about God-manhood it illustrates, or the gospel promises it embodies? Each of these ways of construing the story depends on a distinct interpretive framework (historical, phenomenological, existential, ethical, metaphysical, doctrinal) that specifies the questions asked of the text and shapes the pictures of Jesus that emerge. These pictures may all be formally orthodox in the sense that they are reconcilable with Nicaea, but their implications for religious practice and understanding are radically divergent. Nothing better illustrates the point made in earlier chapters that for most purposes theological issues are more crucial and interesting than doctrinal ones.

The intratextual way of dealing with this problem depends heavily on literary considerations. The normative or literal meaning must be consistent with the kind of text it is taken to be by the community for which it is important. The meaning must not be esoteric: not something behind, beneath, or in front of the text; not something that the text reveals, discloses, implies, or suggests to those with extraneous metaphysical, historical, or experiential interests. It must rather be what the text says in terms of the communal language of which the text is an instantiation. A legal document should not be treated in quasi-kabbalistic fashion as first of all a piece of expressive symbolism (though it may secondarily be that also); nor should the Genesis account of creation be turned fundamentalistically into science; nor should one turn a realistic narrative (which a novel also can be) into history (or, alternatively, as the historical critic is wont to do, into a source of clues for the reconstruction of history). If the literary character of the story of Jesus, for example, is that of utilizing, as realistic narratives do, the interaction of purpose and circumstance to render the identity description of an agent, then it is Jesus' identity as thus rendered, not his historicity, existential significance, or metaphysical status, which is the literal and theologically controlling meaning of the tale.[10] The implications of the story for determining the metaphysical status, or existential significance, or historical career of Jesus Christ may have varying degrees of theological importance, but they are not determinative. The believer, so an intratextual approach would maintain, is not told primarily to be conformed to a reconstructed Jesus of history (as Hans Küng maintains),[11] nor to a metaphysical Christ of faith (as in much of the propositionalist tradition),[12] nor to an abba experience of God (as for Schillebeeckx),[13] nor to an agapeic way of being in the world (as for David Tracy),[14] but he or she is rather to be conformed to the Jesus Christ depicted in the narrative. An intratextual reading tries to derive the interpretive framework that designates the theologically controlling sense from the literary structure of the text itself.[15]

This type of literary approach can be extended to cover, not simply the story of Jesus, but all of Scripture. What is the literary genre of the Bible as a whole in its canonical unity? What holds together the diverse materials it contains: poetic, prophetic, legal, liturgical, sapiential, mythical, legendary, and historical? These are all embraced, it would seem, in an overarching story that has the specific literary features of realistic narrative as exemplified in diverse ways, for example, by certain kinds of parables, novels, and historical accounts. It is as if the Bible were a 'vast, loosely-structured, non-fictional novel' (to use a phrase David Kelsey applies to Karl Barth's view of Scripture).[16]

Further, it is possible to specify the primary function of the canonical narrative (which is also the function of many of its most important component stories from the Pentateuch to the Gospels). It is 'to render a character. . . , offer an identity description of an agent,'[17] namely God. It does this, not by telling what God is in and of himself, but by accounts of the interaction of his deeds and purposes with those of creatures in their ever-changing circumstances. These accounts reach their climax in what the Gospels say of the risen, ascended, and ever-present Jesus Christ whose identity as the divine-human agent is unsubstitutably enacted in the stories of Jesus of Nazareth. The climax, however, is logically inseparable from what precedes it. The Jesus of the Gospels is the Son of the God of Abraham, Isaac, and Jacob in the same strong sense that the Hamlet of Shakespeare's play is Prince of Denmark. In both cases, the title with its reference to the wider context irreplaceably rather than contingently identifies the bearer of the name.

It is easy to see how theological descriptions of a religion may on this view need to be materially diverse even when the formal criterion of faithfulness remains the same. The primary focus is not on God's being in itself, for that is not what the text is about, but on how life is to be lived and reality construed in the light of God's character as an agent as this is depicted in the stories of Israel and of Jesus. Life, however, is not the same in catacombs and space shuttles, and reality is different for, let us say, Platonists and Whiteheadians. Catacomb dwellers and astronauts might rightly emphasize diverse aspects of the biblical accounts of God's character and action in describing their respective situations. Judging by catacomb paintings, the first group often saw themselves as sheep in need of a shepherd, while the second group would perhaps be well advised to stress God's grant to human beings of stewardship over planet Earth.

193

Similarly, Platonic and Whiteheadian differences over the nature of reality lead to sharp disagreements about the proper characterization of God's metaphysical properties, while antimetaphysicians, in turn, argue that no theory of divine attributes is consistent with the character of the biblical God.

Yet all these theologies could agree that God is appropriately depicted in stories about a being who created the cosmos without any humanly fathomable reason, but – simply for his own good pleasure and the pleasure of his goodness – appointed *Homo sapiens* stewards of one minuscule part of this cosmos, permitted appalling evils, chose Israel and the Church as witnessing peoples, and sent Jesus as Messiah and Immanuel, God with us. The intention of these theologies, whether successful or unsuccessful, could in every case be to describe life and reality in ways conformable to what these stories indicate about God. They could, to repeat, have a common intratextual norm of faithfulness despite their material disagreements.

Intratextual theologies can also, however, disagree on the norm. They can dispute over whether realistic narrative is the best or only way to identify the distinctive genre and interpretive framework of the Christian canon, and, even if it is, on how to characterize the divine agent at work in the biblical stories. More fundamentally, they could disagree on the extent and unity of the canon. If Revelation and Daniel are the center of Scripture, as they seem to be for Scofield Bible premillennialists, a very different picture of God's agency and purposes emerges. Further, as current debates over feminism vividly remind us, past tradition or present consensus can serve as extensions of the canon and deeply influence the interpretation of the whole. These extensions can on occasion go beyond the specifically Christian or religious realm. The philosophical tradition from Plato to Heidegger operates as the canonical corpus for much Western reflection on God or the human condition; and when this reflection is recognized as operating with a peculiarly Western rather than transculturally available idiom, it begins to acquire some of the features of intratextuality.[18] In short, intratextuality may be a condition for the faithful description and development of a religion or tradition, but the material or doctrinal consequences of this self-evidently depend in part on what canon is appealed to.

It must also be noted that intratextuality in a postcritical or postliberal mode is significantly different from traditional precritical varieties. We now can make a distinction (unavailable before the development of modern science and historical studies) between realistic narrative and historical or scientific descriptions. The Bible is often 'history-like' even when it is not 'likely history'. It can therefore be taken seriously in the first respect as a delineator of the character of divine and human agents, even when its history or science is challenged. As parables such as that of the prodigal son remind us, the rendering of God's character is not in every instance logically dependent on the facticity of the story.

Further, historical criticism influences the theological-literary inter-pretation of texts. A postcritical narrative reading of Scripture such as is found to some extent in von Rad's work on the Old Testament[19] is notably different from a precritical one. Or, to cite a more specific example, if the historical critic is right that the Johannine 'Before Abraham was, I am' (John 8.58) is not a self-description of the preresurrection Jesus but a communal confession of faith, then even those who fully accept the confession will want to modify traditional theological descriptions of what Jesus was in his life on earth. They may agree doctrinally with Chalcedon, but prefer a Pauline *theologia crucis* to the Christological *theologia gloriae* that is often associated with Chalcedon (and that one finds even in great exponents of the theology of the cross such as Luther). Nevertheless, in an intratextual approach, literary considerations are more important than historical-critical ones in determining the canonical sense even in cases such as this. It is because the literary genre of John is clearly not that of veridical history that the statement in question can be readily accepted as a communal confession rather than a self-description.

Finally, and more generally, the postcritical focus on intratextual meanings does involve a change in attitude toward some aspects of the text that were important for premodern interpretation. The physical details of what, if anything, happened on Mt Sinai, for example, are no longer of direct interest for typological or figurative purposes, as they often were for the tradition, but the basic questions remain much the same: What is the nature and function of Torah? It is in the New Testament custodial in Israel and fulfilled in Christ, but what does this imply for later Christianity and its relations to Judaism? Is not Torah by analogical extension both custodial and fulfilled for Christian communities in this age before the end when fulfillment is not yet final; and does this not make Christians much closer to Jews than they have generally thought? What, furthermore, does the Holocaust have to do with Mt Sinai, on the one hand, and another mountain, Calvary, on the other? As these questions indicate, a postliberal intratextuality provides warrants for imaginatively and conceptually incorporating postbiblical worlds into the world of the Bible in much the same fashion as did the tradition. But the consequences inevitably will often be very different because of changes in the extrabiblical realities that are to be typologically interpreted and because of the more rigorous intratextuality made necessary by a critical approach to history.

In concluding this discussion, it needs to be reiterated that the practice of intratextuality is only loosely related to explicit theory. Just as good grammarians or mathematicians may be quite wrongheaded in their understanding of what they in fact actually do, so also with theologians. There is no reason for surprise if an apparent propositionalist, such as Aquinas, or an undoubted experiential-expressivist, such as Schleiermacher, were more intratextual in their actual practice than their theories would seem to allow. Their performance would perhaps have improved if their theories of religion had been different, but this is true only if other conditions remained equal. Native genius and religious commitment are helpful, but in order to convert these into theological competence one also needs a supportive environment, the tutelage of expert practitioners, and assiduous practice in a complex set of unformalizable skills that even the best theoretician cannot adequately characterize. Where these conditions are lacking, even good theory cannot greatly enhance performance, and where they are present, poor theory may be relatively harmless.

The implications of these observations do not bode well, however, for the future of postliberal theology. Even if it were to become theoretically popular, the result might chiefly be talk about intratextuality rather than more and better intratextual practice. The conditions for practice seem to be steadily weakening. Disarray in church and society makes the transmission of the necessary skills more and more difficult. Those who share in the intellectual high culture of our day are rarely intensively socialized into coherent religious languages and communal forms of life. This is not necessarily disastrous for the long-range prospects of religion (which is not dependent on élites), but it is for theology as an intellectually and academically creative enterprise capable of making significant contributions to the wider culture and society. Further, theology (in the sense of reflection in the service of religion) is being increasingly replaced in seminaries as well as universities by religious studies. There are fewer and fewer institutional settings favorable to the intratextual interpretation of religion and of extrascriptural realities.[20] Perhaps the last American theologian who in practice (and to some extent in theory) made extended and effective attempts to redescribe major aspects of the contemporary scene in distinctively Christian terms was Reinhold Niebuhr. After the brief neo-orthodox interlude (which was itself sometimes thoroughly liberal in its theological methodology, as in the case of Paul Tillich), the liberal tendency to redescribe religion in extrascriptural frameworks has once again become dominant. This is understandable. Religions have become foreign texts that are much easier to translate into currently popular categories than to read in terms of their intrinsic sense. Thus the fundamental obstacles to intratextual theological faithfulness may well derive from the psychosocial situation rather than from scholarly or intellectual considerations. . . .

Concern for the future has traditionally been associated in biblical religions with prophecy. Prophets proclaim what is both faithful and applicable in a given situation, and they oppose proposals that, whatever their apparent practicality, are doomed because of their unfaithfulness to God's future. To be sure, as biblical scholars remind us, prophetic utterances are not predictions in the ordinary sense. Jonah was disappointed by the nonfulfillment of his prophecies against Nineveh, but this did not make him doubt that God had spoken. The repentance that averted the destruction of the city was, so to speak, the point of the prophecy. Similarly, the nonfulfillment of expectations of an imminent Parousia have rarely been taken by those who shared them as evidence that Christ would not return. A similar logic operates in much nonreligious forecasting. The failure of Marxist and other secular anticipations of the early demise of religion does not disconfirm secularism, and the predictive inadequacies of contemporary futurology[21] have not discouraged its practitioners. In all these cases, the purpose is not to foretell what is to come, but to shape present action to fit the anticipated and hoped-for future.

Theological forms of this activity are more like contemporary futurology than biblical prophecy. Unlike prophecy, futurology does not depend on first-order inspiration or intuition, but is a second-order enterprise that draws on the full range of empirical studies in an effort to discover 'the signs of the times'.[22] As we have noted, these signs vary greatly from one overall pattern of interpretation to another – from, for example, Marxist to non-Marxist views. In the case of Christian theology, the purpose is to discern those possibilities in current situations that can and should be cultivated as anticipations or preparations for the hoped-for future, the coming kingdom. In brief, a theological proposal is adjudged both faithful and applicable to the degree that it appears practical in terms of an eschatologically and empirically defensible scenario of what is to come.

In the construction of such scenarios, the crucial difference between liberals and postliberals is in the way they correlate their visions of the future and of present situations. Liberals start with experience, with an account of the present, and then adjust their vision of the kingdom of God accordingly, while postliberals are in principle committed to doing the reverse. The first procedure makes it easier to accommodate the present trends, whether from the right or the left: Christian fellow travelers of both Nazism and Stalinism generally used liberal methodology to justify their positions. When, in contrast to this, one looks at the present in the light of an intratextually derived eschatology, one gets a different view of which contemporary developments are likely to be ultimately significant. Similar practical recommendations may at times be advanced, but for dissimilar theological reasons. A postliberal might argue, for example, that traditional sexual norms should be revised because the situation has changed from when they were formulated or because they are not intratextually faithful – but not, as some liberals may be inclined to argue, on the grounds that sexual liberation is an advance toward the eschatological future. Postliberalism is methodologically committed to neither traditionalism nor progressivism, but its resistance to current fashions, to making present experience revelatory, may often result in conservative stances. Yet there are numerous occasions in which the intratextual norm requires the rejection of the old in favor of the new.

These comments on method, however, leave untouched the question of the possible contemporary relevance of postliberalism. Earlier chapters suggested that a cultural-linguistic approach is supported by intellectual trends in nontheological disciplines, and that it can in its own way accommodate some of the main religious concerns that make experiential-expressivism appealing. Yet we also noted that the present psychosocial situation is more favorable to liberalism than to postliberalism. Sociologists have been telling us for a hundred years or more than the rationalization, pluralism, and mobility of modern life dissolve the bonds of tradition and community. This produces multitudes of men and women who are impelled, if they have religious yearnings, to embark on their own individual quests for symbols of transcendence. The churches have become purveyors of this commodity rather than communities that socialize their members into coherent and comprehensive religious outlooks and forms of life. Society paradoxically conditions human beings to experience selfhood as somehow prior to social influences, and Eastern religions and philosophies are utilized to support what, from a cultural-linguistic perspective, is the myth of the transcendental ego. Selfhood is experienced as a given rather than as either a gift or an achievement, and fulfillment comes from exfoliating or penetrating into the inner depths rather than from communally responsible action in the public world. Thus the cultural climate is on the whole antithetical to postliberalism.

One can argue, furthermore, that there is little likelihood that the cultural trends favoring experiential-expressivism will be reversed in the realistically foreseeable future. If the nations are to avoid nuclear or environmental destruction, they will have to become ever more unified. What the world will need is some kind of highly generalized outlook capable of providing a framework for infinitely diversified religious quests. Experiential-expressivism with its openness to the hypothesis of an underlying unity can, it would seem, better fill this need than a cultural-linguistic understanding of religion with its stress on particularity. Western monotheisms especially appear to be disqualified because, on an intratextual reading, these religions cannot without suicide surrender their claims to the universal and unsurpassable validity of very specific identifications of the Ultimate with the God of Abraham, Isaac, and Jacob; of Jesus; or of the Koran. The future belongs, on this view, to liberal interpretations of religion.

In the speculative domain of futurology, however, it is easy to mount counter-arguments. It can be pointed out that the indefinite extrapolation of present trends is a questionable procedure because any given tendency, if carried far enough, destroys the conditions for its own existence. When liberation from constraints produces chaos, the result is new bondage, and law and order are once again experienced as conditions for freedom. Law and order when unchecked, however, create rigidities that harbor the seeds of their own destruction. Similarly, the viability of a unified world of the future may well depend on counteracting the acids of modernity. It may depend on communal enclaves that socialize their members into highly particular outlooks supportive of concern for others rather than for individual rights and entitlements, and of a sense of responsibility for the wider society rather than for personal fulfillment. It is at least an open question whether any religion will have the requisite toughness for this demanding task unless it at some point makes the claim that it is significantly different and unsurpassably true; and it is easier for a religion to advance this claim if it is interpreted in cultural-linguistic rather than experiential-expressive terms. Thus it may well be that postliberal theologies are more applicable than liberal ones to the needs of the future.

These considerations gain in force when one considers what may be necessary for the viability, not of a world order, but of cultural traditions such as the Western one. If the Bible has shaped the imagination of the West to anywhere near the degree that Northrop Frye, for example, has argued,[23] then the West's continuing imaginative vitality and creativity may well depend on the existence of groups for whom the Hebrew and Christian Scriptures are not simply classics among others, but the canonical literature par excellence, and who are also in close contact with the wider culture. Much the same argument could be advanced in reference to the

Koran and Islamic culture, and perhaps something analogous applies to the religions and cultures of the Far East despite their lack of equally well-defined pre-eminent canons. The general point is that, provided a religion stresses service rather than domination, it is likely to contribute more to the future of humanity if it preserves its own distinctiveness and integrity than if it yields to the homogenizing tendencies associated with liberal experiential-expressivism.

This conclusion is paradoxical: religious communities are likely to be practically relevant in the long run to the degree that they do not first ask what is either practical or relevant, but instead concentrate on their own intratextual outlooks and forms of life. The much-debated problem of the relation of theory and praxis is thus dissolved by the communal analogue of justification by faith. As is true for individuals, so also a religious community's salvation is not by works, nor is its faith for the sake of practical efficacy, and yet good works of unforeseeable kinds flow from faithfulness. It was thus, rather than by intentional effort, that biblical religion helped produce democracy and science, as well as other values Westerners treasure; and it is in similarly unimaginable and unplanned ways, if at all, that biblical religion will help save the world (for Western civilization is now world civilization) from the demonic corruptions of these same values.

These arguments for the applicability of postliberal approaches cannot be neutrally evaluated. Those who think that religions are more the sources than the products of experience will regard a loss of religious particularity as impoverishing, while others will consider it enriching. Comprehensive frameworks of interpretation provide their own standards of relevance, and thus both liberal and postliberal outlooks have no difficulty in reading the signs of the times in such a way as to justify their own practicality.

NOTES

1. E. E. Evans-Pritchard, *Neur Religion*, Oxford: Oxford University Press, 1956, p. 84. This 'notorious ethnographic example' is cited by T. M. S. Evans, 'On the Social Anthropology of Religions', *Journal of Religion*, 62/4, 1982, p. 376.
2. Unlike David Tracy, *The Analogical Imagination*, New York: Crossroad, and London: SCM Press, 1981, I am using 'classic' to refer to texts that are culturally established for whatever reason. Tracy's model, in contrast to mine, is experiential-expressive. For him classics are 'certain expressions of the human spirit [which] so disclose a compelling truth about our lives that we cannot deny them some kind of normative status' (p. 108).
3. This and the following descriptions of intratextuality were composed without conscious reference to deconstructionism, but, given the current prominence of

this form of literary theory, some tentative comments on similarities and dissimilarities may be desirable in order to avoid misunderstandings. First, intratextualism, like deconstructionism, does not share the traditional literary emphasis on a text as that which is to be interpreted, whether (as in the now-old 'New Criticism') as a self-contained aesthetic object or 'verbal icon', or as mimetic, or as expressive, or as pragmatic. (For the meaning of these terms, see Meyer H. Abrams, *The Mirror and the Lamp: Romantic Theory and the Critical Tradition*, Oxford: Oxford University Press, 1953, cited by M. A. Tolbert, *Religious Study Review* 8/1, 1982, p. 2.) Instead, intratextualism treats texts as 'mediums of interpretation', and thus shares the deconstructionist emphasis on texts as constituting the (or a) world within which everything is or can be construed. Related to this, in the second place, is a common concern (as will later become apparent) with what Christopher Norris, speaking of Paul de Man, calls 'the play of figural language', 'the grammar of tropes', and 'the rhetoric of textual performance' (*Deconstruction: Theory and Practice*, London: Methuen and Co., 1982, pp. 106, 108). In the third place, however, the great difference is that for the deconstructionists there is no single privileged idiom, text or text-constituted world. Their approach is *inter*textual rather than intratextual – that is, they treat all writings as a single whole: all texts are, so to speak, mutually interpreting. One result is that what in the past would have been thought of as allegorizing is for them an acceptable mode of interpretation. In an intratextual religious or theological reading, in contrast, there is a privileged interpretive direction from whatever counts as holy writ to everything else. Other differences as well as similarities are discussed by Shira Wolosky in a treatment of Derrida's relation to Talmudic modes of interpretation ('Derrida, Jabes, Levinas: Sign Theory as Ethical Discourse', *Journal of Jewish Literary History*, 2/3, 1982, pp. 283–301). It should incidentally be noted, however, that Derrida's understanding of Christian interpretive method as presented in this article is quite different from the typological approach, which I shall argue was historically dominant. It may be that Derrida's view of what is characteristically Christian in these matters has been influenced by the experiential-expressive hermeneutics of Paul Ricoeur, whose student he once was.

4. Thomas Aquinas, *Summa Theologiae*, 1a, Q. 1, art. 10.
5. For the structure, though not all the details, of my understanding of typological interpretation, see Hans Frei, *The Eclipse of Biblical Narrative*, Yale University Press, 1974, especially pp. 1–39.
6. Charles Wood, *The Formation of Christian Understanding*, Philadelphia: Westminster Press, 1981, pp. 42, 101, and passim.
7. See my review of Gerhard Ebeling's *Dogmatik des Christlichen Glaubens*, in *Journal of Religion*, 61, 1981, pp. 309–14.
8. Frei, *Eclipse*, pp. 39ff.
9. For the general way of looking at the problem of scriptural interpretation presented in this paragraph, though not for all the details, I am indebted to David Kelsey, *The Uses of Scripture in Recent Theology*, Philadelphia: Fortress Press, 1975.
10. This way of putting the matter is dependent on Hans Frei, *The Identity of Jesus Christ*, Philadelphia: Fortress Press, 1975.
11. In addition to Hans Küng's *On Being a Christian* (tr. by Edward Quinn, New York: Doubleday and Co., 1976) see his 'Toward a New Consensus in Catholic

(and Ecumenical) Theology', in Leonard Swidler, ed., *Consensus in Theology?*, Philadelphia: Westminster Press, 1980, pp. 1–17.

12. This is the focus of attack in Hick, ed., *The Myth of God Incarnate*, Philadelphia: Westminster Press, 1980, pp. 1–17.

13. Edward Schillebeeckx, *Jesus: An Experiment in Christology*, tr. by Hubert Hoskins, New York: Seabury Press, 1979.

14. David Tracy, *Blessed Rage for Order*, New York: Seabury Press, 1975.

15. Karl Barth's way of doing this is described and critically but sympathetically assessed in David Ford, *Barth and God's Story*, Frankfurt: Peter Lang, 1981. See also D. Ford, 'Narrative in Theology,' *British Journal of Religious Education*, 4/3, 1982, pp. 115–19.

16. David Kelsey, *The Uses of Scripture*, p. 48.

17. ibid.

18. Richard Rorty partly illustrates this possibility of doing philosophy intratextually, but the inevitable vagueness of his canon of philosophical texts makes him verge on a philosophical version of deconstructionism. See his *Consequences of Pragmatism*, University of Minnesota Press, 1982, especially essays 6 (on Derrida), 8, and 12, and the Introduction.

19. Gerhard von Rad, *Old Testament Theology*, tr. by D. M. G. Stalker, 2 vols., New York: Harper and Row, 1962, 1965.

20. See Lindbeck, *The Nature of Doctrine*, Chapter 1, note 30.

21. For example, the pioneering work, *Toward the Year 2000*, Daniel Bell, ed., (Boston: Beacon Press, 1969) now seems extraordinarily dated.

22. My own two minor exercises in this genre (see *The Nature of Doctrine*, Chapter 1, note 22) are basic to the following paragraphs.

23. Northrop Frye, *The Great Code: The Bible and Literature*, Harcourt Brace Jovanovich, 1982.

# 19

The Nature of Doctrine:

A REVIEW

## David F. Ford

This major work has already created intense debate in USA. It is a short but dense distillation of twenty-five years reflection by a professor at Yale who is one of the most respected academic theologians of his generation. It is a seminal work, in being both the fruit of a long maturation and full of possibilities for new developments. It amounts to a proposed 'paradigm shift' for conceiving the nature of religion, doctrine, and theology.

The basic thesis is simple. Lindbeck presents three 'ideal types' of theory of religion and argues for the superiority, or at the very least the availability and importance, of the third. The first is the 'cognitive–propositional' model which sees religions primarily making truth claims about reality, and their doctrines as informative propositions to be assessed cognitively. This has been the classical Western approach, and is also seen, for example, in much modern analytic philosophy's concern with the informational meaningfulness of religious utterances. The second is the 'experiential–expressive', which in much modern religious thought (especially that under the broad label of 'liberal') has been a response both to the massive post-Enlightenment attacks on the cognitive claims of religion and to the accompanying psycho-social situation of modernity, in which the 'turn to the subject', the privatizing of religion, rapid change, pluralism, and individualism make it very hard for religion plausibly to require the communal acceptance of sets of objectively and immutably true propositions. This model, instead, sees religion springing from the inward depths of the self, rooted in pre-conceptual, pre-linguistic experience or consciousness, and doctrines are understood as noninformative, nondiscursive symbols of inner feelings, attitudes, or existential orientations. The third is the 'cultural–linguistic', according to which religions are seen to resemble languages and their correlative forms of life, or culture. In this, religions are idioms for dealing with whatever is most important, and doctrines are, in analogy with the grammar of a language, the communally authoritative rules of discourse, attitude, and action.

Lindbeck argues that the cultural–linguistic approach need not be relativist (though that is often the implication of it where it is most commonly used, in the fields of anthropology, sociology, and neo-Wittgensteinian philosophy) but that it can take account of the cognitive–propositional concern for truth. He distinguishes 'intrasystematic' truth from ontological truth, and as regards the latter attacks claims that there can be any foundational truth or neutral framework in relation to which the truth of a specific religion can be judged. First-order truth is not so much a property of doctrines (they are second-order 'grammatical' rules) as of the performance of life in which the doctrines plays a part. The emphasis is on 'the performatory conformity of the self to God' (p. 66) which includes a correspondence of the mind to divine reality. In dialogue between different positions the exploration of rationality has all the complexity and particularity of the operation of Newman's 'illative sense'. Apologetics is an *ad hoc* enterprise which presupposes that the grammar of a religion, like that of a language, cannot be explicated or learned by analysis of experience or by reference to translinguistic norms, but only by learning and practice.

The cultural–linguistic model can also take account of the inner depths of experience, but refuses to see these as prelinguistic, precultural or private. Rather, in the complex interplay between 'inner' and 'external' experience, the leading partner is the external, so that the primary direction is from outer to inner. We internalize, through stories, symbols, rituals, behavior, and many other influences, the 'language' through which we experience reality. In Christianity, this is the meaning of 'faith comes by hearing', and of the Holy Spirit understood as giving the capacity to recognize and accept the 'external word' of the gospel.

Lindbeck tests his theory first in relation to the world religions. For a theory to be religiously useful it needs, he says, to be able to allow a religion to claim superiority or unsurpassability, and he argues that this is most appropriately done through the cultural–linguistic approach: this stresses the categories (or 'grammar' or 'rules of the game') of a religion in terms of which truth claims are made and expressive symbolisms employed. It is conceivable that one religion has the categories (e.g. a prophetic revelation or a story identifying God in history) most adequate to what is ultimately important, though this would still permit it to fail in performance to guide its life or its statements by them. This would also allow enrichment of religions by each other even though one might in fact be categorically unsurpassable. Dialogue between religions, in this understanding, is freed from any necessity to postulate a common core experience or an all-embracing criterion of truth, and becomes a variety of *ad hoc* engagements in which participants attempt to share their own religion and learn that of others. They should be open to the possibility that even the reasons one religion finds it worthwhile taking part in dialogue might differ radically from those of others – a Christian's reason may greatly differ from a Buddhist's, but yet the encounter may be fruitful in ways neither can predict. As regards salvation, if one wants to allow for this outside one's own religion one does not have to believe that all religions lead to the same goal or that all are aware of the same variously conceived reality. One can simply hold the hope that just as one's own faith had to be learned and conformed to, so all others will have the possibility of learning 'the true faith'. Without the right categories one can appropriately neither affirm nor deny the truth, and even with them one may be like a toddler just beginning to grasp the implications of what one is learning. This is an eschatological understanding of 'prospective *fides ex auditu*' which for Lindbeck makes sense of the early Christians' 'extraordinary combination of relaxation and urgency in their attitude towards those outside the church' (p. 58).

The other major area in which Lindbeck tests his theory is that of doctrinal differences within Christianity, and he argues that the cultural–linguistic theory does give a non-reductive framework for discussion among those who disagree, as well as a way of accounting for continuity, change, and the often surprising ecumenical reconciliation possible in doctrine. He explores the unconditionality claimed for the classic Christological and Trinitarian affirmations, and, in Roman Catholic dogma, the irreversibility of the Marian doctrines and the issue of papal infallibility. Perhaps most illuminating is his suggestion that the second-order 'rules' operating implicitly in Christological belief in the early Church from its beginning to the climax of Nicaea were:

> First, there is the monotheistic principle: there is only one God, the God of Abraham, Isaac, Jacob, and Jesus. Second, there is the principle of historical specificity: the stories of Jesus refer to a genuine human being who was born, lived and died in a particular time and place. Third, there is the principle of what may be infelicitously called Christological maximalism: every possible importance is to be ascribed to Jesus that is not inconsistent with the first rules (p. 94).

Such a view of doctrine is clearly consistent with a wide range of particular theological positions, just as a vast variety of specific sentences may be generated within the grammar of one language. Overall Lindbeck recognizes that sophisticated modern theologies such as Lonergan's or Rahner's, which combined cognitive–propositional and experiential–expressive elements, may give very similar results to his own theory in practice but he claims that the cultural–linguistic is superior in economy of description and explanation.

The final chapter is a daring sketch of what Christian 'postliberal theology' (one that has rejected the dominance of the experiential–expressive approach) might be like. Systematic theology is seen as primarily descriptive, elucidating postcritically the way in which the Bible is normative for the community ('faithfulness as intratextuality') and showing how this idiom allows all reality to be redescribed in its terms. For Lindbeck it is above all the identification of God through biblical narrative which creates a domain of meaning capable of assimilating other reality. Practical theology becomes 'applicability as futurology' – the attempt to practice the faith by correlating new contexts with eschatological vision but giving primacy to the latter. What this might mean in the realm of the Church is that, in a pluralist society with many pressures against the internalizing and communal practice of a particular faith, the possibility of unity and quality of life

> may depend on communal enclaves that socialize their members into highly particular outlooks supportive of concern for others rather than for individual rights and entitlements, and of a sense of responsibility for the wider society rather than for personal fulfillment. It is at least an open question whether any religion will have the requisite toughness for this demanding task unless it at some point makes the claim that it is significantly different and unsurpassably true; and it is easier for a religion to advance this claim if it is interpreted in cultural–linguistic rather than experiential–expressive terms. Thus it may well be that postliberal theologies are more applicable than liberal ones to the needs of the future (p. 127).

Finally, philosophical and apologetic theology which avoid claims to universal criteria, principles or structures separable from particular religions are defended against accusations of relativism and fideism, and a notion of rationality closely allied with the development of 'unformalizable skill' is suggested.

How is such a comprehensive proposal to be assessed? It has an advantage which is shared with Lonergan's *Method in Theology* (with which the whole book is in critical dialogue) in allowing at the least its use as a model which is helpful to have around while doing theology, while also enabling those who agree with its more controversial implications to follow these through constructively. It also permits influential modern disciplines to contribute to theology, and diagnoses accurately the dilemma of a liberal, experiential method which continues to be attractive for psychological and cultural reasons while becoming increasingly alienated from other academic approaches to religion. Above all, it encourages a more discerning and respectful appreciation of the particularity and integrity of different religions and quasi-religions, and frees them to be themselves and to have their most radical claims taken seriously.

The sharpest critical questions will obviously come from the direction of the two rejected models. Is justice done to the concern for ontological truth and the importance of its propositional expression? The most delicate issue here is likely to be the relationship of categories to truth. There is a Kantian preference both for the priority of our categorical structure and also for resolving its relationship to historical and religious reality in practical, performative terms which are bound to seem unsatisfactory to those impressed by Hegelian and other critiques of Kant. The associated sharp distinction between first-order religion and second-order theological reflection will also seem an unnecessarily practical definition of religion and a division which fails to do justice to first-order involvement of the mind in relating to God. In doctrine this comes to a head in Lindbeck's remark, concerning differences over the economic and immanent Trinities, that 'which theory is theologically best depends on how well it organizes the data of Scripture and tradition with a view to their use in Christian worship and life' (p. 106). This may be to beg the question of the role of cognition in the formation of those data and in the conduct of worship and life. The way in which a doctrine of creation might handle the natural sciences is another area where too cultural–linguistic a theory of religion and too pragmatic a view of truth might show their limitations.

From the experiential–expressive side the most telling criticisms might come from those who see the theory inevitably promoting too conservative a form of Christianity. Yet I think there could be a liberal Christianity in a cultural–linguistic mode. It would need to be rethought, but one hopes that Lindbeck's own rejection of much in liberal Christianity will not prevent others from reconceiving their positions in his terms. In this way there could be a new and vigorous stage of a debate which has become rather stale. Non-Christians, especially those in religions which focus more on inwardness and consciousness, might judge Lindbeck's very categories (giving primacy to the 'thick description' of ordinary life, the perspective in which much of the Bible is written) to be biased towards Christianity, with its concept of God's initiative and involvement in history. Yet this need only be a confirmation of Lindbeck's denial of any neutral framework: just as motives for interreligious dialogue may vary, so the ways of conceiving the various religions may be found to be irreducibly related to the categories of one. This would be a criticism of Lindbeck's way of

207

distinguishing formal, categorical questions from first-order matters of content, but it would confirm his policy suggestions for dialogue.

In conclusion, this seems to me to be one of the most important recent books in theology, well worth lengthy discussion in this country, where, I believe, many of the academic, ecclesiastical, and cultural conditions will make Lindbeck's paradigm more congenial than is likely in USA. It certainly allows a fascinating reinterpretation of the 'Myth of God Incarnate' debate (hinted at in Lindbeck's footnotes) and also of such other media events as the Bishop of Durham affair and Don Cupitt's 'Sea of Faith'. But more significantly there is here a new framework for serious theological and Church discussion in a society with many religions and widespread secularization. After reading it three times I found it was still generating new perspectives, problems and projects in constructive theology, and even its most debatable points served to open up the deepest theological and philosophical issues afresh.

# 20

The Nature of Doctrine:

A REVIEW

## David B. Burrell csc

George Lindbeck has been an unstinting contributor to ecumenical endeavors for a quarter of a century, and his reflection upon that effort has inspired this study of the nature of doctrine. Lindbeck begins his study by asking how his ecclesial experience could be possible given current explanations of the nature of doctrine.

The work, therefore, originates in ecclesial practice, and would help believers understand that practice; hence it is itself a work of theology. Yet, it assumes a position regarding doctrine neatly between that which is prevalent in current philosophical circles, on the one hand, and that of most divinity schools on the other. The view of doctrine most congenial to current philosophers of religion is a *propositional* one, in which doctrines are seen as stating facts about God and the world in relation to God; whereas that typically encountered in divinity schools is called 'experiential-expressive', in which a doctrine is taken to offer symbolic expression of a core religious experience. (This is also the strategy congenial to most liberal thinkers.) Lindbeck offers a 'cultural-linguistic' alternative to these two models; in this model, doctrinal statements function as rules for a language of which the primary uses are prayer and faith-sharing.

The preference of divinity schools for the 'experiential–expressive' theory doubtless reflects their wariness of the more straightforward (and presumably classical) propositional view, as well as their concern to give due weight to religious experience. Lindbeck identifies this approach with 'the liberal theologies influenced by the Continental developments that began with Schleiermacher' (p. 16), while he sees Karl Rahner and Bernard Lonergan attempting to combine it with a propositional view. Yet, while acknowledging the advantage of a hybrid over a one-dimensional view, he proceeds to subsume each of these thinkers under one model or the other, depending upon the subject at hand. (As we shall see, calling their approaches 'hybrid' presumes the accuracy of his own typology, and it is questionable whether he has captured both Lonergan and Rahner in his subsequent depictions.)

In any case, Lindbeck's models offer him helpful ways of posing ecumenical questions; moreover, his approach is careful, irenic, and blessedly free of polemics. His purpose is to settle the propositional versus 'experiential-expressive' controversy, and help create a fruitful exchange between philosophy departments and divinity schools – precisely the role of a university faculty of theology. (His work is manifestly indebted to conversations with colleagues, notably Hans Frei and David Kelsey; thus, it witnesses to that endeavor at Yale.) Furthermore, although he clearly wants to demonstrate the superiority of his alternative formulation, he is, nevertheless, appropriately cautious regarding its viability.

Lindbeck claims that, if we were to regard doctrines as rules governing the grammar of faith-discourse, we would be responding to an ancient sense of *regula fidei*, and subordinating this mode of expression to the ways in which a community puts the first-order language to use. The position may appear minimalist to a propositionist, and sound rather 'external' to an experiential-expressivist; but the initial objections of each can be met by recalling the point of a 'rule of faith'. Since faith always outreaches a set of beliefs by demanding a commensurate way of life, the rules for correct discourse must envisage a coherence between speech and life. First-order discourse has a chance to be true only if it is used in accordance with the 'rule of faith', which includes a way of life. In a fascinating comparison and contrast with mathematics, Lindbeck shows how a rule of faith (like any other rule) is concerned with coherence only; it therefore cannot establish the 'ontological truth' of first-order statements of faith but only the *possibility* of their truth. Yet, coherence in matters of faith entails a consonant way of life as well. So faith-statements stand a chance of being true if they concur with the grammar proper to such discourse (doctrine) *and* are made in the context of the proper form of life. 'God be praised' on the lips of a crusader lopping off Muslim heads cannot be anything but false.

This example helps us to understand the experiential–expressivist's concern with appropriate inwardness as well. It requires a shift in one's starting points regarding knowledge and justification, and Lindbeck patiently develops a Wittgensteinian model of knowing as 'knowing-how', with grammar as a function of our use of language. Like logic, grammar is followed before it is made explicit, so Wittgenstein's 'contrast between interpreting a truth and obeying a rule' is helpful here (p. 107). But this observation does not take into account the concern for *foundations* prevalent in experiential-expressivism. Accordingly, Lindbeck must show the viability of an anti-foundational alternative to knowing-by-faith, as he has offered grammar-in-use as a plausible rendering of inwardness. He

develops the anti-foundational alternative by way of a biblical interpretation which attends to the literary structure of a text as well as to
historical-critical considerations. Relying on the work of Hans Frei, he
explains how an 'intra-textual' understanding of the Scriptures offers a
contemporary analogue to classical Christian typological readings by
showing how the Scriptures can create the world which structures our
lives. (Lindbeck's discussion helped me to pinpoint the differences between
Frei and Ricoeur, as his anti-foundational approach differentiates his own
view of doctrine from that of David Tracy.) It is at this point that the
differences between 'liberal' and 'postliberal' come into play. The
foundationalist strategy is inherently liberal in its attempt to articulate a
level of experience common to all, in which the life and language of faith
might be *grounded*, that is, justified to unbeliever and believer alike. The
'cultural-linguistic' alternative finds such a grounding only in the life and
witness of a community formed by a specific scripture, and so obviates the
need for wider justification.

Ironies abound here, however, for Lindbeck rightly notes that these
broader justifications have usually functioned better for believers than
unbelievers. (Does this observation help explain why experiential-expressive perspectives are so congenial to divinity schools?) What is at stake here
is the old debate concerning the *preambula fidei*. Lindbeck's reading of
Aquinas (like that of Guy de Broglie) notes that the *preambula fidei* function
retrospectively for believers, and not (as baroque theologians often saw
them) as stepping-stones to faith. In fact, it is usually the witness of a
community which impels one to the threshold of faith, and, here,
fascinating logics like Newman's 'converging probabilities' begin to
emerge.

Enough has been said to indicate the clarity with which Lindbeck lays
out the alternatives and the care with which he argues. His involvement in
the life of the Church and in current ecumenical concerns is shown by the
agility with which he relates doctrine to practice. I prefer a 'performative'
reading of Lonergan, whom I see as the one best able to capture the
peculiar genius of *Insight*, as distinguished from the position of Rahner,
who is clearly a foundationalist. (My interpretation makes use of
Lonergan's 'unrestrictive desire to know' to show why one might be
tempted even to entertain the language and life of faith, and follows
Lindbeck's model from that point.) Inwardness becomes a presupposition
of the entire way of life which needs language to proceed, without offering
an independent justification for it. And, I would contend, some such
depth-structure in the human animal must be presupposed to account for

the role which language can play in structuring our lives and the role of grammar in delineating that structure.

Lindbeck's taxonomy of rules for handling different kinds of doctrine should be especially illuminating to theologians, while his test of the 'cultural-linguistic' alternative with regard to Chalcedon, Marian doctrines, and infallibility shows a keen historical and ecumenical sense. Finally, his arresting observations regarding ecclesial patterns and their affinity with specific models for doctrine reflects his characteristic ecclesiological acumen.

# 21

# ECUMENICAL DIMENSIONS OF LINDBECK'S 'NATURE OF DOCTRINE'
## *Geoffrey Wainwright*

A first, quick reading of George Lindbeck's *The Nature of Doctrine* pleased me for its exposure of the weaknesses in modern theological liberalism. On a second, more careful reading I became worried by its own epistemological and ontological timidity and its reduction of doctrine to a merely regulative function. A third reading of this short but materially dense work persuaded me that my initial sympathy towards its cultural-linguistic approach to the Christian faith was not misplaced, provided the approach allowed for a recuperation of doctrinal realism and even the reintegration of a certain active role for experience. On these terms, Lindbeck's proposal might acquire the ecumenical value its author wishes for it.

The main thesis can be very briefly stated. Of three approaches to religions, Lindbeck argues for the superiority of the cultural-linguistic over the cognitive-propositionalist and the experiential-expressivist.

In so far as its application to Christianity is concerned (and this is Lindbeck's chief concern throughout, and he is wanting to be helpful as an insider to the faith), the main fault of the cognitive-propositionalist approach appears – especially when it is designated 'pre-liberal' – to reside in its having been historically overtaken by the criticism that modern thinkers address to all things metaphysical. But more fundamentally, Lindbeck seems to hold that it belongs to Christianity as such to remain content with an economy of salvation rather than attempting to formulate truths about God or ultimate reality as they are in themselves.

'Experience seeking expression' is the characteristically liberal understanding of religion. The principal overt problem Lindbeck has with the experiential-expressivist model is its phenomenological inaccuracy: it reverses observable priorities when it places the experience of individual adherents before the communally available religion itself. Lindbeck concedes the psycho-social attractiveness of this theory for modern apologists: 'The structures of modernity press individuals to meet God in the depths of their souls and then, perhaps, if they find something personally congenial, to become part of a tradition or join a church. . . .

Religions are seen as multiple suppliers of different forms of a single commodity needed for transcendent self-expression and self-realization' (p. 22). The animus of that passage hints at the theological reason for the author's dissatisfaction with the experiential-expressivist approach: he shares a Barthian objection to 'religion' as a universally human 'enterprise'.

The approach with which Lindbeck would like to usher in a postliberal age is labelled cultural-linguistic. Academically, it is most deeply indebted to Clifford Geertz, and particularly his essays in *The Interpretation of Cultures*, but there are also clear and acknowledged influences from Wittgenstein in linguistic philosophy, T. S. Kuhn in philosophy of science, and Michael Polyani in personal epistemology. One advantage for theologians in Lindbeck's favored approach would precisely consist in the possibility of interdisciplinary contact on account of the incipient 'spread of a cultural-linguistic orientation in history, anthropology, sociology and philosophy' (p. 129). Internally, the cultural-linguistic model is held to facilitate a 'rule theory of doctrine' which Lindbeck has come to believe is in any case the one most appropriate in Christianity. The author recounts at the outset that his whole line of investigation was in fact motivated by the need to account for a puzzling result of ecumenical discussions: participants announce themselves to have reached basic agreement even while continuing to maintain their once-divisive convictions. Lindbeck seemingly wants to imply that the solution lies in the fact that the diverse convictions all fall within the rules. At the end, I will return – more explicitly and concretely than Lindbeck himself – to this reading of the achievements of ecumenical dialogues and to the alleged helpfulness of a 'rule theory of doctrine' in further reconciliation. Meanwhile the more general matter of a cultural-linguistic approach to Christianity must be evaluated in its Lindbeckian form.

The approach is, of course, partly defined by what Lindbeck is concerned to reject. We need therefore to look a little more closely at the other two approaches and Lindbeck's understanding of them.

Upon the cognitive-propositional approach he heaps in a pejorative sense the epithets voluntarist, intellectualist, and (above all) literalist. Lindbeck's descriptions of the cognitive-propositionalist position are too simple for it even in its classical or traditional forms, let alone in its sophisticated postcritical versions (a brief, respectful mention is made of Peter Geach). Responsible cognitivists have never held that their propositions speak the truth about God exhaustively. Lindbeck himself comes nearer the mark with a phrase he uses in a quite different context: of propositions concerning God there is no reason why it cannot be said that they are 'entirely yet incompletely true' (cf. p. 49). If the problem lies with the adequacy of *any* statements concerning God, the answer is to be found in the principle of analogy. When the Fourth Lateran Council declared that 'between Creator and creature there is no similarity so great that the dissimilarity is not greater', it was recognizing the ontological condition for both the possibility and the limits of statements about God. Like affirmations about Creator and creature differ according as they refer to the Creator or the creature: God is the source, norm and goal of creaturely values. When we speak of the goodness, justice or love of God, the usage is not equivocal but, precisely, analogical. To accentuate Aquinas' 'agnosticism' (pp. 66–9) is to minimize his cataphatism. If the problem lies with the adequacy of a *single* statement concerning God, a hint can be found in an example given by Lindbeck himself in, again, a different context (p. 83): Gruenewald's agonizing Christ and a Byzantine Pantocrator may *both* be true. What thus applies in the iconic mode can be transposed to the linguistic: various statements concerning God can *all* be, under the conditions of analogy, truthful (assuming we have good reason for each of them and they are not irretrievably incompatible).

For propositions Lindbeck wants to substitute story – the story told normatively in the Bible. We may readily admit the crucial importance of the biblical story, but we have not thereby made the question of epistemological status any easier. Lindbeck writes: 'The rendering of God's character is not in every instance logically dependent on the facticity of the story' (p. 122). But if the story does not *in some instances* at least (which?) narrate real events, then the connection between God and the life of humanity becomes very tenuous indeed and the 'point' of the story is correspondingly weakened. But *if* God 'acts in history' at all, the grounds for advancing true propositions about God are there. Any talk of 'rendering God's character', in however 'non-propositional' a form, in fact raises the ontological question of correspondence to the divine reality.

What, now, does Lindbeck make of the other rejected approach, the experiential-expressivist? His criticisms are often on target. The modern 'turn to the subject', whether one dates it from Descartes (on whom E. Juengel has written very penetratingly in *God as the Mystery of the World*) or from Kant, sounds uncomfortably close to Luther's description of *sinful* humanity as '*homo in se incurvatus*'. Karl Barth was not wrong to oppose what he read in Schleiermacher. But some proper retrieval of experience-expressivism will result if we press upon Lindbeck a question which, curiously, he never adequately faces: where do cultural-linguistic traditions *come from?* For much of the book it would appear that, like Topsy, they just 'growed'. There are a few hints otherwise. Quoting Wilfrid Sellars in *Science, Perception and Reality*, Lindbeck writes: 'The acquisition of a

215

language – *necessarily from the outside* – is a "jump which was the coming into being of man" ' (p. 62, my italics). On p. 39 Lindbeck offers an example of how change, or relative innovation, may occur in an existing tradition: 'Luther did not invent his doctrine of justification by faith because he had a tower experience, but rather the tower experience [if he had one!] was made possible by his discovering (or thinking he discovered) the doctrine in the Bible.' The hint here is that the Christian cultural-linguistic tradition, at least, began somehow 'in the Bible'. But how? On p. 125, in another context, there is an implication that prophecy depends on a 'first-order inspiration or intuition' (which?). The point I am driving at is that, at least according to its own self-understanding, the Christian cultural-linguistic tradition originated in *revelation* (corresponding to the 'from the outside' of p. 62); and the question then becomes that of the place of *experience* in revelation. On p. 33f., Lindbeck is ready to admit, if a little grudgingly, that 'the relation of religion and experience . . . is not unilateral but dialectical'; yet 'in the interplay between "inner" experience and "external" religious and cultural factors, the latter can [and, for Lindbeck, should] be viewed as the leading partners.' And again, on p. 39: 'A religious experience and its expression are secondary and tertiary in a linguistic-cultural model. First come the objectivities of the religion, its language, doctrine, liturgies, and modes of action, and it is through these that passions are shaped into various kinds of what is called religious experience'.

But this won't do in the case of the (relative) *origins* of a religious tradition. I will yield to no one in my affirmation of God's initiative in revelation and salvation and in maintaining an Alexandrian (as opposed to an Antiochene) account of the incarnation; yet Mary's fiat at Luke 1.38 and the humanity of Christ as an active organ of the redemption surely imply a co-constitutive role (responsive, of course) for human *experience* in the *foundation* of the Christian tradition. Then the way is opened for a more '*actively* receptive' view of experience – properly derived and normed – in the continuation of the tradition. Experiencing subjects compose and transmit liturgies, doctrines, and patterns of behavior. I suspect that in this matter Lindbeck has been over-influenced by the Lutheran insistence that, whereas all other Christians are content with the *Allwirksamkeit Gottes* ('God does everything'), God's glory and human salvation require that God 'does everything *alone*' (*Alleinwirksamkeit*).

My attempts to recuperate the cognitive-propositionalist dimension and to retrieve something of the experiential-expressivist have shown, at least indirectly, where I consider the weaknesses of Lindbeck's version of a cultural-linguistic approach to Christianity to reside. Let me now make my criticisms more directly.

To begin with: his theory of truth appears inadequate, at least to the claims Christians have traditionally thought they were making for their message and teaching. Lindbeck sounds like a consensualist (pp. 18, 47f., 63f.), and what has just been suggested about a continuing 'active receptivity' certainly implies epistemological significance for consensus. But what matters is what we consent *to* and *in*. A consensus theory of truth – leaving aside the philosophical objection of the possibility of universal delusion – is of no use to Christianity *without a veridical God.*

A vital element in Lindbeck's truth theory is that of intrasystematic consistency. However, he gives a curious twist to this by emphasizing not rational coherence but rather the successful *performance* of claims in life (pp. 64–9). No one would accuse Lindbeck of perfectionist tendencies (cf. p. 60: 'Christians are just beginning . . .'), and it is therefore ironical that as a Methodist I should feel impelled to throw back at this Lutheran a version of the *'simul iustus et peccator'*. God's truth cannot depend on our perception or achievement of it. A Marxian *making* of the truth ('no longer interpreting the world, but changing it') is not the same as a biblical *doing* of an (existing) truth. And while Lindbeck's apparent attribution here to believers of a *cooperative* role in eschatology is to be welcomed theologically, the primary agent in bringing in the Kingdom – transforming reality – must be God. Both the consensual and the pragmatic theories of truth require, from the Christian viewpoint, an underpinning in a correspondence theory that is finally grounded in the relation between Creator and creation. No account of Christianity can be satisfactory which does not recognize that Christianity's own claims are objectively intended.

The cultural-linguistic approach to religion, and to the Christian faith in particular, is appropriately matched, says Lindbeck, by a 'rule theory of doctrine'. It should be fair to evaluate this feature on the basis of his most significant example, namely the Nicene dogma. According to Lindbeck, Nicea represents no substantive plus beyond – but is rather an instantiation of – three 'regulative principles' that were 'clearly at work even in the New Testament period'. 'First, there is the monotheistic principle: there is only one God, the God of Abraham, Isaac, Jacob, and Jesus. Second, there is the principle of historical specificity: the stories of Jesus refer to a genuine human being who was born, lived, and died in a particular time and place [with no hint at this point of a resurrection]. Third, there is the principle of what may be infelicitously called Christological maximalism: every possible importance is to be ascribed to Jesus that is not inconsistent with the first rules' (p. 94). The difficulty emerges with Lindbeck's interpretation of what Athanasius was about in his explanation of the *homoousion* as 'whatever is said of the Father is said of the Son, except that the Son is not

217

the Father': 'Thus,' says Lindbeck, 'the theologian most responsible for the final triumph of Nicaea thought of it, not as a first-order proposition with ontological reference, but as a second-order rule of speech' (p. 94). But Athanasius is *not*, I would maintain, merely enunciating a 'logical' or 'grammatical' rule of a purely formal kind that would allow an indefinite number of instantiations ('whatever is said of $x$ is said of $y$, except that $y$ is not $x$'). Rather Athanasius, like Nicaea, is speaking precisely of the Father and the Son, so that an indispensable part of the point is that 'whatever is said of the Father', when it is said of the Father, is said precisely *of the Father*, and likewise with the Son. A *subsistent trinitarian relation* is being declared by Nicaea and by Athanasius. It is with this substantive content that the conciliar declaration is intended to give guidance to Christian language concerning God and Jesus Christ.

It would be interesting at this point to compare Lindbeck with the recent work of the German Catholic lay theologian Karl-Heinz Ohlig.[1] In proposing the thesis that 'Christology is a function of soteriology', Ohlig argues that culturally characteristic questions, needs and hopes have set the context in which Jesus has been experienced as the mediator of a transcendent salvation (with its origin and goal in the God of Israel, the Father of Jesus Christ) and have provided the language in which he has been confessed as such. Culturally available superlatives have been doxologically predicated upon him in order to express what is believed and hoped to be his ultimate, comprehensive and universal significance, while the historical Jesus as their subject has – at least in principle and in the long run – in turn functioned correctively upon such predicates. Ohlig is unwilling *systematically* to exclude confessions of Jesus that do not make him 'by nature divine', since *historically* there have been 'Christologies' that do not even functionally imply a 'two-nature' Christology (e.g. ebionite, early Antiochene, and what the author calls modern 'liberal-emancipationist'). Now Ohlig is undoubtedly more inclined to 'experiential expressivism' than Lindbeck would like. But would Lindbeck's christological *rules* – which are remarkably similar to Ohlig's historical *description* – rule out such 'mere-man' Christologies? Certainly the councils of Nicaea and Chalcedon intended the real, *substantial* affirmation that it was God the Son that became human in Jesus Christ.

That brings us to another of Lindbeck's themes that is also of considerable ecumenical importance, namely the question of the irreversibility of doctrine in the Christian tradition. Lindbeck chooses as his example the Marian dogmas of the Roman Catholic Church, and particularly (a neat move *vis-à-vis* the Eastern Orthodox) that of the Immaculate Conception. The question he sets himself is 'whether rule theory allows (but does not require) them to be understood as irreversible' (p. 87: note the 'does not require'), 'whether a regulative approach leaves the theological options open and is therefore capable of accommodating irreversibility as well as reversibility (not to mention the usual Protestant view, which the rule theory also allows, that these doctrines are simply illegitimate)' (p. 96). It might be wondered whether a rule theory that was so elastic could be of any use concretely at all. Lindbeck holds that, on a rule theory, 'irreformable' doctrines would be ones that 'were correct in their original contexts and thus always hold whenever the contexts are in the relevant respects sufficiently similar' (p. 98). Lindbeck suggests that it is *only* – but then perhaps *always* – 'in the context of a questionable Western theology and sense of sin' that the affirmation of Mary's immaculate conception is necessary in order to 'maintain her God-given and God-dependent freedom in saying "yes",' and thus abide by an even deeper set of rules having to do with 'the uncodifiable aspects of the interaction of divine and human freedom' (p. 97). My own (Protestant) sense is that there is ecumenical potential here (albeit in a rather Lutheran formulation, even for another Protestant), but I can imagine a Roman Catholic becoming as substantially worried at this juncture as I myself became – and I think any orthodox Christian would – over the implications of Lindbeck's 'rules' for Christology and the Trinity. Once an authoritative doctrinal decision has been taken and accepted as correctly expressing Christian belief and piety, the terms of that decision make a continuing substantial contribution to the shape of the faith.

The fact is: the 'form' and the 'substance' of doctrines are not so easily separable as may be implied by the remark of Pope John XXIII which Lindbeck cites: 'The substance of the ancient doctrine of the deposit of faith is one thing, and the way in which it is presented is another'. There is indeed a certain possibility of, need for, and value in 'distinguishing' – as 'some modern forms of propositionalism' do (Lindbeck cites Rahner, Lonergan, and Schlink) – 'between what a doctrine affirms ontologically and the diverse conceptualities or formulations in which the affirmation can be expressed' (p. 80). But the picture of kernel and husk – which Lindbeck admittedly does not use although he does come close to implying it (p. 92f.) – is too simple. Or to address the model which is for Lindbeck explicit and important: his notion of 'rule' might have been better applied to doctrine, had he not taken for his primary analogue a whole language or even language as such, where formal rules can rather easily be distinguished from substantive referent, but rather sought comparisons with more specific *games*, where the 'pieces' are given and the 'point' is clear.

Less graphically put, Lindbeck can be reproached for the account(s) that

219

he gives of the relations among (1) such primary activities as worship and confession, (2) church doctrine or dogma, and (3) theology. He so accentuates the distinctions among these three as to minimize their connections. Lindbeck strangely fails to appreciate the significance of the fact that the Nicene bishops chose to insert their *dogmatic* definition in a creed, a genre whose primary use is that of *confessing* the faith at baptism. Nor is the (later) *doxological* use of the Nicene-Constantinopolitan Creed at the Eucharist adequately understood as 'expressive symbolization' (cf. p. 19): the Creed 'belongs' there because its dogmatic *content* had become clarified and confirmed to the Church through, among other things, the *worship* of Father, Son and Holy Spirit. As for *theology* its functions – apart from affording 'intellectual enjoyment' (p. 108) – are said to be the 'explanation, communication, and defense of the faith within a framework of communal doctrinal agreement' (p. 76). That would be fine, if one count count on a more intimate connection between substantive faith and agreed doctrine; but even then, Lindbeck insists on the highly problematic 'distinction between abiding doctrinal grammar and variable theological vocabulary' (p. 113), when in fact the vocabulary question runs right through faith, doctrine and theology because the question of the real referent cannot be avoided at any stage. It is an oddly detached view of theology which is suggested ('organizing', 'using', 'unimportance') when Lindbeck writes on p. 106: 'Which theory [the case under discussion has to do with the economic and the immanent Trinities] is theologically best depends on how well it organizes the data of Scripture and tradition with a view to their use in Christian worship and life. . . . The question of the ontological reference of the theories may often be unimportant for theological evaluation.'

My evaluation of Lindbeck up to now has been predominantly critical. That is due to my concern for things that he feels impelled to deny or diminish. In fact, I share his positive appreciation of a cultural-linguistic approach to Christianity, *provided* it is not set over against cognitive realism or indeed (with caution!) experiential expressivism. My difficulty with Lindbeck is typified by the following sentence, and the italics are mine: 'It is the framework and the medium within which Christians know and experience, *rather than* what they experience or think they know, that retains continuity and unity down through the centuries' (p. 84). For me the tradition of Christianity embraces *both* the 'framework and the medium' (this would be Lindbeck's 'cultural-linguistic system' and 'doctrine as rules') *and* the knowledge *and* the experience; and the ecumenical task consists precisely in *locating* that self-identical Tradition both diachronically and synchronically. (Incidentally, the sentence last quoted illustrates beautifully a prominent characteristic of Lindbeck's mode of argumentation: he proceeds by the method of 'not [sometimes softened by a "primarily"] . . . but . . .'. Here is an echo of the Lutheran 'either/or' as compared to the Catholic 'both/and'!)

We finally come back, then, to ecumenism. The distinction of George Lindbeck's contribution in this field is illustrated by his co-chairing of the Joint Commission between the Lutheran World Federation and the Roman Catholic Church, which has probably done the best work among all bilateral dialogues. Nevertheless, I wonder how far his sense of dialogues having attained 'reconciliation without capitulation' on either or any side should be generalized. It would be better to proceed dialogue by dialogue, and (even within each dialogue) doctrinal theme by doctrinal theme. As between the Roman Catholic Church and the Churches of the Reformation, for example, the progress towards agreement can be read in several ways, apart of course from accusations of a sell-out by any of the parties. On some issues it might be that unfortunate mutual misunderstandings of the sixteenth century are at last being cleared up. On others, the sixteenth-century controversies may be thought to have been real and important enough in their time but to have since, and in changed circumstances, become irrelevant or at least no longer church-dividing. On others again, it may be considered that genuine and substantial differences, which were insoluble when they first arose, can now be reconciled and overcome through the discovery of new insights into the gospel and the faith or the recovery of more original ones that antedate the Reformation.[2] Let us, in any case, examine a couple of examples.

The first is the document *Justification by Faith* produced by the US dialogue between Lutherans and Catholics, in which Lindbeck himself has been active.[3] The group has been able to agree on a 'fundamental affirmation':

> Our entire hope of justification and salvation rests on Christ Jesus and the gospel whereby the good news of God's merciful action in Christ is made known; we do not place our ultimate trust in anything other than God's promise and saving work in Christ. (§§ 4, 157)

It is recognized that this 'fundamental affirmation' is, on the one hand, 'not fully equivalent to the Reformation teaching on justification according to which God accepts sinners as righteous for Christ's sake on the basis of faith alone'; on the other (or perhaps the same) hand, it 'does not exclude the traditional Catholic position that the grace-wrought transformation of sinners is a necessary preparation for final salvation' (§ 157). Not having reached 'full agreement' (cf. § 4) on 'justification by faith (alone)' is not felt

221

by the group to spoil its 'fundamental consensus on the gospel' (§ 164). An outsider is bound to wonder just how fundamental is fundamental. But it is of course up to Lutherans and Catholics themselves to determine whether such a 'fundamental affirmation' as the above would constitute *sufficient doctrinal agreement* for their churches no longer to be divided over the issue that Lutherans have called 'the point at which the Church stands or falls'.

If so, then the remaining differences on the question would be merely 'theological', although they would presumably have to fall within the *substantive* limits of the 'fundamental affirmation'. At the theological level, a strange reversal of roles has in fact been taking place in some quarters – almost a case of ships that pass in the night. Some recent Lutheran thinking, and the dialogue document alludes to it, has gone so far in enhancing the exclusive operation of God that it maintains the 'unconditionality of God's promises in Christ' and, in what the document calls a 'hermeneutical perspective', declares that 'God's word does what it proclaims or, in modern terminology, the gospel message is performative; it effects the reality of which it speaks. The preaching of the gospel has the force of decreeing the forgiveness of sins for Christ's sake. . . . In this hermeneutical perspective, even the faith which receives the promise is not a condition for justification' (§§ 88–9). If thus coming within earshot of the gospel suffices for justification, we seem to have a case of the very '*ex opere operato*' with which Lutherans have reproached Catholics! It is now Roman Catholic theologians who are saying: If justification is to be by faith alone, let it at least be by faith! (cf. § 99). They might even want to insist that the point be positively affirmed in the *doctrinal* consensus.

The second example (and I will be briefer) concerns eucharistic sacrifice. In the forties and fifties it became common for catholic-minded Anglican ecumenists to excuse the Reformers' rejection of 'the sacrifice of the Mass' on the grounds of their *mis*understanding of Roman teaching. Francis Clark, in *Eucharistic Sacrifice and the Reformation* (1960), argued forcefully that, to the contrary, the Reformers knew and understood very well what they were rejecting. In turn Clark can be asked about the adequacy of a teaching that accommodates what were admittedly *mispractices*. But a more promising solution to the historic controversy between Protestants and Catholics over eucharistic sacrifice lies along other lines. It can be argued that the Western Church of the sixteenth century had all but lost the category that made eucharistic sacrifice both possible and necessary. It is a biblically and patristically understood *anamnesis* which is allowing doctrinal convergence concerning the sacrificial character of the Eucharist in the more recent texts of the Anglican – Roman Catholic International Commission, the Lutheran – Roman Catholic international dialogue, and the Faith and Order Commission of the World Council of Churches (Accra 1974/Lima 1982).

It should by now be clear that *doctrinal* issues are inescapably *substantive* issues in the moves of the churches towards reconciliation. If one of the benefits Lindbeck (tacitly) hoped for from his rule theory of doctrine was the easing of the ecumenical burden through the unloading of ontological freight, then he will inevitably be disappointed. His book could nevertheless make an important contribution if it encouraged the ecumenical dialogues to consider the status of doctrine in the respective churches, and also the status of particular doctrines. In the latter respect, something like Lindbeck's 'taxonomy of doctrines' (pp. 84–8) could prove helpful, although I think the churches will continue to believe that doctrine and doctrines make truth claims in a stronger sense than Lindbeck wants to allow. As Luther put it against Erasmus: 'Take away assertions, and you take away Christianity' (WA 18, 603).

To end on a positive note of gratitude for this stimulating book: ecumenical progress would undoubtedly be made if the discussions among the churches could work along certain lines which Lindbeck sees as suited to a cultural-linguistic approach (and which not only remain appropriate even with a more cognitive-propositional understanding of faith, doctrine, and theology but also allow for the importance of experience and expression in their due place).

First, there is Lindbeck's notion of 'faithfulness as intratextuality' or, more specifically, correspondence 'to the semiotic universe paradigmatically encoded in holy writ' (pp. 113–24). Of canonical writings, he says that 'for those who are steeped in them, no world is more real than the ones they create'. Lindbeck favors the assumption of traditional Christian exegetical procedures that 'Scripture creates its own domain of meaning and that the task of interpretation is to extend this over the whole of reality' (p. 117): 'Intratextual theology redescribes reality within the scriptural framework rather than translating Scripture into extrascriptural categories. It is the text, so to speak, which absorbs the world, rather than the world the text' (p. 118). Provided a place is made for postscriptural tradition as a *norma normata* – or, less provincially put, provided Scripture and Tradition can be related along the lines suggested by the Montreal World Conference on Faith and Order in 1963 – then Lindbeck's unifying thrust here can be ecumenically valuable. It will be so not least because of the service it can render to evangelism, which is one of the goals of the ecumenical movement ('that the world may believe . . .').

Second: under the heading of 'intelligibility as skill' Lindbeck argues that 'religions, like languages, can be understood only in their own terms, not by transposing them into an alien speech' (pp. 128–34). For Christianity, that will mean that adherents are gained by a method that 'resembles ancient catechesis more than modern translation' (p. 132). In the early days, converts 'were first attracted by the Christian community and form of life. . . . They submitted themselves to prolonged catechetical instruction in which they practiced new modes of behavior and learned the stories of Israel and their fulfillment in Christ. Only after they had acquired proficiency in the alien Christian language and form of life were they deemed able intelligently and responsibly to profess the faith, to be baptized' (p. 132). A common catechesis of this serious kind would further the ecumenical aims of unity and evangelism. At the doctrinal level we may think already of the 'Common Catechism' drawn up by German-speaking Catholics and Protestants.[4] Potentially more comprehensive still – to the extent that the churches 'can recognize in this [Lima] text the faith of the Church through the ages' – would be the results of the 'guidance' that the churches could take from *Baptism, Eucharist and Ministry* for their 'worship, educational, ethical, and spiritual life and witness'.[5] Such agreed teaching instruments will be all the more necessary if Lindbeck's forecast is realized of the ecumenical Church as a network of scattered small units.

NOTES

1. Karl-Heinz Ohlig, *Fundamentalchristologie: Im Spannungsfeld von Christentum und Kultur*, Munich: Koesel, 1986.
2. See G. Wainwright, 'Is the Reformation over?' in *Theological Students Fellowship Bulletin*, May–June 1984, pp. 2ff.
3. The 'common statement' of 1983 is contained in H. G. Anderson, T. A. Murphy and J. A. Burgess, eds., *Justification by Faith*, Minneapolis: Augsburg Publishing House, 1985, pp. 13–74.
4. Johannes Feiner and Lukas Vischer, eds., *The Common Catechism: A Christian Book of Faith*, New York: Seabury Press, 1975. Tr. from *Neues Glaubensbuch: der gemeinsame christliche Glaube*, Freiburg: Herder, 1973.
5. *Baptism, Eucharist and Ministry*, Faith and Order Paper No. 111, Geneva: World Council of Churches, 1982.

〰〰〰〰〰〰〰〰〰〰〰〰〰〰〰〰〰〰〰〰〰〰〰〰〰〰〰〰〰

# 22

# THEOLOGY AND THE MANY FACES OF POSTMODERNITY
## David Tracy

### Modernity and postmodernity as ambiguous traditions

Réné Descartes spoke for the entire modern era when he pleaded for certainty, clarity, and distinctness. He spoke again on behalf of modernity when he pleaded for a method grounded in the subjects' self-presence, a method, in principle, that would prove the same for all thinking, rational persons. The drive to clarity, the turn to the subject, the concern with method, the belief in sameness – modern thinkers embraced and embrace all these ideals in modernity's working out of its unique history. Indeed history itself, once modern historical consciousness and evolutionary theory were forged by modern thinkers, could also prove more of the same. For the genuine modern, all history leads by inevitable – indeed clear and distinct developmental stages – from the 'ancients' through the 'medievals' to the secret teleology of all history, us, the moderns. Other cultures often do not possess history at all (indeed they are 'primitive', 'archaic' 'pre-historical'). Somehow all other cultures become 'lesser' copies of the modern drive to sameness, the modern 'Western' scientific, technological, democratic culture that *is* culture and history. At the limit, then, history, the last outpost of the other and the different, is, in the modern narrative, finally a secretly evolutionary version of 'more of the same'.

The famous 'turn to the subject' of modernity can now be seen as both emancipatory and entrapping. Its emancipatory character remains for all to see: the triumph of the democratic ideal that great modern, liberal, American thinker, John Dewey, justly saw as the political implication of the scientific ideas and achievements of modernity. All of us who speak an emancipatory, liberating language are moderns at heart. As are all who demand public reason for theology. As are all of us who will always remain, in our lives as much as our thoughts, believers in the democratic ideals of liberty and equality. We all believe, now as then, that the only worthwhile political theology is one that increases both equality and liberty and one that helps us reflect better on how to relate these two great and often conflicting ideals in a politically and economically just society – meaning, finally, a just world society.

Modernity includes all who still acknowledge the modern scientific revolution as not just one more important event in Western culture but as the watershed event that makes even the Reformation and Renaissance seem like family quarrels. All who demand the bracing honesty of an historical consciousness can now also note the further ethical concern with the realities of social location (gender, race, class). They, too, are moderns at heart. All moderns justly see the world of nature and ourselves within it in the context of some form of evolutionary scheme. We moderns tend to find this vision of the whole and our small place within the whole as natural to our thought as many of our ancestors found some version of a Neoplatonic emanationist schema of *exitus-reditus* for understanding their 'ancient' and 'medieval' soul-ful, microcosmic place with the great macrocosm of the universe.

All thinkers who embrace these emancipatory values – as I certainly do, as most readers of this journal are likely to do – are incontestably heirs of the modern era. These modern values, however transformed, cannot be rejected by anyone understanding the ethical-political as well as intellectual stakes in modernity's classical drive to intellectual and political-economic emancipation. Those who claim, as I do, that we are now facing not simply (as almost all concede) late modernity but a puzzling reality named 'postmodernity' must clarify the meaning of that 'post' and the meaning of the 'modernity' it both qualifies and is determined by. Modernity includes all the values, the indispensable values, listed above. These values are familiar to and, I believe, likely to be constitutive of the worldview of any reader of this or similar theological journals. Modernity also includes more negative factors like those hinted at in the introductory description of Descartes' program for modernity.

Many moderns, with a kind of vestigial Enlightenment prejudice against the very category 'tradition', find it hard, perhaps impossible, to believe that modernity itself can now be viewed as one more tradition. But so it is. And like all traditions, modernity is deeply ambiguous. Walter Benjamin's dictum holds for modernity as for every tradition: 'Every great work of civilization is at the very same time a work of barbarism.'

The word 'barbarism' is regrettably accurate for our modern civilization, which can thoughtlessly use its great breakthroughs in science for negative, not only positive, technological achievements. On the positive side, would even the most violent anti-modern prefer to return to the period without, among many such examples, anesthetics? On the negative side, modern communications have helped to level all traditions, all particularities, and, at the limit, the very texture of a culture's life.

Science has also helped to enforce a techno-economic realm where a purely technical reason, as the best defenders of modernity like Jürgen Habermas correctly insist, is now in danger of levelling even the democratic political achievements of modernity.[1] A merely technical reason will inevitably destroy any genuine public realm of modernity by destroying the emancipatory and the communicative character of reason itself.

The harsh word 'barbarism' fits a culture all too willing to unite two of its greatest achievements – historical consciousness in the humanities and evolutionary theory in the natural and biological sciences – into a grand narrative that tells the modern story as one of an inevitable social evolutionary teleology leading up to and finding its glorious climax in us – the 'Westerners', the 'moderns'. This grand and, finally, bogus narrative becomes the subconscious alibi for all the sins of moderns: for example in the *pecca fortiter* version of the 'social Darwinists' (whose number, if not whose name, is still legion). This modern alibi-narrative exists as well in the quieter but finally no less violent forms of the neo-conservatives: Western culture *is* culture; Western classics *are* the classics: where is the Proust of Samoa, etc? This narrative even drives the remaining liberal versions of the story: soon all other traditions, all other cultures will quietly fade away as the grand social evolutionary schema of modern liberalism lulls all to rest with the secret promise of making everything (and everyone) just one more expression of more of the same good liberal worldview.

Any postmodern thinker who believes that she or he can now leave this ambiguous modern scene and begin anew in innocence is self-deluding. There is no innocent tradition (including modernity and certainly including modern liberal Christianity). There is no single innocent reading of any tradition, including this postmodern reading of the positive and negative realities, the profound ambiguities, of modernity.

If there is a postmodernity it, too, is likely to be deeply ambiguous.[2] Postmodernity also needs not merely affirmation but also critique and suspicion. Many forms of thought announcing themselves as postmodern fully merit the suspicion that others cast upon them. The major suspicion, I suspect, is that postmodern thinkers often seem, at best, ethically underdeveloped. It is not only the incurably moralistic who believe this, nor only those moderns who sense life as worth living only if Kant has been right all along. Any thoughtful person can see this ethical difficulty with many of the proponents of the thousand and one banners bearing the title 'postmodernity'.

227

Many of the postmoderns, for example, seem far too academic in the fully pejorative sense, far too convinced that ideas and ideas alone determine history. The combination of Hegel's early modern historicizing of philosophy and Heidegger's early postmodern philosophizing of history have yielded a curious legacy: a plethora of postmodern counter-narratives that are genuinely profound in their central insights, starting with Heidegger's extraordinary 'history of Being' through the new counter-narratives of Derrida and Foucault, of Lyotard and Kristeva. And yet each of these new anti-grand narratives remains both too truncated in its explanatory power and too over-extended in its ambition to merit the kind of affirmation it demands. That kind of academicism towards concrete history is not merely intellectually too ambitious. Any purely academic understanding of history as the history of ideas unites a curious intellectual arrogance with an ethical obtuseness to the massive suffering in concrete history, including the history of the present. There are times when even the best breakthrough ideas are, by their refusal at ethical-political seriousness, in danger of becoming merely academic and ethically both obtuse and finally vulgar (even, at the limit, as in Heidegger's notorious case, morally repulsive).

The postmoderns sometimes seem more determined by ennui than by ethics. They are not, in fact, so much repelled by the ethical barbarism of modernity as bored by liberal modernity's 'gray-on-gray' world. This is perhaps an understandable aesthetic response to liberal modernity. But it is only that – a merely aesthetic response without the moral power of the great aesthetic and ethical traditions of the Good and the Beautiful like Platonism or Romanticism.

Despite these faults, indeed, these barbarisms, postmodernity at its best is a fully ethical response to the ambiguities of modernity. Postmodern thought at its best is an ethics of resistance – resistance, above all, to more of the same, the same unquestioned sameness of the modern turn to the subject, the modern over-belief in the search for the perfect method, the modern social evolutionary narrative whereby all is finally and endlessly more of the self-same.

The real face of postmodernity, as Emmanuel Levinas sees with such clarity, is the face of the other, the face that commands 'Do not kill me', the face that insists, beyond Levinas, do not reduce me or anyone else to your grand narrative.[3] Each of us can accept evolutionary theory for nature and for understanding ourselves as part of that nature. But natural evolutionary theory is not useful for understanding myself as a subject active in history. There, I, like you, am other and different. No one is simply more of the same, simply a moment in the grand social evolutionary teleological schema of modernity.

Genuine postmodernity begins not in ennui but in ethical resistance. Postmodernity begins by trying to think the unthought of modernity. Beyond the early modern turn to the purely autonomous, self-grounding subject, beyond even the more recent turn to language (the first great contemporary challenge to modern subjectism) lies the quintessential turn of postmodernity itself – the turn to the other. It is that turn, above all, that defines the intellectual as well as the ethical meaning of postmodernity. The other and the different come forward now as central intellectual categories across all the major disciplines, including theology. The others and the different – both those from other cultures and those others not accounted for by the grand narrative of the dominant culture – return with full force to unmask the social evolutionary narrative of modernity as ultimately an alibi-story, not a plausible reading of our human history together. Part of that return of otherness, as we shall see below, is the return of biblical Judaism and Christianity to undo the complacencies of modernity, including modern theology.

God's shattering otherness, the neighbor's irreducible otherness, the othering reality of 'revelation', not the consoling modern communality of 'religion', all these expressions of otherness come now in new postmodern *and* post-neo-orthodox forms to demand the serious attention of all thoughtful theologians. Intensity and transgression are frequent entry-points into this unsettling, new reality where sameness dissolves into either a whirlwind of sheer differences or an ethical call to otherness by more and more and more 'others' and 'the other' lurking in the modern unconscious. In such a demanding situation, attention to the forms of theological 'otherness' occurs as one way to try to pay serious theological attention to the change all around us – changes determined perhaps by the Divine Spirit who blows whither She will.

## The turn to the other in Christian theology

The turn to the other takes many forms in postmodernity. Every form is an interruption of the role of the same, more often understood as the reign of the modern. Interruption itself takes many forms. Sometimes it comes as sheer interruptive event, power, gift. At other times it comes as pure revelation and grace. Where transgression often serves as a first sign of a postmodern arrival, the reality of gift and its economy is often a second and more explicitly theological sign of the presence of postmodernity. As with the earlier dialectical theologians (especially Karl Barth), if for very different reasons, both event language and revelation language have returned to theology. Both now return not so much to retrieve some aspect of premodernity (although that too becomes a real possibility) but rather to disrupt or interrupt the continuities and similarities masking the increasingly deadening sameness of the modern worldview. Event is that which cannot be accounted for in the present order but disrupts it by simply happening. Gift transgresses the present economy and calls it into question. Revelation is the event-gift of the Other's self-manifestation. Revelation disrupts the continuities, the similarities, the communalities of modern 'religion'.

The reign of modernity is also the reign of the modern construct 'religion'. The modern academy – precisely through its modernity not its academic status – can accept 'religious studies' as more of the same. It fears 'theology' as other: transgressive and disturbing – a form of thought and life that seems to live on a claim to an otherness (a gift and event of the Other's self-manifestation). When modern theology loses its courage to be other, it retreats to some premodern option. When it acknowledges its own status as a transgressive form of thought dependent upon, because participatory in, an event-gift-revelation of the Other it becomes, in many forms, a transgressive postmodern option.

Many forms of philosophy also begin to partake of such otherness. With the fine exception of that form of analytical philosophy naming itself 'Christian philosophy' (and thereby, considering revelation not only religion) most analytical philosophy seems capable only of further scholasticism or of the relatively untroubled, not to say relaxed postmodernity of Richard Rorty. Moreover, most forms of philosophy of religion (a discipline invented in and for modernity) are far too caught in their own disciplinary modernism even to consider the otherness of revelation as worthy of their attention. On the other hand, all those forms of philosophy in which otherness and difference have become central categories now find modernity more a problematic concept than a ready solution. These philosophies of otherness and difference have become, in fact if not in name, postmodern. Often this occurs through a self-conscious recovery of the non-Enlightenment, even at times the non-Greek resources of Western culture itself: witness Emmanuel Levinas' brilliant recovery of ethics as first philosophy, partly made possible by his recovery of the Judaic strands of our culture; witness Pierre Hadot's and Martha Nussbaum's distinct recoveries of the literary aspect (Nussbaum) and spiritual exercises aspect (Hadot) of pluralistic Hellenistic culture rather than classic Hellenic culture; witness Jean Luc Marion's brilliant recovery of Pseudo-Dionysius or Julia Kristeva's recovery of the love mystics;

witness Jacques Derrida's interest in (and critique of) the traditions of apophatic theology; witness John Caputo's recent Judeo-Christian philo- sophical critique of Heidegger's obsession with the Greeks.

The list of genuinely postmodern philosophical exercises could be expanded easily. Some (as, curiously, with the ancients) make it difficult to distinguish a philosophical from a theological position any longer, for example, Mark C. Taylor, Robert Scharlemann, or Edith Wyschogrod. Others speak their descriptions of the Other in more familiar theological terms – the gift is explicitly named grace; the event of the Other is named the revelation event of the Other's self-manifestation. Indeed those new postmodern theological options have exploded in a hundred new cultural and theological forms.

Surely the very question of form itself is what should command our attention most. My own belief is that across the Christian theological spectrum there is occurring an event of major import: the attempt to free Christian theology from the now smothering embrace of modernity – an event that is as difficult, as conflictual, and as painful as the earlier (equally necessary) attempt in early modernity to free theology from the suffocating embrace of premodern modes of thought. Moderns have now become, in every discipline – including theology – the most defensive and troubled thinkers of all. They always seem to be searching for one more round of the premodern versus modern debate in order to display their honest modern scruples and arguments one more time. Fortunately for them, there are more than enough fundamentalist groups (that curious underside of the modern dilemma) to allow the 'modern' debate to continue.

Unfortunately for the moderns, however, the more serious debate has shifted to one they continue to avoid: the debate on the unthought aspects of modernity itself. Was the modern turn to the subject also a turn to the same? Was the 'religionizing' of all theology more of that same? Is the modern form of argument adequate to understand genuine otherness and difference? Is not modern liberal thought far more engendered, racial, classist, and Eurocentric than it seems capable of acknowledging? These questions begin to haunt the modern conscience like a guilty romance. For some, the only honest option is to find better ways to honor otherness and difference by transgressing the modern liberal pieties, if necessary, in order to honor in thought as in life the otherness manifested in Jesus Christ and the otherness explosively disclosed in all the new theologies of our day.

The question of form itself, I repeat, is one way to begin to address these new theological questions with new resources for thought and action. Christian theology should never be formless,[4] even in its most apophatic, that is, formless moments (for example, Meister Eckhart). Christian theology should always be determined in its understanding of God and humanity by its belief in the form-of-forms, the divine-human form, Jesus Christ – the form that must inform all Christian understanding of God and transform all Christian understanding of human possibility for thought and, above all, action.

There is no serious form of *Christian* theology that is not christomorphic. This is a more accurate designation of the christological issue, I believe, than the more familiar but confusing word 'christocentric'. For theology is not christocentric but theocentric, although it is so only by means of its christomorphism. But my present concern is what form this christomorphism might take in the present situation of the turn to the other. The answer, I believe, is ready at hand in all the new theologies occurring across the whole Christian world (not only in its Euro-American corner). The answer is likely to occur in even more cultural forms in the future. The answer – whether evangelical or mystical, whether Euro-American or African, whether feminist or womanist, whether explicitly postmodern or only implicitly so – is the explosion of what Gustavo Gutiérrez and others have named the mystical-political form contemporary theology needs to take.[5]

My own suggestion is that this now familiar mystical-political naming, although resonant to many of the needs of our moment, is not the most adequate way to describe the fuller range of options for rendering the Other in new forms. For that we may consider the following hypothesis of the fuller spectrum of possible forms needed (and, as it happens, available) for our present question of postmodern theology's turn to the other. Any Christian theology that claims its basic continuity with its biblical roots (as, I believe, Christian theology must if it is seriously Christian) may find what it needs in the full spectrum of forms in the Bible itself. The two most basic religious forms in the Bible are the prophetic and the meditative (wisdom) forms. From these two forms and their dialectic emerge the fuller spectrum of past, present, and likely future forms of Christian theology.

First, the prophetic. The prophet speaks not because he or she wishes to but because God as Other demands it. The prophet speaks on behalf of the other – the neighbor – especially the poor, the oppressed, and the marginal other. Jesus is the eschatological prophet bespeaking the Other for the sake of all others. There is no way around the prophetic core of Christian self-understanding. Even our earliest Christologies come in prophetic form. Not only the liberation and evangelical theologies but all serious Christian theology must maintain that prophetic form or admit that its transformation into some reality has become something perhaps rich and strange but no longer Christian, that is, prophetic.

That prophetic core, in turn, can move in two directions. First, the prophetic insight can be taken in a generalizing direction wherein its religious/revelatory core is seen as, at its heart, also an ethics. This is what Emmanuel Levinas has found in his simultaneous discovery that ethics is first philosophy and that true ethics is grounded in the face of the other. The other – the biblical neighbor – is what no ontological totality can ever control. The temptation to totalizing modes of thought is disrupted once and for all by the glimpse of the Infinite in the face of the other and its ethical command, 'Do not kill me'. Is it really so surprising that Levinas' work has become so central not only for Jewish thought but also for Christian liberation theology with its instinctive prophetic-ethical sense for the other, especially the preferred other of the prophets – the poor, the marginal, and the oppressed.

One or another version of this prophetic move determines the new kind of Christian theological ethics in many postmodern political, feminist, womanist, and liberation theologies across the Christian world. The difference between a postmodern ethics focused on the Other and others and the kinds of ethical positions developed in modern liberal theologies focused on the modern autonomous self and its rational obligations is clear. Some move to ethics (or with the ancients, more accurately, the ethical-political realm) is necessary for Christian theology. Postmodern positions (like Levinas) seem to me far more hermeneutically faithful to the prophetic self-understanding than the more familiar modern deontological and teleological Christian ethical options.

But the prophetic center can also break away from any generalizing move at all in favor of the intensification, indeed transgression, of the prophetic form into a radically disruptive apocalyptic form. 'When prophesy fails, apocalyptic takes over.' And so it may. History then becomes interpreted not as continuity at all but as radical interruption. In philosophy, the apocalyptic urgency of the early Frankfurt thinkers (especially Benjamin and Adorno) will return – as it surely does in the apocalyptic political theology of Johann Baptist Metz, where theology yields great ethical-political urgency driven by the meaning of suffering but does not yield generalizing ethical principles. When apocalypse is understood in and through the forms of excess, transgression, and negation of continuity, then apocalyptic returns as the favored form of many radicalized political theologies.

In the meantime, the other great biblical form, the meditative or wisdom form, may also move in these same two directions. First, at its center, the meditative form turns away from the more historical and ethical prophetic core of the Bible in order to reflect upon our

233

relationships to the cosmos and to face the kind of limit-situations (death, guilt, anxiety, despair, joy, peace, and hope) that human being as human beings will always experience. Job and Lamentations will always speak their meditative, penetrating truth to anyone capable of facing the tragedy that is human existence. The Gospel of John – that meditative rendering of the common Christian narrative – will always describe the beauty and glory of the whole of reality (even the cross as the lifting up and disclosure of glory) to all those capable of genuine meditation on the limit experiences of peace, joy, beauty, and love. Meditative humans, then as now, will turn to intelligence and love, to nature and to cosmos, to mind and to body, to aid their reflections on the vision of life, the wisdom, disclosed by the biblical narratives for our common human limit-experiences.

When these meditative positions make even further generalizing moves, they are more likely to develop profound participatory metaphysics (like Platonism in all its splendid forms). When more ethically oriented, a wisdom ethics will prove an aesthetic ethics of appreciation of the good and of beauty (like Whitehead and Hartshorne). When more historically conscious, these meditative positions will develop into a hermeneutical philosophy disclosing the dialogical character of all reality. A wisdom-grounded metaphysics (never totalizing, if hermeneutically faithful to its biblical core) and an aesthetics will unite to relate themselves to some form of prophetic ethics, more likely in these traditions an ethics of the good, as in Iris Murdoch.

The meditative traditions, however, need not stay in those participatory moments. They, too, may take their own turn to the Other. Then the meditation is intensified to the point of becoming transgressive of all participation – as typically with postmodern recoveries of the more radical mystical traditions. Love then becomes not relationality or overflow but sheer excess and transgression – from Bataille through Kristeva. Radically apophatic Christian mysticism (for example, Meister Eckhart) becomes a genuine option for contemporary thought. The recovery of mystical readings of the prophetic core of Judaism and Christianity is one of the surest signs of a postmodern sensibility. In a similar fashion, the return of the repressed 'pagan' emphasis on nature becomes an equally clear sign, as Scholem insisted, of the presence of a new mystical reading of a prophetic tradition.

This fuller spectrum of a seemingly endless series of new prophetic and meditative forms of new possibilities in new theologies across the globe will surely increase. As both cross-cultural sensibilities and inter-religious dialogue take further hold on serious Christian theology, moreover, this prophetic-meditative spectrum will increase yet again. Theology will never again be tameable by a system – any system – modern or premodern or postmodern. For theology does not bespeak a totality. Christian theology, at its best, is the voice of the Other through all those others who have tasted, prophetically and meditatively, the Infinity disclosed in the kenotic reality of Jesus Christ.

NOTES

1. On Habermas and modernity for theology, see the essays in Don Browning and Francis Schüssler Fiorenza, eds., *Habermas, Modernity and Public Theology*, New York: Crossroad, 1992.
2. I have tried to defend this belief in ambiguity in *Plurality and Ambiguity: Hermeneutics, Religion, Hope*, San Francisco: Harper and Row, 1989.
3. See, especially, Emmanuel Levinas, *Totality and Infinity: An Essay on Exteriority*, Pittsburgh: Dequesne University Press, 1981.
4. The most eloquent defense of this proposition in modern theology remains Hans Urs von Balthasar, *The Glory of the Lord*, seven vols, San Francisco: Ignatius Press, 1982–92.
5. See Claude Geffré and Gustavo Gutiérrez, editors, 'The Mystical and Political Dimensions of the Christian Faith', *Concilium*, 96 (1974).

# 23

# WHATEVER HAPPENED TO THE DOCTRINE OF SIN?
## David H. Kelsey

Published just twenty years ago, Karl Menninger's popular book, *Whatever Became of Sin?*,[1] gave voice to a widespread suspicion that the concept 'sin' was steadily evaporating from everyday life. Culture in general aside, by century's end, people concerned specifically about the health of Christian systematic theology – especially if they had been formed by mid-century theological controversies – are entitled to suspect that the doctrine of sin was somehow evaporating from formal theology as well. After all, by mid-century the clearest line dividing the older, beleaguered Protestant 'liberalism' from the newer, unhelpfully labeled 'neo-orthodoxy' had been the distinction between the 'optimistic' view that human nature was progressively improving beyond sin and the 'pessimistic' view that human nature is inherently and structurally 'estranged'. The last quarter of the century, however, has been dominated by discussions of theologies of 'critical correlation' with general human experience, theologies of 'liberation' and theologies of 'hope'. The doctrine of sin may no longer seem prominent in the conversation. If this suspicion were true, it would be of profound importance for the social as well as the intellectual history of Christianity, because the doctrine of sin is one of those doctrines in which Christian life-forming is held closest to Christian truth-claiming, practical theology closest to dogmatic theology. What has happened to the doctrine of sin?

I want to suggest that the doctrine of sin is vigorously alive but has migrated. It has moved into different contexts provided by various doctrinal *loci*; it has moved under the pressure of subtly different judgments about what the basic gist is of the Christian message; and the effects of the moves are pastorally, morally, and even politically practical. We can broadly map the doctrine's migration by noting its traditional home and sketching three trajectories along which it has migrated.

I

'The' doctrine of sin whose present health and whereabouts are under investigation is broadly Augustinian. It holds closely together two definitions of sin, which it struggles to keep coherent: sin as 'actual sin' and sin as 'original sin'. 'Actual sin' is sin seen (with plenty of support from the Old and New Testaments) as a set of acts done consciously and deliberately against God's will. 'Original sin' (following St Paul's teaching and other Christians' experience of moral conflict) is seen as a state of corruption of the created human will caused in us by the 'actual sin' of the first human couple and, in turn, causing all our own acts themselves to be 'actual sin'. With the latter, we 'inherit' guilt by which we are separated from God until it is removed by baptism; with the former, we incur our own guilt, which, after baptism, needs to be confessed and repented, lest it finally separate us from God.

The insistence on holding these two definitions together has several practical consequences. To define sin as 'actual' is to stress that it most basically is 'against God'. Whatever its further ramifications may be, sin is a theological notion defined theocentrically and cannot simply be interchanged without remainder with psychological, sociological, or cosmological notions. Further, to define sin as 'actual' is to stress our own responsibility for sin. Sin is conscious and deliberate violation of God's will. Whatever 'original sin' implies, sin is not finally a fate before which we are helpless and without responsibility.

However, to leave it at that opens the door to individualistic and moralistic pictures of sin. If sin is violation of God's will, then it is a problem solely between each individual person and God. Furthermore, if each of us is responsible for doing it, each of us could cease doing it by 'trying harder' (and then what we need is more willpower, not a crucifixion).

To define sin as 'original' serves to block both of these inferences. Our actual sins follow from a corrupted state of our wills from which we cannot extricate ourselves by heroic moral and spiritual struggles. Further, our sharing in this corruption is a function of the solidarity of the human family and is not simply the sum total of our individual decisions; sin is a socially shared problem and not isolated individuals' problem with God.

However, to define sin as 'original' is to see sin, if we may use the distinction, in social but not in societal terms. The state of sin may be an intersubjective state shared because of the solidarity of the human family throughout all time, but that 'solidarity' has not been understood in terms of the 'public' realm of actual societies' arrangements of social power.

Hence, the internal logic of this doctrine of sin has tended toward a conservative stand on issues in the public realm. The doctrine has been easily used to support the view that however unjust *status quo* power arrangements may be, injustice is a consequence of sin. Remediation of injustice does not contribute to healing sin, and the elimination of injustice is strictly contingent on the prior elimination of sin. Therefore, those concerned about sin had best leave well enough alone in the public realm.

This entire doctrine of sin rests on a particular formulation of the basic gist of the Christian message. It is justified by a construal of biblical stories that synthesizes and harmonizes them into a single narrative history having three temporally successive moments: First, in love, God created humankind as part of a good world of finite creatures. Then, when some creatures sinned against God, the world as a whole was corrupted. At the right time, the same God, in love, took the initiative to save the fallen world by way of the election of a particular people, among whom God became incarnate and among whom the incarnate one was then crucified and raised in order to restore finite creatures to wholeness.

The 'health-disease-healing' plot-structure of this narrative dictates that the conceptually basic doctrine is the doctrine of creation. Just as the doctrine of sin will set the categories in which redemption will have to be discussed (you can't describe the cure except in terms of the specifics of the disease), so the doctrine of creation will set the terms in which sin will have to be discussed (you can't describe a disease except in terms provided by an account of the healthy state of the ill organism). Thus, the conceptual home of the traditional doctrine of sin is a doctrine of creation, not a doctrine of God, even though sin must be defined in a theocentric way. This is not to say that this doctrine of sin is deduced from a doctrine of creation, but only that the doctrine of creation dictates the conceptual scheme used by the doctrine of sin and lays down some rules about what can and cannot be said consistently in a doctrine of sin.

Housing a doctrine of sin in the larger context of a doctrine of creation allows the doctrine of sin to stress several themes with particular emphasis. Above all, it leads to drawing a sharp line between finitude and sin. The contingency, limitations, and fragility that constitute our finitude are not themselves sin, are not the consequences of sin, and do not fate us to sin. Human creatures, precisely in their finitude and not as escape from it, are both free and knowing and, therewith, changeable in their actions and vulnerable to their consequences. Finitude is precisely what God creates, and it is 'good'.

The converse is that finite creatures are constituted as the type of creatures they are by a relation of absolute dependence on God. The type of creature one is will determine the sort of acts of which one is capable: act follows from being, not the other way around. For free and knowing creatures like us, this entails a relation of absolute accountability to God. This grounds a second major stress in the traditional doctrine of sin: sin incurs 'objective' guilt, that is, guilt as an objective status one, in fact, occupies before God, not guilt as a mode of subjectivity, a type of consciousness, or a feeling. It is also this larger context in a doctrine of creation that allows the traditional doctrine of sin the further theme that sin is best understood as both act and state. As absolutely answerable to God, human creatures' free and knowing violation of God's will is 'actual sin'. As absolutely dependent on God for being, human creatures are the same type of creature, sharing the same nature. If one of the consequences of actual sin (say, by Adam and Eve) is a corruption of human nature, then this corruption is 'original sin'. All who share in human nature will share in the corruption, and, since act follows from being, all who share in the corruption of human nature will commit actual sin.

The difficult intellectual task in this traditional doctrine of sin is to relate each of the two definitions of sin (as 'actual' and as 'original') to the other – in the context of a doctrine of creation – as a check on the other definition's possible religiously unacceptable implications (moralism, individualism, determinism), without falling into incoherence. This requires a dialectical skill with which not all preachers, educators, and thinkers have been equally gifted. The critics (the theological 'liberals' regarding this topic), of course, have argued that it is an inherently impossible task.

## II

The first trajectory along which the traditional, broadly Augustinian doctrine of sin migrated led from creation to theological anthropology as the systematic 'home' of the doctrine. 'Sin' names a condition of human subjects in which they are estranged from themselves, others, and God; a doctrine of sin describes that condition. Its central themes are familiar. The categories to be used in discussing sin and the rules governing what can and cannot be said are provided not by a doctrine of creation but by an analysis of what a subject is. To be a subject is not a gift given but a task to be achieved. What one is 'given' are, on one side, a definite and limiting location (call it 'finitude') and, on the other, capacities to transcend and transform creatively any and every given location (call it 'openness' to transcendence). These are but the possibilities of becoming an actual subject. The task is so to take charge of yourself that you actualize yourself by holding these two in proper balance in all of your other projects. Your acts of self-relating constitute your actual being rather than (as in the traditional doctrine of sin) following from your being. If you fail to keep the two in balanced tension, so that in your life you seek creatively to transcend the given as though you were not rooted in it or, conversely, so that you simply identify yourself with some given *status quo* as though you in no way transcended it, you begin progressively to become less and less a subject. What must be said theologically is that the self-relations that constitute you as a subject can only actually be done in the context of a faith relationship with God. One is actualized as a subject in faith alone. To attempt to do it on one's own amounts to works righteousness; it leads to an inevitable dissolution of the self.

Accordingly, sin may be seen as both 'actual' and 'original'. However, since your actual being follows from your acts of self-relating rather than your acts following from the actual being given you by God's creative act, the two senses of sin cannot be so easily distinguished. The act that counts as actual sin is strictly limited to the 'act' of idolatry, that is, trusting something other than God as one seeks to actualize one's subjecthood. So, too, whereas traditionally the notion of original sin had served both to give a genetic explanation of sin and a description of the state of sin, here only the descriptive power of the notion is retained. Given the internal logic of the doctrine of sin, the two changes need each other. Without the explanatory force of original sin, there is no check on the individualistic and moralistic tendencies of 'actual sin'. Moralism, in turn, entails works righteousness that proponents of this type of doctrine of sin say undercuts the core of the Christian message of grace. Hence 'actual sin' must be limited to the act of idolatry.

This doctrine of sin is funded by the same set of biblical stories of creation and fall, but differently construed and differently interrelated. Now, they are read as myths expressive of different aspects of a single universal human experience. It is an experience of ourselves as so deeply self-contradictory that we are well on the way to self-dissolution. Creation stories express our consciousness that 'what' we truly are is finite and is normative for how we ought actually to be. Accordingly, a doctrine of creation describes not a creaturely cosmos in regard to its actuality but human subjectivity in regard to its possibility, that is, what the features are of subjectivity that make it possible for us to be actual and to be self-contradictory in our actuality. For their part, fall and sin stories express our consciousness that the concrete ways in which we actually live, the 'hows' of our lives, are contradictory to 'what' we truly are. Accordingly, a doctrine of sin describes that contradiction and what is needed to avoid it.

In order adequately to express the one, complex experience of self-contradiction, the two sets of stories must not be held together as two moments in a single temporal sequence, but rather held together as though they were concurrent narratives of the same event (the 'event' of me), each interpreted by reference to the other. The corresponding doctrines of creation and of sin must be held together in the same way in the context of a theological anthropology. One consequence of this is that 'finitude' and 'sin' are so closely tied together that they may seem to be two descriptions of the same reality looked at in two different respects. In that case, the 'goodness' of finite reality, so central to the traditional doctrine of sin, seems to be in question.

Clearly, this was the basic pattern of the doctrine of sin that dominated mid-century American Protestant theology and, in various modalities, is still very influential. Despite deep and important theological differences on other matters, Reinhold Niebuhr[2] and Paul Tillich[3] shared the basic structure of this doctrine of sin. They share it, moreover, with many successor 'correlationist' theologians and with so influential a Roman Catholic theologian as Karl Rahner.[4] That this pattern of thought about sin can still be employed with great power is shown by Edward Farley in his remarkable recent book *Good and Evil*.[5]

Developing a doctrine of sin in the context of this theological anthropology has important practical consequences. By integrating the faith relationship and, indeed, justification by faith so deeply into the very core of a doctrine of sin, it has tended to shift emphasis in pastoral leadership away from programs and structures of worship focused on sanctification and the formation of Christian identity and toward mission on behalf of the neighbor in the public realm and the wider culture shared with the neighbor. Of course, this does not follow of necessity; Karl Rahner's extensive attention to sanctification and spiritual formation alone would be evidence of that. However, especially in American Protestant circles, its systematic undercutting of any theological support for justification by works, pious works in particular, clearly has tended to feed suspicion of expenditures of energy to make us more 'holy'. So too, it opens up space for a less politically conservative stance in two ways: by rejecting the explanatory force of 'original sin', thus making the injustice of the *status quo* look less like implacable fate; and by systematically undercutting all forms of self-righteousness and moralism, which makes the possibility of incurring guilt through action in the public realm seem less ultimately threatening. On the other hand, as feminist theologians especially have pointed out, its stress on sin as willful idolatry tends to provide a better pastoral diagnostic of men's experience of sin than it does for the

241

experience of women who have been socialized into more self-abnegating patterns of action. Finally, it leads to interpretations of guilt as a subjective state rather than an objective status before God (as it is in the traditional doctrine of sin). Indeed, for all of its insistence that it is housed in an ontology of subjecthood, not in a psychology of the dynamics of guilty feelings, this doctrine of sin has – ironically – proved open to a psychologizing of sin. It has readily undergone more or less humanistic psychological 'translations' that allow easy conflation of theologically informed pastoral care with secular psychological counseling.

III

A second trajectory along which the traditional doctrine of sin has migrated leads from creation to redemption as its larger doctrinal context. With the traditional doctrine of sin, it construes biblical stories as one long narrative, but argues (with extensive debts to Gerhard von Rad[6]) that it is, from first to last, a history of God's redemptive acts, of which creation is simply the first among many, culminating in the event of Christ. Indeed, it is God's redemptive action that 'binds' time into a single history, giving it meaning. Hence no topic in theology, from creation to sin, can be properly understood except in terms provided by an understanding of redemption. What the biblical narratives show is that God's redemptive acts always occur in the midst of the 'material' realities of history that generate political conflicts, often occur through radical political change, and are aimed at the relief of those oppressed by unjust power arrangements. In short, on this view redemption is best understood as liberation.

There is room for a variety of characterizations of God's liberating act. Their differences from one another turn in large part on the different ways in which they see time bound by God's redemptive act. As is well known, figures like Gustavo Gutiérrez[7] and James Cone[8] take the Exodus story to be the paradigmatic redemptive act, as though God keeps repeating the same basic pattern of action in a series of redemptive acts in successive moments of history. Johannes Metz,[9] on the other hand, locates God's redemptive act specifically in the past moment of the life and crucifixion of Jesus, which impinges redemptively on subsequent historical moments through our 'subversive memory' of his suffering, a memory subversive of every oppressive power arrangement. By contrast, Jürgen Moltmann[10] locates God's redemptive act in the eschaton, a future event proleptically present in the resurrection of the crucified Jesus, the reality of God's Kingdom of peace and justice that is now genuinely actual but not yet fully actualized, related to the present not as a moment growing out of the present ('*futuram*') but as something radically new impinging on the present from the future ('*adventus*').

In the context of such doctrines of redemption, sin is understood basically to be unjust societal self-contradiction, in contrast to sin as the self-contradictory state of human subjects. Hence sin is at once socially structural (the functional equivalent of 'original sin' as corruption) and individual (the functional equivalent of 'actual sin' as personal act). It is structural in that it is an inherited and shared arrangement of power in society that oppresses some, putting them in conflict with others, in which we continue to be complicit whether as oppressed or oppressing. It is individual in so far as, knowing of God's act to liberate us all from it, we nonetheless willfully refuse to oppose it. Human movements to liberate the oppressed do not bring in God's liberation; only God does that. Redemption as the enactment of God's plan for the world may not be conflated with progressive social action as the enactment of some critical social theory. But refusal to respond in trust to God's act of liberation with our own inadequate efforts to liberate the oppressed and to correct unjust structural arrangements of power is against God and is sin.

The practical consequences of this understanding of sin for a Christian mission of social action are as well known as they are controversial. It is clear in the writings of theologians representative of this view, such as Gutiérrez and Metz, that a theological definition of sin in terms of social conflict no more logically entails a theological justification for the use of violence to liberate the oppressed than does a definition of sin as self-conflict entail a justification of self-violence to heal the self. It is equally clear that this doctrine of sin is nonetheless open to being developed (distorted?) in that direction. What is less often noted is the practical consequences of this doctrine of sin for Christian formation. It requires the cultivation of capacities to perceive and identify sin not only as distortions of one's interiority in specific concrete circumstances but also as structurally at work in specific concrete circumstances in one's society; and it requires cultivation of capacities to engage in specific efforts at liberation without oppressing others (one's enemies) by demonizing them and denying their human dignity.

## IV

A third trajectory along which the doctrine of sin has migrated leads it from creation to Christology as its doctrinal home. The type of Christology in view here agrees with a liberationist doctrine of sin that no theological topic can be understood except in the context of a doctrine of redemption.

However this view, represented monumentally by Karl Barth[11] and his current progeny, holds that redemption has already been accomplished in the resurrection of the crucified Jesus. This rests on yet another construal of biblical stories that sees them as a narrative identity-description of Jesus as God incarnate; the 'history' of God's redemptive acts is simply a story telling who Jesus is. What it tells us is that, as the incarnation of God, Jesus is in himself quite concretely the actualization of God's primordial decision to be in the closest covenant relation with reality that is other than God and that all reality that is not God, including ourselves, is dependent on that decision for its very being. To say that such a Christology is the larger context for a doctrine of sin is to agree with the liberationist theologies that redemption is the necessary context within which properly to understand sin. It is also to go beyond that to claim that, as the incarnation of God, Jesus is the ontological basis of our being creatures who, as it turns out, are sinful.

Formulated in this context, a doctrine of sin defines sin not by reference to a structure of creation that obtains whether or not sin or redemption occur, nor by reference to the structure of subjectivity, nor by reference to the manner in which a history of salvation takes place, but solely by reference to the presence of the risen incarnate Son of God. Sin is defined as willful disrelatedness to the risen Lord present here and now.

Putting it this way has odd conceptual consequences. In one way, sin is ontologically impossible. We would not exist to be 'dis-related' to the risen Lord were we not already related to him by his own gracious decision to include us in the community of his covenant love. Sin only takes place within the context of the covenant relationship with the Son of God and neither breaks off nor neutralizes that relationship. So sin is, at most, a deep delusion we have about ourselves: that we are and can be outside relation to Jesus Christ. Yet, in another way, sin clearly obtains. People do have this delusion. And it has terrible consequences. Not only does it render them incapable of knowing God. It sets them on a kind of slippery slide toward nothingness. Understood in this context, sin is taken very seriously. And yet, given Jesus' resurrection and the realization in it of God's eschatological purposes, neither the ignorance nor the drift toward nothingness can have any ultimacy, for now nothing can separate us from God's covenant love.

This conceptual oddity has correlates in the practical consequences of this doctrine of sin. This comes out in the affective tone fostered by this doctrine of sin. On the one hand, it gravely underscores the objective reality and radically disabling consequences of sin. In sin, we are literally depraved. The affective tone appropriate to this state of affairs is dark, marked by helplessness and terror. Left at that, this doctrine of sin should generate markedly penitential styles of congregational life, modes of piety and strategies of pastoral care that, at best, would cultivate poor self-images and low self-esteem. However, the basic point of the theological strategy of this doctrine of sin is firmly to bracket all of that, without denying its truth in the slightest, in the larger context of the affirmation that sin in all its objectivity has just as objectively been overcome decisively in the resurrection of Jesus. The affective tone appropriate to this state of affairs is sheer joy, a cheerful *hilaritas* as one goes about life in the every day. The strategy of this doctrine of sin is designed to generate patterns of worship, preaching, pastoral care, piety, and mission in the world that instantiate this affective tone in the daily round, not by denying the grave reality of sin but precisely by stressing it as something real but overcome.

The sense that the concept of sin has faded out of the week in, week out discourse of Christian communities does not lack for supporting evidence, of course. This essay has argued that the concept is an important part of a wide variety of types of formal theology, although sometimes under aliases. It may be that otherwise influential formal theologies do not much influence church folk to talk specifically about sin because these doctrines of sin have become too complexly dialectical to be helpful guides to what to say when we pray, preach, give pastoral care, and passionately engage our society. It may be that liturgical movements stressing the centrality in the gospel of Jesus' resurrection and protesting the one-sidedly penitential shape of traditional worship contributes to a muting of sin-talk. Or perhaps what's being sensed is not so much a disuse of the concept of sin as it is an abandonment of the concept of divine wrath, for, if there is no need to talk about the wrath of God, then there is not much need to talk about the sin that incurs the wrath.

NOTES
1. Karl Menninger, *Whatever Became of Sin?*, New York: Hawthorn Books, 1973.
2. Reinhold Niebuhr, *The Nature and Destiny of Man*, Vol. 1, New York: Charles Scribner's Sons, 1941.
3. Paul Tillich, *Systematic Theology*, Vol. 2, Chicago: University of Chicago Press, 1957.
4. Karl Rahner, *Foundations of Christian Faith*, New York: Seabury Press, 1978.
5. Edward Farley, *Good and Evil*, Minneapolis: Augsburg Fortress, 1991. Judging by the way he deals with the topic of sin in his *Anthropology in Theological Perspective*

(Philadelphia: Westminster Press, 1985), I am inclined to place Wolfhart Pannenberg in this group even though the systematically central place of eschatology in his theological project would otherwise suggest that he belongs in the next 'type'.

6. Gerhard von Rad, *Old Testament Theology*, New York: Harper & Row, 1962.
7. Gustavo Gutiérrez, *A Theology of Liberation*, Maryknoll NY: Orbis, 1973.
8. James Cone, *A Black Theology of Liberation*, Philadelphia: J. B. Lippincott, 1970.
9. Johannes Metz, *Faith in History and Society*, New York: Seabury Press, 1980.
10. Jürgen Moltmann, *The Theology of Hope*, London: SCM Press, 1967; *The Church in the Power of the Spirit*, New York: Harper and Row, 1977.
11. Karl Barth, *Church Dogmatics*, Vol. 4, Pts. 1—3, Edinburgh, T & T Clark, 1956, 1956, 1961.

# 24

# AFTER LIBERALISM
## *Don Cupitt*

Until not very long ago theology and the religious scene generally were dominated by the conflict between conservatives and liberals. It was a dispute with ramifications extending far beyond the English-speaking world, and indeed far beyond Christendom. The question at issue was how far traditional religious ways of thinking could or should change in response to the Enlightenment.

There had of course been a period of Enlightenment previously in the Western tradition, during classical antiquity. In that period Enlightened intellectuals who concerned themselves with religion had already explored many of the options available to them – fideism, allegorism, nature-mysticism, syncretism, introvertive or negative mysticism and so forth. But classical antiquity was not democratic, and the Enlightened mentality was a predominantly literary phenomenon, confined to a smallish minority of the population. At first the modern Enlightenment, beginning in early Renaissance Italy, was also a minority affair. The immense power of a persecuting Church obliged it to be relatively discreet and low-key until the late seventeenth century. But then it began to spread rapidly. Democratic and historicist ideologies developed, claiming that before long everyone was going to go over to the Enlightenment mentality. Laws of historical development made the progressive, and ultimately the complete, secularization of culture unstoppable. To survive, it seemed that religion must change. It must come to terms with Enlightenment.

Accepting all this, and being themselves at least half-Enlightened, the liberals set about reshaping religion to make it more humanistic, democratic, progressive and rational. After Descartes the touchstone of truth tended to be located within the subjectivity of the Enlightened individual. The highest court of appeal was the free individual's reason, conscience and experience. So in liberal religion faith duly became more internalized, with more emphasis upon the human Jesus, upon personal religious experience and upon moral action to reform and improve society. In place of the old passive supernaturalism which saw God as having already fully prescribed the whole framework within which human life must be lived, so that nobody but God could bring about any major change in the human condition, it now came to be held that we human beings are historical agents, called upon ourselves to change our world. The Christian individual was invited to join with others in the great work of building the Kingdom of God on earth. This was a Christianized version of the contemporary secular ideologies of historical progress. The liberal God was an inspiring moral ideal, a moral Providence perhaps, a side-of-the-angels for us to be on, and the Goal of the whole historical process; but he was no longer quite the admonitory Voice in one's head, the transcendent cosmic Lord, the dreadful Judge and the loving Heavenly Father of the conservatives. He just wasn't quite so *vivid* as he had been. The liberal view of God was no more than semi-realist, at least so far as divine personality and divine interventions in the world were concerned. Yet in other respects, as many people will have noticed, the liberals are usually found to be determined and tenacious realists. They still stand in the old Platonic tradition, and believe both in one-truth-out-there and in moral-standards-out-there. They are almost without exception scientific realists, and also social-historical optimists who believe, like John Robinson, if not quite in a guaranteed final historical triumph of the Good, then at least in a constant Love-out-there at the root of things. And they use a good deal of traditional vocabulary.

The consequence of this has been that throughout the hundred years and more of sharp conservative-versus-liberal controversy, much though the two sides might dislike each other, they were in many ways still talking the same language. They were frenemies, despite the fact that conservative religion has remained so determinedly medieval (or, in the case of orthodox Calvinism, in a very distinctive manner, *post-medieval*) in its vocabulary and ways of thinking. Religious truth was cosmic-political. We human beings, it was thought, are lost unless our life is anchored and held steady within an immovable framework of objective divine authority, divine law and divine truth. The conservative cosmology is an upward extension of social authority, sacred, hierarchized and animistic. Conservatives lack, or claim to lack, the Enlightened type of consciousness and for the sake of the social order take pains to ensure that they shall go on lacking it, and they view the humanism and the 'laxity', or charitableness, of the liberals with abhorrence.

Yet sharp though the conflict between them could be, I am suggesting that old-style conservatives and liberals seem in retrospect to have been on pretty much the same side and talking much the same language. The conservatives were ironical enough to have themselves at least a tincture of the Enlightenment mentality (enough to enable them to direct their attacks against it accurately), and the liberals were only half-Enlightened anyway

248

because there was still so much realism left in their theories of knowledge and morality. So beneath the superficial disagreements it is not difficult to detect areas of continuing agreement. Conservatives tend to operate in terms of binary oppositions, whereas liberals are usually universalists. Conservatives tend to believe both in Heaven and in Hell, whereas liberals hope for universal redemption; but both parties believe in an otherworldly salvation after death. Conservatives tend to take a realistic view of miracles such as the resurrection, whereas liberals interpret them in more 'spiritual' terms, but both parties believe in 'the myth of the normative Origin'. The liberals may refer back to Jesus' consciousness, his character and the early Christian experience of him, whereas the conservatives refer back to propositions and prodigies, but both continue to appeal to the origins of Christianity as authoritative. Conservatives see sin in more ritual terms, and liberals in more social-moral, but both parties go on using the word. And in general, the conservatives did not by their behaviour seriously threaten the liberals' belief in reason, because the two parties were after all able to reason with each other.

In Britain there are still old-style religious liberals and old-style conservatives, bickering cosily in bed together as they have done for so long. But, I want to suggest, during the 1980s we witnessed their dispute turning into a new and altogether less cosy battle, that between the postmoderns and the fundamentalists. To use Jean Baudrillard's useful term, postmodernism may be seen as the ecstatic form of Enlightenment, and fundamentalism is certainly the ecstatic form of religious conservatism. With the end of realism in our century, the loss of all objective bearings, and the steady erosion of the distinction between the real and the fictional, everything tends to be transformed into an excessive, hyperbolical and superreal version of itself; and both postmodernism and fundamentalism are ecstatic in this sense. As we saw in the Salman Rushdie affair, the two mentalities are still preoccupied with each other – but now, they are locked in mortal conflict. For whereas old-style religious liberals and conservatives had some sort of reciprocal understanding, there can be no accord between postmodern and fundamentalist believers. Those who look in one direction see only blaspheming nihilism, and those who look the other way see only absolutist fanaticism. Each seems like a damned soul to the other. Both have gone over the top.

This total breakdown of communication is fatal to the old liberal belief – today associated especially with Jürgen Habermas – in the possibility through dialogue of achieving universal and complete mutual comprehension. Who today can think that possible? But then, in recent years the liberal creed has been failing article by article. The belief in 'clean' and uncontaminated data of experience by which to check theories, the belief in self-present, self-scanning and undeceived individual consciousness, the belief in universal moral and intellectual standards, the belief in the distinctions between the real and the fictional and between fact and interpretation, the belief in the progressive historical growth of both consciousness and freedom, the belief that language can be used to tell the truth, the whole truth and nothing but the truth . . . And when everything is seen to be invented and the belief in truth is recognized to be only a highly-desirable fiction, then Enlightenment passes completion and begins to turn back upon itself and devour itself. There is no longer anything left, in the name of which we are entitled to set out to deprive other people of their fictions. In any case, do we not often nowadays catch ourselves envying other people the fictions they live by? Why be demythologized? Thus Enlightenment in recent years has seen through even itself, and in becoming hyperbolical has lost all grounds for thinking of its own point of view as being in some sense privileged. So the reflexive difficulties into which it has got itself have transfigured it into its ecstatic form, postmodernism. Nihilistic, self-sceptical, super-enlightenment.

Now, as in the 1840s among the Young Hegelians, the question of religion is the heart and centre of the whole affair. If during these past few years you have watched the difficulties of Enlightenment as from outside and with a certain malicious satisfaction, then you are surely gravitating towards fundamentalism. And indeed, is it not obvious today that in the most advanced countries millions of people are reverting with almost-audible relief to a premodern mentality? But if on the other hand you have in recent years experienced the difficulties of Enlightenment as darkness and travail within your own soul and as epochal religious events, then you will be sympathetic to the new postmodern theologies now appearing.

The difference is something like this: postmodern religion is religion that fully accepts that it is just human, being made of human signs, and which after having gone through the fires of nihilism knows that it must now continually remake itself as art. And indeed, postmodern religious faith is very close in spirit to present-day painting and writing. By contrast, fundamentalist religion is religion that has glimpsed but has repressed as intolerable and unendurable the knowledge of its own humanness. It has glimpsed nihilism because, of course, it arose precisely out of and in sharp reaction against Darwinism and the later Victorian crisis of faith. So to that extent it really does know the alternative. Its brief glimpse into the Abyss has given to it its sense of urgency. It clutches at authority, charisma, tradition and certainty. It desperately needs to think of religious ideas and religious truth as divinely-given, fearsome and uncriticizable. As everyone who has ever belonged to a fundamentalist or ultra-conservative religious group will know, the group goes to great lengths to exclude unwelcome questioning. Literature is controlled, members must speak in stock phrases and have stock experiences, religious meanings are insistently assumed to be univocal, critical reflection is implicitly (and therefore doesn't *need* to be explicitly) ruled out, and individual deviance is sensed and dealt with instantly. All this bears painful and eloquent testimony to the intensity of people's fear of the Abyss, and the high price they are ready to pay to be shielded from it.

By contrast, postmodern religion thinks that we need to train ourselves to look steadily at the Abyss. In fact, the message of both Christianity and Buddhism (*Die to the self*! and *There is no self*!) is that to gaze steadfastly into the Void purges us of anxious egoism, and liberates us for love and creativity. There are plenty of hints of this in the religious tradition: the Wholly Other, the Absurd, the Sea without a shore, the Divine Darkness, the Dark Night of the Soul, the Incomprehensibility of God, dying with Christ. You must collide with something Unthinkable that unselfs you, and it is the Nihil. Poetically speaking, the Abyss is merciful and gracious. It puts us to death and raises us to life again.

Old-style liberal religion was reluctant to let go completely. It clung to at least semi-realism about God, the objective world and moral value. Postmodern religion is ecstatic liberalism in that it insists upon letting go. It says: Nothing is sacrosanct, everything is revisable. There's nothing out there or in here, and we should be truly beliefless. It is spiritually liberating to be free-floating, and to regard all religious ideas as being human and therefore open to criticism and revision. To *hold on* is to risk falling into superstition and fanaticism. The peculiar sort of poise, strength and sanity that religion can give is only to be had if the full price is paid; one must embrace the Void.

Here, there is undoubtedly a considerable gap between the older liberals and the newer radicals and postmodernists. In the language of William James, the liberals were once-born types. Their outlook was in general kindly and optimistic, their universe solid, comfortable and well-furnished. But they now seem dated. Liberalism is being squeezed out, in society, in the Church and in the intellectual world. Western thought has been getting more and more sceptical for a long time. The main theme is very simple: it is the realization that our knowledge-systems, our beliefs, our myths, our norms, our meanings, even our values, are as human and local and transient as we are. *That* is the thought that freezes the blood. The older liberalism could not bear it, and turned away. But the postliberal sort of theology I have been trying to describe will be nihilistic. It will head

251

determinedly into the darkness. It knows that Western religious thought now needs to turn in a somewhat early-Buddhist direction, and it claims that in doing so it will not become any less Christian. Quite the contrary. We are talking about renewal.

# F: CHRIST AND THE ACADEMY

25 EDWARD FARLEY's 'The Structure of Theological Study' comes from his *The Fragility of Knowledge: Theological Education in the Church and the University* (Philadelphia: Fortress Press, 1988, pp. 171–83 and 190). His other books include *Ecclesial Man: A Social Phenomenology of Faith and Reality* (Philadelphia: Fortress Press, 1975); *Theologia: The Fragmentation and Unity of Theological Education* (Philadelphia: Fortress Press, 1983) and *God and Evil: Interpreting a Human Condition* (Minneapolis: Fortress Press, 1990). He has also edited with Barbara G. Wheeler *Shifting Boundaries: Contextual Approaches to the Structure of Theological Education* (Louisville, Kentucky: Westminster/John Knox Press, 1991).

26 ELISABETH SCHÜSSLER FIORENZA's 'Commitment and Critical Inquiry' was published in *The Harvard Theological Review* in January 1989 (Vol. 82, No. 1, pp. 1–11). Amongst her many books are *The Apocalypse* (Chicago: Franciscan Herald Press, 1976); *Bread Not Stones: The Challenge of Feminist Biblical Interpretation* (Boston: Beacon Press, 1984); *In Memory of Her: A Feminist Theological Reconstruction of Christian Origins* (New York: Crossroad, 1983); *Revelation: Vision of a Just World* (Minneapolis: Fortress Press, 1991); *But She Said: Feminist Practices of Biblical Interpretation* (Boston: Beacon Press, 1992); *Discipleship of Equals: A Critical Ekklesia-logy of Liberation* (New York: Crossroad, 1993). She has also edited with Ann Carr *The Special Nature of Women?* (Philadelphia: Trinity Press, and London: SCM Press, 1991).

27 REBECCA CHOPP's 'Emerging Issues and Theological Education' was published in *Theological Education* in Spring 1990 (pp. 107–17 from a total length of pp. 106–24). Her books are *The Praxis of Suffering: An Interpretation of Liberation and Political Theologies* (Maryknoll, New York: Orbis, 1986); *The Power to Speak: Feminism, Language, God* (New York: Crossroad, 1989); and *Liberation Theology and Pastoral Theology* (Decatur, DA: Journal of Pastoral Care Publications, 1990). She has also edited with Mark

Lewis Taylor *Reconstructing Christian Theology* (Minneapolis: Fortress Press, 1994).

28   RONALD F. THIEMANN's 'Toward an Integrated Model of Theological Education' was published in *Harvard Divinity Bulletin* in 1992 (Vol. 21, No. 4, pp. 15, 18–19, extracted from a longer article). His books are *Revelation and Theology: The Gospel as Narrated Promise* (Ind.: University of Notre Dame Press, 1985) and *Constructing a Public Theology: The Church in a Pluralistic Culture* (Louisville, Kentucky: Westminster/John Knox Press, 1991). He has also edited *The Legacy of H. Richard Niebuhr* (Minneapolis: Fortress Press, 1991).

# 25

## THE STRUCTURE OF THEOLOGICAL STUDY
### Edward Farley

I have distinguished between the structure of theological study and the curricula of specific educational programs. Structure, here, means the areas of study that theology, if taught, requires, and the relation between those areas. My thesis is that the *aim* of theological study is to discipline, or rigorize, the basic modes of interpretation that already exist in the situation of faith, and that these hermeneutic modes generate the requisites and criteria for the areas of study and the movement of study in the field. In the present chapter, I shall pursue four problems that arise when my thesis is brought to bear on actual programs of education. I shall discuss (*a*) the relation of the structure of theological study to scholarship and curricula; (*b*) the nature of theological study in congregational education and clergy education; (*c*) the relation between theological study and religious studies; and (*d*) the nature of the propaedeutic studies necessary to the study of theology.

## Theological study and learning

The thesis of these pages may seem to come at a high price. Does the refusal to identify the structure of theological study with an organization of theological sciences end in anti-intellectualism? Does the claim that the hermeneutic modes constitute that structure make the sciences and scholarship irrelevant to theology? The case argued here may be construed as locating theology in the reflective life of the believer and thus as dislocating it from the schools, disciplines, and sciences. It may look as if an opposition is posited between theology and learning. I must try to head off such a disastrous misconstrual, which could empty theology of the critical principle altogether.

I have made a case against restricting learning to clergy education and permitting 'education' in only some lesser sense to congregations.[1] Contending for an ordered learning for the believer as such, I oppose any opposition between theology and learning. Driving my argument is the premise that the believer's faithful life in situations needs not just the kind of interpretation that arises because human responses are as such interpretive but needs disciplined, self-aware interpretation. Such interpretation does not occur automatically but occurs instead through the disciplining and educational processes offered by a community. Ordered learning is appropriate to and needed by believers as such. Believers need not just 'theology' but theological study – theology in the process of being shaped and disciplined by ordered learning. And that means theology as it occurs in a program of study and, thus, in the situation of teaching, with all its constitutive elements: teachers, cumulative knowledge, cognitive criteria, and a curriculum with its movement over time. The setting is *study*, and an environment of pedagogy. What happens when we introduce the structure of the hermeneutic modes into a program of study? The structure manifests itself in the *curriculum*, is pursued with the assistance of *scholarship*, and therefore engenders *disciplines*.

Why is it that the disciplining of interpretation needs and appropriates scholarship and the sciences? The most general reason is the intrinsic commitment of redemptive existence to the truth principle, to grasping and expressing the 'way things are'. Given a commitment to this principle, there is no way the advancing horizon of inquiry can be stopped. What is more, each hermeneutic mode occurs on an ever-moving horizon of inquiry that commandeers whatever cognitive resources are appropriate – from archaeology and linguistics to psychology and ontology. Nor does the allegiance to open-ended inquiry originate with post-Enlightenment modernity. Once faith acknowledges the validity and importance of understanding as such, it cannot say, 'Thus far and no further'. The interrogation of reality can have no terminating point set in advance either for the religious community as a whole or for the individual believer. When the Church sets forth its attestation and claim or when it engages in critical self-interpretation and educates its leadership and its constituency, it can have no grounds for curtailing its concern for the truth about things – even about the things of faith. The disciplining of reflective interpretation must go as far as the capabilities of human finitude permit. It must appropriate all available research, scholarship, sciences, and perspectival emphases. The result is that the disciplining of reflective interpretation must exist in an environment whose aims are centered in science and scholarship – in clergy schools, universities, and graduate schools.

How can the structure of theological study be embodied in a curriculum with disciplinary underpinnings? First, if each basic part of the structure of theological study is a mode of interpretation, the way these parts appear in ordered learning is as areas of hermeneutic. Insofar as schools or programs of study teach theology, they are teaching modes of interpretation. In short, theological study is, in the broad sense of the word, hermeneutic study. It is learning what is involved in the interpretation of tradition, action, truth, and work as they come together in situations. A pedagogical area (e.g. biblical studies) may bring together several disciplines – distinguishable pedagogical, scholarly undertakings – yet may be unified by the aim to thematize and rigorize one of the modes of interpretation (in this case, the hermeneutic of tradition in its originating events and texts).

Second, each of the hermeneutics requires knowledge of the area of concern and makes use of whatever sciences and scholarly resources are necessary for the disciplining of that mode of interpretation. We are familiar with the many humanistic and social sciences that are called on in the interpretation of early Christianity: polity, the philosophy of language, archaeology, history, classics. And in the interpretation of responsible action: sociology, political science, the history of philosophy, analytic or phenomenological methods. The relation between disciplines and the sciences is a pragmatic one: a discipline's pedagogical aim, along with its subject matter, prompts its selection of cognitive resources and methods.

We can see why thinking of the structure of theological study as a pattern for collecting sciences has had an unfortunate, even antiscientific, effect on the schools. By thinking of itself as a discrete science, a guild-supported discipline will immure itself in that science and thus lose the possibility of appropriating what it needs as a hermeneutic, as a disciplining of a mode of interpretation. Thus, we find pastoral psychology annexing psychology as its science and consequently feeling itself relieved of the obligation to read philosophical anthropology and the great 'psychologists' of Western Christianity such as Augustine and Kierkegaard. We find ethicists reading the ethics literature and perhaps the auxiliary literature the graduate school encourages or permits but not the history of philosophy and theology, and not pastoral psychology. It is not that scholars within the disciplines must be totally eclectic and read everything. But the boundaries created for them by their self-understanding as scientists prevent them from crossing the boundaries even when their hermeneutic aims call for it. The pragmatic appropriation of needed scholarly resources is prevented by the guild-drawn boundary. When the disciplines or pedagogical areas think of themselves as sciences, they educate their students by furthering their guild sciences rather than by creating and refining distinctive hermeneutics: the systematic theologian does not teach theological thinking but passes on the texts, lingo, and issues of the guild; the homiletician by marrying biblical exegesis and rhetoric thinks to have gained release from the need to raise the question of the truth of the exegetically exposed material.

Third, the very subject matter, the Christian faith, properly delineates disciplines. In thinking about the Christian faith scholars have traditionally adopted an epochal approach, in which the faith is studied in major and minor periods and in its geographical and cultural distribution. Although there is nothing intrinsically wrong with epochal scholarship, it is not an adequate basis for organizing study of this subject matter, because epochs and regions do not trace the dimensionality of this historical reality. When religion is taught or studied in epochal specialties (New Testament literature, patristics, medieval Catholicism, the Reformation, European pietism, post-Enlightenment Christianity, American Methodism), the problem of understanding the religion is seen as the descriptive one of grasping the sequential movements of events, the contents of literatures, and the origins of movements. But all these together do not touch the religious faith in its claims about truth and reality, as a mythos for action, or as an institution of power, oppression, and traditioning. A more adequate approach organizes the disciplines along lines that yield an understanding of the *dimensions* of the historical Christian faith.

Finally, my interpretation of the nature of theological study calls for new curricular emphases, which in some cases will entail new scholarly disciplines. One new cognitive and pedagogical undertaking that I propose is the hermeneutic description of situations as such. If teaching in this area were developed, it would add a dimension to and perhaps redefine practical theology.[2] In my book 'practical theology' is a comprehensive term, broadened to include three of the five hermeneutic modes: the hermeneutic of action, the hermeneutic of situations, and vocational hermeneutics.

I would give a more central place in theological study to two kinds of studies – perhaps disciplines – that have had a role in earlier periods: studies of world religions, and philosophy. Perhaps for reasons rooted in classical Protestant polemics against scholastic 'natural theology' as well as in the classical Protestant principle of *sola scriptura*, philosophy has had only a marginal place in Protestant theological study. It has become relatively marginal in recent Catholic clergy education as well. This is a serious lapse not because we need to rehabilitate natural theology but because philosophy is the primary means of exposing, assessing, and making thematic the various paradigms of knowledge and reality that are subliminally or explicitly present in the responses of the Church and the believer. Whether present in naive or examined forms, these paradigms dispose faith's interpretation of its own world and reality and of the larger culture. Furthermore, philosophy, which was virtually synonymous with the total human cognitive undertaking until the rise of modern science, has provided the conceptual framework for most of the major Christian theological visions from Christian Neoplatonism to process theology. Most important of all, philosophy, and not just the natural and social sciences, offers linguistic and phenomenological methods for studying the human being in its ontological structure, about which faith makes claims whenever it speaks of the realities of evil or the operations of grace.[3]

## Theological study and the churches

Theology and theological study originate in the religious community, since 'theology' in its primary sense designates the critical, reflective activity of the believer, and 'theological study' the disciplining of that activity. It follows that the structure of theological study will be embodied in both lay, that is, congregational, and professional educational programs.

I have argued that church education should be theological education in the full and rigorous sense of ordered learning. The environment of church lay education is very different, however, from that of the university and the seminary. For one thing, the level of acculturation and formal education in the churches ranges from virtual illiteracy to the attainments of scientists and professionals. Illiteracy must be taken seriously by the Church, since it is systemically connected to societal stratifications created by oppression and social disenfranchisement. Nevertheless, my comments will assume that the constituencies of the majority of North American congregations have a significant amount of public education. A second feature of the church environment springs from the fact that people participate in the church community over a long period of time. In a great many cases, life in the church begins with childhood and continues to adult maturity. So although a church cannot in its educative efforts build on a relative homogeneity of educational background, it can frame long-term educational programs that move from very introductory levels, suited to the education of children, to very advanced levels. The absence of a homogeneous educational background is not an absolute obstacle to ordered learning, learning that is rigorizing, sequential, and cognitively critical.

Ordered learning, however, varies with the environment in which it occurs. Schools of graduate and, some would say, 'higher' education pursue it in conjunction with ongoing scholarly and scientific inquiry. Programs of church education would ordinarily seek a rigor of communication but not of research. Although all learning chases a moving horizon, the horizon of church lay education pertains to the reflective life and understanding of the believer and the community of faith, not the advance of scholarly investigation.

Since theological study is appropriate for the lay believer, the church's ordered learning, or education, should embody the structure and movement of theological study that we have already addressed. Church education, like all theological education, will be a rigorization of the basic hermeneutic modes: of tradition, action, situations, truth, and vocation. After all, the life of the lay person no less than that of the professional clergy is constituted by situations calling for response, interpretation, and understanding. The lay person also interprets situations under the guidance of tradition, responsible to the imperative of truth, serving a primary occupation, and oriented toward action. The very structure of theological study is born of the basic modes of interpretation operating in the believer's situation. It is odd, then, that there are notions of church education that pay no attention to the disciplining of those modes – which tack a Clergy Only sign on the hall of theological study. The idea of vocation that figures in church education is, of course, not that of the vocation of the ordained leadership. In the Church the hermeneutic mode of vocation takes the form of interpreting both work – the primary occupation – and special ecclesial responsibilities. Church education can therefore legitimately include an ordered learning for teachers in the congregation. Nor can church education as theological education avoid rigorous study of theology's subject matter, the Christian faith. Nor can that study be reduced to 'Bible study'. Christianity's historical movement from its beginnings to the present, and in all its dimensions, must be the concern of church education.

Clergy education is a special instance of theological education, because its aim is to prepare a certain kind of church leadership. Schools and programs ordered by this aim need not exclude lay persons whose educational background and objectives require post-baccalaureate theological study. It is possible to envision a time when these schools will not be simply schools for clergy education. Their aims, however, will still cluster around the education of an advanced church leadership. Clergy education, which is in most but not all cases a post-baccalaureate program of studies, pursues theological study and ordered learning in the setting of ongoing scholarly work. It differs from church lay education and from university religious studies in two major respects. First, it teaches the basic modes of interpretation in such a way as to prepare church leaders themselves to teach, explore, and facilitate life in the Church. Second, the total educational program is unified by the anticipated function of the student as a church leader: the focus of clergy education is vocation as a special, ecclesial work. Because of clergy education's vocational focus, ecclesiology should be a part of its foundational or initiating studies. What is disastrous is the idea that clergy education is simply professional training focused on ministerial skills, for that idea allows the distinctive professional aspect of clergy education to displace rather than to shape and supplement, and to be shaped and supplemented by, the structure of theological study. Clergy education, like congregational education, must find its own way of embodying the structure, the basic requirements, set by theology for theological study.

It is apparent that a hermeneutic approach to theological study requires rethinking the educational programs of clergy education. An adequate understanding of the Christian faith in its historical movement and dimensionality, and an adequate disciplining of the hermeneutic modes, pose a complex pedagogical challenge for clergy schools. To use a distinction from medieval Catholic education, present-day clergy educa-tion is only a 'minor course', a series of beginnings, compared with the 'major course' that historical and hermeneutic studies would require. The historical background and originating events of Christian faith cannot be grasped through introductory surveys of biblical literature and courses in exegesis; these courses are part of a pattern reflecting precritical ways of thinking. A vision of the formation, development, and fate of Christianity as a mythos, ethic, or doctrine does not accrete from one or two surveys of church history. An introductory course in ethics or a survey of the literature of liberation theology is only a modest beginning in the shaping of a self-conscious and disciplined hermeneutic of action. A post-baccalaur-eate three-year menu of introductory and survey courses, eked out with courses that focus the interests of several specialty fields, is not sufficient to the needs of the leadership of a religious faith desperately imperiled in the contemporary world. Theological study as advanced hermeneutic education requires a new institutionality of clergy education. If clergy education continues in its present institutional form – the three-year program of seminary studies, with roots in the early nineteenth century – the Church needs to devise also a 'major course' directed to a special type of church leader.

## Theological study and the university

I have built a case for giving theological studies a place in secular universities – in other words, for making them part of university programs in religious studies.[4] But my analysis of the structure of theological study

261

appears to be on a collision course with the case I built. The secular university, private or state-sponsored, has no responsibility for the well-being of specific religions or for serving their institutions and their educational needs. No one expects the local state university to train Jewish rabbis, Catholic priests, or Protestant ministers, nor to sponsor lay theological education for this or that denomination.[5] Yet I have contended that the primary meaning of theology is a wisdom and reflective activity that attend faith, and that faith occurs only through the historical mediation of the specific traditioning of a religious community. How, then, can theological study exist outside that community and its educational institutions? The nonreligious aims of the university seem utterly incompatible with the aims of theological study. To put the problem slightly differently, my view of the conditions, context, and aim of theological study appears to be *fideist*, limiting such study in principle to faith communities, and this fideism seems to undercut any case for theological study in the university.

The apparent contradiction presents us with the question of what is involved in the study – in the understanding, interpretation, scholarly investigation, historical knowledge, critical appraisal – of a specific religious faith. I assume that there is nothing about the study of religion and of specific religions that is incompatible with the scientific and pedagogical aims of the university. I also assume that specific religions are not so mysterious and esoteric that they cannot be studied at all. In other words, I assume that specific religions allow themselves to be understood through a variety of methods, that they are, in short, available to understanding and interpretation.

What is available? Clearly, the history, social reality, and practices of a religious faith can be studied. Early Buddhism, present-day Eastern European Judaism, and Plains Indian religion are all accessible to historical, linguistic, archaeological, and other modes of inquiry. But clearly too, we have not understood Judaism, have not even studied it as itself, if we do not understand it as a *faith*. Nor will Judaism, Christianity, and other religious faiths be understood *as faiths* without grasping the way these faiths are multidimensional realities. Moreover, each faith is multidimensional in a distinctive way that requires its own basic modes of interpretation. If this is the case, any thoroughgoing study of religion will face the tasks set by theological study: the understanding and interpretation of a subject matter (Jewish, Christian, Buddhist faith), and the grasp of basic modes of interpretation. The *interpretation* of a religious faith requires entering into the *interpretations*, that is, the hermeneutic modes, constituting that faith.

There is a difference between theological study that occurs within and on behalf of a community of faith and the more distanced study of that community's faith. Within a faith, the aim of study is the disciplining of faith's actual reflective life; this occurs in the institutions and among the constituents of the religious faith. In the more distanced study of a faith, the aim of theological study is to understand the religious faith; this requires entering into specific hermeneutic modes to the degree that that advances the understanding. The difference, however, should not be thought of as between a personally, existentially oriented and an impersonally, objec- tively oriented study. If it were thought of in that way, theological study within a faith would be permitted interest in questions of the truth of the interpretations studied and of the wisdom of the presented imagery, whereas 'objective' scholarly studies of a faith would be expected to proceed in a posture of indifference to such things. This posture of nonjudgmental neutrality pervades much of present-day humanistic and social-scientific pedagogy, but it is corruptive of the university. The deepest reason for the study of anything is to discipline the modes of interpretation – political, aesthetic, scientific, social, personal, or whatever. One studies ancient Buddhism for the same reason one studies Freud, James Joyce, or Whitehead. Something is being laid claim to in these texts which may have to do with reality and truth, with the way things are, could be, or should be. Utter existential indifference to the truths posed by or laid claim to in the subject matter is a deadly virus, a virtual AIDS of education, any education. Although the educational aims of religious and nonreligious institutions are different, both kinds of institution must include studies that seek to understand and to be shaped by whatever wisdom and truth can establish itself, however historically specific its origin and context.

All religious faiths are socially and historically determinate. Believers in whatever faith exist in situations and respond to and interpret the mystery of things on the basis of the mediations of tradition. Grasping the stars as great hunters is a way of construing things for the African Bushmen, and as such it is an interpretation. Understanding any religious faith requires entrance into the circle of its own self-understanding, into the matters it is serious about, the claims embodied in its tradition-formed experience. The study of any religion therefore entails and requires a study of the dimensions of that religion's faith and of the correlative types of interpretation. The basic hermeneutic modes of that religion must be studied. In reflective interpretation requiring rigorization, the Christian faith comes to self-conscious understanding. To study the religious faith seriously is to be pressed by the claim it sets. But anyone who wishes to grasp the religion at the level of its own claim and self-understanding, in other words, as a *faith*, must appreciate the structure of its reflective interpretations – of its theology. This is why the student must enter into the modes of interpretation that structure the religion's world of faith, and into the study of theology.

If a program of religious studies includes the study of the Christian religion and construes that study to be only a study of classical materials from the faith's origins (Old Testament, New Testament), it has bought into a very truncated vision of its own potential. The teaching and understanding of Christianity will be narrow and abstract if the university student ignores the religion in its truth claims and if no attention is paid to the way its mythos shapes human action or to the distinctive way its believers are prompted to exist interpretively in situations. Thus, the study of a specific religion must attempt to enter into that religion's own hermeneutic structure, in other words, the structure of theological study. Nor is there anything about the effort which is in conflict with the university's critical temper or its commitment to scholarship. On the contrary, to rule out the study of a religious faith's structure of self-interpretation is surely arbitrary and a contravention of the university's cognitive and pedagogical aims.

Each religious faith has distinctive elemental dimensions and distinctive basic hermeneutic modes. Hence, the structure of Christian theological study will not be identical to that of Jewish or Buddhist theological study. There will also be differences between how the study of theology occurs in the Christian Church's educational institutions and how it occurs in the secular university. The truth orientation of the religious community toward the realities to which it attests creates a basic posture in its educational undertakings. In the university, the primary agenda of inquiry concerns religious faiths as *historical* phenomena. Given that agenda and posture, the way the structure of theological study might appear in religious studies in the university reflects the dimensions of a religious faith as a *historical* reality. Religious faiths as comprehensive historical entities offer themselves to study in three dimensions: the historical, the social, and the symbolic-linguistic. Given this, does the Christian faith set requirements on the inquiry and pedagogy of those who would teach it in the university?

Whatever else it is, the Christian faith is an enduring *historical* reality. To the extent that its history is retrievable, it properly evokes historical specialties that focus on origins and epochs of development. Because history is itself multidimensional, these specialties properly reflect a variety of historiographies. The focus, however, must be on the faith as a historical entity and, therefore, on all the matters that make up a historical entity.

Some scholars may think of the *social* study of Christian faith as a special type of historiography. But the sociality of a religion is a particular dimension of its reality and calls for a distinctive approach and conceptual framework. As a social reality, a religious faith is a distinct form of human intersubjectivity. It creates distinctive institutions and distinctive social ways of enduring through time. Furthermore, it is constituted by distinctive social structures of leadership, ritual enactment, and corporate constituency. It occurs in the context of the larger society and stands to society in relationships of opposition, sanction, isolation, and so forth. It can legitimate the oppressive elements of the larger society, oppose them, or paradoxically, do both. The sociality of religion is, in short, a dimension sufficiently complex and important to justify a discrete research agenda, a discipline. To make the investigation of a sociality of religion one of the tasks of some other compartment of labor in the university is probably to bury it.

The Christian faith, like all religious faiths, is also a mythos, a symbolic-linguistic account of reality that brings together themes of the human condition and the sacred. The characteristic language of the mythos, written or oral, is narrational. The primary symbols, narrations, and dogmas of the faith's mythos combine a doxological orientation with an orientation to truth and reality. To grasp the mythos of the faith draws on, but also goes beyond, historical and social inquiries.

Each of these three dimensions of historical Christianity calls forth appropriate resources of scholarship. History requires knowledge and specialty tools pertinent to the epoch. For instance, the study of ancient Hebrew religion will draw on archaeology, on Hebrew and the other languages of the ancient Near East, and on ancient Near Eastern history, as well as on tools dictated by the historiographical emphasis – intellectual history, institutional history, or whatever. The social study of historical Christian faith draws on the sociology of religion, in the sense of a data-oriented social scientific methodology, but it must draw on much more than this. It must call into service social philosophy, social psychology, *Ideologiekritik*, the 'genealogical' methods of Michel Foucault, and the social-world analysis of Alfred Schutz. The symbolic-linguistic study of Christianity must draw on more than simply the philosophy of religion, especially in its narrower sense of rational theology. It must also appropriate the philosophy of language, philosophical anthropology, and the hermeneutics of symbols and myths.

These three dimensions of historical Christianity – the historical, the social, and the symbolic-linguistic – can demarcate pedagogical areas and areas of scholarly study concerning the Christian religion in the university.[6]

They also suggest a general pattern for the study of any specific faith, or even a way of organizing a general program of religious studies.

NOTES

1. In Chapter 5 of *The Fragility of Knowledge*, from which this extract is taken.
2. For thoughts on the expansion of the meaning of practical theology, see the essays in Don Browning, ed., *Practical Theology: The Emerging Field in Theology, Church, and World* (San Francisco: Harper and Row, 1982), especially those by David Tracy, Thomas Ogletree, and Dennis McCann.
3. Karl Rahner makes a strong case for including philosophy in theological study; his approach is different from what he calls the Roman approach, where only philosophy is the propaedeutic predecessor to theology: *Zur Reform des Theologiestudiums*, Freiburg: Herder & Herder, 1969, pp. 40–1. Wolfhart Pannenburg makes a similar case, arguing that the claims of theology imply philosophical hypotheses about reality as a whole: *Theology and the Philosophy of Science*, tr. Francis McDonagh, Philadelphia: Westminster Press, 1976, chapter 5, nos. 3–4.
4. In Chapter 3 of *The Fragility of Knowledge*.
5. This statement is not completely confirmed in fact. A recent study, yet to be published, of theology and religious studies in the Southeast discovered many instances, some in state universities, where the teaching of religion was arranged in such a way that the cause of a particular religion – in this case Christianity – was advanced. There were, e.g., cases where the introductory courses to religion were 'Old and New Testament' courses. And some courses taught by state universities reflected the aims of clergy education or preclergy education. See Stan Lusby and Linda Tober, 'Religion and Theological Studies in the Southeastern United States' (a preliminary report).
6. Under discussion here is how Christian studies might occur in the university. Insofar as any religion possesses these three dimensions, they can serve to organize the field of religious studies itself. The pedagogy fostered by such a division of labor would be oriented toward understanding religion in and through the hermeneutic modes. The unity of the field of religious studies would then lie in its study of religion and religions in their distinctive dimensionality and claims. This unity would make a strong case for considering religious studies a distinctive undertaking irreducible to the occasional undertakings of the study of religion within the various humanistic and social sciences of the university.

╰╮╭╯╰╮╭╯╰╮╭╯╰╮╭╯╰╮╭╯╰╮╭╯╰╮╭╯╰╮╭╯╰╮╭╯╰╮╭╯╰╮╭╯╰╮╭╯╰╮╭╯╰╮╭╯

# 26

# COMMITMENT AND CRITICAL INQUIRY
## *Elisabeth Schüssler Fiorenza*

We are called together here to mark the beginning of a new school year with a symbolic act – a *convocatio*. As cultural anthropologists tell us, such ritual symbolic acts function simultaneously to induct participants into the common life-world of a community and to hold up to them shared values and visions. The convocation address provides an opportunity to reflect critically on the ritual act itself and on the shared visions and values it embodies. Such exploration can uncover tensions and contradictions in how the community sees itself and the world, contradictions that provide openings and challenges for change. By reflecting on these tensions I seek to display the first step in a feminist theological practice. The inclusion of the previously excluded as theological subjects, I argue, calls for a paradigm shift from a value-detached scientism to a public rhetoric, from a hermeneutical model of conversation to a practical model of collaboration.

Thomas Kuhn's categories of scientific paradigms and heuristic models provide a theoretical framework for such an argument.[1] A paradigm, such as theology, articulates a common ethos and constitutes a community of scholars who are formed by its institutions and systems of knowledge. Moreover, paradigms are not necessarily exclusive of each other; they can exist alongside and in corrective interaction with each other until they are replaced by a new paradigm. By envisioning the Divinity School as a heterogeneous public and our work as critical collaboration, I hope to contribute to the conversation on critical theological education and public theological discourse which Dean Thiemann has initiated in his inaugural convocation address and programmatic alumnae/i day lecture of 1987.[2]

I

The contradictions marking this public event are obvious. For instance, we are an academic community in the context of a modern research university, but we have chosen the religious language of ritual to express our common identity and vision. I was asked to select readings from Jewish and Christian Scriptures. At the same time, I was told that the genre of the convocation address is not that of the homily but of the academic lecture.

However, it was to be a short lecture, not longer than twenty minutes, that is, as short as a good sermon is supposed to be. This ambivalence in our choice of language and ritual seeks to do justice, I would submit, to the rich religious, confessional, and academic diversity of the constituency of Harvard Divinity School and at the same time to retain our biblical-historical roots as a Christian divinity school in a university setting.

My own ritual location discloses these contradictions and tensions in the self-presentation of the school. Ritual positions me on high, cast in the role of the authoritative preacher to whom not only students but also faculty must look up in silence. At the same time I wear the insignia of the academic tradition that has replaced the sermon with the lecture. My academic position configures these institutional contradictions. As a New Testament scholar I am to research only what the text meant in its first-century contexts, whereas as a faculty member of practical theology I am to teach the meaning and significance of the Bible for contemporary communities of faith.

I also speak here as a woman scholar. As a biblical scholar I am positioned at the center of the Christian paradigm. As a woman I belong to an outsider group who has not been allowed to speak publicly and for centuries has been excluded from theology by religious law and academic convention. To be sure, my ritual position also signals change. Because of the bitter struggle of our foresisters, women have gained access to ministry, theological education, and scholarship in most, though not all, religious communities. Under the leadership of Constance Buchanan, the Women's Studies in Religion program at Harvard has become a national and international center for gender studies in religion. Year after year it attracts scholars from across the world to teach and do research on women. For many of us it is one of the major reasons why we are here today in such large numbers.

Yet I stand here not simply as a woman scholar but also as a white, educated woman speaking with a German accent. While my gender position marks me as a member of the silenced majority in church and academy, my racial and cultural position designates me as heir to the privileges of white Western Christianity and to the mindset of the Euro-American academy. As a feminist liberation theologian I am challenged by the voices of my Afro-American, Native American, Asian, and Hispanic sisters to use these privileges in the interest of women suffering from multiple oppressions. To this end I need to collaborate with women from different cultural and religious subject locations in articulating a 'different' theological discourse.

Yet such a critical collaboration remains a 'problematic potentiality' as

268

long as women entering religious studies have to adopt the languages of those clerical and academic communities that have silenced us, have defined us as the 'other of the Divine' or as the 'other' of the 'Man of Reason',[3] have relegated us to the status of social, ecclesial, and intellectual non-subjects or — to use the expression of Gustavo Gutiérrez — 'non-persons'.[4] In order to become speaking theological subjects, women must 'master' the clerical and academic discourses of the fathers. For in Kuhn's terms, to become a member of the community of scholars students have to internalize the entire constellation of beliefs, values, techniques, shared worldviews, and systems of knowledge as maps or guidelines for thinking in a 'scholarly' way.

This intensive process of academic socialization could be likened to immersing oneself in the languages and customs of a foreign culture. In the course of this socialization students experience contradictions between their own social or religious life-worlds and those of their discipline until they speak and think in its idiom. Such a process of inculturation, of becoming 'a Harvard man', is less alienating for those who share a gender, racial, social, cultural, or religious background with those who have shaped the discipline.

Women who enter theological education have three choices: either we embrace the languages, traditions, theories, or worldviews of theology which have silenced, marginalized, and objectified us *as women* and risk muting our own theological voice and creativity, or we reject theological inquiry as white male scholarship, because we recognize its destructiveness for women's self-definition and self-affirmation. However, this second choice deprives us of the intellectual skills and tools for finding our own theological voice and for changing theology in the interest of women and all other non-persons. A third option compels us to articulate critically the experiences of contradiction between our own cultural, political, and religious ethos and that of the discipline, and to keep them in creative tension. For, to paraphrase Audre Lorde's dictum,[5] the master's tools will dismantle the master's house as long as we use them for building our own house and not for executing the master's mindset and discursive blueprints.

Feminist liberation theologians who consciously seek to work in the interest of women and other non-persons realize that our existence and practice as feminist liberation theologians and as theological scholars is *contradictory*. As women marked by race, class, and culture we belong to a marginalized and exploited group, whereas as theological scholars we share in the educational privileges of the white male academic élite. This contradictory subject position of feminist liberation scholars in religion

269

provides a rich source of inspiration, energy, and creativity for doing our theological work.[6] By consciously taking the standpoint of 'women' – defined by gender, race, class, culture, and religion – the feminist scholar in religion not only seeks to deconstruct oppressive religious and theological practices but also to reconstruct a religious heritage and theological voice for women. To that end she must not only reconstruct the discourse of her own discipline but also collaborate in articulating a different paradigm of religious scholarship and theological knowledge. Theology in a different key would no longer constitute itself by excluding or silencing the religious experience and theological voice of the subordinated Others. Rather, by constituting itself as a heterogeneous, polyphonic public, theology would be able to develop critical collaboration and discursive practices in the interest of a democratic public no longer confined to élite male citizens in church and nation.

The Divinity School as a public forum for critical collaboration would encourage especially those who have been excluded from theological discourse to articulate their religious self-understandings, to create religious and moral meanings, to find their particular theological voice, to reconstruct religious history, and to reshape the theological knowledge and moral values of the past as a heritage for the future.

Critical collaboration as a metaphor for naming our common task of 'doing theology' from different subject locations and standpoints evokes not only the pains, long hours, and exhaustion of hard labor but also the anticipation, satisfaction, and exhilaration of creative work. It reminds us that our task is not only to understand religious communities and traditions, but also to change them. It insists that as researchers, students, staff, teachers, or administrators we contribute in different ways to the 'common task' of 'doing' theology. Critical collaboration also has negative overtones, as in 'collaboration with the enemy', which warn us that unless theological institutions allow for the equal participation of those previously excluded, collaboration spells either co-optation or treason.

This paradigm of theology as critical collaboration invites study and assessment of religious and cultural practices as rhetorical practices. Religious and cultural practices include not only discursive practices such as language, texts, ideas, or theories, but also nondiscursive practices such as institutions, social systems, or gender, race, and class divisions. Religious and cultural practices are rhetorical practices. By rhetorical I do not mean mere rhetorics as linguistic manipulation, technical skill, or stylistic ornament, but communicative praxis that links knowledge with action and passion and does not deny others or set them at a distance. Rather, it insists that as sociopolitical practices all discourses call for public discussion and moral judgment. Theology understood as rhetorical or communicative praxis unmasks the value-detached, scientistic posture of religious studies as well as the doctrinal certainty of theology narrowly conceived. At the same time, it reconstitutes theology as a religious and ethical practice of critical inquiry and particular commitments.[7]

## II

Allow me to clarify this proposal for a different theological paradigm with reference to Edward Farley's discussion of the university in the Enlightenment tradition in order to indicate the oppositions such a paradigm shift will have to overcome.[8] The ideal of the Euro-American Enlightenment was critically accomplished knowledge in the interest of human freedom, equality, and justice under the guidance of pure reason. Its principle of unqualified critical inquiry and assessment does not exempt any given reality, authority, tradition, or institution. Knowledge is not a given but a culturally and historically embodied language and therefore always open to probing inquiry and relentless criticism. This critical principle of the Enlightenment was, however, institutionalized as the empiricist paradigm of knowledge that gives primacy to experienced data and empirical inquiry. Its 'logic of facts' relies on abstraction for the sake of rigor, evidence, and precision.

The critical principle of the Enlightenment has also engendered three historical correctives that underline the complexity, particularity, and corruption of reality. The aesthetic-romantic corrective stresses intuitive imagination over selective abstraction, the religious-cultural corrective insists on tradition as wisdom and heritage, and the political-practical corrective asserts that there is no pure reason as instrument of knowledge which could lead to a just society. In the beginning was not pure reason but power. The institutions of so-called pure reason – the sciences, scholarship, and the university – hide from themselves their own complicity in societal agendas of power. These three correctives introduce the hermeneutical principle as a second principle of critical inquiry.

However, I would suggest that a fourth corrective is in the process of being articulated. So-called minority discourses, in interaction with postmodernism and critical theory, question the Enlightenment's notion of the universal, transcendental subject as the disembodied voice of reason. These discourses assert that the political-social and intellectual-ideological creation of the devalued Others goes hand-in-hand with the creation of the 'Man of Reason' as the rational subject positioned outside of time and

271

space. He is the abstract knower and disembodied speaker of Enlightenment science.

But in distinction to postmodernism, minority discourses insist that the colonialized Others cannot afford to abandon the notion of the subject and the possibility of defining the world.[9] Rather, the subordinated Others must engage in a political and theoretical process of becoming the subjects of knowledge and history. We who have previously been excluded from the academy have to use what we know about the world and our lives to critique the dominant culture and to construct a heterogeneous public which fosters appreciation of difference.

To be sure, the argument of these four correctives is not with empirical research, analytical scholarship, or critical abstraction itself but with an uncritical conception of reason, knowledge, and scholarship. The atrophy and anorexia of the critical principle in the modern university has engendered a scientistic ethos of allegedly disinterested, impartial research, a proliferation of techniques and specializations in ever narrower fields of professionalization – practices that are reinforced by the university's reward system. Insofar as the scientific paradigm fails to apply the critical principle of the Enlightenment to its own self-understanding and its institutions of knowledge, it cannot recognize its own scientistic character as rhetorical; rather, the scientific paradigm marginalizes its four correctives as 'ideological'. Yet by doing so, the modern research university fails to advance the Enlightenment goal of a just and democratic society. Therefore the voices calling for value-clarification and moral education in higher education can only effect change if the university relativizes its dominant paradigm by institutionalizing rather than marginalizing the four correctives of Enlightenment reason.[10]

## III

Although the research-oriented divinity school has been fashioned in the likeness of the empiricist, scientific paradigm of the modern university, it has nevertheless sought to embrace a more complex paradigm of knowledge, insofar as it has adopted not only the critical but also the hermeneutical and practical principles of knowing. However, as long as doctoral education perpetuates the ethos of specialism and scientism, theological discourse will remain part of the problem rather than contribute to the articulation of public ethics and moral vision.

Traditionally, theology has been understood as the science of God or as the systematic exploration of biblical and church teachings on doctrine and morals. Biblical, historical, and religious studies, in contrast to such a doctrinal or confessional understanding of theology, have developed their own self-understandings as critical, scientific studies in terms of the modern research university. Freed from the fetters of doctrinal commitments and ecclesiastical controls, scholarship supposedly pursues critical inquiry with utmost value-neutrality, detachment, and objectivity. It is descriptive rather than evaluative.

The so-called 'hard' sciences such as biblical and historical studies distinguish themselves from theological studies in terms of descriptive objectivity over against confessional commitment. This posture of value-detached scientism has, however, been thoroughly challenged by philosophical hermeneutics, the sociology of knowledge, and critical theory. Although the progressive vanguard in my own discipline, for instance, utilizes insights from philosophical hermeneutics, the sociology of knowledge, and cultural anthropology for the interpretation of early Christian practices, it often uses them as scientific rules and prescriptions. Insofar as the discipline fails to apply a critical analysis to its own rhetorical practices or to use critical theory for analyzing the function of biblical texts in contemporary church and society, it falls short of its claim to be a critical discipline.

The hermeneutical models of theology as narrative and of theology as conversation focus on the internal story of the community and center on the classics of the tradition. Theology construed as conversation admits of a plurality of voices and disciplines. It allows not only for the participation of those previously excluded from theology, ministry, and the academy, but also seeks to compel the various discrete theological disciplines – or intellectual villages, as Clifford Geertz calls them – to engage in dialogue.[11] This is not an easy task since the specialism of the graduate school encourages, for instance, biblical students to master the technical skills of their area of specialization but does not invite a hermeneutical exploration of their theological frameworks or foster the cultivation of a 'common theological language'.

Theological scholarship that makes its hermeneutical commitments plain for others to examine is not less, but more, scientific; it is not less, but more, critical than an inquiry which hides its own interests and goals or denies its particular social location. Since what we see depends on where we stand, our socio-religious location or rhetorical context decides how we see the world, construct reality, or explore religious practices. When we do theology from a variety of experiences and standpoints we enhance rather than hinder our work.

The creativity and excellence of a theological school rests not simply on technical competence but on the presence of scholars who speak from diverse experiences. Theology as conversation depends on how much we are able to form an intellectual, theological 'rainbow coalition' and to hold our differences in creative tension. If the excellence of a theological school rests on diversity rather than conformity, then, for instance, when evaluating students or hiring faculty members we would not just look for signs of excellence in their respective disciplinary specialties. We also would look for evidence that they are able to cross the narrow boundaries of their disciplinary village, in other words, that they are not *Fachidioten*, 'specialized idiots', but that they have communicative competence and moral vision.

However, liberation and feminist theologies have criticized this model of theology as conversation for mystifying relationships of power in discourse not only by advocating a value-neutral pluralism but also by giving the impression that we all enter the conversation on equal terms. Moreover, by hypostatizing the text as a partner in the conversation, this model obfuscates the real relationship between text and interpreter, between the classics of a culture or religion and structures of domination. By aiming for domination-free conversation and consensus the model of theology as conversation idealizes the practices of theology and religious studies that are embedded in relationships of power. If this is recognized, the distinction between theology as committed confessional theology and religious studies as impartial objective inquiry breaks down. Both constitute political and rhetorical practices that are shaped by the Western 'Man of Reason'.

The 'inclusion' of the previously excluded as theological subjects, I argue, entails a paradigm shift from a scientistic to a rhetorical genre, from a hermeneutical model of conversation to a practical model of collaboration. Since rhetorical practices display not only a referential moment about something and a moment of self-implicature by a speaker or actor, but also display a persuasive moment of directedness to involve the other, they elicit responses, emotions, interests, judgments, and commitments directed toward a common vision.

In my Society of Biblical Literature presidential address I have extended this argument in terms of my own discipline to include not only the rhetorical practices of biblical texts but also the way we understand our function as scholars, and in whose interests we do biblical scholarship. Since the socio-historical location of rhetoric is the public of the *polis*, to be understood today in terms of global interdependence, the rhetorical paradigm shift situates biblical studies in such a way that public discourse and political responsibility become an integral part of our research and educational activities. If, as Krister Stendahl has argued, the Bible has become a classic of Western culture because of its status as Holy Scripture,[12] New Testament scholars must study not only its historical-rhetorical practices but also its functions in contemporary society.[13] Biblical scholarship, in collaboration with other disciplines, must therefore articulate public and ethical criteria for rejecting the religious authority claims and identity formations of destructive religious discourses inscribed in sacred texts. Today, when right-wing political movements forcefully employ the languages of hate encoded in religious scriptures and traditions, as biblical scholars we no longer can withdraw into our academic and clerical ivory towers, but must become critical participants in the competing public discourses on the Bible.

If theological discourse should contribute to a religious critical consciousness and cultural moral imagination it must take seriously the particular social and religious locations of those 'doing theology' in the interest of the 'common good'. Rather than striving for consensus and integration it aims for a pluralistic collaboration that respects the particular social locations and religious reference communities of its practitioners and seeks for connections between diverse theological and cultural dis-courses.[14] Since it invites a plurality of often contradictory responses to the problems at hand it produces deeply felt tensions that will turn into sectarian divisions if they are not articulated in terms of a shared vision of well-being for all.

Let me try to illustrate my point. In his 1982 presidential address to the American Academy of Religion, our colleague Gordon Kaufman reminded scholars in religion of our responsibility to face the possibility of the nuclear devastation of our planet.[15] He called on theologians to decon-struct and reconstruct the central Christian symbols in such a way that Christian theology and community will not foster the mentality and culture of possible atomic annihilation but help to avert them. Sharing Kaufman's conviction, the feminist Goddess theologian Carol Christ has argued that the Christian theology of finitude, body, and nature are at the heart of nuclear mentality.[16] The Christian theologian Sallic McFague in turn has rearticulated Kaufman's project in feminist terms in her book *Models of God*, but has come more and more to understand the ecological deterioration of the earth as the major problem.[17] And liberation theologians of all colors have insisted on the oppression of peoples due to racism, sexism, class exploitation, homophobia, militarism, and colonialism as the practical and ideological condition of nuclear mentality. While a theological conversation between these diverse theologians will never reach consensus because of their fundamental theological differences, they

275

nevertheless can collaborate with each other because they share a common theological commitment, ethos, and passion.

## IV

In place of a *conclusion*, I would like to recall the two women of the biblical readings we have heard (Sir 24.1–8, 12–21; Mark 7.24–30): one human, the other divine. Both represent the religious theological voice that has been excluded, repressed, or marginalized.

Whether we locate the rhetorical practice of the Markan text in the life of Jesus or in that of the early Church, its argument discloses religious prejudice and exclusive identity. The Syro-Phoenician woman is characterized ethnically and culturally as a religious outsider. She enters theological argument, turns it against itself, overcomes the prejudice of Jesus, and achieves the well-being of her little daughter. As distinct from all other controversy stories, Jesus does not have the last word. Rather the woman's argument prevails and her daughter is freed from her destructive spirit.

The other voice is that of Divine Wisdom, 'who speaks with pride among her people'. She offers life, rest, knowledge, and the abundance of creation to all who accept her. She is all-powerful, intelligent, unique, people-loving, an initiate of God's knowledge, a collaborator in God's work. She is the leader on the way out of bondage in Egypt, the preacher and teacher in Israel, a 'people-loving' associate in God's work, and the architect of God's creation. She shares the throne of God and lives in symbiosis with the Divine. Reading the biblical texts that speak of her, one can sense how much the language struggles to characterize Hokma-Sophia as divine in the theological framework of monotheism.

This theology of Divine Wisdom has been suppressed and cut off in both Jewish and Christian theology. Yet traces of her theology, of sophialogy, have been rediscovered by New Testament scholarship. Earliest Christian theology understood Jesus first as Divine Wisdom's messenger and prophet and then as Sophia-Incarnate. Nevertheless, most Christians have never heard of her. The Sophia-God of Jesus could not make her home among her people. Her offer of well-being, beauty, and knowledge presents rich possibilities for the future of theology in a different key.

NOTES

1. Thomas S. Kuhn, *The Structure of Scientific Revolutions*, Chicago: University of Chicago Press, 1962, passim.
2. 'Toward a Critical Theological Education', *Harvard Divinity Bulletin*, 17 (1986), pp. 6–9, and 'Toward an American Public Theology', ibid., 18 (1987), pp. 4–6, 10. See also his 'The Scholarly Vocation: Its Future Challenges and Threats', *ATS Theological Education* 24:1 (1987), pp. 86–101.
3. See, for instance, Genevieve Lloyd, *The Man of Reason: 'Male' and 'Female' in Western Philosophy*, Minneapolis: University of Minnesota Press, 1984; and my 'Politics of Otherness: Biblical Interpretation as a Critical Praxis for Liberation' (forthcoming).
4. See, for instance, his *Power of the Poor in History*, Maryknoll, New York: Orbis, 1983, passim.
5. Audre Lorde, *Sister Outsider*, Trumansburg, NY: Crossing, 1984, pp. 110–13.
6. See also Patricia Hill Collins, 'Learning from the Outsider Within: The Sociological Significance of Black Feminist Thought', *Social Problems* 33 (1986), pp. 14–32.
7. For a fuller development of the notion of biblical studies as rhetorical, see my Society of Biblical Literature presidential address, 'The Ethics of Interpretation: Decentering Biblical Scholarship', *JBL* 107 (1988), pp. 3–17, reprinted in the *Harvard Divinity Bulletin* 18:3 (1988).
8. Edward Farley, *The Fragility of Knowledge: Theological Education in the Church and the University*, Philadelphia: Fortress Press, 1988.
9. See, for instance, Nancy Hartsock, 'Rethinking Modernism: Minority vs. Majority Theories', *Cultural Critique* 7 (1987), pp. 187–206; Linda Alcoff, 'Cultural Feminism versus Poststructuralism: The Identity Crisis in Feminist Theory', *Signs* 13 (1988) pp. 3–17.
10. See, for instance, Harvard President Derek Bok's report for 1986–7 to the Board of Overseers which was issued in April 1988.
11. Clifford Geertz, 'The Way We Think Now: Toward an Ethnography of Modern Thought', in idem, *Local Knowledge: Further Essays in Interpretive Anthropology*, New York: Basic Books, 1983, pp. 147–63.
12. Krister Stendahl, 'The Bible as Classic and the Bible as Holy Scripture', *JBL* 103 (1984), p. 10.
13. See also Helmut Koester's Convocation address: 'The Divine Human Being', *HRT* 78 (1985), pp. 243–52.
14. For the importance of pluralism in theological articulation, see Diana L. Eck, 'Darsana: Hinduism and Incarnational Theology', *Harvard Divinity Bulletin* 17 (1987), pp. 10–11, and in theological education, see Margaret R. Miles, 'Hermeneutics of Generosity and Suspicion: Pluralism and Theological Education', *ATS Theological Education* 23 (1987), pp. 34–52.
15. Gordon D. Kaufman, 'Nuclear Eschatology and the Study of Religion', *JAAR* 51 (1983), 13.
16. Carol P. Christ, *The Laughter of Aphrodite: Reflections on a Journey to the Goddess*, Boston: Beacon Press, 1987, p. 214.
17. Sallie McFague, *Models of God: Theology for an Ecological Nuclear Age*, Philadelphia: Fortress Press, 1987.

# 27

# EMERGING ISSUES AND THEOLOGICAL EDUCATION
## Rebecca Chopp

### The form and deformation of modern knowledge and religion

Since Edward Farley entitled the introduction to his *Theologia*, 'The Travail of the Theological Study', a crisis in theological education has been readily assumed by most other authors writing on this topic.[1] This crisis, as authors point out in various ways, has a great deal to do with the nature and form of theological discourse, such that if we understood what theology was really about, the crisis would be resolvable. I want to look with a somewhat different lens on the crisis, a lens with a wide-angle, in order to suggest that the crisis in our understanding of theology has also to do with the very forms of religion and knowledge in modernity, that is, how religion and knowledge are defined, structured, and assigned sets of values. In sum, I want to suggest that the fragmentation of theological education is related to the way religion (which, in modernity, is primarily represented as Christianity) and knowledge are constructed.

The modern construction of Christianity and knowledge is character-ized by, on the one hand, the acceptance of a particular kind of individualism, where the individual is the contact point and origin of labor and value, and, on the other hand, the modern division of the public and private, where public interests are channeled through the market place and private interests, such as religion, art and tradition, are left as optional choices for the individual. In the public, the citizen of modernity is the laborer, the master of history, while in the private, the individual is the consumer of cultural values such as art, religion, tradition, and family. Knowledge in the public realm becomes formed through a scientific, instrumentalist view while in the private realm, faith is transcendentalized or existentialized, as prior to or outside of the conditions of knowledge. Faith, whether it be in the theological formulations of Barth and Schleiermacher or the religious piety of believers in New York and Kansas is assumed to be largely pre-linguistic, or other than linguistic, prior to or outside of action and knowledge. It may be brought to consciousness and thematized, for instance one may talk about her or his personal relationship to Jesus, but the true and real knowledge of God lies prior to any such talk, and all such talk is at best an inadequate way of expressing faith.

What's interesting about this construction is that it inscribes Christianity into modern knowledge while at the same time allowing Christianity to transgress, silently, without words that can be heard, the confines of knowledge by pointing to a 'something more' or 'something other' that is outside of, or underneath, or at the limits of knowledge. Yet though modern Christianity pointed to this 'something more', theological reflection was engraved within the rules of modern knowledge, and thus required to decenter and devalue pluralistic forms of rationality for the sake of focusing on what Paul Tillich would call theology as technical reason. Theological education had to make illegitimate certain forms of knowledge such as liturgical and mystical knowledge and prohibit certain groups not occupying the dominant anthropological position, such as blacks and women, from offering discourses of knowledge. The illegitimization of certain forms of knowledge can be rendered in a straightforward fashion: forms such as liturgy and mysticism are outside the rules of modern knowledge. Any such religious practice may be understood as expressions of private faith experiences but they cannot be considered as forms of knowledge.

The latter criticism, that modern theological education also served to prohibit knowledge of certain groups of persons, requires a bit more analysis, for such an inquiry can lead us to uncover the relations between power, interest, and knowledge. The subject position of many, usually filled by white, working men, represented the values of knowledge and the power of the public realm. Indeed, 'man' was the constitutive knower and citizen, and knowledge and citizenship were 'manly' affairs. The very value-laden definition of knowledge – objective, rational, logical – was the same definition of man, the citizen, indeed the values of 'man' himself. Furthermore, this relationship of man, knowledge and the public derived its identity from what it was not: woman, religious, the private. As the identity of knowledge depends upon it not being religious, man depended upon not being woman, and the public depended upon not being the private. What is important to see in this patriarchal codification of knowledge is the structural relation of subjectivity, politics and knowledge that formed a unity of man, knowledge and the public through a kind of dualistic dependency on women, religion and the private. In all of this, to use a phrase of Deborah Cameron's 'men can be men, only if women are unambiguously women'.[2]

This patriarchal codification of knowledge created all sorts of problems for theology and Christianity. For if knowledge was located in the public realm, in the subject position of white men, Christianity was located in the private realm, in the subject position symbolized by women. Thus Christianity had to shape its essence in the rules of the private, the subject position of women and its knowledge in the terms of the rules of the public, the subject position of men. The problem for theological knowledge was that man/woman, knowledge/religion, the public/private was related through a kind of dependent dualism, in which the identity of the first term, depended upon the other, but also upon not being the other. We could thus expand the Cameron quotation concerning men being men only if women are unambiguously women, by saying knowledge can be knowledge only if religion is unambiguously religion, and the public can be the public only if the private is unambiguously the private. Supposedly there was a separation, a gap, between men and women, knowledge and religion, the public and private but in reality the gap was a very ambiguous, tenuous relation, for men depended upon women for procreation, nurture, caretaking, and knowledge depended upon religion for motivation, aesthetics, care for the part of existence not rational and objective, and the public depended upon the private for sustenance of that which they said they were not. Theological knowledge, often danced at the edges of this ambiguity, trying hard to maintain loyalties to the modern rules, but also pointing to a kind of knowledge which, if examined, pushed at the subject position of women and men, the private and the public.[3]

Friedrich Schleiermacher's *Christmas Eve: A Dialogue on the Incarnation* is one of the best representations of the modern figuration of religious experience and knowledge, perhaps because the text renders problematic the modern figurations of knowledge, religious experience, men and women.[4] In this text, women obey the modern ordering that places them closer than men to religion, or, more accurately, there is less distance in women between religion and expression than there is in men. Women speak in terms of stories, or in what Schleiermacher would call the rhetorical mode, while men speak in terms of philosophical propositions, in Schleiermacher's sense, the descriptively didactic mode. If, for Schleiermacher, women have an advantage by being closer to the unity of experience and expression, men enjoy the public role of being in the subject position that is most able to reflect on religious experience and expression with detail and precision. But Schleiermacher seems to worry with this 'rule' that faith is to women as knowledge is to men, suggesting in the early part of the dialogues that divisions of women and men are not eternally fixed. Indeed, Schleiermacher renders problematic any rigorous division between men and women, knowledge and faith by figuring the unity of religious experience and expression in the shape of first a child, Sophie, and then a quite childlike man, Josef, both of whom express their religiosity by singing, Schleiermacher's poetic mode, rather than by speaking. As one commentator has recently put it, 'There is no question that the *Christmas Eve Dialogue* seems to favor simple, childlike experience over abstract theological reflection, or that, at least in this text, women appear more suited to the former, while men are inclined to the latter.'[5] Schleiermacher adheres to the modern formulation of religion and knowledge, of women and men, but he does so in the context of calling into question the eternal divisions of men and women, refiguring knowledge or the ability to do abstract reflection on a sliding scale rather than through separate spheres, and allowing a man to represent the return to the origin of all reflection, a position usually represented by women.[6] Schleiermacher does not explicitly criticize the modern formulation of men and knowledge, women and religion, but he renders it problematic and available for questioning.

Yet today Schleiermacher's problematic seems almost a commonplace crisis as we deal constantly with competing subjects and their discourses, and competing claims as to what constitutes knowledge. The rules as to what constitutes and who controls the dominant position in the court of reason are no longer as clear as when Schleiermacher tried to render them somewhat problematic. On the one hand, the narrow definition of knowledge is breaking apart due to factors including the philosophical critiques of knowledge, the technological transformation of knowledge, the renewed interest in relation between knowledge and ethics in public policy, military and scientific research and in the public and private educational systems. On the other hand, the multiplicity of subjects, the diversity of language games, the pluralism of discourses means increasingly that the subjects of knowledge are not one, but plural.[7]

Besides the explosion of knowledge and the awareness of multiple discourses of knowledge, there is another main difference between our day and Schleiermacher's: the loss of belief in major myths of modernity.[8] The myths were the fundamental myths of meaning, the narrative orderings that supported the definitions and practices of modernity. For our analysis we can consider two: one, the myths of the whole, that all the parts fit together, and second, the myth of progress, that the spirit or the true meaning will be realized in history. The narrative of the whole allows for the ordering of parts and hierarchies, while the myth of the origin allows for correct meanings and proper explanations. Schleiermacher could rest with his problematic because of these two myths which made him believe that the difference between men and women, knowledge and religion served the interests of the State which is related to the realization of freedom and progress in history.[9] These myths – that all fits together into an ordered whole, and that there is or will be a correct realization of meaning in history – no longer function to guide the politics of the State, to provide meaning for men and women, public and private, to secure the West's status as big brother of the world.

But the problem must be sharpened even further, beyond the crisis of a secular loss of belief. For the problem of the relations among the myths, rules and roles in modernity is how they have constituted a universal rule of judgment that has functioned to oppress and repress other discourses and subjects. The recent work of Jean Lyotard brings this issue into sharpest focus, and, I think, expresses the current crisis of politics, language and subjectivity. Lyotard analyzes the problem of a universal rule of judgment which forces all other discourses to define themselves in its terms, terms which do not count as legitimate the concerns of other discourses. Lyotard has coined the term, 'the differend' as the case where 'the plaintiff is divested of the means to argue and becomes for that reason a victim' and again, 'a case of differend between two parties takes place when the "regulation" of the conflict that opposes them is done in the idiom of one of the parties while the wrong suffered by the other is not signified in that idiom'.[10] The problem with modernity – with its belief in the great narratives, with its rules of knowledge, power and interests, with its roles of the public and private, men and women, with its definition of knowledge – is that it allowed only one idiom, the patriarchal codification of knowledge, for the adjudication of all claims, and thus ruled out of court the claims and voices of all others. Indeed the present crisis is deeply intertwined with the problems of how not to adjudicate through one discourse or idiom as the universal rule of judgment but how to explode the differences, how to hear other voices, how to learn to live with multiple discourses and multiple ways of being human. It is thus the question of a pluralism which cannot be adjudicated through twin myths of the whole and of progress, but a pluralism in which we must learn to live and flourish. This is the crisis facing us; it is the issue of our meaning, our flourishing, our survival. It has many different expressions: can we know through liturgy, can we hear the meaning of other religions, can we learn to do economic trading with the Japanese, the Brazilians, the Chinese without forcing them to agree to our story of wholeness and identity; can we find ways for men and women to live together where public and private are not sex-segregated, can we find ways for Afro-Americans, whites, Hispanics in public education and church education to learn history through the use of multiple interpretations of historical events, do we know of God as an ultimate giver of openness to pluralism or the closure and ordering of multiplicity?

I want to call this the need to learn to live and flourish with heterogeneous discourses. This is a very awkward and clumsy term. The very thought – that there is no universal rule of judgment, no one final discourse to settle all claims – is quite troubling to us all, even the most postmodern among us! We want to cling, despite all the eloquent pleas from the anti-foundationists – to a belief that we can all talk in the same voice, or at least find an unambiguous form of rationality to adjudicate all our diverse claims. So, perhaps it is best to keep with the awkwardness of the phrase 'the need for heterogeneous discourses' since the very awkwardness reminds us that our task is to find new ways of speaking and living with differences and multiplicities.

This does not mean that we are left forever in our tight little language games, for language itself has a certain openness, an ability to connect, to change, to transform. If we give up the ability of language to gain the true essence of a thing, we can gain the rhetorical function of language to work toward communication, agreement, transformation. To live with hetero-geneous discourses – which is today the crisis for both politics and subjectivity – requires that we find ways for discourses to be open, for communities to nurture differences and solidarity, for each of us to learn that the 'other' has neither to be exactly like us nor exactly the opposite of us.

## New forms of discourse and new forms of community

When facing the crisis of heterogeneous discourses, theology has a role to play in both its locus as a form of 'marginal' knowledge in modernity and in its site as already containing a pluralism of knowledge. Let me consider each in turn.

Certainly theology, as discourses of knowledge in Christianity, holds a marginal status in the modern academy and in knowledge in general. No-where is this so self-evident as in theological education and the academy. Religion is the one area that the well-educated person doesn't have to know anything about, presumably because there isn't anything really to 'know'. Indeed, in some of my favorite theorists, theology is presented as something akin to numerology, superstition, and magical thinking. One of my favorite thinkers, an expert in semiotics, art history, Marxist theory, literary throry and psychoanalytic theory, seems to think that when she can label something as theological, she has proved it as false or not to be taken seriously. A basic reason for the marginality of theology is the definition of knowledge, and its relation to interests and power of dominant subject groups. Yet inside theology we have labored intensely to point out the something more or the something other at the limits of modern knowledge. Take for instance, Schubert Ogden's essay 'The Reality of God', and Paul Tillich's section on reason and revelation in his *Systematic Theology, Volume I*.[11] In very different ways, both texts point out that at the limits, or in the very possibility of modern discourses of knowledge, is a drive and a need for a larger view of knowledge.

One way to pursue our theological analysis of the need for heterogeneous discourses, is to form our analysis of discourses of knowledge: to pay attention to the plurality of discourses in Christianity, to pursue the something more of the theological critique of modern knowledge and modern culture, to be open to multiple discourses within Christian witness.

Much of the material in recent years on theological education hints, and sometimes is quite explicit, about the limits of modern knowledge. Farley's concern for *habitus*, Wood's development of vision and discernment, Hough and Cobb's notion of the reflective practitioner, all can be read as trying to push at the definitions of knowledge. We must unconnect theological explorations of multiple discourses from any metanarrative of the ordered whole or the realization of an original meaning outside of any historical constitution. Finally, we must rethink the work in theological education thus far in light of an imaginative construal of practices such as liturgy, prayer, and the arts. Can we find ways to live with the different ways of knowing in Christian witness not ordering around a centered whole or unpacking to one true meaning but around the possibilities for performative practice in community? We, in theology, are particularly well located for analyzing and criticizing closure of knowledge, the ordering of pluralism, the hierarchy of difference in discourse and we have resources to begin exploring ways of living, speaking, enjoying, flourishing amongst heterogeneous discourses.

Yet if we have much to offer the world in terms of living community with heterogeneous discourses, we also have much to solve in terms of our own problems with prohibiting discourses of certain subjects. If the first set of problems, the acceptance of heterogeneous discourses, has to do with unconnecting our selves from the myths of modernity, the second has to do with resisting the power-knowledge-interests relations of modernity that have so inscribed modern theological education. The place I see this most painfully is the prohibition in theological education for those occupying the subject positions of the 'others' of modernity, persons such as women, blacks, Hispanics, Asians, to multiply the discourses and to expand the parameters of knowledge. It is an irony, isn't it? As much as theology has found ways to criticize the boundaries of knowledge in modernity, it has found ways to instigate the boundaries within its own practices. Theological education, by and large, has tried to address this problem by letting 'others' in, by giving them elective courses, by including occasional lectures or books or voices in foundational courses. But theological education has failed to see the problematic hinted at by Schleiermacher: religion, knowledge, women, men cannot be ordered or contained within the discourse of modern knowledge. What women threaten, in theological education, is the very definition and legitimatization of knowledge, and its complex relations to dominant ordering of politics and subjectivity. The presence of women, as well as the presence of blacks, Hispanics and others, provides the opportunity, gives us the positionality to resist the power, knowledge and interests relationships in modernity and to discover and create new ways, forms, idioms of knowledge.

What is before us is no easy task, for to learn to live with openness and heterogeneous discourses, with specificity and difference without the assumption that we are all the same underneath or there is a whole we can all fit into requires more than just finding new ways of speaking of difference and specificity. For discourses, as I have already pointed out, are dependent upon and bound to community, and the question of finding new discourses of human flourishing is closely related to finding new forms of community. The quest to discover and create new forms of community, ones which live on and nourish the heterogeneity of discourses, may be the greatest political struggle of all. Models of community based on the myths of true meaning, where if we all talk long enough we will agree with the ones in power, or on the myths of the whole where difference is hierarchically ordered, models of community based on rules and roles where certain subject positions legitimize certain powers, will simply no longer serve the needs of the world.

The quest for new forms of community in relation to the flourishing of heterogeneous discourses, is a moral, a cognitive, and a personal problem. It is a moral problem, for in the present world economy we must learn to live in community in which our culture is no longer the big brother or even the major actor. It is a cognitive problem because our modern theories of knowledge are based on models of community which do not easily yield to diversity and difference on a local, let alone a worldwide scale. It is a

285

personal problem, for subjectivity in our culture is closely tied to belonging to a homogeneous community, and to excluding others in order to secure our identity. These problems are our emerging issues in world, church and theological education: the problems of how we can discover and create new forms of human flourishing.

NOTES

1. Edward Farley, *Theologia: The Fragmentation and Unity of Theological Education*, Philadelphia: Fortress Press, 1983. See also Joseph Hough and John B. Cobb, *Christian Identity and Theological Education*, Chico, CA: Scholars Press, 1985; Max L. Stackhouse, *Apologia: Contextualization, Globalization, and Mission in Theological Education*, Grand Rapids: Eerdmans, 1988.

2. Deborah Cameron, *Feminism and Linguistic Theory*, London: Macmillan, 1985, pp. 155–6.

3. For an interesting reading about the attempt to cover up ambiguity in modernity see Donald N. Levine, *The Flight From Ambiguity: Essays in Social and Cultural Theory*, Chicago: University of Chicago Press, 1985.

4. Friedrich Schleiermacher, *Christmas Eve: A Dialogue on the Incarnation*, tr. Terrence N. Tice, Richmond: John Knox, 1967.

5. Dawn DeVries, 'Schleiermacher's *Christmas Eve Dialogue*: Bourgeois Ideology or Feminist Theology?' *The Journal of Religion* 69 (April, 1989), p. 179.

6. This has been talked about in terms of the divided loyalties of modern theology. See Van A. Harvey's excellent rendition of the contradictory position of the modern theologian in his, *The Historian and the Believer: The Morality of Historical Knowledge and Christian Belief*, Philadelphia: Westminster Press, 1966.

7. There are many descriptions of our present 'postmodern' condition. The analysis in this essay is most indebted to: Jean François Lyotard, *The Postmodern Condition: A Report of Knowledge*, tr. Geoff Bennington and Brian Massumi with a forward by Frederic Jameson, Minneapolis: University of Minnesota Press, 1984; Walter Ong, *Interface of the Word: Studies in the Evolution of Consciousness and Culture*, Ithaca and London: Cornell University Press, 1977; Wayne Booth, *Critical Understanding: The Powers and Limits of Plurality*, Chicago: University of Chicago Press, 1979; David Tracy, *Ambiguity: Hermeneutics, Religion and Hope*, San Francisco: Harper and Row, 1987.

8. Lyotard, *The Postmodern Condition*.

9. ibid., pp. 32–3.

10. Jean François Lyotard, *The Differend: Phrases in Dispute*, tr. Georges Van Den Abbeele, Minneapolis: University of Minnesota Press, 1988, p. 9.

11. Schubert M. Ogden, *The Reality of God and Other Essays*, New York: Harper and Row, 1963, pp. 25–37 and Paul Tillich, *Systematic Theology*, 3 vols., Chicago: University of Chicago Press, 1951, vol. 1, pp. 71–159.

# 28

# Toward an Integrated Model of Theological Education
## Ronald F. Thiemann

The basic challenge facing the university divinity schools is to develop a rationale for theological education that links the academic study of religion to the professional preparation for ministry. Only such an integrated rationale will allow these schools to recapture the unity inherent within their dual loyalty to the standards of the research university and the commitments of communities of faith. Unlike their counterparts in law and medicine, however, these schools cannot rely upon an established structure of authority within the profession to link their research aims to professional practice. Rather, these schools must seek to devise a case for theological education that *critically* engages both the mission of the university and the ministries of communities of faith.

In order to provide leadership for the various Christian denominations, university divinity schools must broaden and sharpen their understanding of the distinctive role they play in preparing persons for ministry. While these schools must be responsive to the needs of the churches, they must also take quite seriously their role in setting standards of excellence for the learned ministry. At a time when strong anti-intellectual forces (often under the guise of a concern for 'pastoral care' or 'spirituality') are at work in the denominations, the university schools must represent an unstinting commitment to academic and intellectual excellence in preparation for ministry. These schools must give renewed emphasis to some of the classic disciplines within theological education: biblical studies, history of Christianity, systematic theology, and ethics. At the same time, the curricula of the university schools must seek to develop new models for the integration of theory and practice, models that conceive of theological reflection as arising out of the practices of communities of faith and our broader common public life. University divinity schools must become the essential testing ground for the proposition that the most rigorous forms of theological inquiry can be relevant to issues of practice currently facing communities of faith.

One characteristic of all university divinity schools, even those that retain strong connections to a denomination, is the ecumenical scope of their faculties and student bodies. These schools offer a range and diversity of human resources that the denominational schools simply cannot match. At a time when many denominations have entered a period of economic and confessional retrenchment, the university schools must seek to broaden and strengthen their commitment to a genuinely ecumenical atmosphere for theological education. As universities become increasingly international and multi-cultural in orientation, divinity schools should expand their teaching resources to include coverage of religious traditions other than Christianity. Not only is this expansion essential for the general education of the university student, it is also vital for preparation of Christian ministers. The United States is rapidly becoming a religiously plural nation. The fastest growing religious body in the country today is Islam, and current patterns of immigration indicate significant growth among Buddhist and Hindu populations as well. Ministers must not only gain a knowledge of these traditions, but they must be encouraged to reflect *theologically* on the reality of a religiously plural world. The university divinity schools provide a unique context for this essential form of theological reflection.

In universities that do not have departments of religious studies (Chicago and Harvard, most notably), programs in world religions or history of religions have existed within the divinity schools for many decades. The challenge in these institutions is to integrate these studies with the classical disciplines of Christian theology so that a mutually fruitful dialogue takes place. In universities that host divinity schools and religious studies departments, efforts must be undertaken to form alliances that allow the normative and practical concerns of the theological institutions to engage in critical dialogue with the ostensibly 'value-neutral' approach adopted by most religious studies programs. This dialogue among units of the university with overlapping interests and concerns might then spawn a larger discussion about the 'myth of neutrality' that plagues many of the disciplines throughout the university.

Even the casual observer of the global scene must acknowledge that religious communities exercise exceptional influence, for both good and ill, on world events. Cultural, social, and political values are often decisively shaped by religious convictions and beliefs. Fundamental conceptions of human nature and destiny, of the natural world, of the significance of death implicitly affect policy decisions regarding health care, the environment, and the treatment of the dying. Policies regarding welfare legislation, the conduct of war, and deficit reduction involve questions of justice that often have religious roots and rationales. Professional education, however, rarely prepares students to grapple with the value assumptions that underlie policy decisions, and the role of religion in shaping values is conspicuously ignored in most professional schools.

University divinity schools have a special responsibility to broaden the scope of their practical disciplines in order to address questions of the intersection of religion, values, and policy formulation. The field of practical theology needs to engage questions that have for too long been ignored in other professional schools, questions that are essential to the mission of the university and the churches. Universities and communities of faith seek to be institutions of social responsibility, organizations concerned about the ethical implications of the knowledge and convictions they seek to foster. Yet the separation of disciplines and professions within the contemporary university often makes it difficult to encourage the kind of collaborative research and teaching needed to address the complicated moral issues inherent in the development of public policies. Consequently, medical, law, and business students often lack the most basic orientation to moral reasoning, and theological students are painfully naive about the data, forms of analysis, and assumptions of the policy-related fields. Neither universities nor communities of faith are well served by this unfortunate bifurcation. University divinity schools can serve as the catalysts within the university to encourage new forms of collaboration among professional schools. By regaining a sense of the *public responsibility* of the vocation of ministry, divinity schools can make an important contribution to the overall mission of the university. In so doing, they can take a vital step toward rediscovering the unity inherent in their dual commitment to university and church.

Earlier in this essay I noted that ministry is a peculiar profession because it has not experienced the consolidation of authority that characterized the other 'learned professions'. While this anomalous situation has made it more difficult to devise a convincing rationale for the place of theological education within the university, it has also relieved ministry of some of the burdens of the more centralized professions. The adoption of uniform standards within medicine, for example, also led to a more uniform social composition within the profession. As Starr observes, 'The high costs of medical education and more stringent requirements limited the entry of students from the lower and working classes. And deliberate policies of discrimination against Jews, women, and blacks promoted still greater social homogeneity. The opening of medicine to immigrants and women, which the competitive system of medical education allowed in the 1890s was now reversed.' Between 1900 and 1960, women constituted only five per cent of medical student admissions. A similar exclusion of African

Americans from medical education meant that by the mid-twentieth century only one of every 3,000 black Americans was a doctor, and in the Deep South blacks had one doctor for every 14,000 persons.

The racial and gender diversity within theological education today provides an opportunity to open the conversation about the interaction between the missions of the university and the church to voices and persons previously excluded from those deliberations. As Emory University President James Laney points out, the university needs 'a new sheltering ethos, but one reformed by the definitions and experiences of those among the marginalized who refuse to be bought off by our current power concerns. We need to build an ethos that will make it impossible to conduct business as usual'. As universities face the difficult challenges of the 1990s, their divinity schools have a unique perspective to offer to those conversations that will shape higher education for the twenty-first century. These hybrid institutions, loyal both to the standards of the university and the commitments of communities of faith, can contribute to the intellectual vigor and the moral vision of both communities. In order to make that contribution, however, they will have to reform and broaden their own sense of purpose and mission. In that task they will need the support, both intellectual and financial, of the universities' central administrations.

Universities need vigorous, self-confident divinity schools, institutions devoted to preparing intellectually acute leaders for lives of service in public affairs. In the coming decades, divinity schools will need to reclaim their place of full citizenship within the university, thereby contributing to the university's own effort to maintain the fragile balance between its research and educational mission and its role as an institution of power and responsibility. At a time when difficult decisions must be made about the priorities of the university, a significant investment in the future of the divinity schools will yield genuine dividends for many years to come.

# PART THREE

# Spirit and Community

# G: The Christian Life

29    NICHOLAS LASH's 'Easter Meaning' was published in *The Heythrop Journal* in 1984 (Vol. XXV, pp. 7–18). Amongst his books are *Newman on Development: The Search for an Explanation in History* (Shepherdstown, W.Va: Patmos Press, 1975); *Voices of Authority* (Shepherdstown, W.Va: Patmos Press, 1976); *Theology on Dover Beach* (London: Darton, Longman and Todd, 1979); *A Matter of Hope: A Theologian's Reflections on the Thought of Karl Marx* (University of Notre Dame Press, Ind., 1982); *Theology on the Way to Emmaus: Reflections on Human Experience and the Knowledge of God* (London: SCM Press, and Charlottesville, Va: University Press of Virginia, 1988); *Believing Three Ways in One: A Reading of the Apostles' Creed* (London: SCM Press, and University of Notre Dame Press, Ind., 1993).

30    ROWAN WILLIAMS' 'Resurrection and Peace' was published in *Theology* in November 1989 (Vol. XCII, No. 750, pp. 481–90). Amongst his books are *The Wound of Knowledge: A Theological History from the New Testament to Luther and St John of the Cross* (London: Darton, Longman and Todd, 1979: American title *Christian Spirituality*, Atlanta: John Knox Press, 1980); *Resurrection: Interpreting the Easter Gospel* (London: Darton, Longman and Todd, 1982, and New York: Pilgrim Press, 1984), and *Arius: Heresy and Tradition* (London: Darton, Longman and Todd, 1987). He also edited *The Making of Orthodoxy* (Cambridge and New York: Cambridge University Press, 1989).

31    STANLEY HAUERWAS' 'Some Theological Reflections on Gutiérrez's Use of "Liberation" as a Theological Concept' was published in *Modern Theology* in October 1986 (Vol. 3, No. 1, pp. 67–76). Amongst his many books are *Vision and Virtue* (Notre Dame, Ind.: Fides, 1974); *Character and Christian Life* (San Antonio: Trinity University Press, 1975); *A Community of Character* (University of Notre Dame Press, Ind., 1981); *The Peaceable Kingdom* (University of Notre Dame Press, Ind., 1983, and London: SCM Press, 1984); *Against the Nations* (Minneapolis: Winston Press, 1985); *Suffering Presence* (University of Notre Dame Press, Ind., 1986, and Edinburgh: T & T Clark, 1988);

*Christian Existence Today* (Durham, NC: Labyrinth Press, 1988); *Resident Aliens* (Nashville: Abingdon Press, 1989); *Naming the Silences* (Grand Rapids, Michigan: Eerdmans, 1990); *After Christendom* (Nashville: Abingdon Press, 1991); and *Understanding the Scriptures* (Nashville: Abingdon Press, 1993).

32   SARAH COAKLEY's 'Creaturehood before God: Male and Female' was published in *Theology* in September 1990 (Vol. XCIII, No. 755, pp. 343–54). Her book is *Christ Without Absolutes: A Study of the Christology of Ernst Troeltsch* (Oxford and New York: Oxford University Press, 1988). She has also edited with David A. Pailin *The Making and Remaking of Christian Doctrine* (Oxford and New York: Oxford University Press, 1993).

# 29

# EASTER MEANING
## Nicholas Lash

### The fact of resurrection

The statement 'I believe in the resurrection' can be construed in at least two different ways. It might mean: it is in the light of resurrection, in the grace of resurrection, that I am able to affirm my faith and trust in God. That seems to me an appropriate and sensible thing for a Christian to say. Usually, however, when someone says 'I believe in the resurrection', they are making an assertion about what they think was, is or will be the case. This is how I shall take the statement and, thus construed, it is more like the statement 'I believe that high unemployment is likely to continue for several decades', or 'I believe that the partition of Ireland was a great mistake', than it is like the statement 'I believe in Mrs Thatcher' – where this statement means: 'I trust her and will follow her anywhere.'

I therefore feel entitled to treat the somewhat more specific or circumscribed statement, 'I believe that Jesus is risen from the dead', as a statement of the kind: I believe that X is the case. It follows that, if the resurrection is not a fact, it is unbelievable, not in the sense of being 'really quite incredible', but simply in the sense that, unless it is some kind of a fact, it cannot be an object of belief.

But, what kind of fact is it? The best way to approach this question, I think, is by considering the problem of evidence. If the resurrection of Jesus is a fact, and a fact about Jesus, it can only sensibly or responsibly be believed in if there is good evidence for the fact. Geoffrey Turner, in an article in *New Blackfriars*, dismissed the suggestion that the disciples' belief that Jesus was risen could, in itself, count as 'good evidence'. 'The faith of another man', he says, 'does not count as evidence for me.'[1] Similarly, although he allows that 'in order to believe in the resurrection of Jesus we too need to experience it as something which transcends the past historical event' (we need, as he puts it, 'our own Damascus road experience'), nevertheless such experience alone 'is no basis on which to preach the Easter faith to others'. We must also provide them with what Professor Michael Dummett (quoted at this point with approval by Turner) calls 'real evidence'.[2]

If I understand him, Turner is insisting that that alone could count as good evidence for the resurrection of Jesus to which access could be had, at least in principle, independently of the faith of the disciples or of twentieth-century Christians. And he considers that the evidence for the emptiness of the tomb, and for the fact that 'Jesus was seen (in the ordinary sense) by his disciples and that he spoke to them',[3] is strong enough to count, for his purposes, as good evidence.

Notice that Turner is not requiring that the fact of the resurrection should be *demonstrable* independently of faith. It is, after all, generally agreed that, even if the emptiness of the tomb could be established beyond all reasonable doubt, all that would thereby have been demonstrated was that the tomb was empty!

Nevertheless, what I find unacceptable in Turner's approach (and I have referred to his article only because it seems to me typical of the terms in which the discussion is usually conducted, as least in this country) is the empiricism which underlies it. By 'empiricism', in this context, I mean a philosophical temper which finds it necessary and unproblematic to draw a global or metaphysical distinction between 'objective' facts (what Bernard Lonergan used to call the 'already out there now real') and 'subjective' beliefs, impressions or attitudes ('in here').

Not wishing to interrupt the thread of my argument by entering into philosophical debates with which my readers will be only too wearily familiar, I content myself with asserting that there simply is no good reason why we should accept this Morton's fork of *either* 'brute' facts *or* 'merely subjective' beliefs and impressions (whether those of the disciples or of our Christian contemporaries). Instead, I suggest that we should regard the New Testament writings as a series of invitations to us to consider Jesus' history in one way rather than another. There are, we might say, two ways of 'reading' the story of Jesus, for both of which there is good evidence but yet which cannot both be exhaustively true, cannot both be the last word on the matter. We might, for the sake of convenience, label these two readings the 'story of death' and the 'story of life'.

## Stories of life and death

What is the relationship, in the history of any human being, or of any social group, or (come to that) of the race as a whole, between death and life, between dying and coming alive? The apparently obvious answer, that first we live and then we die, is correct: a person can only cease to be if he or she has previously existed. Birth is the beginning, and death the end, of the historical process.

But although this answer is correct, there is a sense in which it is only trivially true and may be most misleading. At death, our bodily existence is terminated.[4] But what do we mean by our 'bodies'? My body is not simply the lump of matter by means of which I gesture and communicate with other people (or fail to do so). My body is also the world constituted by the personal, social and economic relations in which I share. My language, my family, my city, are parts of my body. When I die, the whole network of domestic and social communication of which I form a part dies a little too. The process of dying starts much earlier than the moment of terminal death. It is not only at the moment of terminal death that our world, our body, dies. Just as the physical constituents which go to make up this lump of matter are changing all the time, and many of the changes that occur amount to irretrievable loss (if you don't believe me, ask your dentist or your hairdresser) so it is with our social relationships. Friends die, relationships wither and, by our failure to communicate and care, our failure to bring each other alive, we contribute daily to each other's dying.

The story of each individual, and of every social group and, indeed, of the human race, is truly told, from start to finish, as a story of death, a narrative of mortality.

It may be objected that this is only part of the story. The story of most individuals, and of many social groups, can surely also truly be told as a story of life, of coming alive: a story of physical strength and prowess, of deepening relationships, of intellectual, practical, emotional and spiritual maturation, progress and achievement?

'This is true. Were it not so, were the story of death the *only* true story, we could not bear to live. But how are these two stories, or these two parts of the story, to be related one to another? Is it possible so to weave them, however tentatively, into a single narrative as to be able to say how it *ultimately* is and will be with the individual, the group and the race?

Before trying to answer this question, there are two more points that need to be made. Firstly, it seems clear, *prima facie*, that the last word must lie with death: every human history is bounded, terminated, by death. Even the most beautiful body corrupts, even the deepest relationship is fractured by mortality, even the most glittering civilizations decay.

The second point is that, without the willingness to die, human existence remains mere 'existence' and cannot flourish, cannot 'come alive'. In our relationships with other people, with new ideas and the challenge of fresh situations, we have continuously to be risking the unknown, the unfamiliar, the disturbing. We have to risk being changed, being transformed. We have to risk the destruction of whatever 'safe little world' we have so far succeeded in carving out of chaos. And the person who has not the courage thus to risk 'dying', throughout his or her life, is unlikely to have the courage to die at the end. The person to tries to live 'privately', to 'hang onto' possessions, friendships, certainties, will die 'privately', alone, and this (perhaps) is hell.

What this suggests is that, even if 'death' and 'life' are antagonistically related, the relationship between them is not straightforwardly antithetical. There seems to be a sense in which acceptance of mortality, engagement in mortality, is a necessary condition of coming alive. Unless a grain of wheat . . .

Nevertheless, life and death are, even if not straightforwardly antithetical, antagonistically related: they are (to put it mythologically) locked in mortal combat.[5] And so, even though the story of death and the story of life can both be truly told, *must* both be told, it is not self-evidently inappropriate or unreasonable to try to weave them into a single narrative and to say (if we can) how it ultimately is and will be with the individual, with the group and with the race; to say where the victory lies.

When we do so, it seems clear (at least if we resolutely avoid all wishful thinking, all utopian dreaming and fantasizing that flies in the face of the evidence which surrounds us on every side) that the last word is with death. Not simply with the mere fact of termination, but with the unravelling of meaning, the destruction of relationship, the lordship of chaos. It is the light which seems ephemeral, the darkness which surrounds, determines and, again and again, 'overcomes' it. We are right to be fearful of death, afraid of the dark, to tremble in the face of chaos.

What would have to be the case for it to be otherwise? What would have to be the case for it to be possible – without illusion, evasion or fantasy – truly to tell the story of the ultimate victory of life, to tell it as a tale most truly told not of mortality but of coming alive? The answer, I suggest, is that we should have to have grounds for supposing that we live and die, although in darkness, yet not into chaos but into unconquerable light. We should have to have grounds for supposing that the ultimate truth, the last word, about all that we do and suffer, enact and undergo, is with the inexhaustible vitality of 'the love that moves the sun and the other stars'.

Which brings me back, at last, to the story of Jesus. The New Testament writings are a series of invitations to us to consider Jesus' story (and, in its light, to consider our own story and that of every human being) as a story of life. It is, of course, a story of failure, suffering and death – hence the centrality of the passion narratives in the gospel accounts. And it does not cease to be so. And yet, in the last analysis, it is the darkness, not the light, which is there declared to be bounded, determined, and 'overcome'.

I suggested earlier that the 'fact' to which the doctrine of the incarnation refers is not simply the *inception* of Jesus' existence, the beginning of his history, but is, quite simply, *Jesus*: that man, that piece of history, of which we say: 'The Word was made flesh and dwelt amongst us' (John 1.14).

Similarly, I now want to suggest that the 'fact', the event, the state of affairs, to which the doctrine of Jesus' resurrection refers is not simply the *termination* of his existence, the end of his history, but is, quite simply, *Jesus*: that man, that piece of history, of which we say: he was glorified, 'we have beheld his glory' (John 1.14).

To adapt Karl Barth's imagery: the doctrine of the incarnation tells the story of Jesus as a tale of 'the way of the Son of God into the far country',[6] and the doctrine of the resurrection tells the story of Jesus as a tale of 'the homecoming of the Son of Man'.[7]

But these two stories are not stories about two consecutive sequences of events. They are the two ways in which we truly narrate one single history, one single sequence of events, the history of Jesus.

I am well aware of the fact that, by now, questions are crowding in as to what all this could possibly mean, and what the evidence for it might be. I shall attempt to attend to such questions in due course. All that I have tried to do in this section so far is to offer a framework within which to indicate what I take to be that fact, or event, or state of affairs, to which the doctrine of Jesus' resurrection refers.

My suggestion has been that, just as the doctrine of the incarnation refers to the fact of Jesus considered in the light of the question: 'who is this man and where did he come from?' so the doctrine of the resurrection refers to the fact of Jesus considered in the light of the question: 'how did it go with this man, what was the sense of his ending?' Both doctrines are interpretations of Jesus. But thus to interpret Jesus' fact and significance is thereby to confess one's faith in the mystery of the God who thus acts in and transforms Jesus' history and ours. It makes no more sense to say 'I believe that Jesus rose from the dead but I don't believe in God' than it does to say 'I believe that Jesus is the Word incarnate but I don't believe in God'. (This last point may seem obvious, and yet much discussion of the resurrection, and especially of the evidence for the resurrection, proceeds as if the former affirmation might make sense.)

If the doctrine of the resurrection is true, it is factually true, and the fact to which it refers is a fact about Jesus. He is not here. Nor is he simply remembered. He is risen. But, once again, what *kind* of 'fact' are we speaking about? Is it an 'objective' fact? Many theologians, under the influence of the kind of empiricism that I mentioned earlier, find this an awkward question to handle.[8] But, frankly, I know of no other kind of fact. 'Facts are what statements (when true) state; they are not what statements are about.'[9] If the statement 'Christ is risen' is true, it states a fact. And, if *Jesus* is the Christ, the statement states a fact about Jesus.

Is that fact which the doctrine of the resurrection states an 'historical' fact? Inasmuch as the doctrine purports truly to state how it went with Jesus, how his story is to be most truly told, the answer must be 'Yes', at least in the sense that no attempt to estimate the truth of stories about Jesus can ignore the historian's testimony. If the historian could demonstrate that what we know about Jesus is such as to render the Easter story utterly implausible, then the truth of the doctrine would have thereby been impugned. With all respect to Harry Williams, the 'real and important truth' does *not* remain 'whatever the status as history of the story in which it is represented'.[10]

If we have good reason to suppose that what the doctrine of the resurrection states about Jesus is false, then to continue to tell it as a tale about 'spiritual reality, always contemporary, within the hearts of the worshippers' (ibid., p. 370), is to issue a licence for the kind of self-indulgent fantasy which has done damage enough in human history. I have no doubt that the Nazis found the myth of the master-race deeply 'meaningful', profoundly descriptive of 'inner realities'. To suppose, however, that 'meaning' can thus be simply divorced from publicly testable fact, significance from history, is to open the door to destructive lunacy.

Of course, the doctrine of the resurrection says *more* about Jesus than the historian is in a position to consider. But the same is *also* true of the alternative version: of the story of death, of the unravelling of meaning and the ultimacy of chaos. The historian is not in a position to make what we might call 'metahistorical' judgements concerning what is 'ultimately' the truth concerning the history of Jesus, or of any one else.[11]

## Evidence and Easter

If the doctrine of the resurrection states a fact about Jesus, on the basis of what kind of evidence does it do so? Here, the first thing that needs to be said, if only because it is too often not said, is that the evidence for Jesus' resurrection is the evidence of his life and teaching and the manner of his death. If Jesus, and the message which he announced and embodied, is not to be trusted on the basis of this evidence, then neither he nor his message are to be trusted at all.

If the manner of his living, and teaching, and dying, affords no basis for that trust in him which is, simultaneously, trust in the One who sends him and speaks to us through him, then nothing that happens to the disciples (or to us) after Jesus' death can be such as to warrant confessing him as the

Christ of God, the Lord's anointed, him whom God raised up, him in whom the glory of God is glimpsed.

It does not follow that the evidence which the manner of his living and dying affords is *sufficient* to warrant the confession of Easter faith. Not that something was 'missing' from that life, that teaching, that costly fidelity. But that we have to be *shown* the 'sense of his ending'; we have to be shown that, not in spite of Calvary but because of it, his story can be most truly told as the story of God's unconquerably creative love, of the victory of the light which the darkness could not overcome.

How are we to be shown this? By that 'conversion process' which Edward Schillebeeckx calls 'the Easter experience'.[12] How else could we know, except by the healing gift of God's Spirit, that the fruit of his silencing was peace, of his rejection forgiveness; that the 'end' of his death was not chaos, but daybreak; that Jesus had died, not into the darkness, but into the light of God? If that is not 'where' Jesus went, the story that we tell of him is false, and the 'Easter experience' a delusion. But, if this *is* where he went, then what else but such change, such 'conversion' could show us where he had gone, enabling us to 'find' him whom we had thought, like us, to be 'lost'? As Schillebeeckx puts it, evoking the visual metaphors that play a large part in the gospel narratives: 'Apart from this experience of Christian faith the disciples had no organ of sight that could afford them a sight of Jesus' resurrection'.[13] And I think that Karl Rahner is saying much the same thing when he says, in a much-discussed passage, that 'the resurrection of Christ is not another event *after* his passion and death . . . the resurrection is the manifestation of what happened in the death of Christ'.[14]

But in what might such 'experience' consist? How and where might such 'manifestation' occur? If we are not to fall back on unintelligible and unacceptable appeals to some kind of incommunicable 'private' experience, the answer must be sought in some public, intersubjective event or state of affairs. Here, as elsewhere, God's self-gift has created contingent 'form' or occurrence. Perhaps the pervasiveness of eucharistic imagery in the resurrection narratives provides us with a clue. Perhaps it was, above all, in common meals shared in his memory that the disciples were 're-called', that they came to know themselves forgiven, re-called to the presence of the crucified. And perhaps the insistence on the fact that the risen Christ first 'appears' as a 'stranger' is, in part, a comment on the perceived lack of any appropriate language, ready to hand, in which they could say what they had come to 'see'.[15]

Two footnotes, before moving on. In the first place, the account I have sketched seems to satisfy Geoffrey Turner's requirement that there should be evidence for the resurrection which is, in principle, accessible independently of the faith of the disciples. The difference between Turner's form of the requirement and mine is that I would shift the weight of the evidence to that which occurred before and at, rather than after, Jesus' death. The language in which the disciples tried, after his death, to say what they had come to 'see' is also 'evidence of resurrection', but only in the indirect sense that it constitutes an invitation to us to see what they saw; an invitation to construe Jesus' history (and hence our own and that of every human being) as a story the sense of whose ending is given by the inconquerable power of God's transforming grace.

In the second place, I disagree with Harry Williams' claim that 'there isn't a single shred of historical evidence for the corporeal assumption of our Lady'.[16] There is historical evidence, however slender, of Mary's obedience and trust, from Nazareth to Calvary. And this seems to me just the kind of evidence that we would need in order to be able to see in her the 'image' of the faithfulness of Israel and thus, in the light of our faith in her son's resurrection, to trust that she, too, was brought by the grace of God to die into his glory.

## The meaning of Easter

It will not have escaped your notice that, so far, I have said nothing about the question of the empty tomb. Geoffrey Turner is quite confident that even if stories about the empty tomb only came to feature in Christian proclamation of the resurrection relatively late, 'the fact of the empty tomb must have been accepted from the beginning, given Jewish beliefs at the time'.[17] He may be right, I am simply not sufficiently well-informed, historically, to pontificate on the matter. But I notice that there seem to be quite a number of learned and sober historians of the New Testament who do not share his confidence.

I take it, however, that the emphasis on 'bodily' resurrection (or 'corporeal' assumption) is, fundamentally, an emphasis on wholeness and personal identity. It is *we*, human persons, human beings, who, by God's grace, die into his glory, not some wraith-like element or partial feature of whatever constitutes our personal identity. I doubt if we can sensibly say much more. Geoffrey Turner may be correct in supposing that the emptiness of the tomb was a necessary condition of the first Christians expressing their Easter faith in terms of 'resurrection', but I am not convinced that the emptiness of the tomb is amongst the truth-conditions of the proposition 'Jesus is risen from the dead'.

This brings me, finally, to the question of what the doctrine of the resurrection *means*. I intend, by this question, to invite consideration of two problems: firstly, concerning the range of terminology and imagery that is available to us for expressing our conviction; secondly, concerning how much we can hope to *understand* of that which, in confessing the doctrine, we declare to be true.

Even if, as I suggested earlier, questions of meaning and questions of truth cannot and must not be dissociated, nevertheless they can and must be distinguished. Thus, for example, whatever we take to be the truth-conditions of the proposition 'Jesus is risen from the dead', I suggest that the unique appropriateness of the metaphor of 'resurrection' is not amongst such truth-conditions. In other words: it is, in principle, possible to make true statements about that to which the language of resurrection refers without using the terminology, or imagery, of 'rising' from the dead.

To anyone even as cursorily familiar as I am with the New Testament evidence, this may seem obvious. And yet, theologians sometimes give the impression that a decision not to use the terminology of 'resurrection' is tantamount to a denial of the truth of the doctrine. But the early Christians used other metaphors: 'exaltation', 'glorification', and so on. And even if in terms of linguistic history, 'resurrection-talk' is closely related to meta-phors of 'waking from sleep', this notion is clearly distinguishable from that of 'resuscitation', with which 'resurrection-talk' is still too often dis-astrously associated. On the general issue, Léon-Dufour has argued the historical case, in some detail, for saying that 'rising metaphors only gradually came to occupy the dominant and apparently normative place which, by and large, we continue to ascribe to them.[18]

There are, to be brief, four points that I should want to make on these matters. In the first place, to say that, in our attempts to make true statements about that to which the doctrine of resurrection refers, we are not restricted to the imagery of 'rising from the dead', is not to say, or to imply, that how we decide to tell the story (of Jesus, of ourselves, and of all mankind) is simply a matter of arbitrary choice or personal preference. It could not be so: we are constrained (as in any interpretative enterprise) by the *interpretandum*. We may, indeed, be very tightly constrained, if we are not to float free of the particularities of that which occurred and was transacted into some 'idealist' fantasizing of our prospects and predica-ment. We are constrained by what we know of Jesus' history, and by our own continuing, and continually unfinished, experience of desolation and forgiveness, tragic circumstance and obscure hope. There is, nevertheless, a crucial difference (however resistant it may be to theoretical expression) between telling a story differently and telling a different story. My only concern is to suggest (and the suggestion has considerable catechetical implications) that to refrain from speaking of 'rising' is not necessarily to tell a different story.

In the second place, I am not suggesting that the expression of Easter faith could ever be a simple, unproblematic or straightforward affair. Such straightforwardness is ruled out by the fragmentariness and 'illegibility' of our circumstance, and by the fact that our 'conversion' (individually and communally, personally and politically) lacks the purity and completeness which might render our 'sight' less occluded and our speech less questionable.

In the third place, whatever imagery we employ, the story that we try to tell (and, corporately and individually, to enact) can never be, as it were, a direct transcript of its referent. Because we seek to speak of that which 'transcends' and heals all time and circumstance, we can only do so tentatively, indirectly, metaphorically, in language drawn from our present experience, which is that of a history that has *not* yet ended, not yet been given its final 'resolution', 'shape' and identity.

Therefore, fourthly, we should never lose sight of how *little* we can glimpse and understand of that of which we seek to speak. The consequent restraints upon speech and imagination work in two directions. On the one hand we need, again and again, to allow the exuberance of unwarranted optimism to be chastened and broken by the dark facts of human experience. The 'story of death' has not ceased to be true even if it is not, perhaps, the last word. On the other hand, however, finding it too easy to say too much about the future is not the exclusive prerogative of optimism. There is also a self-indulgence of despair, a fantasy of egotism, which is or may be silenced and healed by Easter hope. The important thing is not to be able to utter that hope, to speak of resurrection, with facility, but to be able to do so at all.[19]

I have suggested that what the doctrine of the resurrection – of Jesus' resurrection and, in the light of Easter hope, of ours and of every human being – attempts to state is that the story of human history is ultimately to be told in terms, not of death, but of life, not of chaos but of God's unconquerably effective love.

It follows that, if the doctrine of the resurrection is true, then nothing whatsoever, no circumstance, no suffering, no cracking by chaos of sanity and dignity, no betrayal, no oppression, no collapse of sense, structure or relationship, can justify despair, can justify the admission that, at the end of the day, the darkness has the last word. Those who know *this* know, I think, all that it is yet possible for us to know of what 'resurrection' means.

NOTES

1. G. Turner, 'He Was Raised and Has Appeared: Evidence and Faith', *New Blackfriars* 58 (1977), p. 161. Turner was responding to Fergus Kerr, 'Exegesis and Easter', *New Blackfriars* 58 (1977), pp. 108–21, who, in turn, was replying to Michael Dummet (cf. note 2, below).

2. Cf. Michael Dummet, 'Biblical Exegesis and the Resurrection', *New Blackfriars* 58 (1977), p. 64.

3. Turner (note 1, above), p. 166. I am not at all sure what would count as 'seeing', in 'the ordinary sense', a dead man walking through walls.

4. In the next few paragraphs, I have made use of material in N. L. A. Lash, *Theology on Dover Beach*, London, 1979, pp. 174–8.

5. I have in mind the phrase from the Easter Sequence: '*Mors et vita duello conflixere mirando*'.

6. Karl Barth, *Church Dogmatics* 4/1, Edinburgh: T & T Clark, 1956, pp. 157–210.

7. *Church Dogmatics*, 4/2, pp. 20–154.

8. Cf. for instance, M. F. Wiles, *Faith and the Mystery of God*, London, 1982, p. 59.

9. P. F. Strawson, *Logico-Linguistic Papers*, London, 1971, p. 196.

10. Williams (note 2, above), p. 371.

11. The historian is a specialist and such judgements are not, fundamentally, 'specialist' judgements at all: see N. L. A. Lash, 'What Might Martyrdom Mean?', in W. Horbury and B. McNeil, eds., *Suffering and Martyrdom in the New Testament*, Cambridge, 1981, p. 195.

12. E. Schillebeeckx, *Jesus: an Experiment in Christology*, London: Collins, 1979, p. 645.

13. Schillebeeckx, (note 12, above), p. 645. Aquinas's treatment of the matter suggests that the 'experience' in question is to be understood in terms of (we might say) 'seeing the point' about something. That metaphor seems neatly to indicate the *cognitive* element in that to which the visual imagery refers. Cf. *Summa Theologiae* 3a, Q. 55, art. 2.

14. Karl Rahner, *Theological Investigations* 4, London, 1966, p. 128.

15. Cf. Rowan Williams, *Resurrection*, London, 1982, pp. 76–97; on the resurrection meals, pp. 39–40, 108–9, 115–16. I am grateful to Dr Williams for his perceptive comments on an earlier draft of this paper.

16. H. A. Williams, *Some Day I'll Find You*, London, 1982, p. 369.

17. Turner (note 1, above), p. 165.

18. See X. Léon-Dufour, *Résurrection de Jésus et Message Pascal*, Paris, 1971, Cf. G. O'Collins, *The Easter Jesus*, London, 1973, p. 51.

19. On the distinction implied here between 'optimism', 'hope' and 'despair', cf. N. L. A. Lash, *A Matter of Hope*, London, 1981, pp. 85–7, 268–73; 'All Shall be Well: Christian Hope and Marxist Hope', in *New Blackfriars* 63 (1982), pp. 404–15.

# 30

# Resurrection and Peace
## Rowan Williams

There is a New Testament passage used rather too frequently in the Week of Prayer for Christian Unity and on other occasions when we are being urged to be conciliatory to each other – the verses in Ephesians 2 about Christ as our peace.

> Gentiles and Jews, he has made the two one, and in his own body of flesh and blood has broken down the enmity which stood like a dividing wall between them; for he annulled the law with its rules and regulations, so as to create out of the two a single new humanity in himself, thereby making peace . . . . So he came and proclaimed the good news: peace to you who were far off, and peace to those near by; for through him we both alike have access to the Father in the one Spirit (Ephesians 2.14–18).

The words are echoed in Colossians (1.20): 'Through him God chose to reconcile the whole universe to himself, making peace through the shedding of his blood upon the cross' – though here the 'peace' in question is primarily a new relation with God rather than a new relation with each other. In any case, what is clear is that there is one important strand in the New Testament, associated with Paul and his reflections on the effects of Jesus' death, that sees the result of the cross as a drawing together of the human world, an overcoming of hostility: because of the death of Jesus, God and the world are no longer strangers to each other, and thus too the world is not divided into communities that are for ever strange to one another. Peace is practically identical with the condition of the new universe, the wholeness that now exists where before there were only fragments of human reality at odds with each other. The further implication that this wholeness does not stop with the human world only, but involves some kind of renewal of human relations with the rest of the universe is not explored, nor is it now our primary theme; but we should keep it in view as we reflect on the consequences of this in the immediate human context.

What is often missed in the reading of the Ephesians passage, though, especially in contexts where its use is a bit sentimental and unreflective ('reconciliation' is such a seductively comfortable word, fatally close to 'consensus' in common usage), is that the writer of the epistle associates the new possibility of a world of non-strangers with the annulment of the Law and of the sense of an *exclusive* covenant between God and God's people. The human starting point for the writer is that there is a community that has received promises and commitments from God on the one hand, and a sort of shapeless human conglomerate on the other – not really a 'people' at all, not possessed of a firm corporate identity. There is Israel, which has a clear source for its sense of itself, and there is the 'non-community' of the Gentiles, who have no name of their own, and no sense of a future that is distinctively theirs, no awareness of a security in promise. But the problem which forms the subtext of these words is that the security of Israel has become ambiguous: the Law and the covenant are matters of gift; but because they are expressed in terms of clear and identifiable demands, it is possible to think that, as a recipient of this gift, you gain some kind of secure control over your identity. How do we know who we are? In doing what is required of us, in performing a set of measurable duties that will define in unmistakeable terms a secure belonging, an image of 'rightness', a place in the universe. The moral or spiritual risk in this comes in at this point: what *we* do establishes us in the world. It is the distinctive practices of this group as distinct from others that guarantees our life to be meaningful – not passive, anonymous, vulnerable to circumstances. So, to recast the original polarity, we have a set of people who are actively constructing meanings by actions that they are assured are right and approved, and another set who are incapable of so acting: they are at the mercy of their own momentary states of body or mind ('we . . . obeyed the promptings of our own instincts and notions' Ephesians 2.3).

The writer to the Ephesians claims that *both* these conditions are to be put behind, that they are locked in a demonic symbiosis of hostility. The life that defines itself confidently in its ordered doing, *and* the life that steps aside from the painful question of meanings and continuities together form a pathology of the human world. They are the roots of violence and mutual rejection between people; they are both challenged and transformed in encounter with the crucified Jesus, and the 'peace' that we may hope for as a result of the act of God in the death of Jesus is something that stands against each of them alike.

But how does this symbiosis work? On the one hand, the idea of a life that defines itself by successful performance commonly involves the presence of unsuccessful performance as something to measure itself against, define itself against. I or we can *know* what it is to be successful performers because we have a clear picture of what it is to lack this success, provided by the lives and experiences of others; and the energy that fuels the pursuit of good performance is supplied by an anxiety generated by the familiar prospect of failure. The Pharisee in the gospel parable thanks God for his virtue, as he should, but it is given added public definition by the presence of someone who lacks virtue, who has no claim in the company of the good performers. Performance demands such a public measure, demands therefore that there be failures. And the failure is both necessary to the culture of success, and threatening to it: we need to have it there, yet it is also something that is capable of making inroads upon us and weakening or spoiling our own clarity. The result is that we defend the 'territory' of success with great energy and commitment; the Other, the 'failure', is both enemy and ally, a necessary enemy who supports and confirms the project of succeeding, in an oblique or negative way, the shadow that picks out the sharp contours for us.

On the other hand, the life that steps out of the whole business of patterns, meanings, intelligible wholes, carries with it the assumption that there is such a thing as a natural independent selfhood buried in each of us, a spiritual essence whose liberty is infringed by the insulting limits of time and language and other realities, by death and the body and all that is not consciously chosen by this immaterial ego. It works with no less intensive a model of competition for limited space than the order and success model, though its language about this is more muted. In presupposing that we are answerable only to an 'inner truth' of instinct or the claims of the moment, this perspective risks obliterating any awareness of belonging in a context that has not been chosen or invented, and so also risks losing the knowledge of that characteristically human tension that has to do with learning creativity through engagement with the limits of the world and other subjects. Those limits are seen primarily as negative, as menacing. There is a lack of sense that there might be a work to be shared, a future that can be corporate as well as individual, and so too a lack of resources to deal with necessary loss or postponement – an impatience with time. Yet here too, energy is commonly generated by protest or refusal, by the active battle to avoid being formed by a context, belonging to or with others; a curious kind of activity designed to protect the idea of responsiveness to the sheer process of the moment, of the inner motion.

Of course, what I have been trying to describe is not precisely what the writer of Ephesians had in mind in talking about Jews and gentiles! But once we start asking why the making of peace should have something to do with the removal of both law and lawlessness, we are bound to look at the wider questions of what these apparently simple religious disjunctions are saying about the divisions in human self-perception, individual and collective. Just as in Romans Paul sees law and lawlessness at work in a single self, so here we are dealing with more than a distinction between two visibly different groups of human beings. This is actually fairly clear if you look at the curious fact that the writer is both addressing gentiles, those who are simply ethnically non-Jewish, as if they were distinct from him, and speaking of a 'we' who share the gentile condition. The mention of outward or 'fleshly' identification as Jew or gentile in v. 11 is a caution to those who believe the distinctions being discussed are primarily those between empirical groups. So, between the lawkeeper and the lawless is a gulf of enmity that is not simply ethnic or cultural prejudice. The careful ambiguity over 'we' and 'you' urges towards a recognition that the conflict and the violence are bound up with the world of human self-interpretation and social construction overall. This is a world, then, in which there is no peace because it seeks for clarity and self-identification in ways that are necessarily fragmenting and destructive. The active world-shaping impulse, creating order by the imposition of patterns and regularities, requires in practice the contrast of disorder or failure to achieve its own definition; it looks for and when necessary creates its opposite, generating images of disorder, rebellion, irrationality, projected on to others and attacked. The 'freedom' of the life of passion, the organization of life around gratification, is intrinsically incapable of producing a properly social sense at all (witness the erosion of community sense in the wake of advanced capitalism), yet can foster a picture of human living together that is rigid and oppressive in its very resistance to the possibility of a shared future for which it is necessary to reflect, plan or sacrifice. In deferring or refusing the problem of common human language, shared meanings, it also refuses to question its own conflicts, imbalances and exclusions. Law and lawlessness equally issue in an acceptance, tacit or admitted, of strife as humanly necessary; both work with the assumption that the world is irreducibly a place of victory or defeat, in which it is unthinkable that there should be a common future. The two models of human practice have a hidden alliance; and to look at actual human societies is to see generally a fusion of these two impulses – just as to look at individual human beings is to see the interweaving of the hunger for order and the hunger for fulfilment beyond external control.

What these ideal fictions of human life together both insist upon is, ultimately, that human identity is for humans to *control* – either in the overt form of the construction of successful human performances, or, more subtly, in the enacting of the desires of a given and unconstrained selfhood. Both therefore have two denials in common: they resist the vision of a universe in which reasoned control or liberated desire is not ultimate – in other words they resist the idea of a *belonging* that cannot be dictated or constructed by the human self (personal or social); and they have no room for the awareness of *gift* in the relation of humanity to its total environment. If we are to explore further what might be involved in seeing peace as the overcoming of the polarity of law and lawlessness in the building of another sort of humanity, it seems that peace has something to do with the creation of this dual awareness, of belonging and gift. In the rest of what I have to say, I shall turn to the question I am meant to be addressing, of how this kind of peace is rooted in or conditioned by the event of Easter, on which the confession of Christian trust rests.

The life of Jesus – insofar as it can be characterized in a few brief phrases – has to do with proclaiming and enacting a disturbing truth: that achievement in the terms of a religious ordering of things is not of itself decisive in forming the reaction of God to the human world, and that what *is* decisive is a commitment of trust in God's compassion that shows itself in costly and painful letting go of the obsessions of the self – both the obsessive search for the perfectly satisfying performance and the obsessive search for the perfectly unconstrained experience. Indeed, these two apparently antithetical urges are shown to have an uncomfortable amount in common: the unprincipled rich man, the unreflectively vindictive servant, the person who unquestioningly indulges aggressive or lustful fantasy are close kin to the accumulator of religious merit. They have not learned to lose what they believe to be crucial to their identity, they work in different but recognizably related modes of acquisitiveness. To all such, the word of judgement is addressed: the person who faces and acknowledges inner contradiction, failure, the breakdown of performance and the emptiness of gratification, is the person who is capable of hearing and answering the invitation to loss and trust.

The invitation is in practice an invitation to accept the 'hospitality' of Jesus himself – often literally as well as figuratively. And so it is that the challenge of this invitation is put at its baldest and most alien when Jesus himself *fails*. His actions and words are sufficiently inflammatory, sufficiently a relativizing of the existing forms of political and religious sense, that the administrators of political and religious power, the governing élite of priestly aristocrats and the occupying forces of Rome, combine to bring about his death; and he is left to die alone and despairing, because his failure is too difficult and strange to continue with. The incipient 'new Israel' of the Twelve is scattered as Jesus is taken to his execution. The Twelve have hoped for a gratification of longings for power – the fire of judgement from heaven for their enemies, the positions of influence and authority in the new age (what Jesus himself calls the 'gentiles' or 'the nations', modes of governance in Mark 10). They have looked for a restoration of God's people that will involve fuller and better answers to the problem of what performance is required of them (Peter's famous question about how often he must forgive). Jesus in yielding to his failure, his appalling mortality, finally refuses these projections – as if only *by* this failure of all that has been fantasized and longed for can he at last 'say' what is to be said; as if the silence of his dying is the only rhetoric for his gospel. In this sense, the cross is the end of both 'law' and 'lawlessness' as defined already; the roots of human enmity are here brought to nothing.

But: to be able to *say* this depends upon a transformation of self-perception. The writer to the Ephesians rightly speaks of the central event as the shedding of Jesus' blood; this is what provokes the final crisis for trust in Jesus. In the aftermath of the cross, the friends of Jesus are left stripped both of their inherited identities (they have become marginal in the world of public law-keeping) and of the confused and embryonic new identities they had begun to learn in the company of Jesus. The inadequacy and weakness of those new selves are exposed as they find they cannot survive his failure and dereliction. Any identity, any reality they now have will have to be entirely gift, new creation; not generated from their effort or reflection or even their conscious desire. To be able to speak at all about the cross as a moment where meaning is given is to speak from the gift of new perception. Jesus has taken his friends beyond the normal bounds of law and lawlessness, and they have found that beyond those bounds they cannot survive in their own resource; the loss that threatens is too sharp and humiliating to be borne. So life beyond law and lawlessness must be the life of God's gift, the assurance that failure and loss do not mean final destruction or emptiness. Meaning, promise, the future, the possibility of continuing to live in freedom and in the resource to love – all these are 'held' in the being of God, which is communicated to us as mercy, absolution. 'Because I live, you will live' (John 14.1).

These constipated and abstract words are an attempt to say what I think the New Testament documents conceive to be the nature of 'resurrection' life. I have tried to set out elsewhere at greater length the ways in which I believe the actual narratives of the resurrection of Jesus work to show the centrality of forgiveness, restoration and gift in the apprehension by the apostles of the risenness of Jesus, and am here assuming such a reading of the stories, and of some of the reflection on resurrection to be found elsewhere than in the narratives. The essential point is that resurrection is the transaction in human beings that brings about the sense of a selfhood given, not achieved – as well as an event that bridges the history of Jesus and the history of the Church; or rather, it is this latter in that it is the former. Otherwise it would simply be a rather exceptional 'paranormal' occurrence, whose historicity or non-historicity could be debated in isolation from the creation of community involved. The resurrection of Jesus may be (as I for one believe) at least the empty tomb, but it is most importantly the overcoming of the loss, the death-of-identity, in the experience of those who had followed and then abandoned Jesus, and the proclamation to his executioners of hope or salvation through their victim. Resurrection, the new life from a moral and material nothing, is judgement upon the attempt to construct a system of action and understanding so impregnable that it cannot live with prophetic criticism, and judgement too upon our sentimental assumption that we can sustain newness of life beyond the regularities of 'law' independently of relation to a 'giving' reality, a point of personal love and affirmation. Peter's promise of fidelity even to prison and death is harshly exposed as this kind of illusion; he becomes capable of that sort of witness when he has discovered the extreme vulnerability of his emotional commitment, and discovered beyond that a continuing vocation, discovered that he is still trusted.

These things are said in the New Testament in an individual register, and are most readily comprehensible to us perhaps in terms of the stories of particular persons. But in fact they have to do no less with our societies. To look at our own nation at the moment is to see, in some important respects, the kind of tension I have been trying to explore. We have a public rhetoric in which repentance, provisionality, openness to judgement, the acknowledgement of failure, are all apparently unthinkable. And we see also a 'humanist' opposition, a conglomerate of alternative patterns of human living together, sceptical of the possibilities of social organization and law as we know them, sharply and accurately critical of the self-serving processes of political power (exercised by left or right), yet apparently stuck in a permanent minority position, without the means to establish and sustain their vision for a society at large, rather than just a self-selecting sub-culture. The failures and divisions of this amorphous 'opposition' are a major source of that temptation to cynicism that regularly overtakes anyone not hypnotized by the claims of organization for success; and this is something the Peace Movement has to confront with particular urgency, committed as it is to the kind of change that can only be effective on a more than personal level, yet so often finding its supreme moments in the intensity of experience offered by a sub-culture type of group (I suppose that this tension is especially painfully focused in and around Greenham and all that it stands for).

Our social experience (there is nothing very original or profound in noting it) suffers from the non-communication between competing ways of constructing human identity: an ideology of achievement that punishes failure, and a utopian hope of justice and reconciliation that is consistently vulnerable to its own failure to transform more than the interpersonal, and thus tempted to reinterpret failure as success (the classic reaction of the left after an election defeat, the reiterated insistence on the felt warmth of companionship at a peace demonstration that fails to touch public opinion . . .). Both styles of living find strangeness in speaking of what lies beyond failure as gift or trust or entrustment; which is to say that both have difficulties with the idea of a creative forgiveness. Law can allow for reparation, lawlessness can sidestep the issue of accountability, of a life that is morally connected within itself, and so can devolve the idea of failure on to fate, the operation of process we are not answerable for. But a vision that can hold to the reality of personal and corporate tragedy, the possibility of betrayal and inadequacy unleashing powerfully destructive processes, *and* also continue to affirm that our individual resources, even the sum of our individual resources, are not the only resources for life or renewal in the world – this is a vision that may keep us from the urge to 'master' our identity in the world, whether by the orientation towards performance and satisfaction of 'law' or by the orientation towards immediacy and transparency – (transparency of acts to passions, transparency of persons to each other, transparency of social order to personal claim) of utopian opposition, personal and political.

This is not to say (God forbid!) that the gospel of the resurrection, as represented by the practice of the Church, offers a quick solution to the tensions of our social life. Indeed, once you have put the tensions in the sort of way I have suggested, you can see that the Church itself is divided by exactly the same polarity, urged into the same 'solutions' by way of law and by way of experiential utopianism. The Church is itself unsure of how to handle forgiveness, reducing it to the possibility of reparation or drowning it in a rhetoric of a forgiving and forgetting God, so that the notion of offence itself evaporates, and there is no real injury to be healed by mercy. However, this is to be expected if the Christian community remains an historical human community; these are, quite simply, part of what it is to be beings whose identity is in process of formation rather than unprob-lematically given in a non-historical 'nature'. What is different in the community of belief is the story told of its origins in a paradigmatic discovering of a gift over and above the attempts of human beings to settle by human resources the question of their truth or reality, a gift we can variously call absolution, conversion, transformation (even, for one ancient and reputable Christian tradition, deification), but which is firmly

313

anchored in the unique and particular narrative of betrayal, cross and resurrection. The community exists in distinctive, perceptible shape because of this, its self-identifying actions in the sacraments are celebrations of what is given in this. Christian language states that failure is both real and not final, and so offers the possibility of a corporate or individual self-perception that can cope with honesty above the past and thus imagine a future in which all of that past can be held together; but the discovery of such a possibility depends not on ingenuity and effort, nor on a release of 'natural' energy from the depths of pre-existent selfhood, but on the contingency of someone's history, or rather of the histories of a whole nexus of persons and forces in conflict around the figure of Jesus.

What the gospel of the resurrection has to say about peace, then, seems to me to be most clearly audible if we grasp that the resurrection promise has something to do with the roots of our mistrust and violence in our unwillingness or inability to receive our human identity from God as a gift, at every juncture in our experience. This means being able to leave behind the fantasy of a decisively successful performance as a human being, or a human society: building into my projects and hopes a provisionality that acknowledges the possibility of defeat and thus the possibility of repentance. It means leaving behind no less the fantasy of life in untrammelled immediacy of experience and expression, or life in transparent companionship with those like myself: building into my sense of myself the unavoidability of conflict, the lack of resolution in any effort to transform the human world, the reality of moral and spiritual error, limitation and exhaustion. These are fantasies that have a lot to do with where and how 'enmity' begins. Not to recognize our creatureliness, our incapacity to master all the conditions under which we are becoming what we shall become, is close to the heart of our unfreedom, since this refusal binds us to pervasive struggle. We need, as I have said, to take on the reality and inevitability of conflict; our error is often to see this as a kind of metaphysical statement about the inevitability of mutual exclusion and strife, rather than about the ways in which we are formed in the hard tasks of responding to the resistance, the otherness of the world (people and things), and in the accepting of our inability to guarantee ourselves or anyone an untroubled passage through it. The assumption that strife is an absolute 'given' in the world grows from the conviction that we possess a territory to be safeguarded, whether of law-based achievement or naturally given essential selfhood. The gospel of the resurrection proposes that 'possession' is precisely the wrong, the corrupt and corrupting, metaphor for our finding place in the world. What we 'possess' must go; we must learn to be what we receive from God in the vulnerability of living *in* (not above) the world of change and chance.

It must be said again that this is not a claim to be able to point to some realization of 'resurrection' life; it is certainly not a blueprint for 'reform'. It is that by which we may judge all our efforts at life together, and that which prevents us from giving up on the hope of non-destructive human living – a hope that has nothing at all to do with our ability to realize it for ourselves. Let me quote some words of Peter Selby (from a talk given at Leeds during a 'teaching week' at the University in 1985):

> Christianity has to start with confronting the notion of our self-understanding that is produced by an ideology of victory and defeat; and to confront that, of course, means to re-evaluate all our defeats . . . . [T]hey no longer have to be forgotten, they no longer have to be your enemies, but can in fact become the building blocks from which you make a new future. Life under that kind of promise is what Christianity is all about, and the process which it offers people – prayer, worship, meditation – are about the possibility of getting in touch with your own defeats and putting those defeats in touch with the defeat of Jesus, in order that, like his life, your life can become part of the new and better future which is promised to us . . . . Your self-understanding and mine, corrupted as they are by our involvement in the processes and the ideologies of victory and defeat, have to be turned round so that we come to see them alongside the defeat of Jesus as the world's ultimate friend, so that the world is befriended by its defeat, and not by victory achieved at the expense of other people's defeat.

We began with the Epistle to the Ephesians on the overcoming of enmity, and noted too the language of Colossians about peace being made with God. If the foregoing pages make sense, and if we follow Peter Selby's powerful characterization of what is fundamental in Christianity, it is clear that the enmity we know in the world is grounded in our urgency to forget defeat, because it speaks to us of what we have not successfully controlled. When we can shed this enmity towards our failures, we have taken a step towards the end of enmity between people. And the discovery of this possibility is the discovery of the friendship of God. How do we 'make friends' with defeat? As Peter Selby proposes, we do so by setting it alongside the defeat of Jesus, in the knowledge that that defeat is absorbed in life – the knowledge of the resurrection gospel. God in Jesus is the friend of the world, shown to be so by the fact that Jesus' death in desertion is not the end of God's promise of absolution and renewal through his life and action. For God, no defeat is final, and that is the ground for *our* trust that no defeat is final. It is, then, possible to stop fearing defeat as if it meant the dissolution of all possible reality for us; it is possible to look at other human beings and understand that they too face the traps of fear, that they share a vulnerability with us that they are incapable of admitting. If we can find, in the light of the gospel, a language for us and for them to *communicate* this common vulnerability, we shall have realized the 'new humanity' that is in Jesus. We shall have accepted the impotence of our fantasies of control; or, as you might say, we shall have repented and believed the gospel.

# 31

# SOME THEOLOGICAL REFLECTIONS ON GUTIÉRREZ'S USE OF 'LIBERATION' AS A THEOLOGICAL CONCEPT
## Stanley Hauerwas

## On getting the issues straight

I have been asked to address the issue of the 'role of "total liberation" as a theological concept for a Christian autonomous ethic'. I must begin, however, by confessing a good deal of skepticism about such a task. For I am not at all sure what issue or set of issues are meant to be addressed. I have no idea where or how one should begin in order to say something constructive about the 'role of "total liberation" ' in Christian ethics. Indeed I am not even sure I know what is being asked since I am unsure what the crucial phrases in the statement mean. Why, for example, is 'total liberation' used rather than simply 'liberation'? Can one be liberated without the liberation being 'total'? Does 'total liberation' have a theological connotation in contrast to liberation understood in social or economic terms?

But if that is the case why is 'total liberation' identified as a theological concept? Though it is often asserted that liberation is equivalent to the notion of salvation that has remained more an assertion than a carefully worked out argument. Is the use of the qualifier 'total' meant to suggest that liberation as a theological concept is a fuller and/or more complete concept than its use in social, political, and economic contexts?

Equally puzzling is the idea of a 'Christian autonomous ethic'. Is it assumed that such an ethic exists and if it does so who are its proponents? It is by no means clear what is meant by a 'Christian autonomous ethic'. Is such an ethic one that is independent of all other forms of morality? Or is a Christian autonomous ethic one, in a Kantian fashion, that is based on no metaphysical or anthropological presuppositions? Or is a Christian autonomous ethic one that maintains a sense of autonomy for the individual in opposition to all forms of heteronomy?

Though I have argued for the distinctiveness of Christian ethics I have not, thereby, understood myself to be trying to develop or defend a

Christian autonomous ethic – that is, an ethic that is the mirror image of Kant's attempt to ground morality in rationality qua rationality.[1] Indeed I have tried to suggest that the very idea that ethics needs such a ground or foundation is a mistake. Rather Christian ethics, like all ethics, draws its substance from sets of convictions about the nature and good of human kind carried by a historic community. Christian ethics is committed, therefore, to exposing the pretensions of any ethic that claims to be 'autonomous'.

I suspect, however that the issue I am being asked to address is that raised by liberation theology. For the notion of 'total liberation' is sometimes implied, if not explicitly advocated, by liberation theologians. For example under the heading, 'Christ and Complete Liberation', Gustavo Gutiérrez distinguishes three levels of meaning: political liberation, the liberation of man throughout history, liberation from sin and admission to communion with God. These three levels mutually affect each other, but they are not the same. One is not present without the others, but they are distinct: they are all part of a single, all-encompassing salvific process, but they are to be found at different levels. Not only is the growth of the Kingdom not reduced to temporal progress; because of the Word accepted in faith, we see that the fundamental obstacle to the Kingdom, which is sin, is also the root of all misery and injustice; we see that the very meaning of the growth of the Kingdom is also the ultimate precondition for a just society and a new human being. One reaches this root and this ultimate precondition only through the acceptance of the liberating gifts of Christ, which surpasses all expectations. But, inversely, all struggle against exploitation and alienation, in a history which is fundamentally one, is an attempt to vanquish selfishness, the negation of life. This is the reason why any effort to build a just society is liberating. And it has an indirect but effective impact on the fundamental alienation. It is a salvific work, although it is not all of salvation. As a human work it is not exempt from ambiguities, any more than what is considered to be strictly 'religious' work. But this does not weaken its basic orientation nor its objective results.[2]

Gutiérrez seems to suggest, therefore, that 'liberation' from sin is the most fundamental, the 'total' liberation on which all other forms of liberation depend. Thus he says

> Liberation is a precondition for the new society, but this is not all it is. While liberation is implemented in liberating historical events, it also denounces their limitations and ambiguities, proclaims their fulfillment, and impels them effectively towards total communion. This is not an

identification. Without liberating historical events, there would be no growth of the Kingdom. But the process of liberation will not have conquered the very roots of oppression and the exploitation of many by man without the coming of the Kingdom, which is above all a gift. Moreover, we can say that the historical, political liberating event *is* the growth of the Kingdom and *is* a salvific event; but it is not *the* coming of the Kingdom, not *all* of salvation. It is the historical realization of the Kingdom and, therefore, it also proclaims its fullness.[3]

Gutiérrez, thus, argues that salvation cannot be protected by trying to lift it from the midst of history where people struggle to liberate themselves from slavery and oppression. Such a liberation 'partakes in', is 'integral to', the liberation of Christ yet the latter is nonetheless more complete. For the salvation of Christ is a 'radical liberation from all misery, all despoliation, all alienation'.[4] It must, therefore, be 'total'.

At least one of the critical questions raised by Gutiérrez's claims about liberation is whether he has not, in the name of the salvation offered by Christ, underwritten an account of liberation that is profoundly anti-Christian. For at times his account of liberation sounds far more like that of Kant and the Enlightenment than it does of the Kingdom established by Christ. Thus he says it is important to keep in mind that the object of the struggle against misery, injustice, and exploitation is 'the creation of a new man'.[5] The liberation of the Latin American continent

> means more than overcoming economic, social, and political dependence. It means, in a deeper sense, to see the becoming of mankind as a process of the emancipation of man in history. It is to see man in search of a qualitatively different society in which he will be free from all servitude, in which he will be the artisan of his own destiny. It is to seek the building up of a new man.[6]

Though perhaps not intending it, phrases such as 'free from all servitude', 'artisans of our own destiny', have the ring of the Enlightenment. Thus Kant defines enlightenment as 'man's release from his self-incurred tutelage. Tutelage is man's inability to make use of his understanding without direction from another. Self-incurred is this tutelage when its cause lies not in lack of reason but in lack of resolution and courage to use it without direction from another. *Sapere aude!* "Have courage to use your own reason!" – that is the motto of enlightenment.'[7] Of course Gutiérrez can rightly object that he is not talking about liberation from 'self-incurred tutelage', but liberation from unjust social, political, and economic oppression by forces and people outside the self. But yet it seems his ideal society, a society of the 'new man', at least draws its inspiration from this Kantian ideal insofar as we seek to be free from all servitude except, perhaps, that which we voluntarily accept.

But if that is the case then has Gutiérrez, perhaps unwittingly, underwritten a sense of liberation at odds with the gospel? For the salvation promised there is not a life free from suffering, free from servitude, but rather a life that freely suffers, that freely serves, because such suffering and service is the hallmark of the Kingdom established by Jesus. As Christians we do not seek to be free, but rather to be of use, for it is only by serving that we discover the freedom offered by God. For we have learned freedom cannot be had by becoming 'autonomous', free from all claims except those we voluntarily accept, but rather freedom literally comes by having our self-absorption challenged by the needs of another.

Yet the dominant account of freedom since the Enlightenment has denied such an understanding of freedom. As Iris Murdoch has suggested we live in

> the age of the Kantian man, or Kantian man-God. Kant's conclusive exposure of the so-called proofs of the existence of God, his analysis of the limitations of speculative reason, together with his eloquent portrayal of the dignity of rational man, has had results which might possibly dismay him. How recognizable, how familiar to us, is the man so beautifully portrayed in the *Grundlegung*, who confronted even with Christ turns away to consider the judgment of his own conscience and to hear the voice of his own reason. Stripped of the exiguous metaphysical background which Kant was prepared to allow him, this man is with us still, free, independent, lonely, powerful, rational, responsible, brave, the hero of many novels and books of moral philosophy. The *raison d'etre* of this attractive but misleading creature is not far to seek. He is the offspring of the age of science, confidently rational and yet increasingly aware of his alienation from the material universe which his discoveries reveal; and since he is not a Hegelian his alienation is without cure. He is the ideal citizen of the liberal state, a warning held up to tyrants. He has the virtue which the age requires and admires, courage. It is not such a very long step from Kant to Nietzsche, and from Nietzsche to existentialism and the Anglo-Saxon ethical doctrines which in some ways closely resemble it. In fact Kant's man has already received a glorious incarnation nearly a century earlier in the work of Milton: his proper name is Lucifer.[8]

I am certainly not suggesting that Gutiérrez's 'new man' can be identified with that which Murdoch so trenchantly critiques. Yet I think that Gutiérrez's rhetoric does not sufficiently guard against such possible misunderstanding. Indeed I would suggest that to make the metaphor of 'liberation' central or overriding as a description of the nature of Christian existence, as is done in much of 'liberation theology', is a mistake given the background of much of our recent intellectual history. For when the metaphor of liberation determines or controls all other ways of understanding the Christian life, the uncompromising commitment of Christians to work to make our societies more nearly just and peaceful can be distorted. Thus I hope to show that the stress on liberation by the liberation theologians has in some ways resulted in misdirecting some of their most basic concerns. In the rest of this essay, therefore, I want to try to show the limits of liberation as a central theme for Christian ethics by suggesting how liberation only makes sense as a means to a more profound sense of fellowship and justice.

However before I do so I need to guard against a possible misunderstanding. By criticizing Gutiérrez's use of liberation I am not denying his central claim that there is a close connection between salvation and social practice. Indeed in that I think he is exactly right as the Kingdom brought by and through the ministry of Jesus fundamentally entails the establishment of a new order which just is our salvation.[9] The issue is not whether there is a connection between salvation and social justice, but whether liberation is a sufficient image or metaphor to depict adequately the nature of that social salvation. There is no question that what Christians mean by salvation includes some sense of liberation, but liberation is clearly only one of the images used in the New Testament.

Moreover it may be the case that our inability to exploit those other images of salvation in the Scripture has meant that liberation has been made to do more than its share of the work. Part of our task, therefore, must be to try to find other images as compelling as liberation to depict the salvation we believe accomplished in Christ. I cannot pretend to make much headway on that large task here though I hope my analysis will at least suggest some of the issues that must be considered for accomplishing that task.

## Freedom, equality, and power

At the beginning of *A Theology of Liberation* Gutiérrez explains why liberation is the primary theme of his theology. It is the term that best expresses in our times the struggle to construct a just and fraternal society, where people can live with dignity and be agents of their own destiny. It is our opinion that the term *development* does not well express these profound aspirations. *Liberation*, on the other hand, seems to express them better. Moreover, in another way the notion of liberation is more exact and all-embracing: it emphasizes that man transforms himself by conquering his liberty throughout his existence and his history. The Bible presents liberation – salvation – in Christ as the total gift, which, by taking on the levels we indicate, gives the whole process of liberation its deepest meaning and its complete and unforeseeable fulfillment. Liberation can thus be approached as a single salvific process. This viewpoint, therefore, permits us to consider *the unity*, *without confusion*, of man's various dimensions, that is, his relationships with other men and with the Lord, which theology has been attempting to establish for some time.[10]

The great difficulty with this kind of claim is its fatal abstractness. 'Liberation' is simply made to do more work than one term can bear as we are left unsure what kind of liberation is implied and/or if it is consistent with other values Gutiérrez desires. For example Gutiérrez suggests that the primary goal is to construct 'just and fraternal societies', but a society that tries to make every person 'the agent of their own destiny', indeed the oft stated aim of the capitalist societies Gutiérrez finds so oppressive, may in fact be inconsistent with any meaningful sense of 'fraternity'.

This is not to imply that becoming 'an agent of our destiny' is inherently incompatible with the achievement of more nearly just and fraternal societies, but if such claims are to avoid ideological manipulation we need a more definite sense of how such a society is to be institutionalized and structured. In particular missing from Gutiérrez's account of liberation is a crucial element of all significant social movements – power. For the 'stuff' of liberation involves taking power from some and giving it to others. Unless we have some sense how that is done justly calls for liberation can too easily result in false consciousness.

That is why liberation is insufficient as a single term of social analysis or strategy. If liberation is to serve for the creation of more nearly just and fraternal societies, we need equality and power as crucial categories. No one, I think, has seen this better than R. H. Tawney in his still classic *Equality*. Tawney notes that liberty and equality have usually been considered antithetic by Western political and social theorists; and fraternity has not been considered at all. And to be sure if liberty means that every individual should be free to indulge without limit his appetites, it is clearly incompatible with economic, social, and political equality.[11]

Yet Tawney argues that the fatal mistake of this line of reasoning is its failure to recognize that there is no freedom in the abstract.

> For freedom is always relative to power, and the kind of freedom which at any moment it is most urgent to affirm depends on the nature of the power which is prevalent and established. Since political arrangements may be such as to check excess of power, while economic arrangements may permit or encourage them, a society, or a large part of it, may be both politically free and economically the opposite. It may be protected against arbitrary action by the agents of government, and be without the security against economic oppression which corresponds to civil liberty.[12]

Writing from the perspective of an industrial society Tawney argued in *Equality* that the urgent task for such societies was to extend the liberty gained in the political sphere to the economic. Moreover the necessity to do so shows clearly that the claimed antithesis between liberty and equality is invalid. On the contrary liberty does not conflict with equality but requires it. For

> when liberty is construed, realistically, or implying, not merely a minimum of civil and political rights, but securities that the economically weak will not be at the mercy of the economically strong, and that the control of those aspects of economic life by which all are affected will be amenable, in the last resort to the will of all, a large measure of equality, so far from being inimical to liberty, is essential to it. In conditions which impose co-operative, rather than merely individual, effort, liberty is, in fact, equality in action, in the sense, not that all men perform identical functions or wield the same degree of power, but that all men are equally protected against the abuse of power, and equally entitled to insist that power shall be used, not for personal ends, but for the general advantage.[13]

For the creation of a fraternal society Tawney argues, therefore, what is required is that power over public matters should be public power. For power is but 'the capacity of an individual, or group of individuals, to modify the conduct of other individuals or groups in the manner which he desires, and to prevent his own conduct being modified in the manner in which he does not.'[14] In industrial societies, however, by permitting some disparate power over economic holdings in the name of freedom, the public good has been subjected and controlled by private interests. Thus the necessity to equalize such power is the means to increase freedom of those subject to economic power. But the increase in their freedom is not to make them 'agents of their own destiny', but rather make them more capable of performing services for the creation of a fraternal society. Such a society is one that aims 'at making the acquisition of wealth contingent upon the discharge of social obligations, which seeks to proportion remuneration to service and deny it to those by whom no service was performed, which inquires first, not what men possess, but what they can make or create or achieve.'[15]

The attempt to develop such a society does not deny that people have different natural endowments or gifts, but yet more fundamentally, it is claimed, we share something more elementary and commonplace. For

> it is a fact that, in spite of their varying characters and capacities, men possess in their common humanity a quality which is worth cultivating, and that a community is more likely to make the most of that quality if it takes into account in planning its economic organization and social institutions – if it stresses lightly differences of wealth and birth and social position, and establishes on firm foundations institutions which meet common needs, and are a source of common enlightenment and common enjoyment. The individual differences of which so much is made will always survive, and they are to be welcomed, not regretted. But their existence is no reason for not seeking to establish the largest possible measure of equality of environment, and circumstance, and opportunity. On the contrary, it is a reason for redoubling our efforts to establish it, in order to ensure that these diversities of gifts may come to fruition.[16]

Such a view of society Tawney derives from the Christian affirmation that all men and women are the children of God and thus the rights of all men and women are equal. But by affirming that people are people and nothing more, Christianity

> is a warning that those rights are conditional and derivative – a commission of service, not a property. To such a faith nothing is common or unclear, and in a Christian society social institutions, economic activity, industrial organization cease to be either indifferent or merely means for the satisfaction of human appetites. They are judged, not merely by their convenience but by standards of right and wrong.[17]

It may be objected that this brief discussion of Tawney's analysis of the relation between freedom, power, and equality does little to advance

Gutiérrez's account of liberation. For there is nothing in Tawney's position that Gutiérrez cannot accept and yet stay perfectly consistent with his own account of liberation. Yet I think such a response is far too cavalier once we remember the issue is the adequacy of liberation as a theme to guide Christian interpretation and strategy of the current social crisis. For Tawney reminds us that social analysis, if it is not to lose touch with the actual forms of societal organization, requires an account of power and equality so that our understanding of liberty does not become idealistic or utopian.

Perhaps a more serious objection to my introduction of Tawney is that he simply is irrelevant to the kind of challenge that the societies that Gutiérrez is trying to address. Tawney was writing presupposing advanced industrial societies, and insofar as his work is still relevant, it is only relevant to such societies. In contrast Gutiérrez is writing from and to societies that lack the advantages and disadvantages of industrialization and, thus, whose forms of oppression and injustices are quite other than those with which Tawney was concerned. For Gutiérrez the problem is not simply economic inequality but the structural injustice build into his societies and complicated by the economic and political dominance of foreign powers. In such a context liberation as a single term of analysis makes more sense since what it requires is a much more thorough overturning of social structures than that envisaged by Tawney's analysis.

Such an objection, however, fails to acknowledge the essential point that my use of Tawney was meant to make – namely, that liberation as a social goal must be displayed by locating those concrete forms of oppression that are to be challenged. To do that requires more concepts than simply liberation in and of itself for we must have some account that gives us the means to name the injustices we actually confront. If we lack such an account, calls for liberation can too easily be interpreted not simply as challenges to specific injustices but as an attempt to deny our status as finite creatures who are rightly subject to many limits and claims by others.

Gutiérrez quite rightly desires a 'just and fraternal society, where people can live with dignity and be agents of their own destiny'. He is, moreover, quite right to claim that Christians have an obligation to work for the development of such a society, not as something incidental to their faith, but as integral to the very meaning of that faith. The difficulty, however, is that at least as it is stated such ideals are fatally abstract so that we are unable to determine what social strategies or institutions are compatible with them. For certainly capitalist social orders have as much claim as more socialist to be the exemplification of such a society. What is required, therefore, is a more fulsome account of the nature of Gutiérrez 'fraternal' society and how it is best accomplished.

## 'Total liberation' as a theological concept

Finally it may be objected that the argument I have been developing, even if correct, is beside the point. For the issue is not simply whether liberation is an adequate concept or theme for social analysis and strategy, but its status as a theological concept in Christian ethics. Have I not in fact avoided that issue? Whether I have or not depends on how one understands the relation between theological and ethical analysis. If, as Gutiérrez argues, there is a close relation between liberation as a theological concept and liberation as a social and political concept, which certainly seems to me to be correct, then the kind of analysis I have provided must be relevant. However it must be further said that Gutiérrez's claim in this respect would be stronger if we had a better sense of the relation between the 'levels' of political, historic, and theological liberation. Or perhaps even more important one may wonder if the metaphor of levels is the best for distinguishing between these kinds of liberation.

Yet the question still remains as to the role that liberation ought to have in Christian ethical concerns. As I have already indicated there is no question that a sense of liberation is central to any account of the Christian life. As Paul constantly reminds us 'For freedom Christ has set us free; stand fast therefore, and do not submit again to a yoke of slavery' (Gal. 5.1). Yet that freedom that we have as a gift from Christ is of a very distinct kind. For in effect it is a freedom from the presuppositions and powers of the old world, a world determined by law and order. The freedom given us in Christ is that of a new age which Christ has brought through his cross and resurrection. It is therefore not just a freedom from, but a freedom to. 'For you were called to freedom, brethren; only do not use your freedom as an opportunity for the flesh, but through love be servants of one another. For the whole law is fulfilled in one word, "You shall love your neighbor as yourself." But if you bite and devour one another take heed that you are not consumed by one another' (Gal. 5.13–15).

Thus freedom, at least in Paul, is not an end in itself but rather it is the means in which it is made possible for us to serve one another. Any account of liberation in Christian ethics must be tested against this norm. Moreover this also means that the kind of liberation that Christians experience and hopefully learn to live may not be easily translated into or identified with the liberation desired and sought in other contexts. For too often the liberation is sought not as a means to serve, but as a means to dominate.

That does not mean, however, that Christians have little to contribute to liberation struggles. But their contribution may be more demanding than simply underwriting or approving of such struggles in the name of 'liberation'. Rather, Christians' most important contribution to such struggles is to be a community of the liberated who can witness to paradigmatic forms of service. For in truth there are 'ideal' models for knowing how power is best distributed in societies to offer the greatest freedom and equality. What is required is the experience of a people who pioneer ways of social relation that give concrete expression to liberty and equality. For without such experience our imagination either withers or is perverted by flights of fancy. The Church, as a society of the liberated, is thus the necessary paradigm that can offer us imaginative possibilities of social relations otherwise not thought possible.

What is important, therefore, is not that Christian ethics be autonomous, but that it have the courage to draw on the integrity of the Church's experience of liberation. For if we are to ever know what liberation means surely it is there that we will learn it. That does not mean that God only liberates within the Church, but if we are ever to discriminate between the kinds of liberation found in the world we will be able to do so only by first having experienced it through a body of people who have found freedom through learning to serve one another and the world.

NOTES

1. See for example my *A Community of Character: Toward a Constructive Christian Social Ethic*, Notre Dame, Indiana, 1981.
2. Gustavo Gutiérrez, *A Theology of Liberation*, New York: Maryknoll, pp. 176–7.
3. ibid., p. 177.
4. ibid., p. 178.
5. ibid., p. 146.
6. ibid., p. 91.
7. Immanuel Kant, *Foundations of the Metaphysics of Morals*, tr. by T. N. Beck, New York, 1959, p. 85.
8. Iris Murdoch, *The Sovereignty of Good*, New York, 1971, p. 80.
9. See for example John Howard Yoder, *The Politics of Jesus*, Grand Rapids: Eerdmans, 1972.
10. Gutiérrez, op. cit. p. x.
11. R. H. Tawney, *Equality*, London, p. 164.
12. ibid., p. 167.
13. ibid., p. 168.
14. ibid., p. 159.

15. R. H. Tawney, *The Acquisitive Society*, Brighton, Sussex, 1982, p. 31.
16. Tawney, *Equality*, pp. 55–6.
17. Tawney, *The Acquisitive Society*, pp. 185–6.

◈◈◈◈◈◈◈◈◈◈◈◈◈◈◈◈◈◈◈◈◈◈◈◈◈◈◈◈◈◈◈◈◈◈◈◈◈

# 32

# CREATUREHOOD BEFORE GOD: MALE AND FEMALE
## *Sarah Coakley*

'The human soul comes directly from God, and therefore finds its happiness by returning direct to God', writes Thomas Aquinas (X *Quodlibets*, viii.I). The Christian tradition presents no single normative understanding of what it means to be a creature; indeed it is not even clear to me that there exists a *uniquely* 'Christian' standpoint on creatureliness: the quotation from Aquinas is sufficient to remind us of the lasting entanglement of the Neoplatonic theme of 'return' with the Nicaean insistence on a free personal creation *ex nihilo*; and further paradoxes confront us with the realization that even creation *ex nihilo* is difficult to justify from Scripture alone.[1] But at the heart of any Christian doctrine of creaturehood must surely lie, as perhaps Aquinas' theology illuminates above all, the notion of a radical, and qualitatively distinct, *dependence* of the creature on God. It is this constellating theme of creaturely dependence, along with what I shall argue have been its fatal cultural admixtures for women in Christian patriarchal society, which I wish to explore in this article.

My analysis will employ what may seem to some an untidy combination of themes from Christian iconography and spirituality, psychoanalytic theory, and secular and theological feminism, as well as from the more usual resources of biblical and systematic theology. Such messiness is however nothing but the methodological counterpart of the equally messy entanglement of the theme of creaturely dependence on God with *different* sorts of human dependence. Official doctrinal formulations and theological discussion on 'creatureliness' traditionally ignore or repress reflection on these entanglements, and hence the need to probe to the 'soft underbelly' of the doctrine, to expose by reference to popular symbolism and spiritual practice the wider ramifications of the theme of 'dependence'. Dorothee Soelle has posed the necessary questions succinctly:

> It seems to me that at the core of all feminist philosophy or theology there lies this matter of 'dependency' . . . . Is it a good thing to make

oneself emotionally independent, or would this only lead us to the position of the male with his superficial ties who would not dare attack the ideological independence of the male heroes? What does it mean anthropologically to be dependent? What does it mean in social life? The area covered by this interfeminist debate is also the area where decisions have to be made in theory. Is this dependency only a repressive inheritance from the past or is it part of the simple fact that we are created?[2]

I have elsewhere[3] sought to describe and explicate – in Trinitarian terms – the unique sense of creaturely dependence that silent prayer inculcates, a dependence unlike any other, for in it what is experienced as noetic blankness is theologically explained as 'that-without-which-there-would-be-nothing-at-all'.[4] This then is radical, absolute – and so intellectually ungraspable – creaturely dependence; to grasp it would be to make God into an entity. But God is by definition ungraspable, and towards God the dependent creature yearns inchoately, with 'the restless heart' of quasi-erotic unfulfilment. The recurring metaphor is that of 'ascent' to divine intimacy (whether Gregory of Nyssa's dark operation of the 'spiritual senses', for instance, or Bernard of Clairvaux's more openly erotic 'kiss of the mouth'); and the undeniable interconnection of sexual desire and contemplative desire for God is celebrated in the elaboration of the themes of the *Song of Songs* from Origen to St John of the Cross. But the unresolved antinomy between the (acceptable) erotic desire for the divine on the one hand, and actual relationships with people of the opposite sex on the other, is as tense, if not tenser, than in the Platonic writings from which Christianity inherited it.[5]

Now the paradox for the feminist who surveys this material, and who herself experiences the tug of the dependent heart on the Divine, is this. The metaphor of 'ascent' is a metaphor of power and hierarchy; the Cappadocian doctrine of the Trinity announces on the one hand the absolute equality of the 'persons' according to the *homoousion* principle; but in describing the incorporation of the soul into the divine life through prayer, Basil of Caesarea's debt to Neoplatonic subordinationism is scarcely veiled:[6] the Spirit catches one *up* so that one may ascend to the level of the Son, and then via him glimpse something of the dizzier heights of the Father's glory. The Father, of course, is in this Eastern vision the convergent 'source' and 'cause' of the other two 'persons'. This hierarchical Godhead is however symbolically charged with social implications for women: for how is the ceding to the Spirit in the contemplative quest not also implicitly, for a woman, the ceding to potentially repressive and patriarchal structures in Church and society?

In the medieval West, as we shall explore a little later, the same trend of dominance is associated with a particular, negative stereotyping of 'female mysticism', arising out of the male mystic's quest to transmute his sexual energy towards God. In search of the dependent creaturely perfection of his ('female') soul, the male contemplative projects on to the real women who might deflect him from this goal all the negativity of his still unresolved desires. Even Bernard of Clairvaux, lauded by Jean Leclercq for his wondrously healthy 'sublimation' of the erotic towards God,[7] can warn his monks that it is quite impossible to have a normal relationship with any woman without it ending in an illicit sexual liaison. This reflects the Western Augustinian background we shall explore briefly below: if woman is intrinsically 'bodily', then she is either a temptress or a 'female' type of saint, also bodily, emotional, 'hysterical'.

We must attempt, then, to *distinguish* more clearly and consciously between different sorts of dependence; not, I believe, because we can ever hope finally to disentangle them, to arrive at the tidy isolation of a pure contemplative dependence on God; but because it is as well to bring to consciousness how easily one fades into another, how the infinitely 'subtle' and 'obscure'[8] operation of the Divine on the dependent creature is entwined with the deepest hopes and fears about family relationships, about sexuality, power and death.

Consider then the following distinguishable types of 'dependence'. Alongside what we have called the 'absolute dependence' of the creature on God brought to special consciousness in contemplation, we must range: the complete physical dependence of the newborn infant on the mother (or other primary caretaker) for nourishment, warmth and cleanliness; the no less significant emotional and psychological dependence of small, growing, and even grown-up children on parents and parental figures; the economic dependence of families (and so often women) on the wage-earner and bread-winner (or in the case of the unemployed or disabled, on the state or charity); the 'dependence' of servile subjugation or imprisonment in countries subject to oppressive regimes; the dependence of prisoners on their captors; of the tortured on their torturers; the emotional, psychological and sexual dependence of the spouse, the lover – or rather differently, the infatuated – on the beloved; the 'dependence' of slothful mental habit and failure in critical thinking which is the opposite of 'independence of mind'; the arrested infantilism of neurotic dependence; the dependence on drugs (of whatever kind); the dependence we are all subject to, in events beyond our control – the elements, accidents, disease; the dependence on others for sustenance and care in sickness, handicap or mental disturbance; and finally the yielding to the unknown in the 'dependence' of death.

These intertwined themes of dependence find Christian iconographic expression. A vivid example of the sense of the cosmic significance of the mother is to be found in Georgios Klotzas' icon of the Virgin and child at the heart of the world, the spirals of the mandala shape centring in on the supreme mother on whom all are dependent. The fragility of the baby Christ dandled on her knee presents another variation on this theme, whether the Virgin is portrayed as full of concern and foreboding or, more usually, as rapt in pure absorption. This theme may itself contain a pointed reminder of him on whom the Virgin in turn is dependent, and to whom she is submissive: consider, for instance, Stephan Lochner's 'Madonna in a Rose Bower' where the papal Father figure lurks half-hidden at the apex.

In the 'dependence' of death, the cycle comes full circle and the son is again cradled on his mother's knee; but in the Orthodox representation of the Virgin's 'Dormition' the roles are reversed, and the mother's soul is held by Christ as a dependent baby itself now, while the saints mourn over her physical body.

Mary's role as protector and intermediary, a favorite theme of the late medieval West, suggests not only continuing dependence on the approach-able maternal figure, but the desire to flee the dangers of the world and of a potentially vengeful Father God. Thus in the 'Virgin of Mercy' type, Mary both shelters the faithful under her robe and acts as point of safe contact with the heavenly realm. In Piero della Francesca's unique representation of this theme, however, Mary achieves the stature of what one might call 'proto-feminist' assurance, and her followers, significantly, are more respectful than cowed. More common, however, are the distinctly neurotic overtones of the hierarchy in which the Virgin *replaces* the (ineffectual?) Spirit; the penitent may safely approach the awesome papal Father only via the Virgin and then the Son, both of whom plead to the Father by reference to their own points of vulnerability and tenderness (Christ's wounds and Mary's breast).

But the Virgin also can be a dominating, awesome, mother-type, to whom submission in turn is due, as powerful, perhaps as overwhelming, as some of the pagan Mother goddesses she replaces. She can also be herself dependent on her own mother, bespeaking that probably universal experience of new mothers of their own fundamental fragility and exhaustion, of their need for being mothered again upon their entry into the awesome responsibilities of motherhood. The chain of dependence creates another hierarchy (in the 'St Anne Trinity' of St Anne, the Virgin, and the Child), perhaps an unwitting pastiche of the visual form of the

Eastern hierarchical Trinity discussed above; here, perhaps, is the *matriarchal* power-structure of the Greek extended family centred on the grandmother, a hierarchy no more releasing, I would argue – and doubtless more fearful to a man – than its counterpart in the 'male' Trinity. The tables are turned, only to repeat the subordinationist pathology in reverse.

The Virgin can be represented also as Christ's lover, sexually as well as religiously dependent on his superior divine status. According to Bernard, the Virgin 'ascends to the throne of glory', 'sings a nuptial hymn' and is greeted with 'kisses of [Christ's] mouth'.[9] On this however Marina Warner comments, more with sadness than bitterness, that 'The icon of Mary and Christ side by side is one of the Christian Church's most polished deceptions: it is the very image and hope of earthly consummated love used to give that kind of love the lie.'[10] Likewise, the Assumption, greeted by C. G. Jung as an implicit acknowledgement of the 'equality of women' and as a transformation of the Trinity into a properly balanced quaternity, is again not all that it seems. The Virgin is welcomed into the magic mandala, certainly, but it is visually clear in Fouquet's representation of this scene that she remains in a subordinate and fully dependent submissive position, again as befits a woman.

Finally, but most symbolically redolent of all of Christian prayer and practice, we have the Annunciation, Mary's 'fiat' of ready submission and acceptance of divine will. Despite brave and promising efforts by contemporary feminist theologians to find in the Annunciation a symbol of right 'cooperation' and response to God,[11] or even, more backhandedly, an event at least without active intervention from a human father,[12] we can have no doubt of the implications of the more traditional interpretation for dependent women. Although there are many lovely exceptions, where for instance the Virgin exhibits self-composure as well as obedience, contemplative absorption rather than cowed submission before the angel, the themes of fear, humility and submission in the face of divine command are predominant, and a natural enough interpretation of Luke 1.26ff. Mary, recapitulating and reversing the disobedience and carnal knowledge of Eve, accepts the announcement of the Father God's intentions in obedient, and this time pure, sexual submission. Indeed, it is her willing *passivity* (whether or not this is wholly true to Luke's original intentions)[13] which has so exercised the proponents of 'dependent', contemplative prayer. In the eighteenth-century Pière de Caussade's theory of 'abandonment to divine providence', for instance, the theme of contemplative acceptance is woven specifically around the Annunciation story.[14] It is worth remembering, as I have remarked elsewhere,[15] that de Caussade, a Jesuit director of considerable influence and intellectual flair, wrote for nuns already enjoined to a double submission: to their own superiors, and to male confessors and directors. It is not particularly reassuring to find him warning them against 'intellectual curiosity' and recommending yet more 'humble submission'.

Thus we conclude: 'all creatures are dependent, but some are more dependent than others'. The message has had unchartable spiritually stultifying effects for women of many generations; but for men, too (and arguably most acutely since the creation of the Cartesian cultural ideal of the heroic, lonely, cogitating self), the effects of this adage have been both equally dehumanizing and desiccating. In a brilliantly insightful essay, Mary Midgley has shown how the very creation of such a vision of the self could rest on *unconscious* dependences – in Kant's case, for instance, the domestic dependence on his man-servant![16] The *denial* of creaturely 'dependence', then, is as misleading as is its subordinationist misuse in human hands.

But what then of male creaturely dependence? Does not the Christian tradition provide resources for a riposte to the Enlightenment distortion of the self-sufficient (male) individual? We have already illustrated something of the double-sidedness of this theme in tradition: the urging of the submission of the (significantly 'female') soul to God or the Virgin on the one hand, but the implicit legitimation of male power over female subordination on the other. Jesus' ultimate yielding on the cross in death is the supreme locus for such a theme of male dependence, and as some Christian feminists have urged,[17] this symbolic *depotentiation* of male control, this breaking of societal stereotypes, is what makes for them the retention of a male saviour not only bearable but thoroughly pointed. But again, if we look to the iconographical evidence, especially from the West, we find this theme complicated by the (male) power-play implicit in the relationship between Father and Son at the point of Christ's death. Thus, in the late medieval *Gnadenstuhl* ('throne of grace') type of representation of the Trinity, the Father dispassionately holds up the Son at the moment of death, accepting the just punishment for human sin absorbed into the body of the Man of Sorrows. The paradoxes for the male beholder are evident, and indeed still being played out in modern Western theology. For with whom does the male (whether consciously or unconsciously) most easily identify? Is it with the yielding, depotentiated Son, or more truly with the impassive and all-powerful Father, bent on justice and punishment? The paradoxes are only partly relieved by the later reinterpretation of this type in the so-called *Not Gottes* representation of the Trinity:[18] here the Father, with increasingly compassionate visage, supports the dead body of his son, whom he has however still abandoned to a lonely and agonizing death.

Themes of male power and subordination are still lurking here then, as too, I believe, are sexual connotations. The symbolic connection between male sexual release and death is well documented in literature; and von Balthasar's argument in his essay 'The Christian and Chastity' is based precisely on this male sexual symbolism:

> In its origin [the New Testament] presents to man and woman a glorious picture of sexual integrity: the Son of God who has become man and flesh, knowing from inside his Father's work and perfecting it in the total self-giving of himself, not only of his spiritual but precisely also of his physical powers . . . . What else is his eucharist but, at a higher level, an endless act of fruitful outpouring of his whole flesh, such as a man can only achieve for a moment with a limited organ of his body?[19]

This line of connection, whatever one thinks of von Balthasar's particular argument here, is one that I suspect is worthy of bringing to greater consciousness.

Yet the seamier side of such a sexual connection is a tendency to sado-masochism; it is essential that we should expose any distorting and destructive aspects of spiritual practice that have been based on such hidden sexual agendas of a punitive type. Sara Maitland, reviewing some pertinent evidence from female saints (Rose of Lima, Margaret Mary Alacoque, and most worryingly, the canonized Maria Goretti, who chose death over loss of 'honour' at the hands of a rapist), poses the right question: 'What can possibly lead women [such as these] to believe that they are more "conformable", more lovable to the God of creation, love and mercy, bleeding, battered and self-mutilated, than they would be joyful, lovely and delighted?'[20] The question applies no less poignantly to men who have trodden this path; but, as Maitland's essay shows, the frenetic quality of some of the evidence relating to women in this area alerts us once more to the hierarchical context in which women have sought with desperation for spiritual equality and perfection.

But the 'hierarchy' – as we have already hinted – is differently enunciated in East and West Christendom, and it is well to be clear about this, if only to highlight the fallibility of some supposed corrections to the problem. In a now classic article, Rosemary Radford Ruether outlined the difference between Gregory of Nyssa's and Augustine's understanding of creation, and of the implications thereof for the place and understanding of female creatureliness.[21] According to Gregory, there is a double creation: in the first intance a non-sexual and purely spiritual creation (for it is assumed by Gregory that to be truly 'in the image of God' the creature must be angelic, non-physical); only in the second instance – and 'with a view to the Fall' – is bodily nature added, both male and female. On this

335

view, then, the female creature is not regarded as intrinsically more physical or bodily than the male; but both the origins and goal of perfect creatureliness lie in a sort of humanoid state, where sexual differentiation is *irrelevant*. In Augustine, by contrast, the existence of the sexes is from the start 'intrinsic to creation', and sexual relations – without passion, however! – are part of God's good intentions. This might appear to be potentially a more promising picture for women, were it not for the sting in the tail: the disjunction of spirit and corporeality, with woman being fatally identified with the latter. Augustine sees the male, alone, as the proper and full image of God. He contains both 'male' spirit and 'female' bodiliness within himself, whereas the woman is *intrinsically* carnal, subordinate to the male, and in the image of God only insofar as she conjoins herself with her husband. The result, as Ruether shows, is that 'woman is not really seen as a self-sufficient, whole person with equal honor, as the image of God in her own right, but is seen, ethically, as dangerous to the male.'[22]

Now if we align this material with the insights already gleaned from attending to the different emphases of Eastern and Western Trinitarianism, we may arrive at some interesting results. In the East, first, there emerges a fascinating correlation between the *ideology* of *homoousion* equality in the 'persons' of the Godhead on the one hand, and creaturely equality of humanoid souls on the other. But we cannot help asking whether the *realities* are not in both cases actually more hierarchical and subordinationist than the ideology allows. For all its appeal to the natural and fortuitous inclusiveness of its *anthrōpos* language, the Greek Church – we could surely all agree – is not noted for its granting of equal ministerial roles to women; and it is these *practical* issues which are the acid test in the long run. Even such a moving visual correction of the hierarchical image as Rublev's icon – which employs what is indeed the older and for the East the mainstream, typology of Genesis 18 in attempting a visualization of God – still combines in subtler form the two distinctively Eastern characteristics we have highlighted; the de-sexed or humanoid view of the 'person', and the simultaneous bowing to the Father's monarchy, however delicately done in this case.[23] Thus too the apophaticism for which the East is justly lauded is sometimes capable of being a mask for complacency or a pat response to the feminist challenge. Let anyone who claims that he has passed well beyond the need for 'male' or 'female' images into God, or that (more ingeniously) 'Father' to him means nothing whatever to do with ordinary human fathering,[24] examine his actual relations with women in Church and society. Things are not always what they seem.

In the West, however, one may suggest a different point of correlation between the Trinitarian theology of Augustine and his views on male and female creatureliness, but one that is perhaps also telling. Running through the various different psychological analogies of the *Die Trinitate* is the insistence on the right operation and *harmony* of the faculties of the soul (memory, understanding and will) which mirror the co-inherent relations of the divine triad. It is not insignificant, I suggest, that what most offends Augustine about normal sexual activity is the failure of the male will to effect total dispassionate control over the phallus; the harmonious ordering of the soul is disrupted: the body revolts. (The contrast here with Gregory of Nyssa, as Peter Brown has recently illuminated, is of some importance: for Gregory the sexual act itself is apparently not intrinsically worrisome, but rather the implications of human reproduction for the continuing cycle of births and deaths in a persisting social order.[25]) In Augustine, however, it is not the hope of eschatological flight to a non-sexual realm that is held before us, but rather *actual* sexual relations without loss of control. In this (somewhat joyless) vision of paradise the woman nonetheless remains intrinsically 'bodily' and subordinate to her husband's leading spirit. Now when such assumptions are carried over, much later, into the problematic inner-Trinitarian relations of an Anselmian substitutionary atonement theory, a (bodily) female figure may occasionally be brought in visually as the *vinculum amoris*, effecting a *rapprochement* between Father and Son, whether directly as Holy Spirit or, more usually, as the Virgin replacing the Spirit and warding off the wrath of a vengeful Father. Christian feminists may again well ask, however, whether these spontaneous projections of female figures into the Godhead, retrieved and welcomed with enthusiasm by some, are really a viable way forward, recapitulating as they do the Western stereotype of bodily, subordinate dependence for women.

To sum up: if in the East we have detected a tendency to announce a spurious (and de-sexed) equality for female creatureliness, in the West a more explicit stereotype of subordinate female bodiliness has been the norm. From a Christian feminist standpoint clearly neither of these solutions is agreeable as a systematic view of female creatureliness. In concluding I shall make some brief programmatic suggestions about a way forward.

We may first note a suggestive convergence of themes from secular feminist psychoanalytic theory on the one hand, and Christian feminist atonement theory on the other. In the work of Nancy J. Chodorow,[26] the Freudian theory of the 'castrated', incomplete female is turned on its head. By examining the different implications of the mother-child relationship for gender development in little boys and girls, Chodorow stresses that while girls are encouraged to continue in a state of relational identification

337

with the mother, boys must forge an effective separation from her in order to develop as male 'individuals'. *Contra* Freud, it is this male urge to individuate that needs explaining, not the connectedness of the female identification with the mother. The results however are those gender characteristics thoroughly sanctioned by our society: the 'relational' capacity for empathy and feeling in the female, and the propulsion to autonomy and control in the male. Chodorow's conclusions have found interesting corroboration in Carol Gilligan's study of ethical decision-making.[27] Her surveys (on, for instance, decisions over abortion) brought to light in the 'different voice of women . . . an ethics of care, the tie between relationship and responsibility, and the origins of aggression in the *failure* of connection'[28] (my emphasis).

This line of approach – not uncontentious in contemporary secular feminism, for it has a tendency to smack of the essentialism it is trying to surmount – finds its theological counterpart in Christian feminist work on 'female' sin and atonement. Thus, in a pioneering article originally published in 1960, Valerie Saiving urged that the 'temptations of women *as women* are not the same as the temptations of men *as men*', and that whereas 'pride' and 'will-to-power' are the creaturely faults that come naturally to men, in women sinning is more likely to be associated with

> Frivolity, distractability, and diffuseness; lack of an organizing centre or focus; *dependence on others for one's own self-definition*; tolerance at the expense of standards of excellence; inability to respect the boundaries of privacy; sentimentality; gossipy sociability, and mistrust of reason – in short, underdevelopment or *negation of the self*.[29]

Moreover, note again how the cultural effects for women are not just different but *negating*; as a Jungian psychotherapist recently remarked to me (and she deals with a substantial number of women religious): 'It is the combination of *overdependence* and self-*hatred* which is so fatal'.

If we accept the broad picture of modern female 'creatureliness' outlined here, then obviously some form of compensation for actual stereotyping is an urgent necessity. In part, but only in part, the Christian tradition has thrown up its own spontaneous corrections, and a comparison of the equally extraordinary, twelfth-century figures Bernard of Clairvaux and Hildegard of Bingen is particularly instructive here. In Bernard we see a male saint asserting in a new way the importance of *feeling* in spiritual development; along with this goes a frank and even daring delight in the erotic metaphors of the *Song of Songs*: the soul is 'female' and passive before its lover; and in the iconography of St Bernard his devotion to the Virgin is celebrated as his feeding at her breast, returning, as Freudians would say, to a pre-oedipal identification with the mother. In the connected Cistercian idea of *Christ* as mother, there is a similar turn to tenderness and passivity. Whatever one may make of this, these connected themes all indicate an unusual urge to 'relatedness'; whereas in the visions of Hildegard, Bernard's contemporary and correspondent, there is an opposite compensation towards female authority and power. Awesome female figures appear as Wisdom or 'Ecclesia'; conversely, however, the Spirit is celebrated not as submissive 'female' mediator but as a fiery (phallic) 'tower'. Yet, as Barbara Newman's brilliant analysis shows,[30] Hildegard's remarkable *sui generis* symbolism has its remaining gender paradoxes: just as Bernard's compensating themes break down at the point of accepting normal social relations with real women, so Hildegard too remains in thrall to societal assumptions about the 'weakness' and unreliability of women, whilst manifestly managing herself to be the exception that proves the rule.

To conclude: if we are to grope towards a more equitable representation of male and female creatureliness before God we shall indeed be doing a new thing. Selective retrieval from the tradition will be instructive, but not, I suggest, wholly convincing without further critical reflection. Corrective 'androgynies' may still mask unacknowledged sexism;[31] the simple throwing up of compensating 'feminine' divine imagery may leave societal relationships between the sexes largely untouched; false apophaticism may leap to the place of 'unknowing', leaving curiously intact the sexual stereotypes it claims to overcome. The safer test for sexism overcome is not so much the purity or balance of an official doctrinal formulation, but the *practical* outworkings of the relationship between the sexes in society and Church.[32]

It has been the burden of this paper to suggest – against the more radical of the post-Christian feminists[33] – that an 'absolute dependence' is indeed at the heart of true human creatureliness and the contemplative quest. But such *right* dependence is an elusive goal: the entanglements with themes of power, hierarchy, sexuality and death are probably inevitable but also best brought to consciousness: they are an appropriate reminder that our prayer is enfleshed. In that sense the lessons of such reflection may yet be revealingly 'incarnational'.

NOTES

1. The interpretation of 2 Macc. 7.28 is disputed.
2. In J.-B. Metz and E. Schillebeeckx, eds., *God as Father?*, Edinburgh and New York, 1981, pp. 73–4.

3. In *We Believe in God*, London, 1987, ch. 7, as a member of the Church of England Doctrine Commission.

4. Here I acknowledge my indebtedness to Sebastian Moore's argument in 'Some Principles for an Adequate Theism', *The Downside Review*, 95 (1977), pp. 201–13.

5. See for instance Diotoma's speech in Plato's *Symposium*: one 'ascends' from actual love affairs finally to the vision of the 'beautiful'.

6. See *On the Holy Spirit*, 9.23.

7. Jean Leclercq, *Monks and Love in Twelfth-Century France*, Oxford, 1979.

8. The language is that of John of the Cross.

9. *In Assumptione Beatea Mariae Virginis*, *PL*, 183, col. 996; quoted in Marina Warner, *Alone of all her Sex*, New York, 1976, p. 130.

10. Warner, op. cit., p. 133.

11. See for example Rosemary Radford Ruether, *Sexism and God-Talk*, London, 1983, ch. 6.

12. So (the earlier) Mary Daly, *Beyond God the Father*, Boston, 1973, p. 84.

13. See the interesting argument to the contrary by my colleague Deborah Middleton in 'The Story of Mary: Luke's Version', *New Blackfriars*, December 1989, pp. 555–64.

14. See Père de Caussade, *Self-Abandoment to Divine Providence*, London, 1971, pp. 31ff.

15. Sarah Coakley, ' "Femininity" and the Holy Spirit?', in M. Furlong, ed., *Mirror to the Church*, London, 1988, p. 129.

16. Mary Midgley, 'Sex and Personal Identity: The Western Individualistic Tradition', *Encounter*, June 1984, pp. 50–5.

17. Notably Angela West, 'A Faith for Feminists?', in J. Garcia and S. Maitland, eds., *Walking on the Water*, London, 1983, pp. 66–90.

18. For both these types see G. Schiller, *Iconography of Christian Art* II, London, 1972.

19. Hans Urs von Balthasar, *Elucidations*, London, 1975, p. 150.

20. Sara Maitland, 'Passionate Prayer: Masochistic Images in Women's Experience', in L. Hurcombe, ed., *Sex and God: Some Varieties of Women's Religious Experience*, London, 1987, p. 127.

21. Rosemary Radford Ruether, 'Misogynism and Virginal Feminism in the Fathers of the Church', in Ruether, ed., *Religion and Sexism*, New York, 1974, pp. 150–83. I concur with Ruether's general conclusions in this article as summarized here, but would want to urge that Augustine's position especially in Book 12 of the *De Trinitate* is more complex and double-sided than Ruether allows.

22. op. cit., pp. 156–7. Much of the relevant material from Gregory and Augustine is conveniently available in Elizabeth A. Clark, *Women in the Early Church*, Wilmington, Delaware, 1983.

23. It is usually assumed that the figure on the left of the icon is the Father (for this reason).

24. See the line of approach in *The Forgotten Trinity 1: The Report of the BCC Study Commission on Trinitarian Doctrine Today*, London, 1989, p. 39. I was a member of this commission, but I was unconvinced by this particular argument.

25. Peter Brown, *The Body and Society*, New York: Columbia University Press, 1988 and London: Faber and Faber, 1989; see Chaps. 14 (on Gregory of Nyssa) and 19 (on Augustine).

26. Nancy J. Chodorow, *The Reputation of Mothering*, Berkeley and Los Angeles, 1978, and, more recently, *Feminism and Psychoanalytic Theory*, Oxford, 1989.
27. Carol Gilligan, *In a Different Voice*, Cambridge, Mass., 1982.
28. ibid., p. 175.
29. Valerie Saiving, 'The Human Situation: A Feminine View', reprinted in Carol P. Christ and Judith Plaskow, eds., *Womanspirit Rising*, New York, 1979, p. 37. My emphasis.
30. Barbara Newman, *Sister of Wisdom: St Hildegard's Theology of the Feminine*, Berkeley and Los Angeles, 1987.
31. See the illuminating section in Rosemary Radford Ruether, *Sexism and God-Talk*, London, 1983, pp. 127–30.
32. See the remarks of Mary Daly in *Beyond God the Father*, Boston, 1973, p. 20: 'Even when the basic assumptions of God-language appear to be non-sexist, and when language is somewhat purified of fixation upon maleness, it is damaging and implicitly compatible with sexism if it encourages detachment from the reality of the human struggle against oppression in its concrete manifestations.'
33. See especially Mary Daly's trenchant and apposite remarks about Rom. 8 and Gal. 4 in *Pure Lust*, London, 1984: 'We do not wish to be redeemed by a god, to be adopted as sons, or have the spirit of a god's son artificially injected into our hearts, crying "father".'

# H: CHRISTIAN COMMUNITIES

33   ROSEMARY RADFORD RUETHER's 'Renewal or New Creation' was published in *Religion and Intellectual Life* in Winter 1986 (Vol. III, No. 2, pp. 7–20). For her books see entry (5).

34   ROBIN GILL's 'Churches as Moral Communities' was extracted from my *Moral Communities: The Prideaux Lectures 1992* (Exeter: Exeter University Press, 1992, pp. 63–80). Amongst my other books are *The Social Context of Theology* (Oxford: Mowbrays, 1975); *Theology and Social Structure* (Oxford: Mowbrays, 1977); *Prophecy and Praxis* (London: Marshall, Morgan and Scott, 1981); *A Textbook of Christian Ethics* (Edinburgh: T & T Clark, 1985: revised 1995); *Beyond Decline* (London: SCM Press, 1988); *Competing Convictions* (London: SCM Press, 1989); *Christian Ethics in Secular Worlds* (Edinburgh: T & T Clark, 1991); and *The Myth of the Empty Church* (London: SPCK, 1993). I have also edited *Theology and Sociology: A Reader* (London: Geoffrey Chapman, 1987) and *Michael Ramsey as Theologian* (London: Darton, Longman and Todd, 1995).

35   STEPHEN SYKES' 'An Anglican Theology of Evangelism' was published in *Theology* in November 1991 (Vol. XCIV, No. 762, pp. 405–14). Amongst his books are *The Integrity of Anglicanism* (Oxford: Mowbrays, 1978) and *The Identity of Christianity: Theologians and the Essence of Christianity from Schleiermacher to Barth* (London: SPCK and Philadelphia: Fortress Press, 1984). He has also edited a number of books including *Christ, Faith and History: Cambridge Studies in Christology* (with J. P. Clayton, Cambridge and New York: Cambridge University Press, 1972); *Authority in the Anglican Communion* (Toronto: Anglican Book Centre, 1987); *The Study of Anglicanism* (with John Booty, Philadelphia: Fortress Press, 1988); *Karl Barth: Centenary Essays* (Cambridge and New York: Cambridge University Press, 1989); and *Sacrifice and Redemption: Durham Essays in Theology* (Cambridge and New York: Cambridge University Press, 1991).

36  DANIEL HARDY AND DAVID FORD's 'Hope and Churches' is extracted from their book *Jubilate: Theology in Praise* (London: Darton, Longman and Todd, 1984: American title *Praising and Knowing God*, Philadelphia: The Westminster Press, 1985, pp. 145–152). Among his other publications Daniel Hardy has edited with Colin Gunton *On Being the Church* (Edinburgh: T & T Clark, 1989) and with Peter Sedgwick *The Weight of Glory: Essays in Honour of Peter Baelz* (Edinburgh: T & T Clark, 1991). For David Ford's books see entry (19).

# 33

# Renewal or New Creation?
## Rosemary Radford Ruether

More than a century ago Karl Marx described religion as the opiate of the people. What he meant by that famous phrase was that religion was a tool of the ruling classes which served to pacify oppressed people and alienated them from their own critical responses to unjust social systems. Religion sacralizes the existing social order as an expression of the will of God and deflects the anger of the oppressed into pipedreams of an otherworld transcendent to their own. What Marx hoped to accomplish by his critique of religion was to de-alienate those very real hopes expressed in religious visions of redemption from their sublimated or transcendental expression and to bring them back to earth where they could fuel real struggle against social evil and real efforts to transform life on earth.

If the industrial proletariat of Marx's day could be seen as the victims of the religious opiate, women have been doubly the victims of religious pacification. All the major historical religions, not only Christianity, but also Islam and Judaism as well as Buddhism and Hinduism, have been male-dominated in religious leadership and have promoted a system of religious law and symbolism which marginalizes women. I believe this is also true of the earlier forms of religion which Judaism and Christianity have called 'pagan' (a word that means 'religion of the countrypeople', although it has been construed by Jews and Christians to mean a worshipper of false or evil powers). In the texts, rituals and oral traditions known to me – the ancient Greek and Near Eastern materials – these religions also appear to be essentially androcentric.

Contemporary feminists have sometimes assumed that these non-Biblical religions were feminist because they contain female personifications of deity. But the presence of goddesses in a religion does not necessarily mean that that religion is genuinely gynecentric, that is, defined and led by women and upholding full female personhood. Christianity also has in the Virgin Mary a powerful female figure which functions as an object of devotion, but that female cult object serves overwhelmingly to sacralize the auxiliary and submissive role of the female *vis-à-vis* male humanity and the male God. Figures such as Isis, Astarte, Athena or other goddess figures known to us from classical antiquity have elements of power and autonomy that have been supressed in the more patriarchalized Virgin Mary. But they also seem to function as part of an androcentric worldview; that is to say, a world where the ultimate divine figures are male and where the goddess as mother, sister or spouse functions to rescue and restore male kingly power, rather than to uplift the power of women.

It has sometimes been argued that this patriarchalized version of goddess religion is a later stratum and conceals the earlier form of these religions which were truly gynecentric. But if we have no archeological or textual survivals of these religions and no living community that represents them, we have no way of knowing whether such earlier levels existed or not. One can judge only from the evidence that survives. That evidence shows some ups and downs of women's participation in religion, as also their participation in society. There were earlier periods when they seem to have participated more, as well as later periods of liberalization, when more rigid patriarchal systems were relaxed, as in the Hellenistic era that followed the rigidity of Hellenic Athens. What has not been proven, in my opinion, is that there was, once upon a time, a great era when women were either equal or dominant in society, and when religion expressed this dominance in a genuinely gynecentric religion.

Those religions known from pre-Christian antiquity show clear elements of androcentrism. The sacred mysteries of Eleusis were the only mystery religion in antiquity to lift up the mother-daughter relationship by celebrating the finding of the raped daughter by her goddess-mother. Nevertheless the Eleusinian mysteries were led by hereditary colleges of male priests. Isis attracted many female adherents, although not necessarily more female than male devotees. Although women were priestesses in all periods, they held secondary rank compared with male priestly roles. American Indian religion has sometimes been upheld as a mother-and-nature-centered religion, but those elements of mother-right are clearly auxiliary to male power. For example, the *kivas* or holy underground chambers of the Pueblo Indians, which duplicate in some way the maternal womb of woman as earth mother, can be entered only by males.

Indeed, the more one studies different religious traditions and their early roots, the more one is tempted to suggest that religion itself is essentially a male creation. The male, marginalized from direct participation in the great mysteries of gestation and birth, asserted his superior physical strength to monopolize leisure and culture and did so by creating ritual expressions that duplicated female gestating and birthing roles, but in such a way as to transfer the power of these primary mysteries to himself. This would perhaps explain why mother-goddess figures predominate in early religion, but do not function to give women power. This ritual sublimation

345

of female functions, as transfer of spiritual power over life to males, is continued in Christianity. The central mysteries of baptism and the Eucharist duplicate female roles in gestation, birth and nourishment, but give the power over the spiritualized expression of these functions to males, and only males who eschew sex and reproduction.

In the religious traditions with which I am familiar in the Ancient Near Eastern, Greco-Roman, Judaeo-Christian and modern developments, there seem to me to be three stages of androcentric use of religion. In the first stage, the male sublimates female procreative functions into a great Mother-Goddess, situates himself as the son and beloved of this Mother-Goddess, and is rescued from death and enthroned as king through the power of the Mother. One finds this pattern in the Ancient Near Eastern myths and rites of Innana, Ishtar, Anath and Isis, and remnants of it in Christian Mariology.

In the second stage, the great Mother is dethroned and subordinated as the creaturely Mother Earth and Church, created and ruled over by a Father God who now assumes transcendency outside of and above the cosmos. Here the female becomes the symbol of that which is to be dominated, ruled over and ultimately shunned by the transcendent, spiritual male Mind.

In the third stage, the male leadership class emancipates itself from religious tutelege and assumes direct power over the cosmos through science, while relegating religious piety to a private world identified with women. In classical patriarchal religion, i.e. orthodox Judaism and Islam, males dominated not only the priestly and teaching functions, but even the required prayers, thus relegating women to the margins. Now, in privatized religion, women monopolize the practices of the religion, while the official leadership and teaching authority remains vested in a male clerical class.

This evaluation of known religions as androcentric is not an argument against feminists exploring non-biblical religions, such as Buddhism, or Goddess traditions from the Ancient Near East, Greece or the Germanic world, in preference to the dominant religion of American society, i.e. Christianity. There may be stories and symbols in such traditions that appeal deeply to those who have been alienated from the patriarchalism of the dominant Biblical religions. Such explorations are, in my view, perfectly legitimate from the point of view of religious authenticity. It is simply to say that whether one seeks to be a feminist within the religious traditions of Judaism, Christianity or Islam, or within Buddhism, or by a renewed encounter with Isis and Ishtar, one is faced with somewhat parallel problems of androcentrism. The dominant priesthood was male.

The female divine symbols, where they exist, have generally played an auxiliary role to male social power.

This means that whatever elements of a particular religious tradition appear to be positive for women have to be carefully analyzed for their androcentric import. One has to ask how the story or symbol can be translated from its androcentric context into a context that is interpreted from the side of female experience and which will affirm the empowerment of women as subjects of their own histories. This means, it seems to me, that feminists today have to ask, first of all, whether religion or spirituality is what they should be about at all. What function can it play that enhances the liberationist transformation of history, rather than the sacralization of male domination? Secondly, we have to ask how stories and symbols drawn from past religious traditions can be translated from their androcentric form into one defined by and for women (although not necessarily against men, i.e. not necessarily a female reversal of androcentrism). Thirdly, we need to ask at what point we need to go beyond reinterpretation of past traditions into the generation of new stories and rituals from our own experience, and what norms we can use to discern the good from the destructive in such new story-telling and ritual-making. Finally, we might ask whether such feminist restatements of older traditions must go along on separate paths, corresponding roughly to the religious divisions of male culture, or whether feminists engaged in religious critique and revisioning can begin to come together in some new synthesis of the perspectives traditionally set against each other.

What I wish to do now is to trace the course of these four steps of feminist critique and revisioning from the context of the Christian interpretation of biblical religion. Christian tradition appropriates and builds on the Jewish religious tradition embodied in Hebrew scripture. So it is appropriate to start by asking what distinctive expressions of religion are found in Hebrew scripture. Feminist critique of Yahwist religion has focused on the partiarchal ordering of society and the imaging of deity in terms of patriarchal leadership roles, such as king, warrior, shepherd (a kingly title) and judge. These aspects of Hebrew religion are parallel to patterns also found in Ancient Near Eastern religions. To imagine that the Jews invented patriarchalism and patriarchal religion to suppress a matriarchal faith of other Near Eastern people is based on historical myopia. I agree with Judith Ochshorn that the rejection of polytheism for monotheism strengthens patriarchalism to the extent that the one God is presumed to be male and represented by males, thus setting up the hierarchy of God over human as analogous to male over female. Hebrew monotheism leaves open the alternative possibility that the one God is

347

beyond gender and is imagable as both male or female, and one finds some female imagery for God in Hebrew scripture and Jewish tradition.

I believe that the distinctive elements of Hebrew faith lie elsewhere than in the strengthening of patriarchalism. Characteristic of Hebrew religion is the shift from mythically to historically rooted religion. Whereas Babylonian and Canaanite religion focuses on myths that represented mythical primordial events (such as the slaying of Tiamat, personifying primal chaos, by Marduk, representing human order in the city state), or the recurring cycles of drought and rain, death and renewal in nature, in the stories of Anath and Baal, the Hebrew tradition recalls the liberation of Israel from bondage in Egypt, the giving of the Law in the desert, the trek through the wilderness to the Promised Land. When the festivals of the nature cycle are taken over into the Hebrew liturgical year, they are overlaid with new interpretation drawn from these historical commemorations.

These historical paradigms function not simply as ritual mimesis, but as the spur to historical action. 'Because these things happened to you, you shall or shall not do certain things.' Historical precedent becomes ethical paradigm for living historically in community. In the prophets one also sees a social shift in the function of religion emerging, placing it over against royalist religion that serves to sacralize existing systems of power and wealth. The prophets also assume that kings represent the deity, as keepers of social order, but they can pass judgment on kings who fail in these tasks, particularly when they do not protect the weakest members of society — the poor, widows and orphans.

Rapacious economic power, which inflates prices and steals the subsistence of the poor, is placed under divine judgment. This social shift of religion from panegyric of the powerful, in the name of the gods, to social criticism and calling to account is of great significance. It lays the basis for the language of social criticism and historical transformation in those cultures which trace their roots to the Bible. The prophetic paradigm not only criticizes unjust and oppressive power, but also criticizes the use of religion to sacralize such oppressive power. This is, in fact, the ancient biblical root of the Marxist critique of religion. In both the prophets and the gospel one finds a decrying of the use of law or ritual in order to create a privileged priestly or scribal élite and in order to institutionalize forms of cult seen as salvific in themselves without regard to social concern for justice and mercy. This critique of religion is not directed at paganism, but is directed at the Jewish temple or scribal leadership. It is a self-criticism that aims at the renewal of the ethical content of religious practice.

The prophetic paradigm also contains the language of radical social transformation. God is seen as active in history overthrowing oppressors, bringing into being a new social order of justice and mercy. Hope is directed toward a historical future where the wrongs of the present system will be righted. Modern social movements of liberation draw on this prophetic paradigm, even if in secular form. However, modern social and political liberation movements also restate this prophetic paradigm in the framework of a modern recognition that social structures are human creations. Ancient societies assumed that existing social systems were part of the order of the cosmos. So they could only be changed by an intervention of the Creator of the world to recreate the cosmos itself. Humans could only wait for such transformative intervention of God into history to create a new heaven and earth; they might hasten the day by ethical obedience, but could not really transform these systems themselves.

Modern social movements are born in the new consciousness that institutions like kingship, feudal hierarchy and slavery are human creations which violate justice, i.e. the true nature of things. The concept of 'Nature' ceases to be used to justify these social systems, but rather to refer to an ideal of original equality in the light of which these social hierarchies are judged as alienation from nature. Humans in history are thus empowered to change such systems themselves. However, the creation of a truly just and harmonious society still eludes us, as much as it eluded the ancient peoples who awaited a messianic intervention of God. Which is to say, we have not solved the root problem of sin, which is the desire for domination itself.

Feminism is a restatement of the prophetic paradigm in its modern form in the context of women's oppression and hope for liberation. We too cry out against oppression and stand in judgment on religious systems that justify oppression. But unlike ancient Hebrew prophecy, feminism decries the patriarchal oppression of women and envisions the liberation of women. Hebrew prophetic criticism remained confined to the concerns of oppressed males in an oppressed nation, *vis-à-vis* the powerful males of the society or the imperial powers that surrounded Israel. Although it might seek to alleviate the oppression of slaves or women in the patriarchal family, prophetic critique did not originate from these groups nor did it express a consciousness of patriarchy itself as contrary to nature or God's will.

Modern social movements, such as liberalism or socialism, or Black and Third World liberation movements, also have tended to express the concerns of oppressed males. While they might assail monarchy, feudalism, bourgeois class hierarchy, slavery and racism, they have tended to continue the assumption that the subordination of women was part of an unchangeable 'order of nature'. Feminism extends modern revolutionary consciousness by naming patriarchy as a human (male) construct and as an expression of unjust power that distorts the true nature and capacities of women and also of men, turning gender-relationality into domination and subordination. Patriarchy is named as something that both can be changed and should be changed.

Feminism thus can appropriate the biblical prophetic paradigm and claim it as its source only by a radical recontextualization. It applies the language of critique of oppression and of oppressive religion, and the language of future hope to questions of patriarchy and the liberation of women; these were not addressed by the ancient authors. This is, of course, also true of all modern liberation theologies. Not only do these modern liberation theologies assume the human origin of and control over social systems in a way that goes beyond ancient consciousness, they also apply this language to the racial oppression of American blacks, or to the Latin American victims of monopoly-capitalism, neither of which is literally addressed in the ancient text. Such application of ancient language to modern issues is not historical exegesis, but analogical *midrash*, the retelling of ancient paradigms in the context of modern issues and modern consciousness. (This is also true of any sermonic application of ancient stories.) Historical exegesis may be useful to delineate the ancient meaning and context, and thus make more sophisticated the translation to the modern analogy. That this is not historical exegesis should be quite obvious, but it has been concealed by the modern preoccupation with historical meaning as the only legitimate form of exegesis, and the concomitant discrediting of analogical forms of interpretation.

This means that feminist use of the prophetic paradigm has to be even clearer since it is not simply exegeting the ancient text. It is retelling the story in new ways. Latin American liberation theologians can imagine when they take a text about the oppression of the poor that the word 'poor' in antiquity meant something similar to their critique of poverty in Latin America. Black theologians can use texts about the elect nation, apply them to oppressed black people in America, and imagine that they are talking about something similar or even identical to what was referred to by the language about ancient Israel as the elect nation. Feminists can have no such illusions of liberal continuity. We need to be clear that when we apply language about oppression and liberation to patriarchy and to women, we are not exegeting the ancient meaning of the text, but retelling the story in a new way. Feminist hermeneutics thus claims the power to retell the story in new ways, a power which has not been owned by other liberation theologies.

One fairly familiar way of retelling old stories consists in a careful study of the original context of the biblical story and a recontextualization of it in a parallel contemporary setting. For example, in a paper which I wrote in 1983 on feminist hermeneutics, I studied the account of Jesus's commentary on the text of Isaiah 61.1–2 which appears in Luke 4.17–27. In this paper I noted that Jesus himself radically revised the meaning of the text as it was spelled out in Isaiah 61.5–7. In the Isaiah text, 'good news to the poor, liberty to the captives' was understood to mean that a dejected and captured Israel would triumph over its foes, the gentile nations around it: 'strangers will become your servants and you will eat the wealth of the nations.' In Luke, Jesus rejects the understanding of this text as national triumph. Instead, he uses it to direct a rebuke against the ethnocentric complacency of the synagogue by declaring that the lepers and widows from among the despised gentile people around Israel would hear God's Word and be healed, and that the people of the synagogue would remain closed to it.

A contemporary feminist liberation *midrash* on this text might similarly use it to criticize the sexism and class bias of the affluent church by suggesting that bag ladies and homeless people in their midst are the special objects of God's love and care, while they, the self-righteous church people, fall under divine judgment for their hardness of heart to the poor. This kind of claiming and retelling of biblical stories depends on discerning a liberationist intention in the original story and recontextualizing that liberationist element, while avoiding any tendency to import a Christian chauvinism that would scapegoat the Jewish people as the butt of the story.

Another way of retelling traditional stories consists of study of stories that have a specifically misogynist intent, in order to turn them inside out and release the power of women that is repressed through the old story. A brilliant example of this type of *midrash* is found in Judith Plaskow's retelling of the Lilith story. The rabbinic commentary on Lilith conflates the two creation stories of Genesis 1 and 2 by supposing that Adam must have had a wife prior to Eve who, like Adam, was created at the same time as he from the earth. But this earlier wife, Lilith, refused to lie under Adam, and when he complained to God about her, she left him and went out into the waterless places. There she became a demoness who haunts male wet dreams and threatens newborn babies.

Plaskow retold the story of Lilith and Eve by making Lilith represent the repressed power and autonomy of women, feared by patriarchy and driven out beyond the boundaries of patriarchal culture. There it is demonized by telling women fearful tales of monstrous viragos who come to a bad end. The 'return of Lilith' in Plaskow's *midrash* is the story of women's

351

reappropriation of their own repressed potential by a reconciliation and consciousness-raising session between Lilith and Eve.

Another way of telling new stories plumbs the dimensions of primary religious experience which I would call 'revelation' and thus goes beyond a simple retelling of old stories through study and discussion. I believe that whenever one hits on a meaningful new storytelling, even of traditional material, there is an element of inspiration. I believe, however, that revelation, in the sense of primary religious vision, happens today and is not confined to some privileged period of the past. This is another way of saying, theologically, that the Holy Spirit is present and is not simply the tool of historical institutional structures limited to the past. Most of these primary visions remain private and are only occasionally shared in such a way as to take on the function of a communal paradigm, expressing a new consciousness among a community that is being born. I would suggest that religious feminism is generating many new visions of this kind today, some of which are taking hold as new communal paradigms.

One such new paradigm that is in the process of being born is the image of the Christa or the crucified woman. There has been a remarkable proliferation of such images of crucified women as statues and paintings recently. Whenever they have been publicized in the Christian community, there has been a storm of hostile protest. The usual argument is to say that since Jesus was a male one cannot represent the Crucified as a woman. But the vicious level of the protest clearly goes beyond a mere statement of historical fact. What is being challenged is that the sufferings of a male God are regarded as redemptive for both men and women, while the sufferings of women are regarded not only as nonredemptive, but as pornographic. Images of tortured women abound in male sexual fantasy as objects of sadism. Thus to suggest that the image of a tortured woman represents the presence of redemptive divine power jars the patriarchal mentality deeply and is experienced as blasphemy against the sacred.

It is not at all clear how salutary it is for women to claim this image of the Crucified to interpret their own sufferings under patriarchy. The image of Christ's crucifixion has for so long functioned as a tool of passive acceptance of victimization that for most people, especially women, it has lost its meaning as the divine presence in human suffering, empowering the explosive protest against and overthrow of the unjust powers that proliferate violence and victimization. Mary Daly, in her book *Gyn/Ecology*, tells a story of women's victimization through a long history of sexual surgery, rape and battering. This story of torture is intended to generate women's anger and, in that sense, the power to overthrow victimization.

But tortured women remain only victims. One experiences no depth of divine presence in female suffering itself.

A story told by a woman in a class I taught recently on women and violence dramatizes this deeper appropriation of women's sufferings in what I would call primary religious vision. The woman told the story of how she had been raped by an unknown man in a wood and experienced her own death as a conviction that he would kill her. When he departed and she found herself still alive, she experienced herself as surrounded by a vision of God as a crucified woman. This filled her with a sense of relief since she knew she would not have to tell a male God that she had been raped. God was a woman who knew what it was like to be raped. Such a story astonished and compelled us. Like all primary religious visions, it goes beyond mere interpretation or theological restatement. It wells up from a depth of inarticulated female experience, disclosing many dimensions of meaning. But what is stated most primarily in this vision is that the Divine is present where the Divine has never been allowed to be present in patriarchal religion, in female sexual victimization by men. The Divine is present here, not as representative of the male who is the victimizer, but on the side of the female victim, one with the female victim, one who knows this anguish, who is a part of it, and who also heals and empowers women to rise from the dead, to be recreated beyond and outside the grasp of this negative power.

How have women begun to claim their power to do feminist *midrash*, to recast traditional stories in feminist retelling, and to communicate new primary visions as collective paradigms? I believe that the power to do this is being claimed in the Women-church movement. The Women-church movement represents women's spirituality moving from the secondary level of theological critique of patriarchal symbols to the primary level of liturgical mimesis of religious experience. Here women not only claim the right to preach, that is, to interpret traditional texts. They claim the right to write the texts, to generate the symbols and stories out of their own religious experience. Feminists of the Christian tradition here no longer petition the patriarchal Church to respond to women's call to ministry, and for inclusive language and relevant practice. Rather they depart from the institutional turf controlled by the patriarchal Church to engage in building alternative communities of worship and mutual support where one is free to shape the language, community dynamics and practice in a way as fully expressive of women's visions of redemption from patriarchy as we can imagine.

Such feminist liturgies and communities rising from women of Christian heritage parallel the feminist *minyan* movement among Jewish feminists, where women take power not only to be a *minyan* for prayer, but also to shape the language of prayer itself. There are also parallels with feminist liturgies that are an integral part of neo-pagan gatherings. Priestesses of the Wicca movement, such as Starhawk, in her book, *The Spiral Dance*, lay out a pattern of feminist ritual that focuses on the planetary cycles of the year and the rhythms of the female body. The ritual casts circles of power for women and men that heal the wounds of the present system and send the magical power of collective intention to blast the works of patriarchal violence.

There are significant differences between neo-pagan and biblically-based feminists, as well as between Jewish and Christian feminists; they call for serious and objective discussion. For example, there seem to me to be fundamental differences between how one relates to myth as distinct from history, and how one understands the relationship of one's community to a historical tradition. There are also differences in the interpretation of ritual as magic, as distinct from the understanding of prayer and ritual as response to divine initiative. There also seem to me to be basic differences in the perception of human nature and its relation to nonhuman nature or the cosmos around us, and in the definition of the causes of evil and the basis for a struggle against evil.

I don't believe it has been possible here to discuss these issues in a meaningful way because there is too much sense of hurt and threat on both sides; questions are interpreted as attack and as an attempt to discredit one or another, rather than as seeking a fuller vision of what we are doing. Yet it is also the case that many in the Christian feminist context, and perhaps the Jewish as well, are adopting elements from the neo-pagan movement into their own liturgical work as helpful contributions, even though these critical questions of divine-human relationship, anthropology and historical accountability remain not only unresolved, but largely undiscussable. Thus a feminist liturgy with recognizably Christian elements, such as reflections on biblical texts, and blessing and sharing bread and wine, might also use a guided meditation from Mariechild's *Motherwit*. Or a croning liturgy, done to celebrate the seventieth birthday of long-time Grail member Janet Kalven, might adopt from Wicca the casting of the circle of power as a way of gathering the liturgical community.

This practical eclecticism seems to me to indicate that such Jewish and Christian feminists stand on a boundary, facing two directions, and refuse to opt simply for one against the other. On the other hand, they affirm a responsibility to their historic faith communities. Despite all the patriarchal elements, they claim the essential liberationist message of this tradition and seek to translate its riches into expressions liberating for women, and also to call these communities themselves to liberate themselves from patriarchal forms and to recognize feminist restatement as a larger future of their own best insights. In this way they also insist on remaining rooted in real historical communities and traditions, rather than floating in a rootless world of what might be and what might have been but about which we have no discernible memory.

At the same time, these Jewish and Christian feminists are open to new possibilities, generated from new religious experience, which may derive from an imaginative recapturing either of repressed options that never really were, but are only hinted at, in early human beginnings. It is these options of primary religious imaginations that are being explored particularly by neo-pagan women.

Perhaps what is in the process of being born through this dialectic is a feminist resynthesis of the various layers of the religious tradition itself. Such a resynthesis is looking for an integration of religion based on mimetic experiencing of the rhythms of nature; of religion shaped by historical responsibility and the striving for obedience to law, in order to create a just society; and, finally, of religion shaped by ecstatic encounter with redemption from historical ambiguity and a proleptic entrance into the blessedness of harmonious integration of human history and nature.

One of the barriers to positive encounter between these various approaches to religion lies in the biblical concept of historical revelation that suggests that Judaism rises above and supersedes paganism. Christianity took this over and saw itself as rising above and superseding both Judaism and paganism. The new religious perspective situates itself against the old as superior to inferior, truth to falsehood, authentic knowledge of the divine against idolatry. Neo-paganism perhaps has a reversed version of this pattern when it sees itself as representing an original good state of humanity and its harmony with Nature, over against Judaism and Christianity which are seen as expressions of fall into alienation and patriarchal oppression, a variant of the Paradise-Fall myth of Christianity.

There may be elements of truth in both these myths of historical relationship, the first seeing the gains in the new religious point of view and the second seeing the losses. I believe that there were indeed both gains and losses in this history of shifts of religious perspective. While historical faith gains a new sense of human autonomy and ethical responsibility, it also tends to lose a sense of respect for our integration into the cycles of nature and thus to set the stage for a destructive relationship between humans (ruling class males) and dominated nature – dominated nature which includes both women, dominated races and non-human nature.

Christianity, while moving to a new universalism and an anticipation of the eschatological, loses a respect for the particularities of people and place and falls into an a-historical spiritualism which negates the need for social ethics as part of the redemptive task. I see this dialogue as a new opportunity to get beyond these classical ways of setting religious options against each other as truth and falsehood, anticipation and fulfillment. It is an opportunity to recapitulate this whole historical journey and seek a new dynamic integration of the cyclic, the historical and the eschatological.

As feminist theology finds itself on the boundary, facing toward a reinterpretation of past historical tradition and also forward to the creation of new possibilities, it will find that it is already involved in a dynamic resynthesis of this journey. This seems to me evident in the spontaneous interaction among these three dimensions of our religious tradition already happening among the three communities. It remains, however, for women to become more consciously reflective and theological about this process. There needs to be more reflective analysis of what it is we are doing and how we can become genuinely accountable to the past, to each other and to a just and sustainable future for all of earth's beings in this project.

# 34

CHURCHES AS MORAL COMMUNITIES
*Robin Gill*

1

Christianity has always had a heavy investment in communities. Yet an important distinction must be made. Christian communities may be better harbingers and carriers than exemplars of Christian values. Of course some may at times be exemplars of Christian values, but all too often they are sinful and/or socially constrained. Christian communities may need to be reminded, by the media and others, that they are harbingers of values which they frequently flout, misunderstand or just fail to notice. Yet their Scriptures, lections, liturgies, hymns and accumulated sources of long-refined wisdom continue to carry these values despite their own manifest frailties. Worshipping communities act as such moral harbingers and carriers whether they realize this or not. They then may spill these values more widely into society at large, again whether they realize this or not. Ironically, the very moral judgements so frequently offered by the media of Christian communities may act as an important reminder that Christian values are already scattered in society at large.

Some words of caution are necessary. An emphasis upon the crucial role of moral communities does not of itself commit Christian ethics to a theory of social determinism. This is an emphasis not a strait-jacket. I have argued elsewhere[1] that both Christian ethics in the 1960s, and moral philosophy more generally, were over committed to the idea that values could be derived solely from individual rational inspection. In Joseph Fletcher's influential account of situation ethics this led to the quirky result that debates about moral issues became debates about outrageous paradigms.[2] In order to show that there were no moral rules apart from specific moral situations, Fletcher argued time and again that there were always conceivable exceptions to any moral rule. So notions such as sacrificial adultery (in which a woman in a concentration camp deliberately got pregnant by a guard in order to return to the family she really loved) or justifications of human cloning, in order to have the most pugnacious fighting soldiers possible (presumably they would all be clones of Mike Tyson), were offered by Fletcher as serious examples of Christian ethics.

This does not mean that individual rationality is simply abandoned. My

357

point is about the adequacy of individual rationality in moral debates. It is not an excuse for individuals who have faith to stop thinking for themselves, as some forms of fundamentalism might encourage. In his inaugural lecture as Regius Professor of Divinity at Cambridge very recently, David Ford argued this point powerfully. He saw that there were good reasons for the suspicion of intellectualism that has often character-ized people of faith in modern Britain. But he also argued that it is actually a profound and dangerous mistake:

> From the side of the communities of faith there are . . . fears and prejudices . . . . The dominant modern academic discourses have, on the whole, given some cause to religions to be defensive. Yet it is sad to the point of tragedy when this leads, as so often, into a suspicion of intellectual life as such, as if faith might be unintellectual or anti-intellectual. The main religions present in this country, Judaism, Christianity, and Islam, all have distinguished intellectual heritages. They are also at present involved in complex and rapid transformations. For them not to think about these matters is not an option.

I would endorse this wholeheartedly. Pointing to the importance of moral communities in fashioning and sustaining values in our society need not become an excuse for irrationality. It is rather a claim that individual, isolated rationality is quite simply, in itself, an insufficient resource for a profound morality. Moral communities without the critique of rationality can become tyrannical, arbitrary and perhaps even demonic. But atomized rationality without moral communities seems incapable (despite many attempts) of fashioning and sustaining goodness beyond self-interest.

Again, it is important not to hypostasize Christian communities. Communities are by their nature dynamic, and even the most moribund Christian communities change over time. It is one of those quirky ironies that some 'heresies' result from traditionalist attitudes which refuse to change. Faith communities change, but a minority refuses to change and are then dubbed 'heretics' by the majority (Archbishop Lefebvre was a recent example). In an age of postmodernism changes are especially likely. Faith communities living cheek by jowl can avoid mutual influence only with difficulty and few are immune to secular pressures. Perhaps it is the influence of feminism, or liberation models, or popular music. Or, just as importantly, it might be counter-cultural reactions against feminism, liberation models, popular music, or whatever. Either way faith communi-ties respond (even if negatively) and in the process change. Christian communities mutually influence each other and all are influenced by society at large. A complex series of interactions is likely to characterize scholarly accounts of the way Christians may influence, and are influenced by, society at large.[3] Most social processes are indeed complex, and few are more complex than those of faith in a postmodern society.

Of course churches are not the only moral communities in society. I have no intention of following the patronizing line of French functionalism – through Voltaire, Comte, Durkheim and Sartre – which held in effect that the phenomenon of religion in some form is essential to the stability of society, whilst at the same time remaining profoundly sceptical of any theological claims. It seems to say, in effect, 'the masses need religious faith, but I personally realize that it is spurious'. In reality the world today abounds with moral communities that owe little to religious faith – from delinquent gangs to the strong communities fostered by wars. It has long been known to sociologists that deviance can foster strong counter-cultural communities. Prisoners, for example, have strong internal codes and norms which fellow prisoners defy at their peril. Child molesters are subjected to particular moral indignation amongst prisoners, as are those who grouse on other prisoners. And Tyneside joy-riders do not lack moral codes – it is just that their moral codes do not include respect for the general public's cars, let alone for public safety.

In contrast to the claims of *Habits of the Heart*, religious institutions in advanced capitalist societies, and especially in postmodern societies, may foster not some overall moral unity but highly diverse moral perspectives, ranging from the most conservative to the most radical.[4] The competing forces of Islam in the Middle East over the last decade have demonstrated this again and again, as have the sharp divisions attached to traditional religious affiliations emerging within the former Soviet Republics. Antagonisms between Christians and Jews, between both of them and Muslims, between Muslims and Muslims, and between Christians and Christians – but, above all else, antagonisms between all of them and atheistic Marxism – have all been features of the new-found 'freedoms' of some of these Republics.

Where monotheistic communities differ from their secular counterparts is not in their ability to generate and nurture specific values, but in their grounding in worship. They are thus communities – Jewish, Christian, or Islamic – responding in worship to Another, not communities simply manufacturing and then maintaining values. There is a correspondence between what they believe is or is not moral behaviour and their view of the world as being created not fortuitous. Goodness beyond self-interest is believed, by Jews, Christians and Muslims alike, to be a reflection of an all-loving Creator. Morality is ultimately grounded in a metaphysic and intimately linked to worship.

It is at this point that I find Don Cupitt's recent books most challenging and also most frustrating. He too shares in regular worship, takes morality very seriously, and is fully aware of the possibilities and frailties of historical churches. Yet his apparent rejection of traditional theism leads him to a mirror image of my own thesis. Thus in his *The New Christian Ethics* he spells out at some length the culture-boundness of Christian communities and points to their tendency to justify positions simply because they have become established (sometimes by force). Yet finally I would want to part with his bleak dictum that 'we make truth and we make values'.[5] In worship I believe that we are actually confronted with truth. Even though our articulations of this truth are inevitably culture-bound (human language can never be culture-free), it seems to be the experience of most worshippers that we are in the presence of Another. Furthermore, I would regard it as a confusion to believe that moral values are the *teloi* of worshipping communities (as Cupitt appears to believe). Most practising Jews, Christians or Muslims would appear rather to hold that the principal object of liturgy is to worship God. Values that are generated in the process are a consequence of worship and not its object. What is more, most might argue that if you finally remove the object then you may also remove the *telos* of the whole.[6]

It could just be that worship offers a firmer foundation for communities than most alternatives. This is especially the case if the community is defined in Bellah's terms as, 'a group of people who are socially interdependent, who participate together in discussion and decision making, and who share certain practices that both define the community and are nurtured by it'.[7] Obviously worship is not the only way that a group of people can achieve interdependence. Nevertheless, it is a particularly intimate way of doing so, and it is clearly a form of activity based upon deep-held and long-maintained practices. Without being regarded as the reason for worshipping, it might still encourage others to treat worshipping communities with a new moral seriousness – especially in the midst of some of the shallower fragmentations of postmodernism.

2

But none of this resolves the problem of internal diversity within Christianity. How can Christians seek to change society, when churches and denominations are so internally divided on moral issues? Raymond Plant's scepticism about the possibility of a corporate political theology in a fragmented society is important again at this point in the argument. Plant contends that society itself, the social sciences and theology are all too pluralist today for there to be any longer a convincing corporate political theology. If this is the case, he maintains, then 'the Church's interventions in politics are not in fact well rooted in a theological understanding of modern politics and to that extent their status is somewhat insecure'.[8] This is a challenge, I believe, which should be taken very seriously indeed.

The thoroughgoing, world-denying sect provides an obvious solution to this challenge. As mainstream churches continue to decline in Britain so such sects seem to become more visible. Although small, they – together with sectarian tendencies within churches – almost alone seem to be growing numerically. Mormons appear to be amongst the most successful.[9] In the United States their membership increased from some two million in the early 1970s to nearly four million by the mid-1980s. In Britain they increased from some 70,000 to 125,000. Jehovah's Witnesses are also growing numerically at a fairly rapid rate: by the mid-1980s they had nearly three-quarters of a million members in the United States and over 100,000 in Britain. And the balance given in many book-shops in either country to New Age literature at the expense of more conventional Christian literature suggests similar changes. Academic theology, in contrast, is, I am afraid, just a minority pursuit.

In a postmodern age of fragmentation and bewildering choices, the thoroughgoing, world-denying sect offers certainty, salvation and manifest religious commitment. It also offers an oasis of care. The American sociologist and Anglican priest, Richard Fenn, has suggested that in a time of increasing cognitive differentiation and specialization, such sects uniquely offer unambiguity and 'truth'.[10] To depict them for the moment in stereotypical terms, thoroughgoing sects are exclusive in both belief and membership. They demand much of members, but in return they offer a total way of life; they offer members total care. To become a Jehovah's Witness is usually to be expected to become a door-to-door evangelist – with all of the attendant risks of ridicule and abuse that that involves. It may also mean (as in Hitler's Germany) to become a martyr for the faith. And it is to enter a world of strong community – a community *par excellence* on the Bellah understanding – which is frequently at odds with society at large. To be a Jehovah's Witness is to be a part of one of the most complete religious counter-cultures available in contemporary Britain.

It is not difficult from all of this to understand why such sects may appeal to minorities and why sectarianism is an obvious temptation for declining churches. Bryan Wilson's books are invaluable in trying to understand this appeal. Reader in Sociology at Oxford University and Fellow of All Souls, he is the leading authority on this subject and has a unique knowledge of the complexities of sectarianism. His earliest work

*Sects and Society*,[11] written almost forty year ago, was a milestone in scholarship. It studied in detail the life of three sects in Birmingham. His *Religious Sects*[12] provided a system of classification which has been used by most sociologists working in this area. His *Magic and the Millennium*[13] extended his work into Third World movements and his *Religion in Sociological Perspective*[14] into Japanese sects. Most recently in *The Social Dimensions of Sectarianism*[15] he has gathered together a series of studies in sectarianism written over the last fifteen years.

This most recent book well represents some of the challenging themes that run through Wilson's writings on sects. The first is concerned with how sects survive in an often hostile world. Particularly interesting are the chapters which describe the legal obstacles (in Britain and elsewhere) which have confronted sects in their attempts to gain the tax advantages enjoyed by other religious bodies. Wilson's mask of sociological objectivity (quite rightly I believe) drops somewhat when he reviews some of the legal judgements that have denied them these advantages. In the second section he focuses on the evolution, diffusion and appeals of sectarianism. One of the chapters presents the findings of a unique questionnaire-survey that he carried out on Belgian Jehovah's Witnesses. He must have used considerable charm to have achieved this and he admirably conveys the attraction that the movement has for its followers. The final section looks at New Religious Movements (as they are often called), with sustained studies of the Unification Church (the 'Moonies') and Scientologists.

In addition to his writings on sects, Wilson has also been a leading exponent of the secularization thesis over the years.[16] There is an important link between these ideas in his writings. He has frequently argued that the sect is the most likely form of religious institution to withstand the erosions of secularization. The rigorous sect can remain morally and doctrinally pure even in a hostile or indifferent secular society. But, of course, it pays a heavy price for this purity. It is effectively marginalized by society at large. In technical terms, it is without social significance. Furthermore, once a sect does genuinely attempt to influence society especially in areas of care – the Salvation Army today is an obvious example – it soon becomes denominationalized in the process. By taking this step, so Wilson argues, such a sect is likely to become secularized itself.

Recent resurgences and declines in the House Church Movement, and more generally in what are sometimes called Independent Churches, illustrate this process. In the MARC Europe surveys[17] of English churchgoing and church membership in 1979 and 1989, it is this movement particularly which is highlighted as being the hope for Christianity to come. These surveys suggest that during the decade measured, churchgoing declined most sharply amongst Catholics. Anglicans and a majority of the mainstream Free Churches (especially Methodists and the United Reformed Church) also experienced heavy losses in most parts of the country. However, the Independent Churches, and within them particularly the House Church Movement, showed significant increases of membership and attendances. MARC Europe predict that in the next decade they will become a dominant force amongst British churchgoers. The Free Churches taken as a whole will, they believe, continue to grow, whilst Catholics and Anglicans continue to decline. Taken together with Evangelicals in other Churches (particularly Anglicans) they will then represent a majority of active Christians in Britain.

There are some very serious methodological and historical problems involved in this analysis.[18] The authors of the MARC Europe reports consistently fail to notice that brief resurgences of independent churches, in a context of overall Free Church decline, have been a feature in Britain since at least the 1880s. They also play down the extent to which these resurgences are heavily dependent upon transfer growth from other denominations and, as a result, find growth difficult to sustain. In my own empirical research, it becomes clear that even a very successful movement like the Salvation Army was experiencing acute problems within two decades of its being established. Today there are already indications that the House Church Movement is beginning to find its own initial growth difficult to sustain.

Be that as it may, Independent Churches do tend to be more sectarian than many other forms of organized Christianity. They do tend to stress doctrinal and moral purity and are especially concerned to eradicate internal pluralism and to resist the tides of secularism. And, in the last decade or so in England, they do seem to have been increasing in strength relative to other denominations.

Yet can thoroughgoing, world-denying sects really influence society? The perennial problem for such sects is that they are socially marginalized. Within some of the most rigorous, world-denying sects – the Exclusive Brethren for example – care is readily available, but it is care for members alone. It is in this sense that the sect provides an oasis of care in a postmodern world. If you wish to drink at the water, then usually you must become a member first. Indeed, in some urban areas today (such as High Barnet in North London) members of the Exclusive Brethren have moved house to live closely together. They live as a strongly caring community, worshipping together several times a day. They are very conscious of each other's needs, but nevertheless they are as detached as possible from the world at large.

However, it will certainly not do to generalize about Evangelicals (or even all sects) in this way. Recently there have been signs that some British Evangelicals are once again becoming more socially conscious. In the United States this new social concern has tended to take the right-wing form of the so-called Moral Majority (although the much smaller Sojourners are an exception even there). In Britain Evangelicals are not so predictably conservative. The umbrella organization, the Evangelical Alliance, puts almost equal stress on evangelism and social care, and includes structural change within the latter. In a recent interview, its General Director, Clive Calver, argued as follows:

> There needs to be a challenge to what society accepts as true. If all the Evangelical Alliance is doing is talking to nice cosy Christians, keeping an institution happy and a hundred-and-five-year-old tradition alive, that's useless. But we have a platform for challenging a secular society with the fact that there is a God who can be known and loved and served, and he has a way for society to be run. If we're not using it as the platform to challenge slavery, if we're not using it to change the hours and conditions of work for women and children as our forebears did in the nineteenth century, then we're missing it. Social action without evangelism is sanctified humanism. Evangelism without social action is words without deeds.[19]

Of course the Evangelical Alliance itself is well aware of internal pluralism. In the interview in question, Clive Calver admitted as much. Its members are drawn from many shades of political and moral opinion and it has proved exceedingly difficult to unite it around specifically moral issues. But Wilson might argue that it is actually attempting to combine the impossible – a sharp distinction from secular society and an attempt to change that society. In reality Evangelicals found it very difficult to sustain the united moral action that characterized part of their work in the nineteenth century. Generalized attacks on immorality, gambling or alcoholism caused few problems. But specific attacks on, say, the Contagious Diseases Acts, proved far more contentious even in the nineteenth century, as might a specific attack on the commissioning of a fourth Trident submarine today. Even opposition to the Abortion Act fails to unite evangelicals today.

The thoroughgoing sect does offer one option for Christians who wish to maintain moral purity in the context of what they believe to be a purely secular society. However, I am not wholly convinced by the Wilson thesis. If we live in a fragmented, postmodern society, and not in a uniformly secular society, then the rigorous, world-denying sect may be both an excessive reaction to society and by no means the only way still available today to maintain a distinctive moral stance. There are, I believe, at least three other options: the individual prophet, the interchurch movement, and the transposing church. They each have different strengths and weaknesses and cannot readily be combined into a single whole. But they do each suggest that the sect is not the only, and perhaps not even the most effective, way for Christians to care in a fragmented world.

3

The individual prophet and the interchurch movement share a number of characteristics and can be usefully compared. Both usually have a single dominant moral issue as their central aim – frequently an issue at odds with conventional opinion. The influential individual prophet in the world today may even initiate an interchurch movement. In the ancient world such a prophet would more typically have initiated a sect.

The sociologist who gave clearest shape to the social function of the prophet was Max Weber.[20] For him the notion of the charismatic prophet was what he termed an 'ideal type'. That is to say, the notion was an intellectual concept which helped the sociologist to interpret reality, but did not necessarily exist in all of its purity in the actual world. The charismatic prophet was to be distinguished sharply from the priest. The prophet was typically a lay person at odds with religious authorities and institutions. The charismatic prophet received a specific and self-authenticating revelation. The priest, in contrast, was a functionary of religious authorities and institutions, maintaining a revelation which had been passed down and mediated through a community. The priest's orders were legitimated, not by any self-authenticating revelation, but by religious authorities. Whereas the prophet could be radical and iconoclastic, the priest was essentially conservative and intent upon fostering a community. Whereas the prophet tended to disrupt, the priest was more concerned to heal. If the sort of care offered by the priest was concerned with the patient nurture of caring communities, that offered by the prophet might rather take the form of founding new communities or challenging existing communities to change radically.

To make the contrast between priest and prophet in this way is of course to exaggerate. Those regarded as priests can be very disruptive at times (as the Church of England is currently discovering) and it has for long been recognized that some of those regarded as 'prophets' in the Jewish Bible were also involved in the cult. In addition, effective care within a complex urban society is bound itself to be complex – requiring an ever-interacting mixture of challenge and nurture often from the same people. Yet critics of Weber do sometimes forget that he regarded such sharp contrasts as heuristic devices through which to interpret reality, not as themselves direct depictions of reality. They were tools, not the end product.

Viewed in this way, I have often found this distinction between priest and prophet helpful. It fits particularly well an example I have used on several occasions, namely that of Josephine Butler. She provides a vivid illustration of how a single-minded, but exceedingly caring, individual Christian can effect social change despite massive hostility. As a socially active evangelical, she campaigned for some thirty years against the mid-nineteenth century Contagious Diseases Acts and, despite a genteel upbringing, befriended numerous prostitutes. The Contagious Diseases Act required women suspected of prostitution in certain ports to have compulsory venereal inspections. They were of course designed to reduce infection amongst troops, but Josephine Butler maintained that they considerably infringed the rights of the women involved, as well being ineffective in reducing infection amongst men. She spoke, campaigned and lobbied, often at extremely hostile meetings, in a tireless effort to get the acts repealed. When they were, she set about trying to get similar changes elsewhere in Europe and, most ambitiously of all, in France. I am afraid that France finally defeated her!

Remarkably, she was married throughout this campaign to a Church of England clergyman, who was first headmaster of Liverpool College and then a residentiary canon at Winchester Cathedral. Less surprisingly, her work was greeted by those in authority in the Church with embarrassed silence. It took the best part of a hundred years for the Church of England to recognize the importance of her caring work in its calendar. Yet, although thoroughly marginalized by her own Church, she remained convinced throughout that this work was a part of her Christian vocation. Her writings show a classic pattern of self-authenticating revelation which she felt impelled to follow. In true prophetic style, she believed that she must defy conventional opinion, both within the Church and in mid-Victorian society at large, and work vigorously on behalf of prostitutes. This was for her, quite literally, 'a calling'.

As AIDS continues to spread in the West, and particularly once it is discovered by the public that it is primarily a heterosexual disease, so the coercion of prostitutes may be one of the policies increasingly sought.[21] Josephine Butler's work may become highly instructive once again. At-risk groups might well become the targets of legislators. Butler believed, in contrast, that it was far more important, and distinctly more Christian, to attempt to change the moral behaviour of the men involved. The long incubation period of HIV infection may considerably strengthen the cause she defended. The search for infection-free prostitution, in order to service voracious male appetites, may turn out to be just another patriarchal El Dorado.

Of course Josephine Butler did not achieve all of this on her own. Like-minded people from a number of churches joined her in the campaign to repeal the Contagious Diseases Acts, just as they had joined Wilberforce in a previous generation to combat the slave trade. In the late twentieth century, the interchurch movement surely represents the nearest parallel to this. Christian CND, the pacifist Fellowship of Reconciliation, Christian activists against animal experimentation, or even the Gay Christian Movement, all represent examples of such movements.

Characteristically, interchurch movements draw together committed people from across denominations who are then united within a single caring cause. In other respects members of such movements might be quite different from each other. So, in terms of the definitions drawn earlier from *Habits of the Heart*, interchurch movements are probably more lifestyle enclaves than communities as such. In contrast, thoroughgoing sects are clearly communities. Members of an interchurch movement are typically united on just a single issue, although the stance they adopt on the issue in question is usually at odds with the majority within their own denomination. Indeed, this is probably the reason they feel impelled to join a Christian organization outside their own denomination. However, unlike genuine communities, members of interchurch movements are not characteristically interdependent in other respects and the movements themselves can be quickly formed and (once their task is completed or surpassed) can be quickly disbanded.

Precisely because the individual prophet and the interchurch movement tend to adopt moral positions at odds both with mainstream churches and with society at large, they are likely to inspire counter-movements. Some of the sharpest moral debates within the Church of England have become polarized in competing groups. Tony Higton is perhaps a predictable response to the Gay Christian Movement, and the Bishop of Oxford to Christian CND. Interchurch movements which campaign on contentious platforms on issues of care must expect to inspire counter-movements. The series of books that have followed Anglican reports on such contentious issues as nuclear deterrence and urban deprivation are clear evidence of this.

Yet most interchurch movements would probably rather inspire counter-movements than simply be ignored. Their primary aim is not to be liked by others, but to care by effecting social change. They are self-consciously crusades with a strong mission. They would probably respond to the title that Paul Ramsey gave to one of his more polemical books – *Who Speaks for the Church?*[22] – with the retort 'Not us – we are seeking to change the Church'. Like postmodern society itself, such movements are fragmentary, pulling in different moral directions from each other. The shared aims of each movement, or enclave, are explicitly to further care in a specific area, to support fellow believers against what is seen as the dominant consensus elsewhere, and then to change that consensus.

4

The final option for care is quite different and relies more upon the notion of community rather than that of lifestyle enclave. Again it was Weber who offered a clue to this option with his notion of the transposition of values. The notion emerges in Weber's famous thesis which dominated his extensive writings on world religions – what is often called the Protestant Ethic Thesis.[23] I am sure that it is far too well known to need expounding here. But in essence it posited a link between some of the theological changes that resulted from the Reformation and the rise of the spirit that helped to generate the development of modern capitalism. Weber saw a connection between Calvinist emphases upon vocation, election and predestination, and some of the moral values of thrift, honesty and hard-work that characterized early capitalists.

The secondary literature on the Protestant Ethic Thesis is now vast.[24] Even if the thesis is largely ignored by historians (who were seldom convinced by the connections Weber made), it is still debated by sociologists of religion and now by some within business studies. At the very moment when Western capitalism seems to be losing its main ideological competitors, and yet appears beset by ethical dilemmas, it is perhaps not surprising that Weber is still much discussed. Despite numerous critiques and some very obvious lacunae, the thesis remains fascinating. Turning classical Marxism on its head, it suggested the outrageous possibility that modern, rationalistic capitalism (not to be confused with the simple age-long process of accumulating wealth) owed at least a part of its existence to a series of moral and theological changes.

The thesis never was as simple and straightforward as many would seem to imagine. It did not credit Calvin himself with making these moral changes. Rather it was perceived Calvinism – something far more subtle – that was seen by Weber as oddly connecting personal thrift and hard-work. And it was Benjamin Franklin's utilitarian account of honesty in business-practice that captured Weber's attention. Perceived honesty, not private honesty, was what was required for good business. Perceived honesty generated business confidence, but in private it might be thoroughly dishonest. In contrast, private honesty which remained private was quite literally use-less. The rogue who was perceived in public to be honest was good for business, whereas the privately scrupulous person, who was nonetheless suspected in public, was not. For example, had the extent of Robert Maxwell's private dishonesty in syphoning money from his own newspaper's pension fund been made public in his lifetime, it is difficult to imagine that he would have retained any credibility whatsoever in the business world. Perceived honesty – something Maxwell evidently craved for and indeed paid for, even if he did not quite attain – need not actually be honesty at all in any serious moral sense.

This extraordinary possibility points, I believe, to an issue that is frequently ignored by ethicists. It is perceived ideas which may be more influential than intellectually purified ideas. Precisely because academics are usually in the business themselves of purifying ideas, they may have tended to overlook the public role of mediated ideas. Yet it is the latter which may be more socially significant. For example, it is not so much pure monetarist or Keynsian notions that may effect changes in the world, but rather monetarist or Keynsian notions that are first mediated through politicians. Since few politicians are themselves political theorists, the notions may well be changed through this mediation. Once mediated in this way, they may be almost unrecognizable to their intellectual exponents. Similarly, perhaps, with theological ideas. Perceived, mediated theology may in the end be far more influential than the theology studied by most theologians. Yet this popularized version of theology may in the end be far more socially influential than academically 'respectable' theology.

I puzzled over this phenomenon in my early writings on the social influence of *Honest to God*.[25] I was fascinated at the time by the fact that a book so replete in unexplained Latin tags should have sold so widely in the mid-1960s and should have caused such a furore. From these investigations, I concluded that it was actually the popular perception of what was seen as a radical book written by a bishop, rather than the actual contents of the book, that seemed to have caused much of this furore. Similarly today, it can only be a minute proportion of Muslims protesting against *The Satanic Verses* who have actually read the book. What surely has outraged most Muslims is Rushdie's provocative title and a perception of his apostasy. Linked to this are doubtless other social and cultural factors – the ambivalent immigrant status of many British Muslims, counter-cultural reactions to racism and sometimes overt racialism, new-found orthodoxy in a context of fragmented postmodernism, Arab antagonisms to what is viewed as Western decadence, etc. Yet the role of perceived apostasy is both clear and clearly perplexing to a secular, literary intelligentsia in the West. Tragically, a novelist whose craft it is to change perceptions becomes literally a prisoner of perceptions which he never intended but was nonetheless instrumental in effecting.

Once ethicists start to focus on popularly perceived values, and not simply upon intellectually articulated values, then quite fresh possibilities emerge. Since the issue of the rise of modern Capitalism (or, more accurately, modern capitalisms) has now become overwhelmed with secondary literature, Weber's task might more fruitfully be taken up in new areas. In a postmodern society it need not be assumed that there are still underlying values with religious roots shared by all. We are perhaps too fragmented in Britain today to expect that. Nevertheless, there may well be values which are still widely dispersed but which are largely invisible to those who hold them. In short, moral values with Christian roots – and care is surely one of these – may have become embedded in society and may still be held by many who are now largely oblivious to these roots. More than that, these values may finally make full sense if these roots are once again included within their meaning in our society.

All of this is far too abstract; perhaps I can give a small illustration of what I mean. Recently I produced a little Lent book with a slightly saccharin title, *Gifts of Love*.[26] Since it was written as a Lent book it was necessarily untechnical. However, the theme it contains was first conceived as a technical theme. What it attempts to suggest is that everyday language still carries the notion of 'gifts' within it, and that this language is typically used to denote unusual experiences. Many parents still speak of the birth of their first child as a 'gift'. They did so little to create the child (men even less than women) and yet here it is as a new life – a gift. Very appropriately the acronym GIFT (gamete intra-fallopian transfer) is used to denote one of the means of biotechnology. Parents who conceive through GIFT may feel that this acronym is especially suitable. After years of struggling to have their own child, this technique at last makes it possible for them to do so.

Furthermore, we still frequently refer to people with very special abilities – particularly in mathematics, art and sport – as being 'gifted'. We are even slightly frightened of the prodigiously 'gifted' child. And finally, the word *data* is firmly present in the natural and social sciences. The notion of the world as given – perhaps as God-given – still abounds even within a postmodern society.

Of course there is no *necessary* connection between borrowed Christian language and the Christian communities that once nurtured it. It clearly does still survive even within apparently alien contexts. Presumably in the process it assumes a much more metaphorical status. However, what I attempt to show in *Gifts of Love* is that there is ambivalence to the experiences that underlie gift-language which finally makes fuller sense within communities of faith. So, after discussing gifts of love at some length, I turn instead to gifts of poison. Within any society gift-relationships are complex and can sometimes be highly destructive. By giving too generously to those we love we can actually ruin their lives. By giving aid thoughtlessly some Northern countries have actually made life more difficult within some Southern countries. Individuals who are gifted in one area can sometimes be thoroughly immature and spiteful in other areas (as we were frequently reminded last year about Mozart). Hitler and Stalin were both highly 'gifted' men who used their gifts to dominate and destroy others. Appropriately, in German the word *gift* means 'poison'.

I hope that this bleaker side to gifts rescues the book somewhat from its saccharin title. It also points to an ambivalence in everyday experience which finds many echoes in the New Testament. In the Synoptic Gospels, Jesus is surrounded by gifts, some benign but some clearly demonic. If the Magi bring 'gifts' to Jesus in the second chapter of Matthew, the satanic figure offers gifts in the fourth chapter. In all three Synoptic Gospels the rich young man is told to give away his possessions and cannot, but Jesus at the Last Supper does give both his body and his blood. The communal implications of all of this for gifts as well as for care are made clear in 1 John 3: 'This is how we know what love is: Christ gave his life for us. And we in turn must give our lives for our fellow-Christians'.

NOTES

1. See my *Christian Ethics in Secular Worlds*, Edinburgh: T & T Clark, 1991, ch. 1.
2. J. Fletcher, *Situation Ethics*, London: SCM Press, 1966.
3. See my *Competing Convictions*, London: SCM Press, 1989.
4. R. Bellah, R. Madsen, W. M. Sullivan, A. Swidler and S. M. Tipton, *Habits of the Heart: Middle America Observed*, New York: Hutchinson, 1985.
5. D. Cupitt, *The New Christian Ethics*, London: SCM Press, 1988, p. 5.
6. See my *Beyond Decline*, London: SCM Press, 1988.
7. *Habits of the Heart*, p. 333.
8. R. Plant, 'Pluralism and Political Theology', Centre for Theology and Public Issues Publication, New College, Edinburgh University, 1991, p. 5.
9. See B. Wilson, *The Social Dimensions of Sectarianism: Sects and New Religious Movements in Contemporary Society*, Oxford: Oxford University Press, 1990.

10. R. Fenn, *Towards a Theory of Secularization*, Society for the Scientific Study of Religion, 1978, and *Liturgies and Trials*, Oxford: Blackwell, 1982.
11. B. Wilson, *Sects and Society*, London: Heinemann, 1955.
12. B. Wilson, *Religious Sects*, London: Weidenfeld & Nicolson, 1970.
13. B. Wilson, *Magic and the Millennium*, London: Heinemann, 1973.
14. B. Wilson, *Religion in Sociological Perspective*, Oxford: Oxford University Press, 1982.
15. See note 8.
16. For instance, B. Wilson, *Religion in Secular Society*, Watts, 1966, and *Contemporary Transformations of Religion*, Oxford: Oxford University Press, 1982.
17. P. Brierley, ed., *Prospects for the Nineties: Trends and Tables from the English Church Census*, MARC Europe, 1991, and *'Christian' England: What the English Church Census Reveals*, MARC Europe, 1991.
18. See my *The Myth of the Empty Church*, London: SPCK, 1993.
19. *Church Times*, 7 February 1992, p. 7.
20. See M. Weber, *The Sociology of Religion* (1920), ET, Boston: Beacon Press, 1963.
21. See my *Christian Ethics in Secular Worlds*, Edinburgh: T & T Clark, 1991, ch. 8.
22. P. Ramsey, *Who Speaks for the Church?*, Abingdon, 1967.
23. M. Weber, *The Protestant Ethic and the 'Spirit' of Capitalism* (1904–5), ET, London: George Allen & Unwin, 1930.
24. e.g., G. Marshall, *In Search of the Spirit of Capitalism: an Essay on Max Weber's Protestant Ethic Thesis*, New York, Hutchinson: 1982; and G. Poggi, *Calvinism and the Capitalist Spirit*, London: Macmillan, 1983.
25. See my *The Social Context of Theology*, London: Mowbrays, 1975, and *Theology and Social Structure*, London: Mowbrays, 1977.
26. *Gifts of Love*, London: HarperCollins, 1991.

# 35

# AN ANGLICAN THEOLOGY OF EVANGELISM
## Stephen Sykes

I begin by talking about God, not about evangelism (a word with formidable and in the end unavoidable drawbacks), nor about Anglicanism (a Johnnie-come-lately in the long history of God's patience with his people). 'God loved the world so much', said an unknown writer living in one of the communities of the early Jesus movement, 'that he gave his only Son' (John 3.16). With that gift came the possibility of believing in the Son, believing in such a life-transforming way that he spoke of it (as he had himself doubtless experienced it) as new birth. Believing in the Son, he held, was a whole-person inhabiting of the truth. It amounts to the occupation of a standpoint on absolutely everything, and for this the only analogies are adoption, in-grafting and marriage.

But this is no easy process, because of the continuous presence of an antagonistic realm with its corresponding structures, a realm which he designates 'the world'. The world is the resisting heart of unbelief. It is enticing to the eyes and panders to the appetites, and is rooted in the arrogant imperviousness of wealth (1 John 2.15–16); and the world can become the object of an exclusive and rival love.

Is it then an accident that God is said to love the 'world'? Is this a case of a single word having two utterly contrasting meanings which only contexts can enable us to distinguish? Or is there, in the perception of this remarkable author and the view of the group to which he belonged, a recognition precisely of the ambivalence of the world, of its being both loved by God, and yet a threat to the children of God? I have learned in biblical study to be chary of exegetical over-subtlety; but if there is any work in the New Testament repaying extra sophistication of interpretation it is the Gospel of St John. 'God loved the world so much that he gave his only Son.' There is, then, on God's side an undeviating and fundamental attitude of benevolence towards the human environment, and to human-kind within it; and it is out of that attitude that the gift of God's Son proceeds, a Son who is closest to the Father's heart (leaning, as it were, on his breast, as did the beloved disciple at the Last Supper, John 1.18; 13.23).

373

But that self-same world is not coerced by God's benevolence, and may reject it. The objects of love may resist his love and structure themselves into hostility, such a hostility as to constrain and oppress the very people of God themselves, so that they are forced to become, as it were, the residual legatees of God's fundamental benevolence, holding on trust God's love in the context of betrayal, default and death.

The construal of the context for the proclamation of the gospel is one of the most pressing tasks of any Church at any time; and it is in the first instance a theological task. 'Our struggle', said the writer of the Letter to the Ephesians, 'is not against human foes' (6.12). He has unmasked the phenomena which were depressing enough, the hostility and persecution of rival creeds, the venality and unreliability of the official administrators of justice, the gross immorality of rampant paganism, and (as if the external trials were not severe enough) ambition, factiousness and greed within the Church. 'Our struggle is not against human foes, but against cosmic powers, against the authorities and potentates of this dark age, against the superhuman forces of evil in the heavenly realms.' But, again, is it an accident that God is said elsewhere to have created all existing authorities (Rom. 13.1)? Is there not the same dimension of ambivalence about the here-and-now profoundly hostile forces which manipulate the immediate context of the Church's mission? Are not those very powers over which Christ triumphs in the cross, and of which he makes a public spectacle, made by and beloved of God himself? And if we ask who are those powers, whether they are actual historical figures, institutions and social processes, or, perhaps, fallen angels out of some obscure cosmological myth, we may well answer that they are both, that good theology allows us to say there is no contradiction between the activity of the angels of the nations, and that of Pontius Pilate or of some harassed and corrupt provincial magistrate. The world of the powers is ambivalent. It is created and loved by God. But it is not coerced by him; and under some circumstances it may form itself into structures of resistance and opposition of such mighty and terrifying potential, that the people of God see themselves as a beleaguered remnant, bearing around in their hearts God's love for the world, but frustrated of their task to express it.

As we address the matter of the Church of England's response to, and participation in the Decade of Evangelism, elements of this Johannine realism begin to speak powerfully to our situation. Realism and honesty compel us also to admit that it is not self-evident for Anglicans to speak enthusiastically about evangelism. Despite an honoured tradition of Evangelicalism, we have not been the most evangelistically minded of Churches. This has been not infrequently admitted, not least in our own century in the post-war endeavours 'towards the conversion of England'. But I believe this present decade is an opportunity for us corporately to study and acknowledge the strengths and weaknesses of our own tradition with a view to deepening our grasp upon evangelism, and to do so without anxiety or over-cautious definition. We *know* that we are not going to launch ourselves into the deplorable antics of the Elmer Gantrys of this world; what we do not yet know is whether we have the courage and the resolve to rise to the real opportunities of the Decade.

I am struck by the way in which this thought has been expressed by Professor William Abraham in his impressively balanced work *The Logic of Evangelism*. He notes with understanding how some churches with 'fine ecclesiastical pedigrees' are embarrassed by evangelism. They lose interest in it in a welter of other activities; they forget how evangelism used to be done in their tradition; they develop a distaste for it and ridicule those who press for its rightful place. But the consequences are finally disastrous:

> Again and again evangelism has been driven to an underground group or even movement or ecclesiastical body. When this happens it is a tragedy for all concerned. The Church is no longer apostolic, for it has ceased to repeat the works of the apostles. Those driven underground or driven out are cut off from the full life and faith, and they invariably end up reinventing the wheels of ancient ecclesiology or falling into superficial conceptions of faith or into outright nonsense or heresy. In the meantime the world fails to be encountered by the full signs of the coming Kingdom of God.[1]

I shall come to a definition of evangelism in due course, but let us for the moment assume a thoroughly positive view, and ask from what fundamental motive it might proceed in the case of those nurtured within the Church of England in the last fifty years. Have I not already quoted from the heart of the Paschal Mystery, in the words familiar to generations of Anglicans as the Comfortable Words, spoken to those who with hearty repentance and true faith have turned to Christ, Christ our Passover sacrificed for us, in whose praise we keep the feast?

For the cover of our collected work, *The Study of Anglicanism*, John Booty and I chose Marc Chagall's marvellous window in Chichester Cathedral illustrative of the text, 'Let everything that hath breath, praise the Lord.' In aspiration at least may not Anglicans think of themselves as a people of praise? 'Let all the world in every corner sing, my God and King', wrote George Herbert, nurtured on the piety of the 1552 Book of Common Prayer.

> Thou that hast giv'n so much to me,
> Give one thing more, a grateful heart . . .
>
> Not thankful, when it pleaseth me;
> As if thy blessings had spare days:
> But such a heart, whose pulse may be
> > Thy praise.[2]

Would it not be consistent with the Anglican tradition to see the Church of England as offering on behalf of a part of the world which God loves, namely England, the praise which it has largely forgotten how to express? In this surrogate role the Church would act on behalf of a whole population in much the same way as Herbert thought humanity should speak on behalf of the physical and animal creation, as the 'Secretary' of God's praise. Not that Herbert had any illusions about the zeal of the Church of his own day. Carelessness in God's service was something Herbert well understood. In 'Misery' he seriously considers resigning the task of praising God to the angels, so hopeless is humanity:

> Lord, let the angels praise they name.
> Man is a foolish thing, a foolish thing,
> > Folly and Sin play all his game.
> His house still burns, and yet he still doth sing,
> > *Man is but grass*
> > *He knows it, fill the glass* . . .
>
> As dirty hands foul all they touch,
> And those things most, which are most pure and fine:
> > So our clay hearts, ev'n when we crouch
> To sing thy praises, make them less divine.
> > Yet either this,
> > Or none, thy portion is.[3]

The alternative, 'Yet either this, or none, thy portion is', still confronts the Church in our decade. I want to explore this theme, the way in which the love of God for his world elicits our praise, as the fundamental motive for evangelism arising out of our tradition. I do not claim that this is in any way distinctive of Anglicanism as compared with other Christian traditions; that would simply be untrue. My argument rather is that it is consistent with our tradition and thus with the way in which our Church has nurtured all its members, in whatever tradition they have been raised.

The varieties of contemporary English Anglicanism confront us in all parts of the land, and the task of leading and supporting evangelism in the Church cannot wait upon their reduction. This conviction has determined my method in what follows, which is to argue from the accumulated stock of memories forming the natural language of Anglicans. If I lay weight upon the Book of Common Prayer it is not because I am ignorant of the degree to which it has in practice been replaced. I acknowledge that I am not undertaking a descriptive exercise. I want there to be family resemblance between the varieties of Anglicanism; and I want Anglicans to engage in mutual recognition of each other, and not to define themselves with the partisan exclusiveness that comes so easily to our urban culture. My claim is that all these differences have historic roots in the past, and that to consider our inheritance of faith in love and loyalty is a way of bringing the grace and truth of Christ to this generation, and of strengthening the bonds which hold us together. For a portrait of our Church as a people of praise I turn without hesitation or apology to the Book of Common Prayer.

Let us consider, first, Morning Prayer, a liturgy of showing ourselves glad in him with Psalms (*Venite*), prefaced by the confession of sin and deliverance from guilt which, according to Psalm 51, is the precondition for the opening of the lips so that the mouth shows forth God's praise. Consider *Te Deum Laudamus*, the irresistible articulation of an entire universe in a song of acknowledgement of the Trinity; or consider *Benedicite, Omnia Opera*, the Church's own ecological canticle. Morning Prayer is an assembling 'to acknowledge our sins before God', 'to render thanks for the great benefits that we have received at his hands, to set forth his most worthy praise, to hear his most Holy Word, and to ask those things which are requisite and necessary as well for the body as the soul', all of them aims of enduring validity, and as Donald Allchin has rightly pointed out, embodying a true offering of the sacrifice of praise and thanksgiving.

Consider too the sacramental offering of the body and blood of our Saviour in the Holy Communion. It is for the whole world that our Lord made his one oblation of himself once offered, through the merits of which and through faith in which the whole Church receives remission of its sins and all other benefits of his passion. Our modern liturgies, as we know, now rightly speak of 'the eucharistic prayer', and of the giving of thanks over the gifts of bread and wine. They have brought out the sense in which those who have praised God for going out to meet us 'when we were still far off', nurture a hope that 'we and all your children shall be free, and the whole earth live to praise your name'. The eucharistic heart of the life of the Church confirms the Johannine conviction of a world loved by God and of a Church holding God's love on trust on its behalf. Nor has this departed from a tradition which exhorted the congregation assembling for the sacrament to give most humble and hearty thanks to God, the Father, the Son, and the Holy Ghost, for the redemption of the world by the death and passion of our Saviour Christ, both God and man.

And at the fountain-head and heart of it all stood the Sacrament of Baptism, signifying the very profession of the Christian life itself, which is

to follow the example of our Saviour Christ, and to be made like unto him; that as he died and rose again for us, so should we, who are baptized, die from sin, and rise again unto righteousness; continually mortifying all our evil and corrupt affections, and daily proceeding in all virtue and godliness of living.

For this reason, of course, baptism was commanded to be administered 'when the most number of people come together', and to be spoken 'in the vulgar tongue'. In baptism, as Herbert was to put it, 'Redemption measures all my time, and spreads the plaster equal to the crime'.[4]

My contention is, then, that gratitude for all God's 'goodness and lovingkindness to us and all men' (General Thanksgiving) is the atmosphere in which our tradition has schooled members of the Church of England. I have deliberately quoted from the Book of Common Prayer, but every quotation could be matched, paralleled, and in some cases enhanced, by quotation from the Alternative Service Book of our last decade. Nonetheless, it is no part of my argument to suggest that our liturgies already contain all that we need for the Decade of Evangelism. My point is rather that we may engage in evangelism (and, please God, not just for a decade) on the basis of deeply laid common traditions and instincts, without strain, pretence or flimsy theological novelties.

But we have an obvious problem, and it is brought to us by the Prayer Book itself, which provides not just for a baptism of infants, but for baptisms of 'such as are of riper years', made necessary 'through the licentiousness of the late times crept in among us', and 'useful for the baptizing of natives in our plantations, and others converted to the faith' (Preface to the Book of Common Prayer). The problem is that most of the rest of the Prayer Book treats baptism in infancy as the normative mode of entry into the Christian life. Baptism implied regeneration; and thereafter the problem was spiritual obtuseness. Almost the entire energy of the ministry envisaged by the Prayer Book is poured into the pastoral problem of enabling the baptized people of God to understand and be moved by the wonder of God's graciousness, his 'manifold and great mercies'. 'See', says the bishop to those about to be ordained priests, that you never cease your labour, your care and diligence, until you have done all that lieth in you, according to your bounden duty, to bring all such as are or shall be committed to your charge, unto that agreement in the faith and knowledge of God, and to that ripeness and perfectness of age in Christ.

Growing up into Christ (as described in the Ordinal's Epistle, from Ephesians 4) is the goal of Prayer Book spirituality. The basis is, I believe, Augustinian, and it shines through numerous collects which address themselves to the desires of the believer – 'pour into our hearts such love toward thee', 'graft in our hearts the love of thy name', 'make us to love that which thou dost command', 'nourish us in all goodness'. The Prayer Book confronts a people of very mixed spiritual capacity and insight, and invites and coaxes them to risk more of themselves in their response to the love and grace and mercy of God; and it does so in much the same way as did St Augustine of Hippo with the obtuse, recalcitrant and half-converted congregations addressed in his sermons. What the Prayer Book envisages may, in a certain way, be called 'slow conversion'. As a result it creates a pattern of Christian life structured by the rhythm of contrition and praise, contrition and praise, supported by a primarily pastoral ministry whose task it is to promote genuine contrition for sin and reconciliation, and then to lead the praise of the community.

Our problem may be put very simply. It is that not enough parents bring their children to baptism; that many who do so do not then commit themselves to nourishment in the Church; and that the world has devised many powerful ways of pulling even those children who have persisted for some years into an alternative love. So we are confronted by the primary need for adult conversions, which is not what our old Prayer Book has in mind, though, it is true, the Alternative Service Book treats adult baptism as the norm.

But we are not helpless in this situation. Nor need, nor should our attitudes to the tasks of evangelism entail policies or practices strange to, or remote from, the mind schooled upon our Prayer Book. There are, however, certain important provisos, the first of which is that a praising community *is* an agent of evangelism. We shall have to set aside the intimidating thought that we are only ready for evangelism after we have taken this or that course of instruction. I do not wish to be misunderstood. Lay education in the faith and increasing people's ability to be confident about the articulation of the faith is a continuous task of the Church, and it is *one* of the ways of being equipped for evangelism. But another is getting an existing Church to understand that praising God with heart and voice is also an essential aspect of evangelism.

Part of the challenge of the Decade, I believe, is the empowering of the people of God in the congregations *as they are*, by setting before them something achievable related to the overall goals of the Church. So many of the connotations of the word 'evangelism' conjure up the unachievable and the inconceivable; it postpones tasks until after elaborate preparations have been undertaken; or it entails visits from exotic speakers who will not be present when the PCC is trying to decide whether to launch an organ fund; or it involves fantasies about the impact of the existing worship of the Church upon new converts who have been through the spiritual equivalent of a trip to Mars. But to get a congregation to examine all that it is and does as a people of praise, and then to see that from the standpoint of a non-attender, is both salutary and realistic and may lead to the setting of achievable goals. In such a way a community may itself become the major agent of evangelism.

The second proviso has to do with construing the context for the proclamation of the gospel. We have to unmask the patent facts which confront us in the revolutions of our time, in sexual mores, entertainment, transport and communications. The contraceptive pill, the car, the television set and the computer are facts about our world which are deeply ambivalent. God loves this world, but there is a way in which it lures people away from the truth; and, as ever, wealth is there to harden the heart and deaden the perceptions. The people of God need to know the world in which they are living at some depth, because it is inside our heads, not external to us; and if we do not understand it we become the unwitting agents of our own oppression.

The importance of this last proviso I wish to underscore. One of the historic legacies of some nineteenth- and twentieth-century evangelistic practice is the assumption that it is carried out by those who have made a firm distinction between the saved and the lost, to enable the former to target the latter. This is a deeply objectionable procedure, and contradicts in a number of ways the standpoint I have developed. On the model of slow conversion, those reared in our tradition will have come to understand that the world impinges mightily upon them too, and that God has some difficulty in correcting them. As a people of contrition and praise, they will have come to experience a peace and joy which the world cannot give, and will want to share it with others. And if they have studied their Scriptures they will realize that God alone knows the identity of the saved, and denies to human beings the presumption of judgement. One of the advantages of the form in which the doctrine of predestination is treated in the Thirty-nine Articles (Art. xvii) is that God's counsel in the matter of salvation is 'secret to us'. The article does not teach a *particular* predestination of named individuals; there is simply the decree to save 'those chosen in Christ'.[5] The people of God are carriers of a blessing which is intended for the whole world and which they will want to share with others from the motive of gratitude, not out of anxiety or a desire to dominate. A royal priesthood, a chosen race, a dedicated nation, a people claimed by God for his own, 'to proclaim the glorious deeds of him who called (them) out of darkness into his marvellous light' (1 Pet. 2.9), *is* an agent of evangelism.

And it hardly needs to be mentioned, so obviously is it consistent with this formulation, that such a people praises God not only with its lips but in its life. The penitential practice envisaged in the Prayer Book involved forgiveness, social reconciliation and restitution as a precondition of the partaking of Holy Communion. The object of prayer and aspiration for the State was that a whole people might be (simultaneously) preserved in wealth, peace and godliness. The advancement of public education was a natural concern of Cranmer, and Latimer was fiercely critical of an avaricious gentry. John Booty has argued to good effect that the Book of Common Prayer was designed in part to bring about social reform in sixteenth-century England.[6] A self-congratulatory stance on the score of our social witness over the centuries is, I need hardly say, spectacularly inappropriate; and thank God we have not found it impossible from time to time to be penitent about our corporate failures as a Church. The point I wish to make is a modest one, namely that Anglicans have always had a whole-life view of the tasks of a Church in its social context, and that the tradition does not require us to see any kind of competitive stress between evangelism and social witness. We do not need, even, to follow the WCC Bangkok Conference of 1973 in speaking of 'holistic evangelism'. It is the same motive, namely the praise of God, which compels, or should compel, the people of God into evangelism and into the confrontation of social disorder and oppression.

This is a necessary accompaniment of evangelism if the praises of the people of God are not to become an expression of the cheaply purchased satisfaction of the comfortable. As Professor Walter Brueggemann has reminded us,[7] praise disconnected from real liberations is in danger of degenerating into the legitimation of a dominant terrestrial order. Psalm 102 is one of those which sees the connection between liberation and praise:

> This shall be written for those that come after: and the
> people which shall be born shall praise the Lord.

> For he hath looked down from his sanctuary: out of heaven did
>    the Lord behold the earth;
> That he might hear the mournings of such as are in captivity: and
>    deliver the children appointed unto death;
> That they may declare the name of the Lord in Sion: and his
>    worship at Jerusalem.[8]

What, then, finally, *is* evangelism? I come to this question last, partly because most modern definitions carry an in-built persuasive agenda, and partly because the noun form is never used in the New Testament. At the start of this article I invited you to assume a positive understanding of evangelism; and I now tell you why. At the end of Luke 4, Jesus is said to have retired to a remote spot after an exhausting day's preaching and healing. The crowds found him and begged him not to leave them! 'But he said, "I must give the good news of the kingdom of God to the other towns, also, for that is what I was sent to do" ' (Luke 4.43).

On the basis of the Greek verbs used here, *euangellizomai* and *apostello*, we would not be very far wrong to précis that verse with the words. 'I must engage in evangelism, for that is my apostolic mission.' But the noun form, 'evangelism', is a little misleading, and not merely because it comes trailing clouds of unattractive or frankly disreputable modern history. It may confuse us into assuming that evangelism is one activity. If we were to use the word 'evangelizing' we might be less misled. There are, in fact no rational grounds for supposing that evangelism or evangelizing amounts to a single task or enterprise. Professor Abraham puts the point well:

> Evangelism is necessarily a polymorphous activity. It is more like farming or educating than like raising one's arm or blowing a kiss. It is done in, with, and through a host of other activities that are intimately related to the specific circumstances in which the evangelist is working.[9]

What makes all these activities evangelism is, he argues, that they are governed by the goal of initiating people into the Kingdom of God. It has, on his analysis, a variety of dimensions, corporate, cognitive, moral, experiential, operational and disciplinary. So it will necessarily involve a very large number of discrete tasks (which justifies the simile of farming), held together by what he calls the logic of the Kingdom of God, God's own activity within human history.

I endorse this standpoint. The people of God, who find themselves in our churches Sunday by Sunday, hear, if we are faithful to the good news, that before the foundation of the world they were chosen in Christ to be his own adopted people, to be full of love, to be forgiven through the sacrificial death of Christ and to have wisdom and insight lavished upon them, so that God's glory might be praised in the Church (Ephesians 1). Evangelizing is simply the consequence of wanting as many as possible to share as fully and as explicitly as possible in that belief and in all its consequences. We know that this is good news for the whole world, and that it entails a whole-person inhabiting of the truth. We are not in the least surprised or discouraged by the fact that the 'world' which God loves is capable of deciding that other things are more interesting; and that this world is not simply external to us, but internal, undermining commitment, distracting our singleness of vision and sowing discouragement. But a people of praise, schooled in the disciplines of penitence and constantly reminded of the great and tender mercy of God, is moved by God's love to lift up its heart, a heart whose very pulse is the praise of God. And if praise is the pulse of our heart, then the Church of England, as it now is, is no more than a heart-beat away from every member participation in the Decade of Evangelism.

NOTES

1. William Abraham, *The Logic of Evangelism*, London: Hodder & Stoughton, 1989, p. 179.
2. 'Gratefulness', *The Works of George Herbert*, Oxford: Oxford University Press, 1941, p. 123.
3. 'Misery', ibid., p. 100.
4. 'Holy Baptism', ibid., p. 44.
5. Oliver O'Donovan, *On the Thirty-Nine Articles*, Exeter: Paternoster Press, 1986, p. 86.
6. John Booty, 'Church and Commonwealth in the Reign of Edward VI', *Anglican Theological Review*, Supplementary Series no. 7, Nov. 1976, pp. 67–80.
7. Walter Brueggemann, *Israel's Praise*, Philadelphia: Fortress Press, 1988.
8. Psalm 102.18–21, Book of Common Prayer Psalter.
9. Abraham, op. cit., p. 104.

∽◠∾◠∾◠∾◠∾◠∾◠∾◠∾◠∾◠∾◠∾◠∾◠∾◠∾◠∾◠∾◠∾◠∾◠∾◠∾◠∾◠∾

# 36

# HOPE AND CHURCHES
# Daniel W. Hardy and David F. Ford

## The God of hope

Joy in God transposed into a vision of the future becomes hope in God. In the face of problems, miseries and stubborn evils, knowing God entails trusting him for the future and being open to his decisive encouragement. The encourager is the Holy Spirit. The Holy Spirit is the greatest realist about evil, sin and all problems, exposing them to their depths. But, even deeper than all of these, the Spirit reveals Jesus Christ, crucified and risen. He is the demonstration of a hope that gives us the heart to tackle the problems.

This is not an optimism. It does not claim that the world is necessarily improving or that the freedom to do evil will not wreak havoc. It recognizes the possibility of an appalling fate for both individuals and the world if they resist God and his goodness. Christian apocalyptic sees the fate of the world as an analogy with the fate of Jesus Christ in crucifixion and resurrection, culminating in an unprecedented intensity of evil before the new creation of God. The final Christian historical perspective is a hope which, like resurrection of the dead, relies on God alone. Yet the Holy Spirit is the presence of this God in history and the cosmos now, inviting to shared responsibility. The scope of the Spirit's work is as wide as the cosmos and is concerned for every aspect of history, institutional as well as individual. For every area there is a message of hope. It is not simply to be identified with the great hope in Jesus Christ, but, before him, it embraces innumerable lesser hopes inside and outside the Christian Church. The Spirit brings the taste of a better future into the present and creates a thirst for more.

There is the universal hope for justice. In itself it can be grim and stoic, but a look at movements of liberation shows how essential they find the overflow of songs, sacrifices and ideals. There are also hopes for love, for beauty, for meaning and for knowledge, and all are notoriously ambiguous, the most powerful as usual being the most vulnerable to going wrong. In relation to all of them the experience of praising and knowing God gives rise to prophetic insights. We take as an example just one area, that of meaning and knowledge.

Most of the pressures in our educational system are towards gaining knowledge for practical reasons, especially finding employment. This is a proper role of education, but when it is idolized there is a corruption of motivation which poisons the deepest spring of learning. The capacity simply to wonder, to ask questions from a desire to know and to have the joy of discovery, is one of the fundamental human orientations. It is practically very useful, but it also opens the way beyond immediate needs and beyond what can be justified functionally.

The dynamic of wonder follows the same logic of overflow that we have seen in praise. Wonder continually questions, explores, compares, and delights in the use of all faculties in order to invent and discover. It is a realm of freedom yet definiteness, and it unites heart and mind in a movement of transcendence. The act of questioning has been described as our basic mode of transcendence, because it leads us beyond brute experience into understanding. An education which fails to nourish non-utilitarian wonder deadens one of the roots of human dignity and freedom. Ironically, it may also even fail practically, because it does not make the mind adaptable enough for rapid developments or changes of career. Worst of all is the betrayal of the increasing numbers who can find no employment. For them an education whose chief motivation is towards finding a job is a training for despair. The right education for the mind is a condition for hope.

Embracing all this is the question of the meaning of the life for which education is a preparation. The utilitarian tendency is to equate one's role in society, especially the economy, with one's vocation. This is always a fraud, but it is more obvious when the economy is in trouble and offers less attractive roles, or none at all. Then the despair of a useless life can grip millions, in quiet or violent forms. The good news that vocation does not depend on the state of the economy but on the call of God, which is for every single person, needs to be acted out prophetically by those who proclaim it. The massive assurance is: you do have a vocation, you are respected and called by God to very definite tasks, and to joy in doing them. Ironically, again, this can be the liberation which frees for a more effective role in society. The lesser hopes tend to be fulfilled as one risks living for the larger hopes.

## Hope for the Church

The largest hope of all is at the heart of praising and knowing God. Paul expresses it:

> We rejoice in our hope of sharing the glory of God. More than that, we rejoice in our sufferings, knowing that suffering produces endurance, and endurance produces character, and character produces hope, and hope does not disappoint us, because God's love has been poured into our hearts through the Holy Spirit which has been given to us (Rom. 5.2–5).

The Holy Spirit in the Church produces that mature, tested hope which Paul describes, oriented towards the ultimate hope of sharing God's glory. It is a lively movement with three basic dynamics which have also emerged in the previous chapters: the overflow of praise to God, offering him everything; the overflow of love in a community that shares in the Holy Spirit; and the overflow in mission to the world. As those three interweave, the Church becomes what it is meant to be, a prophetic community whose vocation is to witness to the love of God in Jesus Christ. The prototypical Church described by Luke in Acts (especially Acts 2.43–7) shows all three in action, and they have been there at the origins of every major tradition in church history.

The prophetic signs of our times are that Christian praise, community and mission are being integrated in new ways.

The explosion in praise which has happened in this century has, as we have shown, had its prophetic dimension. It has held up the God of joy as the truth of life, and so confronted all that negates joy. Yet there is a further, more explicitly prophetic element in this praise. All over the world Christian communities have been rediscovering what was the experience of both the Old and New Testament communities: that prophecies can be given in worship. Wholehearted engagement with God in praise is the ideal context for clearly receiving his communication. He reveals both who he is and what he wants.

The recovery of this gift on a large scale is a revolutionary innovation. As the Bible and church tradition are acutely aware, prophecy's importance is matched by its dangers. It is only reliable in an ecology that includes openness to correction by Scripture, tradition and contemporaries. But the New Testament rightly saw the gift of the Holy Spirit as the fulfilment of the Old Testament hope that all receivers of the Spirit should be able to prophesy (cf. Acts 2.17). Paul tells the Corinthians to 'make love your aim, and earnestly desire the spiritual gifts, especially that you may prophesy' (1 Cor. 14.1). It is an expectation of receiving communication from God as part of normal Christian exprience. As Paul's discussion shows, it both springs out of worship and can lead even unbelievers to worship (1 Cor. 14.24f.).

Prophecy in worship can act as a critical check on the community. It discerns complacency or hypocrisy in praise. It sharpens moral awareness, as hearts and minds are opened in worship of the God of peace, goodness and justice. Self-protective narrowness of concern is dissolved in the expansion of appreciation of the God who loves the whole of creation. Prophecy that lives in praise can also give a vision of the proper shape of life in the Kingdom of God, and can offer inspiration, encouragement and direction to realize it. All of this is a sign of the presence of the God who speaks, and is intrinsically linked to the three dynamics of praise, upbuilding the community and mission.

This century has also seen new developments in Christian community. There have been periods in which inherited forms of the Church proved more or less satisfactory, but today that is not so. We are in a period of disintegration and fresh creativity. Every level of church life, from international and ecumenical organization to congregational and family life, is in transformation. The demonstration of Christian community has become a form of prophecy for which there is a deep desire and hope. The first Christians, numerous religious orders, the parish systems, several churches springing from the Reformation, the early Quakers and the Methodists, and many other movements and societies have in the past been such prophetic signs. It is not hard to find parallels today, mostly new variations on old themes. Friendship, family, and the idea of 'covenanting' together in communities are continually taking fresh forms and finding new prophetic directions. Without such environments, praise of God and Christian mission lose their depth and power. The God of joy gives the Holy Spirit in order to be loved by a community of joy, and praise of God is the strongest and most objective of bonds between people.

Finally, there is the third dynamic, the Christian mission, which has at its heart the respectful invitation to share in praise and community. We conclude with a consideration of this.

## The spread of praise and knowledge of God

In Thomas Mann's novel, *Joseph and his Brothers,* Jacob at the end of his life talks about his wife Rachel:

> Anyhow, he simply loved to speak of her, even when there was no point
> at all – just as he loved to speak of God.[1]

This overflow of appreciation and delight is the master-spring of Christian
mission and evangelism.

The Song of Songs has perhaps more to teach about the right spirit in
this than any other book of the Bible. The Song has all the urgency, joy,
agony and mutuality of love, but the main note is the pure praise of the
beloved:

> your name is oil poured out . . .
> We will exult and rejoice in you;
>> we will extol your love more than wine . . .
> Behold, you are beautiful, my love;
>> behold, you are beautiful . . .
> Your lips distil nectar, my bride;
>> honey and milk are under your tongue;
>> the scent of your garments is like the scent of Lebanon.
> A garden locked is my sister, my bride,
>> a garden locked, a fountain sealed (1–4).

Then the right sort of communication to others can happen:

> Awake, O north wind,
>> and come, O south wind!
> Blow upon my garden,
>> let its fragrance be wafted abroad (4.16).

Praise is the primary form of the communication of the gospel, the sheer
enjoyment and appreciation of it before God 'even when there is no point
at all'. All other communication is an overflow of this, the spread of its
scent, affirming in appropriate ways, in various situations, the content and
delight of praising God.

It is of the greatest importance to the whole of Christian communication
that it be praise-centred. This is in contrast with the problem-centred
approach that has often been dominant. One popular image of evangelism
is of it sniffing out sin and misery, making people feel guilty and
inadequate, and then offering the gospel as the answer. Instead, the essence
of mission and evangelism is in the intrinsic worth, beauty and love of God,
and the joy of knowing and trusting him. This of course brings to light all
sorts of things that are wrong, but it is not to be reduced to the solution of
problems. Problem-solving lacks the logic of overflow, and easily lets the
problem be the centre of attention, whereas praise puts what is wrong in a
wider perspective from the start. Praise recognizes the primacy and reality

of the love of God, and in its desire to share delight in this it becomes evangelical and missionary.

This approach is in line with a transformation in the understanding of mission by many Christian Churches in the twentieth century. There has been a change in the dominant perspective. Beginning as the mission of the Western Church to the rest of the world, it shifted to the mission of the worldwide Church, and finally to the 'mission of God' in both Church and world. This can be traced in the great missionary conferences (starting with Edinburgh in 1910) and on into the World Council of Churches, the Second Vatican Council and some representative Evangelical statements. The God-centred understanding has many versions, in which the old problems inevitably recur in new forms, but the energetic discussion and experiment of this century have begun to produce a convergence of the main traditions, and in this the perspective of the mission of God is vital. Its emphasis on who God is and what he is doing means that praise and thanks become the starting-point for mission. As a by-product, the words 'evangelism' and 'mission' can begin to be liberated from exclusive association with their more shallow and manipulative forms.

The reasons why evangelism and mission have a range of bad connotations for many people are not just because they have often been carried on badly, insensitively or from doubtful motives. That is true, but to leave the criticism at that might imply that it was a matter of the perversion of something basically sound. Yet the very conception of much Christian communication has been questionable. It has often presented the good news in functional terms: it is useful for meeting needs, crises, limitations or other problems. It has been a gospel that fills gaps in one's life, or repairs things that have gone wrong, or is essentially practical in a host of ways. The seductiveness of this is that there is indeed good news for every problematic situation and person. The flaw lies in its missing the free praise of God, the generosity, the foolish abundance far beyond all need and practicality. The gospel is that all sin, evil and suffering, all need and want, can now be seen in the perspective of the resurrection of Jesus Christ in which God acts in such a way that the realistic response is joy. Even beyond this, it is the joy of love between us and God, the ultimate mutuality and intimacy. That is why the Song of Songs is the best expression of the communication that flows from it.

Recognizing and responding to this God inevitably leads to evangelism and mission as acts of love and celebration, longing for others to share in something whose delight increases by being shared. Yet expressions of praise easily become overbearing and triumphalist, and so does evangelism. When this happens, there is a contradiction of the message. The history of

389

evangelism is extremely painful, full of examples of the message being falsified by the way it is spread. The crucifixion of Jesus is the only essential guard against this. It contradicts all glib praise and preaching. It continually demands the repentance, reconversion, suffering and even death of the evangelist. This is not just a matter of method, but a fundamental truth about the unity of message and method, as Paul passionately maintained throughout his Second Letter to the Corinthians. The temptations of Jesus show the classic traps of evangelism – use of worldly incentives, spectacular events and manipulative power. The alternative is the way of the cross, from which the true ethic of evangelism springs: an ethic of radical respect which refuses any coercive communication, preferring to suffer and die; but which also refuses to compromise on what is communicated.

The classic New Testament case of the ethic of respect in evangelism is in the story of the spread of Christianity beyond Judaism, as told in Acts 10–11. This was the most revolutionary event in the history of the early Church, and it meant a conversion for those who were evangelizing as well as for those who were listening to them. Peter, the story says, had a vision in which he was told to go against his Bible, his upbringing and his whole Jewish culture and religious practice: to break the law by eating food forbidden as unclean. This prepares him to respond to the request of Cornelius, who has also had a vision, to visit him and accept his hospitality even though he is a gentile. It is when both men follow their visions and meet in this atmosphere of respect that Peter can share 'the good news of peace by Jesus Christ' (Acts 10.36), and there is an explosive event as faith comes alive in praise of God and in speaking in tongues.

God is already ahead of all evangelism, carrying on his mission in the world, and this adds further dimensions to the ethic of respect. It means that the abundance of God is poured out way beyond the boundaries of the Church, and a vital task is in discerning this abundance and accepting it with joy. There is no Christian triumphalism in a theology of the all-sufficiency and abundance of God. More often than not, respectful discernment will demand drastic changes of heart and mind, as for Peter with his own traditions. Christians are only beginning to glimpse the comprehensive repercussions of this in relation to the various sciences, other religions, philosophies and ways of living. It would take many books (for many of which the experience is not yet available for them to be written) to describe those implications. But without the right content and mode of affirmation of God the horizon is lacking within which all that can take place.

The crucified and resurrected Jesus Christ is therefore at the heart of the method as well as the content of Christian mission. He is also at the heart of Christian community and of Christian praise and knowledge of God. Jesus is our praise, and through him the God of living perfection invites others deeper into his life, dealing with everything that spoils it, and promising in prophecy that

> he will rejoice over you with gladness,
>     he will renew you in his love;
> he will exult over you with loud singing
>     as on a day of festival (Zeph 3.17f.).

A chapter of the Bible that has had an extraordinary influence through the centuries, including giving the terms in which Jesus announced his mission, expresses both the hope and joy of praise. It begins by setting the problems of life, such as poverty, broken hearts, imprisonment, bereavement, lack of confidence, and the destruction of cities and social fabric over generations, in the context of good news and praise, and the glory of God. There is then a repeated promise of joy and justice, and the culmination is a vision of the 'new dress' and the universal network of praise and respect which is the hope of faith:

> I will greatly rejoice in the Lord,
>     my soul shall exult in my God:
> for he has clothed me with the garments of salvation,
>     he has covered me with the robe of righteousness,
> as a bridegroom decks himself with a garland,
>     and as a bride adorns herself with her jewels.
> For as the earth brings forth its shoots,
>     and as a garden causes what is sown in it to spring up,
> so the Lord God will cause righteousness and praise
>     to spring forth before all the nations (Isa. 61.10–11).

NOTE

1. Thomas Mann, *Joseph and his Brothers*, London, 1978, p. 1181.

# Epilogue

Although this Reader is just a snapshot of modern theology, it does, I hope, show something of the vigour of the discipline in American and British academies. By studying modern theology, students are encouraged to debate and think deeply about some of the most important issues in life. Can we know or talk about God? What makes Christian belief distinctive? How can Christians understand other faiths? What is truth in the midst of all the fragmentations and pluralisms of postmodernity? How do communities protect, shape or fashion beliefs? Where do values come from? What makes a life Christian? These and many other crucial questions.

Of course there are disagreements on the answers given to all of these questions. Modern theology would hardly be a critical discipline if this were not the case. What a dull world it would be if we all reached an assured consensus on such issues. Theology would simply become a subject to be learned not a subject that challenges us to think and to debate. But perhaps I can conclude with a few personal observations about some of the key issues raised in each section. This is an editor's final privilege.

## God as Creator

There is an exciting form of apologetic that seems to be increasing at the moment. It is not committed to a naive teleology, but it does believe that physical and moral order is highly consonant with theism. That is to say, the theist has every reason to believe that the universe will be rationally ordered. This applies to perceptions both of the physical world as well of the moral world. Peter Berger has appealingly termed these 'signals of transcendence'. The wise theist is not claiming that physical and moral order can *only* be explained in terms of a belief in God as Creator. All that is necessary to claim is that theism does offer a coherent account of the sort of physical order which is a requirement of practical science – and possibly an account which is more coherent than many of its rivals. It also provides a coherent account of the sort of moral order that is always presumed by deep moral outrage. In contrast, some secular accounts of morality give little reason to believe that deep moral outrage (say at child abuse or at the degradations of the Holocaust) is anything other than an expression of personal feeling. There is much to be explored here, but I believe that it could well be a highly productive path for theological apologetics.

## Models of God

The observant theologian has always known that if God really is God then human language is never adequate to depict God. At best it is analogical or metaphorical – univocal language about God is always a mistake, even Trinitarian language. However it is a mistake that is constantly made – whether by theologians becoming too dogmatic or by congregations becoming too rigid. Sallie McFague's challenge has been an important reminder that this is so. It has real theological sophistication and seldom relies upon easy rhetoric. I doubt whether the issues will be easily resolved, especially within church congregations (a concern which she evidently shares). Nevertheless, by exploring some of the female divine images in the Old Testament, I believe that Christians can be led gently to see that patriarchy is not an essential ingredient of the Godhead.

However, just one note of caution. Radical theological critiques can sometimes render Christian heritage almost unusable. Perhaps it is the radical critique which argues that historical Christianity is inescapably patriarchal. Perhaps it is the radical Jewish critique which argues that historical Christianity is inescapably anti-Semitic. Or perhaps it is the radical ecologists who strongly implicate theism with the domination and destruction of the environment. If a more vigorous Christian apologetic is increasing, then these three forms of radical critique are also on the increase at present. I am sure that they should be taken seriously (as, for example, LaCugna clearly does). Yet perhaps theologians should also be more conscious than at present that each of them was first developed within Christian theology, but are now increasingly used from without as a means of dismissing Christianity in its entirety. What an impoverishment to theology it will be if we can no longer read Augustine because of his views on the environment, Aquinas because of his views on women, or Luther because of his egregious attitudes to Jews. And to implicate all of Christianity in the process will hardly be justice.

## Christ and other faiths

My points about order and theism apply equally to Judaism and to Islam as they do to Christianity. If Ursula King envisages a new alliance between women across faith traditions, then perhaps a broader alliance may be seen amongst theists generally. There is an increasing recognition that no faith tradition is well served by pretending that real (and probably irreconcil-able) differences do not exist – a point stressed by Keith Ward. If once some religionists thought that a meta-faith was possible, uniting differing faith traditions, today few academic theologians talk in such terms. Most of us are more conscious of the particularities of different faith traditions (even if social factors are identified in these particularities). Nonetheless, it could be that there will be limited and specific alliances between otherwise very different faith traditions. Such alliances have already begun to emerge on such moral issues as euthanasia or peace, both in Britain and in the United States. Perhaps they might also increasingly extend into apologetics. If belief in God really does make a difference to human lives, then this is a difference presumably shared by a number of faith traditions. At an even more general level, an openness to transcendence and to a world which is not viewed simply in functional terms unites theistic and Eastern faiths.

## Christ and postmodernism

It was stressed several times in the Introduction that various forms of postmodernism offer an important challenge to modern theology. Mani-festly those following George Lindbeck have a very different response to those following theologians such as David Tracy. There is something tidier about Lindbeck. He responds clearly to the challenge of philosophers such as Alasdair MacIntyre and has inspired Christian ethicists such as Stanley Hauerwas to advance positions quite distinct from secular forms of ethics. Lindbeck also gives an emphatic role to the Bible in Christian formation and helps to explain why a new generation that knows little of the Bible can make less and less sense of Christian faith. In contrast, David Tracy appears confusing and perhaps confused. His analogical imagination seems to share many of the fragmentations, and much of the eclecticism, of postmodern-ism itself.

Yet my own preference is finally more for Tracy than for Lindbeck – tempting though the latter undoubtedly is. My problem finally lies with thoroughgoing anti-foundationalism. Don Cupitt is the clear warning here. Like Lindbeck and Hauerwas, he is a confirmed anti-foundationalist. He too believes that there is no way of knowing 'the real' outside particular communities. It is the narratives within communities that shape their beliefs and values. And, since all three have had their lives shaped by specifically Christian communities, perhaps their visions are not that far apart. Of course this conclusion is outrageous. The vision of Christian ethics offered by Cupitt, with no belief in a personal God or in any personal survival beyond death, seems quite opposite to that of Hauerwas. Yet thoroughgoing anti-foundationalism risks reaching Cupitt's solipsism.

Natural law theory provides an instructive example. The well-known problems with this theory – social determinism, human diversity, and elusive principles – have led many ethicists to abandon it altogether. Perhaps it never was a very productive way of convincing non-theists. Yet, for those who do believe in God as Creator, surely the logic is different. Unless theists believe that the human (and perhaps nonhuman) world is completely corrupted by sin, then perhaps it is reasonable to suppose that something of the Creator's will can still be glimpsed from creation. Similarly in the foundationalist/anti-foundationalist debate. Attempting to convince a pluralistic and fragmented world of foundationalism is never going to be easy. Yet theists addressing other theists might not find this so difficult. Viewed from the perspective of theism, something like Tracy's analogical imagination makes more sense. It listens sensitively to the secular whilst still being firmly rooted in a Christian community.

## Christ and the academy

I do not wish to take sides in the American academy debate, but I think it is worth affirming one issue that arises from it. My own experience as a modern theologian within a secular university has convinced me that there is indeed a wider academic role for theology. There has been a collapse of many of the positivist presumptions that haunted a previous generation of university theologians. Whilst my colleagues may or may not be sympathetic to Christian faith, they do seem to be increasingly concerned about values. There does seem to be a wider awareness, especially amongst scientists, that research is seldom value-free and that some of the most exciting research, particularly in genetics, is raising very profound moral issues. It is no longer simply assumed that what can be done should be done. Within this changed environment a professional member of a moral community seems to be surprisingly welcome – not of course to dictate, but certainly to listen and to discuss. I do not even feel obliged to hide my clerical identity within the modern university. This too is new.

## Spirit and community

There is an increasing emphasis upon communitarianism within modern theology. In the United States this has recently taken the form of stressing that theology itself is a communal activity. Perhaps part of the recent vigour of American theology is a fruit of this. However both British and

American theologians tend to contrast the communal nature of faith with the atomized and individualistic nature of much secular thought. I welcome this development very strongly, but also believe that it should be accompanied by a frank analysis of actual communities. There is a tendency in the Lindbeck/Hauerwas tradition to present an idealized understanding of church communities which bears little relation to the frailties of actual congregations.

It is precisely at this point that the social sciences can be used judiciously within theology. James Mackey has done this to real effect in his analysis of power within churches and within society at large. Feminist and liberationist perspectives are also crucial for understanding better the social pressures that shape congregations. A clearer vision of worship, of the knowledge of God that can be gleaned through worship, and of the distinctiveness of Christ that lies at the heart of Christian worship, can help to guide and clarify theological vision. All of this is an activity that assumes involvement in a worshipping community. For me, and indeed for many in the present generation of modern theologians, theology itself makes little sense without this.

# Index